LONELY PLANET PUBLICATIONS

☑ **W9-ACH-404**

DANIEL C SCHECHTER
JOSEPHINE QUINTERO

MEXICO CITY
CITY GUIDE

Celebrate Mexico's pre-Hispanic heritage with the Concheros (p52) outside the Templo Mayor

On a crisp October evening, families crowd the Zócalo to look at tombstones. Rows of these mock monuments stand on a carpet of colored sawdust strewn with marigolds and painted skulls.

French poet André Breton famously called Mexico the surrealist country par excellence, and the capital seems to revel in its strangeness. The world's third largest urban area (by some estimates) fills a highland basin 2240m above sea level, so you might already feel a bit light-headed upon arrival. Often described as a malevolent maelstrom of unbreathable air and rampant crime, the city nevertheless impresses visitors as a wonderfully weird and welcoming world, and captivates them with its year-round springlike climate, bubbling street life and abundant cultural offerings.

Like any great metropolis, Mexico City presents a mosaic of scenes. One moment you're knocking back tequila at a grand old cantina, the next you're grooving to world-class DJs on a rooftop terrace. Breakfast on tamales and *atole* (a drink made from corn) from a street corner vendor, dine on fusion cuisine by one of Polanco's acclaimed chefs. After an afternoon spent sharing the anguish of artist Frida Kahlo, watch masked wrestlers inflict pain on one another at the *lucha libre* (wrestling) arena downtown.

To be sure pollution and crime remain real concerns for Chilangos, but since the turn of the millennium, there's been a palpable sense that the capital has turned a page. Rather than heading for the apocalypse, it now seems destined for a renaissance.

MEXICO CITY LIFE

Mayor Marcelo Ebrard is committed to bringing the city into line with worldwide urban trends. Many residents are enthusiastic about his campaign to remove thousands of *ambulantes* ('informal' street vendors) from the historic center. At last, *capitalinos* can shop along the center's grand boulevards and admire its architectural beauty without having to dodge vendors of novelty underwear and pirated porn. It wasn't the first time such a campaign had been waged, but Ebrard seems serious about enforcing the restrictions, employing hundreds of police to keep the *ambulantes* away.

'Rather than heading for the apocalypse, Mexico City now seems destined for a renaissance.'

Chilangos seem encouraged by the new mayor's progressive attitude. Ebrard has displayed a get-tough stance toward illicit activities, bulldozing tenements reputed to be centers of the narcotics trade in the notorious Tepito district. He's started to address the city's horrendous traffic congestion by encouraging bicycling as an alternative mode of transport. The mayor himself rides his bike to work from his Condesa apartment the first Monday of every month.

These measures have been regarded with cynicism by some residents, but Mexico City seems to be on the upswing. After a prolonged period of economic malaise and high crime rates, the city is enjoying an image makeover. No longer seen as a smog-choked nightmare where kidnappers pounce upon every taxi, it is lately perceived as a paragon of chic, where innovative chefs set the course for world cuisine, fashion designers create edgy streetwear, and *lucha libre* figures fly across the ring. If some of this is hype, Chilangos want to believe it.

A blend of colonial architectural styles, the Catedral Metropolitana (p50) was built over the ruins of an Aztec temple

HIGHLIGHTS

FOOD

Morning tamales at the market, midday comida *at a family-run dining hall, fusion cuisine at one of Polanco's exclusive restaurants and tacos beneath the freeway at 3am – the capital's multifaceted foodscape is legendary among culinary adventurers.*

❶ Markets
Some of the best eating in Mexico City is not found in any restaurant but in the big covered *mercados* (p156).

❷ Tacos
Mexico's salsa-seasoned signature snack, available all over town (p147).

❸ Regional Cuisine
Jalisco, Puebla, Yucatán and other regions contribute to the capital's culinary mosaic (p144).

❶ Cantinas
Tequila, served with *sangrita* and lime, is the favored drink at these classic watering holes (p137).

❷ Lucha Libre
Mexico's iconic masked marauders clash in the wrestling arena (p192).

❸ Condesa Café Society
The intelligentsia gather in the city's trendiest quarter (p163).

CITY STYLE

The Chilango vibe borrows freely from a cavalcade of folk imagery. You'll see it in the hand-painted signage on the corner locksmith, the Virgin of Guadalupe trinkets on the bus dashboard and the primary colors on apartment-block facades.

ARCHITECTURE

The city's vast architectural catalog covers five centuries of building styles, from preconquest pyramids to modern monoliths. Its historic core is studded with gems from various eras, with colonial fortress-palaces alongside Parisian-style mansions.

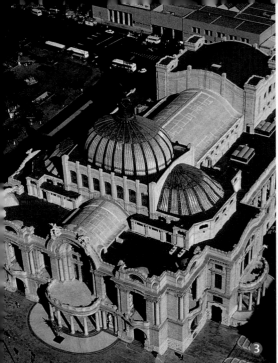

➊ Pre-Hispanic
Pyramids and temples give glimpses of an ancient metropolis (p31).

➋ Modern
Ricardo Legorreta's designs are bold assertions of modern Mexican identity (p67 & p209).

➌ Porfiriato
Dictator Díaz' obsession with European opulence yielded the Palacio de Bellas Artes (p60).

➍ Early 20th Century
The cosmopolitan aspirations of Polanco (p83) and Condesa's (p86) elite are reflected in the districts' ornate architecture.

➎ Colonial
Churches, monasteries and palaces meld Spanish designs with indigenous decoration (p31).

① Museo Frida Kahlo (Casa Azul)
Home of the country's internationally renowned artist in the Coyoacán district (p96).

② Museo del Templo Mayor
Dedicated to Aztec Tenochtitlán and its formidable ceremonial center (p52).

③ Museo Nacional de Antropología
Superbly arranged collection of Mexico's indigenous legacy (p80).

MUSEUMS

History, popular culture, handicrafts and food are just a few of the collections held in the city's museums (many housed in historic buildings). For art buffs, everything from pre-Hispanic symbolism to postrevolutionary social realism is on display.

CONTENTS

Continued from previous page.

THE AUTHORS

Daniel C Schechter

Definitely swimming against the tide, native New Yorker Daniel C Schechter migrated *al otro lado* southward in 1994 to take a peso-salaried teaching post at a university in Mexico City. Shortly afterward, Mexico experienced its worst peso devaluation in decades. Rather than cut and run, Daniel found an even less lucrative job as an editor at Mexico's English-language daily newspaper, launching a midlife career as a writer and translator. After more than a decade in Mexico, Daniel and his wife Myra are back in the USA, though the border is a reassuringly quick drive from their adopted city of Austin, Texas. Daniel was the coordinating author and wrote the Introducing Mexico City, Highlights, Getting Started, Neighborhoods, Drinking, Nightlife, Gay & Lesbian Mexico City, Sleeping, Transportation and Directory chapters and contributed to the Background, Eating and Day Trips & Excursions chapters.

Josephine Quintero

Josephine was married for many years to a Mexican American with a large extended family, leading to a healthy exposure to mariachi music and margaritas. She made frequent trips to Mexico, visiting various Quintero relatives in the DF (Federal District), and continues to be enthralled by the heady mix of vibrant culture, wonderful people, fabulous food and all that history. Now living in Andalucía, Spain, Josephine wrote the Shopping, Arts and Sports & Activities chapters and contributed to the Eating and Background chapters.

Contributing Authors
TOM MASTERS
Tom is a travel writer, journalist and documentary producer based in London. His first experience of Mexico was in the jungles of Chiapas on a two-week filming stint in Palenque, and since then he has fallen particularly hard for Malinalco, Valle de Bravo and José Cuervo Black Medallion. Tom's research of the wonderful towns around Mexico City for the 11th edition of *Mexico* was used for this book's Day Trips & Excursions chapter. You can read more of Tom's work at www.mastersmafia.com.

MAURICIO VELÁZQUEZ DE LEÓN
Mauricio Velázquez de León was born in Mexico City, where he was given boiled chicken feet and toasted corn tortillas to soothe his teething pains. Since then, he has developed an enormous curiosity for food. As a journalist, Mauricio has worked for the Mexican newspaper *Reforma*, *Críticas* magazine, the New York daily *El Diario la Prensa* and the magazines *Escala*, *Viceversa*, *Cinemania* and *Travel Guide*. His food writing has been published in *Saveur*, *Gourmet*, *Leite's Culinaria*, and by Lonely Planet. Like anybody else with a heartbeat, Mauricio has a blog: Josefina's Kitchen (http://josefina-food.blogspot .com). He currently lives in New York City, working as an editor, writer and full-time father of twin toddlers, whose teething pains had been soothed using toasted corn tortillas. According to the internet, his favorite *taquería* is 2094 miles from his current home. Mauricio wrote the 'Drinks (& Great Food) in the Cantina' boxed text in the Eating chapter.

LONELY PLANET AUTHORS
Why is our travel information the best in the world? It's simple: our authors are independent, dedicated travelers. They don't research using just the internet or phone, and they don't take freebies, so you can rely on their advice being well researched and impartial. They travel widely, to all the popular spots and off the beaten track. They personally visit thousands of hotels, restaurants, cafés, bars, galleries, palaces, museums and more – and they take pride in getting all the details right, and telling it how it is. Think you can do it? Find out how at lonelyplanet.com.

11

A trip to Mexico City need not require much planning. Hotel rooms in all price categories are in abundant supply, so accommodation availability is rarely an issue. Since Mexico City is not a standard holiday destination, direct flights to cities throughout the Americas and Europe aren't usually booked far in advance. ATMs on global networks are scattered around town, so you'll always have access to your funds. And there's rarely a slow period in this kaleidoscopic capital. Perhaps the best preparation you can do is to pick up a bit of Spanish before your departure; every word you learn will help you to communicate with Chilangos.

WHEN TO GO

The weather is temperate or warm all year, and mainly dry. It can be cool on autumn and winter nights, and from July to September you can expect afternoon downpours most days. The city bustles year round, though the holiday periods of Christmas–New Year and Semana Santa (Holy Week; the week before Easter Sunday and the couple of days after it) are not good times to get much business done here. Many Mexicans also take holidays in July or August. On the plus side, the relative lack of congestion during those periods makes it a more pleasant time to move around.

Perhaps the best months to visit Mexico City are April, with pleasant temperatures and lilac-colored jacaranda blossoming all around, and October, when the rains have tapered off and the city is awash in Day of the Dead displays.

FESTIVALS
January
DÍA DE LOS REYES MAGOS – THREE KINGS' DAY (EPIPHANY) January 6
Mexican children traditionally receive gifts this day, rather than at Christmas. Between Christmas and January 6, the Santa Clauses around the Alameda Central are replaced by the Three Kings, who are equally popular and look, if anything, even more ill at ease. Families flock in, and stalls selling anything from tacos to music tapes pop up, too.

March & April
FESTIVAL DE MÉXICO EN EL CENTRO HISTÓRICO
www.festival.org.mx
The Centro Histórico's plazas, temples and theaters become performance venues for

a slew of international and Mexican artists during this three-week program of classical and popular music, dance, exhibitions and other cultural events.

SEMANA SANTA – HOLY WEEK Easter
The most evocative events of Holy Week are in the Iztapalapa district, 9km southeast of the Zócalo, where more than 150 locals act out a realistic Passion Play. The most emotive scenes begin at noon on Good Friday, when Christ is sentenced, beaten and crowned with real thorns. He then carries his cross up Cerro de la Estrella, where he is 'crucified.'

July
FERIA DE LAS FLORES Mid-July
San Ángel's annual flower festival takes place when the poppies traditionally bloomed along the banks of the Río de Magdalena (though these days the river runs underneath the traffic). Hundreds of stalls display flowers and plants at the Jardín de la Bombilla (p102), and there are concerts, parades and awards for the best flower arrangements.

September
GRITO DE LA INDEPENDENCIA September 15
Thousands gather in the Zócalo on the eve of Independence Day to hear the Mexican president's version of the Grito de Dolores (Cry of Dolores; Hidalgo's famous call to rebellion against the Spanish in 1810) from the central balcony of the Palacio Nacional at 11pm. Afterwards, there's a spectacular fireworks display over the cathedral. For the best views, reserve dinner at one of the terrace restaurants facing the palace.

FOTOSEPTIEMBRE

In odd-numbered years, this month-long photography summit highlights the creative efforts of hundreds of photo artists from Mexico and Latin America, with exhibits held at museums, galleries and cafés around town.

November

DÍA DE MUERTOS – DAY OF THE DEAD
November 2

Mexico's most characteristic fiesta; the souls of the dead are believed to return to earth this day. Families build *ofrendas* (altars) in homes and visit graveyards to commune with their dead on the preceding night and the day itself, taking garlands, gifts of the dead one's favorite foods and so forth. Sweets resembling human skeletons and skulls are sold in almost every market. In the weeks leading up to the holiday, elaborate *ofrendas* show up everywhere from public markets to metro stations. Some of the best are at the Universidad del Claustro de Sor Juana (p59) and the Museo Dolores Olmedo Patiño (p113), while a contest for the most creative *ofrenda* is held at the Zócalo. Major vigils take place in the Panteón Civil de Dolores cemetery, west of Bosque de Chapultepec, and at San Andres Mixquic, in the extreme southeast of the Distrito Federal.

FIESTA DE SANTA CECILIA
November 22

The patron saint of musicians is honored with special fervor at the Plaza Garibaldi, where a stage is set up for continuous performances by mariachi ensembles.

December

DÍA DE NUESTRA SEÑORA DE GUADALUPE – DAY OF OUR LADY OF GUADALUPE
December 12

At the Basílica de Guadalupe (p116), the Day of Our Lady of Guadalupe caps 10 days of festivities honoring Mexico's religious patron, who appeared to an indigenous Mexican, Juan Diego, on the hill Cerro del Tepeyac in 1531. On December 11 and 12, groups of indigenous dancers and musicians from across Mexico perform in uninterrupted succession on the basilica's broad plaza. The number of pilgrims reaches the millions by December 12, when religious services go on in the basilica almost around the clock.

COSTS & MONEY

A single traveler, staying in budget accommodations and eating two meals a day in restaurants, can expect to pay from M$250 to M$300 a day for those basics. Add in other costs (such as snacks, soft drinks, entry to museums), and you'll spend more like M$400 to M$450. If there are two or more of you sharing a room, costs per person come down considerably. Double rooms are often not much more expensive than singles, and triples or quadruples are available in many hotels for only slightly more than doubles.

In the middle range you can live well in Mexico City for M$600 to M$700 per person per day. Two people can easily find a clean, modern room with private bath and a TV for M$450 to M$600, and have the rest for food, admission fees, transportation and incidentals.

At the top of the scale, a few hotels charge more than M$3000 for a room, and there are restaurants where you can pay M$600 or more per person. But you can also stay at very comfortable hotels for under M$1200 a double, and eat very well for M$300 to M$600 per person per day.

Keep your costs down by having a *comida corrida*, a three- or four-course set lunch served by many restaurants, or make a meal of the tasty *botanas* (snacks) served by cantinas along with each drink you order. Almost all Mexico City museums are free on Sundays and many cinemas have half-price shows on Wednesdays (of course, those places will also be more crowded then). The city regularly stages free concerts on the Zócalo on weekends and many museums offer music recitals and films – check *Tiempo Libre* magazine for listings. Finally, use the metro and the Metrobus to get around instead of taxis.

HOW MUCH?

Liter of unleaded gas M$7
Liter of Herradura tequila M$230
Liter bottle of purified water M$8
Bottle of Corona beer M$20
Set of six tequila glasses M$150
Taco de bistec (beef taco) M$8
Kilo of tortillas M$8.50
Taxi ride from Zócalo to Zona Rosa M$70
Metro ride M$2
Movie at Cineteca Nacional M$40

INTERNET RESOURCES

The following sites compile oodles of information on the capital. Some offer their pages in English, but the English pages are often not as thorough or are sometimes barely comprehensible.

Artes Visuales (www.artesvisuales.com.mx, in Spanish) Covers DF galleries and museums, including links to many of their own sites.

Chilango (www.chilango.com, in Spanish) Online version of glossy what's on mag with extensive restaurant and nightlife listings.

Consejo Nacional Para la Cultura y las Artes (www.cnca .gob.mx, in Spanish) Up-to-date guide to DF museums, libraries, theaters and other cultural institutions, including a *cartelera* (calendar) of current happenings.

DFiesta en el DF (www.dfiestaeneldf.com) Tourism department's exhaustive listings with plenty of practical information.

Secretaría de Cultura del Distrito Federal (www.cultura .df.gob.mx, in Spanish) DF festivals and museum events.

Sistema de Transporte Colectivo (www.metro.df.gob.mx, in Spanish) All about the Mexico City metro.

SUSTAINABLE MEXICO CITY

The mayor of Mexico City, Marcelo Ebrard, seems intent on turning around this ecologically dysfunctional metropolis (see p35). No matter how short your stay, you can join other progressive-minded Chilangos in supporting the mayor's quixotic efforts. Here are a few suggestions.

Instead of driving a car or taking taxis, use the metro and the metrobus to get around town. If you just need a quick dash around the city center, bicycle taxis are a good alternative to gas-powered vehicles. If you are traveling elsewhere in the republic but aren't pressed for time, travel by bus instead of flying.

The city produces colossal quantities of trash, but you can slightly reduce the flow. Instead of buying multiple bottles of purified water, refill the first one from the drinking-water cooler provided by some hotels. Juice stands want to give you styrofoam but bring your own cup or bottle and have them fill it. Buy a shopping bag (available in an array of tantalizing colors at the nearest market) to put your souvenirs or snacks into.

Despite the voluminous rain that falls upon the Valle de México, the city's underground aquifers are not being replenished fast enough to meet the voracious demand for drinking water, and some 30% of the water supply is lost through leaks in the pipe network. You can avoid contributing to the impending crisis by being conscious of your water use while in the city. Don't run taps unnecessarily – for instance, when shaving or brushing your teeth – and cut down on your shower time.

HISTORY

Driving over the sea of asphalt that now overlays this highland basin, you'd be hard pressed to imagine that, a mere five centuries ago, it was filled by a chain of lakes. It would further stretch your powers to think that today's downtown was on a small island crisscrossed by canals. Or that the communities who inhabited this island and the banks of the lake spoke a patchwork of languages that had as little to do with Spanish as Malaysian or Urdu. As their chronicles related, the Spaniards who arrived at the shores of that lake in the early 1500s were just as amazed to witness such a scene.

Water covered much of the floor of the Valle de México when humans began moving in as early as 30,000 BC. Eventually it started shrinking back, and hunting became tougher, so the inhabitants turned to agriculture. A loose federation of farming villages had evolved around Lago de Texcoco by approximately 200 BC. The biggest of these, Cuicuilco, was destroyed by a volcanic eruption three centuries later.

Breakthroughs in irrigation techniques and the development of a maize-based economy contributed to the rise of a civilization at Teotihuacán, 40km northeast of the lake. For centuries Teotihuacán was the capital of an empire whose influence extended as far as Guatemala. However, unable to sustain its burgeoning population, it fell in the 8th century. The Toltecs, possibly descended from the nomadic tribes who invaded Teotihuacán, arose as the next great civilization, building their capital at Tula, 65km north of modern-day Mexico City. By the 12th century the Tula empire had collapsed as well, leaving a number of statelets to compete for control of the Valle de México. It was the Aztecs who emerged supreme.

AZTEC MEXICO CITY

The Aztecs, or Mexica (meh-*shee*-kah), arrived a century after the Toltecs' demise. A wandering tribe that claimed to have come from Aztlán, a mythical region in northwest Mexico, they initially acted as mercenary fighters for the Tepanecas, who resided on the lake's southern shore, and they were allowed to settle upon the inhospitable terrain of Chapultepec. After being captured by the warriors of rival Culhuacán, the Aztecs played the same role for their new masters. Cocoxtli, Culhuacán's ruler, sent them into battle against nearby Xochimilco, and the Aztecs delivered over 8000 human ears as proof of their victory. They later sought a marriage alliance with Culhuacán, and Cocoxtli offered his own daughter's hand to the Aztec chieftain. But at the wedding banquet, the ruler's pride turned to horror: a dancer was garbed in the flayed skin of his daughter, who had been sacrificed to Huizilopochtli, the Aztec god of war.

Fleeing from the wrath of Culhuacán, the tribe wandered the swampy fringes of the lake, finally reaching an island near the western shore around 1325. There, according to legend, they witnessed an eagle standing atop a cactus and devouring a snake, which they interpreted as a sign to stop and build a city, Tenochtitlán.

TIMELINE

30,000 BC–1200 BC	AD 150	1325
Human beings begin to populate the Valle de México, living off the plants and animals around Lago de Texcoco. As the larger game animals start dying off, hunting is gradually replaced by agriculture.	World's third-biggest pyramid, the Pirámide del Sol, completed at Teotihuacán. At its height, the city northeast of Lago de Texcoco counted 125,000 inhabitants and practiced intensive agriculture.	Nomadic Aztecs spot an eagle devouring a snake while perched atop a cactus on an island in Lago de Texcoco. The vision was their cue to establish their capital, Tenochtitlán, at this site.

Tenochtitlán rapidly became a sophisticated city-state whose empire would, by the early 16th century, span most of modern-day central Mexico from the Pacific to the Gulf of Mexico and into far southern Mexico. The Aztecs built their city on a grid plan, with canals as thoroughfares and causeways to the lakeshore. At the city's heart stood the main Teocalli (sacred precinct), with its temple dedicated to Huizilopochtli and the water god, Tláloc. In the marshier parts of the island, they created raised gardens by piling up vegetation and mud, and planting willows. These *chinampas* (versions of which can still be seen at Xochimilco in southern Mexico City) gave three or four harvests yearly but were still not enough to feed the growing population.

To supplement their resources, the Aztecs extracted tribute from conquered tribes. The empire yielded products such as jade, turquoise, cotton, paper, tobacco, rubber, lowland fruits and vegetables, cacao and precious feathers, which were needed for the glorification of the elite and to support the many nonproductive servants of its war-oriented state. In the mid-15th century they formed the Triple Alliance with the lakeshore states Texcoco and Tlacopan to conduct wars against Tlaxcala and Huejotzingo, which lay east of the valley. The purpose was to gain a steady supply of prisoners to sate Huizilopochtli's vast hunger for sacrificial victims, so that the sun would rise each day.

When the Spanish arrived in 1519, Tenochtitlán's population was an estimated 200,000 to 300,000 – far bigger than any city in Spain at that time – and that of the whole Valle de México was perhaps 1.5 million, already making it one of the world's densest urban areas.

THE SPANISH CONQUEST

The Aztec empire, and with it nearly 3000 years of ancient Mexican civilization, was shattered in two short years – 1519 to 1521. A tiny group of invaders brought a new religion and reduced the native people to second-class citizens and slaves. So alien to each other were the two sides that each doubted whether the other was human (the Pope gave the Mexicans the benefit of the doubt in 1537).

From this traumatic encounter arose modern Mexico. Most Mexicans, being mestizo (of mixed indigenous and European ancestry), are descendants of both cultures. But while Cuauhtémoc, the last Aztec emperor, is now an official Mexican hero, Hernán Cortés, the leader of the Spanish conquistadors, is seen as a villain, and the native people who helped him as traitors.

The Spanish had been in the Caribbean since Columbus arrived in 1492. Realizing that they had not reached the East Indies, they began looking for a passage through the land mass to their west but were distracted by tales of gold, silver and a rich empire there.

The Aztec ruler at the time was Moctezuma II Xocoyotzin, a reflective character who believed (perhaps fatally) that Cortés, who arrived on the Gulf Coast in 1519, might be the feathered serpent god Quetzalcóatl. According to legend, Quetzalcóatl had been driven out of Tula centuries before but had vowed to return one day and reclaim his throne.

Cortés' Expedition

In 1518 the Spanish governor of Cuba, Diego Velázquez, asked Hernán Cortés, a colonist on the island, to lead a new expedition westward. As Cortés gathered ships and men, Velázquez became uneasy about the costs and Cortés' loyalty, and tried to cancel the expedition. But Cortés ignored him and set sail on February 15, 1519, with 11 ships, 550 men and 16 horses. The Spaniards landed first at Cozumel off the Yucatán Peninsula then moved round the coast

1487	1519	1521
The Aztec king Ahuízotl has no less than 20,000 prisoners sacrificed for the dedication of Tenochtitlán's newly rebuilt main temple, the Templo Mayor.	A small group of Spanish explorers led by Hernán Cortés arrives on Mexico's Gulf Coast, then makes its way through the sierra, entering Aztec Tenochtitlán on November 8.	Cortes' men, bolstered by 100,000 native allies, conquer the Aztecs. After razing Tenochtitlán to the ground, they set about establishing their own capital, Mexico City, upon the ruins.

to Tabasco. There they defeated some hostile locals and Cortés gave the first of many lectures to Mexicans on the importance of Christianity and the greatness of King Carlos I of Spain. The locals gave him 20 maidens, among them Doña Marina (La Malinche), who became his interpreter, aide and lover.

The expedition next put in near the site of the city of Veracruz. In Tenochtitlán, Moctezuma began hearing tales of 'towers floating on water' bearing fair-skinned beings. Lightning struck a temple, a comet sailed through the night skies, and a bird 'with a mirror in its head' was brought to Moctezuma, who saw warriors in it. Unsure whether or not Cortés was the returning Quetzalcóatl, Moctezuma tried to discourage him from traveling to Tenochtitlán by sending messages about the difficult terrain and hostile tribes that lay between them.

Cortés apparently then scuttled his ships to prevent his men from retreating and, leaving about 150 men on the coast, set off for Tenochtitlán. On the way, he won over the Tlaxcalans as allies. After an unsuccessful attempt to ambush the Spaniards at Cholula, about 120km east of Tenochtitlán, Moctezuma finally invited Cortés to meet him. The Spaniards and 6000 indigenous allies thus entered Tenochtitlán on November 8, 1519. Cortés was met by Moctezuma, who was carried by nobles in a litter with a canopy of feathers and gold.

The Spaniards were lodged in luxury – as befitted gods – in the palace of Axayacatl, Moctezuma's father. But they were trapped. Some Aztec leaders advised Moctezuma to attack them, but Moctezuma hesitated and the Spaniards took him hostage instead. Moctezuma told his people he went willingly, but hostility rose in the city, aggravated by the Spaniards' destruction of Aztec idols.

The Fall of Tenochtitlán

After the Spaniards had been in Tenochtitlán for about six months, Moctezuma informed Cortés that another fleet had arrived on the Veracruz coast. This had been sent from Cuba to arrest Cortés. Cortés left 140 Spaniards under Pedro de Alvarado in Tenochtitlán and sped to the coast with his remaining forces. They routed the bigger rival force, and most of the defeated men joined Cortés.

Meanwhile, things boiled over in Tenochtitlán. Apparently fearing an attack, Alvarado's men struck first and killed about 200 Aztec nobles trapped in a square during a festival. Cortés and his enlarged force returned to the Aztec capital and were allowed to rejoin their comrades, only to come under fierce attack. Trapped in Axayacatl's palace, Cortés persuaded Moctezuma to try to pacify his people. According to one version, the king went on to the roof to address the crowds but was mortally wounded by missiles; other versions say that the Spaniards killed him.

The Spaniards fled on the night of June 30, 1520, but several hundred, and thousands of their indigenous allies, were killed on the Noche Triste (Sad Night). The survivors retreated to Tlaxcala, and prepared for another campaign by building boats in sections that could be carried across the mountains for a waterborne assault on Tenochtitlán. When the 900 Spaniards re-entered the Valle de México, they were accompanied by perhaps 100,000 native allies.

Moctezuma had been replaced by his nephew, Cuitláhuac, who then died of smallpox brought to Mexico by a Spanish soldier. Cuitláhuac was succeeded by another nephew, the 18-year-old Cuauhtémoc. The attack started in May 1521. Cortés resorted to razing Tenochtitlán building by building, and by August 13, 1521, the resistance ended. The captured Cuauhtémoc asked Cortés to kill him, but was denied his request.

1531	1629	1810
On December 12, a vision of the Virgin of Guadalupe appears before indigenous peasant Juan Diego on Tepeyac Hill at the site of an Aztec religious shrine.	Torrential rain leaves Mexico City submerged under water for five years, until 1634, when the drainage canal is finally expanded and improved. Residents either flee for higher ground or take up rowing.	After declaring independence from Spain at Guanajuato, the priest Miguel Hidalgo leads 80,000 troops to Mexico City. They defeat the loyalist forces outside the capital, but the War of Independence continues for another 11 years.

CAPITAL OF NUEVA ESPAÑA

Establishing their headquarters at Coyoacán, on the southern shore of the Lago de Texcoco, the Spaniards had the ruined Tenochtitlán rebuilt as the capital of Nueva España (New Spain), as the new colony was called. The city's central plaza (today the Zócalo) was laid out next to the former site of the Aztecs' Teocalli. Beside the plaza Cortés had a palace (today the Palacio Nacional – the presidential palace) and a cathedral built.

From this capital, the Spanish sent out expeditions to subdue not only the rest of the Aztec empire but also other parts of Mexico and Central America that had not been under Aztec control. By 1600 the territory ruled from Mexico City stretched from what's now northern Mexico to the border of Panama (though in practice Central America was governed separately).

COLONIAL GOVERNMENT & SOCIETY

The Spanish king Carlos I denied Cortés the role of governor of Nueva España, and the crown waged a long, eventually successful struggle through the 16th century to restrict the power of the conquistadors in the colony. (Cortés returned disillusioned to Spain in 1540 and died there in 1547.) In 1527 Carlos I set up Nueva España's first *audiencia,* a high court with governmental functions. Then in 1535 he appointed Antonio de Mendoza as the colony's first viceroy, his personal representative to govern it. Mendoza, who ruled from Mexico City for 15 years, brought badly needed stability, limited the worst exploitation of indigenous people, encouraged missionary efforts and ensured steady revenue to the Spanish crown.

By 1550 the city emerged as the prosperous, elegant capital of Nueva España. Broad, straight streets were laid out along the Aztec causeways and canals. Indigenous labor built hospitals, palaces and a university according to Spanish designs with local materials such as *tezontle,* a red volcanic rock which the Aztecs had used for their temples. The various Catholic orders (the Dominicans, Augustinians, Franciscans and Jesuits) had massive monastic complexes erected.

While the Spaniards prospered, the conquered peoples declined disastrously, less because of harsh treatment than because of a series of plagues, many of them new diseases brought over from the Old World, such as smallpox and measles. The native population of the Valle de México shrank, by most estimates, to less than 100,000 within a century of the conquest.

The indigenous people's best allies were some of the monks who started arriving in Nueva España in 1523 to convert them. Many of these were compassionate, brave men; the Franciscan and Dominican orders distinguished themselves by protecting the local people from the colonists' worst excesses. The monks' missionary work also helped extend Spanish control over Mexico. Under the second viceroy, Luis de Velasco, indigenous slavery was abolished in the 1550s. Forced labor continued, however, as indigenous slavery was partly replaced by African slavery.

Building continued through the 17th century but problems arose as the weighty colonial structures began sinking into the soft, squishy lake bed. Furthermore, lacking natural drainage, the city suffered floods caused by the partial destruction in the 1520s of the Aztecs' canals. Lago de Texcoco often overflowed, damaging buildings, bringing disease and forcing thousands of people to relocate.

Urban conditions improved in the 1700s as new plazas and avenues were installed, along with sewage- and garbage-collection systems and a police force. This was Mexico City's gilded age. But

1824	1833–55	1847
After the overthrow and execution of Emperor Iturbide, the Constitution of 1824 is adopted, declaring Mexico a republic with a representative legislature and a popularly elected president.	Mexican presidency changes hands 36 times, with 11 terms going to one general, Antonio López de Santa Anna.	During the Mexican–American war, US forces invade Mexico City, storming Chapultepec Castle. Six heroic teenaged Mexican cadets perish rather than surrender, assuring their place in martyrdom.

the shiny capital was mainly the domain of a Spanish and criollo (people born of Spanish parents in Nueva España) elite who made their fortunes in silver mining. The masses of indigenous and mixed-race peasants who served them were confined to outlying neighborhoods.

INDEPENDENCE

Spanish king Carlos III (1759–88), aware of the threat to Nueva España from British and French expansion further north, sought to bring his colony under firmer control and improve the flow of funds to the crown. He reorganized the colonial administration and expelled the Jesuits, whom he suspected of disloyalty, from the entire Spanish empire.

In 1804 the Spanish crown decreed the transfer of the powerful Catholic Church's many assets in Nueva España to the royal coffers. The church had to call in many debts, which hit criollos hard and created widespread discontent. Then, in 1808, France's Napoleon Bonaparte occupied most of Spain, and direct Spanish control over Nueva España evaporated. Rivalry in the colony between peninsulares (those born in Spain and sent by the Spanish government to rule the colony in Mexico), who remained loyal to Spain, and criollos, who sought political power commensurate with their economic power, intensified. Criollos began plotting rebellion.

On October 30, 1810, some 80,000 independence rebels, fresh from victory at Guanajuato, overpowered Spanish loyalist forces just west of the capital. But they were not sufficiently equipped to capitalize on this triumph, and their leader, Padre Miguel Hidalgo, chose not to advance on the city – a decision that cost Mexico 11 more years of fighting before independence was achieved.

After independence, Mexico was ruled by a long succession of short-lived governments, with an ongoing struggle between proreform liberals and antireform conservatives. The presidency was occupied repeatedly by General Antonio López de Santa Anna, who is best remembered for losing large chunks of Mexican territory to the USA. It was under Santa Anna's watch that the Mexican–American War broke out, following the US annexation of Texas. During the conflict, US troops briefly captured Mexico City after a fierce battle at the Ex-Convento de Churubusco in Coyoacán.

The liberal government that finally replaced Santa Anna in 1855 attempted to dismantle Mexico's conservative state and break the economic power of the church. Under the reform laws instituted by President Benito Juárez, the monasteries and churches were appropriated by the government, then sold off, subdivided and put to other uses. This anticlerical stance precipitated the internal War of the Reform between the liberals and conservatives. The liberals won, but in 1862 France's Napoleon III decided to invade a weakened Mexico. Despite a May 5 defeat at Puebla (still celebrated every year as Cinco de Mayo), 130km east of Mexico City, the French occupied Mexico City in 1863. The following year Napoleon installed the Austrian archduke, Maximilian of Hapsburg, as emperor of Mexico. Juárez and his government retreated to the provinces.

Maximilian and his wife, Empress Carlota, moved into the Castillo de Chapultepec (instead of the Palacio Nacional on the Zócalo, traditional residence of Mexico's heads of state). They had Paseo de la Reforma, still the city's grandest boulevard, laid out to connect Chapultepec with the city center. But their reign was brief. Under pressure from the USA, Napoleon withdrew his troops and in 1867 Maximilian – a noble but naive figure – was defeated and executed by republican forces at Querétaro, 215km northwest of Mexico City.

1877–1911	1900	1910
Porfirio Díaz rules Mexico with an iron fist for three decades. The city is transformed by Díaz' infrastructure projects and monuments, but his repressive government sets the stage for the revolution.	Grand drainage canal finally completed, 300 years after its inception, finally drying up the Lago de Texcoco and greatly reducing the threat of floods in the sealed Valle de México basin.	Francisco Madero runs against Díaz for president. Díaz throws his opponent in prison and wins the race. After Madero is released, he declares Díaz' presidency illegitimate, thus launching the Mexican Revolution.

THE PORFIRIATO

Mexico City entered the modern age under the despotic Porfirio Díaz, who ruled Mexico for most of the period from 1877 to 1911 and attracted much foreign investment. Díaz ushered in a construction boom, building Parisian-style mansions and theaters, while the city's wealthier residents escaped the center for newly minted neighborhoods toward the west like Roma and Polanco. Some 150km of electric tramways threaded the streets, industry grew, and by 1910 the city had more than half a million inhabitants. A drainage canal and tunnel finally succeeded in drying up much of Lago de Texcoco, allowing further expansion.

Díaz kept Mexico free of the wars that had plagued it for over 60 years, but at the price of political repression, foreign ownership of Mexican resources, and appalling conditions for many workers. Wealth became concentrated in the hands of a small minority. Such extreme economic disparity led to the Mexican Revolution, a confusing sequence of allegiances and conflicts between a spectrum of leaders and their armies, in which successive attempts to create a stable government were wrecked by new outbreaks of devastating fighting.

THE REVOLUTION

When rebels under Francisco 'Pancho' Villa took Ciudad Juárez on the US border in May 1911, Díaz resigned. The liberal Francisco Madero was elected president in November 1911, but found himself in conflict with more radical leaders, including Emiliano Zapata in the state of Morelos, south of Mexico City, who was fighting for the transfer of land from large estates to the peasants.

In February 1913 two conservative leaders – Félix Díaz, nephew of Porfirio, and Bernardo Reyes – were sprung from prison in Mexico City and commenced a counterrevolution based in La Ciudadela, a building 700m south of the Alameda Central (Map p64). This brought the Decena Trágica, 10 days of fierce fighting, to the capital. Thousands were killed or wounded and many buildings were destroyed. The fighting ended only after US ambassador Henry Lane Wilson negotiated for Madero's general, Victoriano Huerta, to switch to the rebel side and help depose Madero. Huerta became president; Madero and his vice president José María Pino Suárez were executed.

The unpopular Huerta himself was soon deposed and the revolution devolved into a confrontation between the liberal 'Constitutionalists,' led by Venustiano Carranza, and the forces led by populist Villa and the radical Zapata. But Villa and Zapata, despite a famous meeting in Mexico City in 1914, never formed a serious alliance, and the fighting became increasingly anarchic. Carranza emerged the victor in 1917, but in 1920 former allies including Álvaro Obregón and Plutarco Elías Calles ran him out of office and had him assassinated. The revolutionary decade had devastated the economy – starvation was widespread, including in Mexico City – and an estimated 1.5 to two million Mexicans, roughly one-eighth of the country's population, had lost their lives.

RECONSTRUCTION & GROWTH

The 1920s ushered in peace and a modicum of prosperity. The postrevolution minister of education, José Vasconcelos, commissioned Mexico's top artists – notably Diego Rivera, David Alfaro Siqueiros and José Clemente Orozco – to decorate numerous public buildings in Mexico City

1910–20	1917	1985
Almost two million die and the economy is shattered in the Mexican Revolution. As fighting degenerates into factional struggles, popular revolutionary heroes Francisco 'Pancho' Villa and Emiliano Zapata are superseded by the liberal constitutionalists.	A new constitution is drawn up, guaranteeing civil rights for all Mexicans and recognizing the nation's indigenous identity. Freedom of speech and the press are also declared.	On September 19, an earthquake measuring 8.1 on the Richter scale strikes Mexico City, killing thousands and destroying numerous buildings. Emergency relief effort is led by citizens as city government fails to address the crisis.

ECHOES OF TLATELOLCO

Nineteen sixty-eight marked a pivotal moment for Mexican democracy. Perhaps due to the subversive mood of the era, unrest was rife and students took to the streets to denounce political corruption and authoritarianism. Mexico had been chosen to host the Olympics that year, and President Gustavo Díaz Ordaz was anxious to present an image of stability to the world. Known for his authoritarian style, Díaz Ordaz employed heavy-handed tactics to stop the protests, in turn generating further unrest from a broader coalition of middle-class *capitalinos* (residents of Mexico City).

On the afternoon of October 2, a week before the Olympics were to begin, a demonstration was held on Tlatelolco's Plaza de las Tres Culturas. Helicopters hovered overhead and a massive police contingent cordoned off the zone. Suddenly a flare dropped from one of the choppers and shots rang out, apparently from the balcony that the protestors had made into a speaker's platform. Police then opened fire on the demonstrators and mayhem ensued. Later, government-authorized newspaper accounts blamed student snipers for igniting the incident and reported 20 protesters killed, although the real number is acknowledged to be closer to 400. News of the massacre was swept under the rug and the Olympic Games went on without a hitch.

There are numerous theories as to what actually occurred that October day. But the generally accepted version is that the government staged the massacre, planting snipers on the balcony to make it seem as if the students had provoked the violence. Many Mexicans viewed the killings as a premeditated tactic by the government to suppress dissent, permanently discrediting the postrevolutionary regime.

Four decades later, the Tlatelolco massacre was still recalled bitterly by a generation of Mexicans after an investigation authorized by President Vicente Fox, the country's first opposition-party president in modern history, failed to yield any new revelations. Meanwhile, a new museum was inaugurated beside the scene of the carnage (see p116) to commemorate and document the epochal incident.

with vivid, semipropagandistic murals on social, political and historical themes. This was the start of a major movement in Mexican art, with a lasting impact on the face of the city.

Following the Great Depression, a drive to industrialize attracted more money and people, and by 1940 the population had reached 1.7 million. Factories and skyscrapers rose in tandem with the population surge in the following decades. But the supply of housing, jobs and services could not keep pace, and shantytowns appeared on the city's fringes as Mexico City began to grow uncontrollably. Economic growth continued in the 1960s, but political and social reform lagged behind, as was made painfully evident by the massacre of hundreds of students in the lead-up to the 1968 Olympic Games (see the boxed text, above).

Mexico City continued to grow at an alarming rate in the 1970s, as the rural poor sought economic refuge in the capital's thriving industries, and the population of the metropolitan area surged from 8.7 to 14.5 million. Unable to contain the masses of new arrivals, the Distrito Federal (DF; Federal District, the geographic entity that comprises Mexico City's territory) spread beyond its boundaries into the adjacent state of México, which eventually became more populous than the DF proper. The result of such unbridled growth was some of the world's worst traffic and pollution, only partly alleviated by the metro system (opened in 1969) and by attempts in the 1990s to limit traffic. On September 19, 1985, an earthquake measuring over 8.0 on the Richter scale hit Mexico City, killing at least 10,000 and displacing thousands more. Still, people kept pouring in.

Today the metropolitan area counts an estimated 22 million inhabitants, around a fifth of the country's population. Though growth has slowed in the last decade, there are still some 100,000

1997	2000	2006
Mexico City gains political autonomy; opposition party candidate Cuauhtémoc Cárdenas becomes first popularly elected mayor in city's history.	National Action Party (PAN) candidate Vicente Fox elected president, releasing Mexico from one-party rule after seven decades. Popular politician Andrés Manuel López Obrador elected mayor of Mexico City.	López Obrador is defeated in presidential election by PAN candidate Felipe Calderón. Marcelo Ebrard becomes mayor of Mexico City.

newcomers and 150,000 births annually. Mexico City is the industrial, financial and communications center of the country; its industries generate a quarter of Mexico's wealth, and its people consume two-thirds of Mexico's energy. Its cost of living is the highest in the nation.

POSTMILLENNIAL OPTIMISM

The year 2000 marked a watershed in Mexico's political development. After 70 years of continuous rule by the Partido Revolucionaria Institucional (PRI; Institutional Revolutionary Party), an opposition candidate, Vicente Fox of the National Action Party (PAN), was elected president. Furthermore, Andrés Manuel López Obrador (commonly known as AMLO), a member of the left-leaning PRD (Party of the Democratic Revolution), was elected mayor of Mexico City. Under López Obrador's administration, the face of the capital began to change for the better, starting with a massive renovation of the Centro Histórico. Financed in part by Carlos Slim (the world's richest man as of 2007), the city launched renovations of the zone's cobblestone streets and building facades, installing new lighting, bolstering security and sweeping thousands of unauthorized vendors from the streets. Similar face-lifts have been performed on the Paseo de la Reforma corridor and in the Alameda Central area. The urban landscape has been further transformed by a wave of new construction, attributed to low interest rates, a stable currency and renewed attention by foreign investors. Among the more architecturally impressive new structures are the new Foreign Relations Secretariat building (p66), alongside the Alameda Central, and the 59-storey Torre Mayor (p73), Latin America's tallest building.

The DF's notorious smog has been significantly curtailed thanks to tougher emission controls, while traffic congestion has been relieved by the construction of elevated highways along various sections of the city's freeways (a project that was poignantly documented in the 2007 film, *In the Pit)*. Meanwhile, the installation of the metrobus along Av Insurgentes, the city's principal north–south corridor, has displaced an unruly, polluting fleet of buses, further reducing congestion (though the increased volume of vehicles on the road somewhat offsets those improvements). Crime, though still a persistent concern for *capitalinos* (residents of Mexico City) and visitors, has significantly dropped off since the 1990s.

PRD candidate Marcelo Ebrard won a sweeping victory in Mexico City's mayoral elections of 2006, consolidating his party's grip on the city government. Also registering an overwhelming takeover of the Federal District's legislative assembly, the PRD passed a flood of progressive initiatives, including the sanctioning of gay unions and the legalization of abortion and euthanasia. Though Ebrard doesn't inspire the sort of fervor demonstrated by AMLO's followers, his work may have longer-lasting effects. Whether due to the city's recently won autonomy or the country's exhilaration after being released from the grip of seven decades of one-party rule (see p36), the turn of the millennium marked an improvement in Mexico City's mood.

Not content with having a safer, cleaner city, current Mayor Marcelo Ebrard is also striving to make the DF a more fun place, providing a slew of new recreational options for stressed-out Chilangos. Every Sunday morning, skaters and cyclists have the run of Paseo de la Reforma and other thoroughfares that have been closed to auto traffic. The city has poured truckloads of sand alongside various public swimming pools to create 'urban beaches,' much to the delight of residents who lack the means to get to the coasts. And during the winter holidays, an enormous ice-skating rink is installed on the Zócalo, with thousands of pairs of skates loaned free of charge.

ARTS

It's hard to think of Mexico in black and white. This is a country where dazzling color is never far from view. Just as the dull green skin of a fresh fig is peeled to reveal a seductive crimson flesh, so an otherwise drab urban street can suddenly explode with color from a mural, a market store or a vividly painted building. The capital's art world is similarly heavy hitting and dynamic, reflecting the lifestyle and extremes of society here, where wealth and poverty stand side by side in edgy and controversial partnership.

While Diego Rivera is considered equal only to Picasso in terms of his range of painting technique and style, it is Frida Kahlo who has achieved global cult status and helped publicize Mexican art. Many of today's tourists have included DF on their itinerary quite simply because they cannot admit to anyone back home that they missed seeing the Museo Frida Kahlo (better known as the Blue House; see p96) on their trip to Mexico or, of course, genuinely want to enjoy the experience firsthand. Inevitably, they subsequently discover that this is only scratching the canvas' surface as far as the depth and richness of the city's art world is concerned. Art is, in general, also very accessible in Mexico City with museums exhibiting grand works of historical art, as well as contemporary art galleries that easily equal those in New York or London in terms of cutting edge innovation. And then there are the murals which are both proudly displayed in palaces and museums, as well as in obscure corners all over the city (see the boxed text, p26).

Mexico's heritage in the arts extends to its literature and music; the latter ranging from the traditional folk of the southwest to the Latino ska of the city. Music is played at any excuse and every occasion, ranging from the cheerful cacophony of several mariachi bands touting for business (simultaneously) in Plaza Garibaldi to the blind man on the metro selling pirated CDs of the latest Lila Downs release. Dance is similarly an important part of Mexican culture, particularly the traditional indigenous dances enjoyed at fiestas and which can be experienced in all their glory at the Palacio de Bellas Artes' *Ballet Folclórico de México* performance (see p180).

PAINTING

Mexico City is a fabulous destination for art buffs. Since pre-Hispanic times, remarkably talented painters have lived and worked here. Many of them share a love for vibrant colors, clearly displayed in their dramatic landscapes, portraits and murals. More recently, the city has become a base for international artists clearly stimulated by the light, the colors and the culture. There are numerous museums and galleries where you can enjoy Mexico's paintings, both past and present.

Pre-Hispanic

The earliest Mexican murals, found at Teotihuacán, are outstanding. Here, within a reconstruction of a temple, is the sumptuous *Paradise of Tláloc* mural which depicts, in detail, the delights awaiting those who died at the hands of the water god Tláloc. The people of Cacaxtla near Puebla (AD 650 to 900) also left some vivid murals depicting battle scenes. The surviving art of the Aztecs (circa 1350 to 1521) is more sculpture than painting, but some frescoes survive. The Maya of southeast Mexico and Guatemala, at their cultural height from about AD 250 to 900, were ancient Mexico's most artistic people and created some marvelous multicolored murals and pottery. They have undoubtedly inspired subsequent generations of artists, sculptors and muralists across the country.

Colonial Period

Mexican art during Spanish rule was heavily influenced by the colonizers and became chiefly religious in subject, though portraiture grew in popularity under wealthy patrons. The Academia de San Carlos, founded in Mexico City in 1783 by Spanish royal decree, had its students learn by copying European masterworks. The 18th-century painters Juan Correa and Miguel Cabrera were leading figures of the era in Mexico. Correa was one the most accomplished and productive painters of his era, undertaking many important religious commissions, including that of the famous Virgin of Guadalupe (the patron saint and beloved icon of Mexico City). Although you have to travel to Santa Monica, California to view this emblematic painting, examples of Correa's work can be viewed at Mexico City's Metropolitan Cathedral. Miguel Cabrera was an equally famous painter of his time, favored particularly by the Archbishop and of the Jesuit order, earning him many commissions. His style follows that of the Spanish painter Bartolomé Estéban Murillo, with a sureness of touch lacking in the more labored efforts of many of his contemporaries. In 1753 he founded and presided over Mexico's first Art Academy. Stunning examples of Cabrera's work can be found at the Church of San Francisco Javier, the Jesuit monastery in Tepotzótlan.

Independent Mexico

Juan Cordero (1824–84) began the modern Mexican mural tradition by expressing historical and philosophical ideas on public buildings. The landscapes of José María Velasco (1840–1912) captured the magical qualities of the country around Mexico City before it was swallowed up by urban growth.

The years before the 1910 revolution saw a break from European traditions and the beginnings of socially conscious art. Slums, brothels and indigenous poverty began to appear on canvas. The cartoons and engravings of José Guadalupe Posada (1852–1913), with his characteristic *calavera* (skull) motif, satirized the injustices of the Porfiriato period and were aimed at a much wider audience than most earlier Mexican art. Gerardo Murillo (1875–1964), known as Dr Atl, displayed some scandalously orgiastic paintings at a show marking the 1910 centenary of the independence movement.

The Muralists

In the 1920s, immediately after the revolution, education minister José Vasconcelos commissioned leading young artists to paint a series of murals on public buildings to spread awareness of Mexican history and culture and impel social and technological change. The trio of great muralists were Diego Rivera (1885–1957), David Alfaro Siqueiros (1896–1974), and José Clemente Orozco (1883–1949).

Rivera's work carried a clear left-wing message, emphasizing past oppression suffered by indigenous people and peasants. He had an intense interest in native Mexico and tried hard to pull together the country's indigenous and Spanish roots into one national identity. Typically, his murals are colorful, crowded tableaux depicting historical figures (like Cortés) and events or symbolic scenes of Mexican life, with a simple, clear-cut moral message. They're realistic, if not always lifelike. To fully appreciate Rivera's subtleties you need some knowledge of Mexican history and, preferably, a guide or some know-it-all friend to explain the finer details.

Siqueiros, who fought on the Constitutionalist side in the revolution (while Rivera was in Europe), remained a political activist, spending subsequent time in jail and leading an attempt to kill Leon Trotsky in Mexico City in 1940. His murals lack Rivera's detailed realism but convey a more clearly Marxist message through dramatic, symbolic depictions of the oppressed and grotesque caricatures of the oppressors. Some of his best works are at the Palacio de Bellas Artes, Castillo de Chapultepec and Ciudad Universitaria.

Orozco focused more on the universal human condition than on historical or political specifics. He conveyed emotion, character and atmosphere. More of a pessimist than Rivera or Siqueiros, by the 1930s Orozco grew disillusioned with the revolution. Some of his most powerful works, such as those in the Palacio de Bellas Artes, depict oppressive scenes of degradation, violence or injustice but do not offer any simplistic political solution.

Rivera, Siqueiros and Orozco were also great artists. A number of their portraits, drawings and other works can be seen in various art museums in Mexico City.

The muralist movement continued well after WWII. Rufino Tamayo (1899–1991), from Oaxaca, was relatively unconcerned with politics and history but absorbed by abstract and mythological scenes and the effects of color. Many of his works, some of which are held in the Palacio de Bellas Artes, are easily identified by his trademark watermelon motif (his father was a fruit seller). Juan O'Gorman (1905–82), a Mexican of Irish ancestry, was even more realistic and detailed than Rivera. His mosaic on the Biblioteca Central at Mexico City's Ciudad Universitaria is his best-known work, though atypical of his usual style.

Other 20th-Century Artists

Mexico City–born Frida Kahlo (1907–54; see the boxed text, opposite), physically crippled by an accident and mentally tormented in her tempestuous marriage to Diego Rivera, painted anguished, penetrating self-portraits and grotesque, surreal images that expressed her left-wing views and externalized her inner tumult. After several decades of being seen as an interesting oddball, Kahlo struck an international chord in the 1980s, almost overnight becoming hugely popular and as renowned as Rivera. Thanks to the 2002 Hollywood biopic *Frida*, she is now better known worldwide than any other Mexican artist.

Since WWII, Mexican artists have moved away from muralism, which they saw as too didactic and too obsessed with *mexicanidad* (Mexicanness). They opened up Mexico to world trends such as abstract expressionism, op art and performance art. The Museo José

FRIDA & DIEGO

A century after Frida Kahlo's birth and 50 years after Diego Rivera's death, the pair's fame and recognition are stronger than ever, both internationally and within Mexico. In 2007, a retrospective of Kahlo's work at the Palacio de Bellas Artes attracted more than 440,000 visitors. Though attendance at the Rivera survey that followed was not so phenomenal, the show reminded visitors that the prolific muralist had been an international star in his own lifetime. Their memory is inseparably linked, and both artists were frequent subjects in each other's work.

Diego Rivera first met Frida Kahlo, 21 years his junior, while painting at the Escuela Nacional Preparatoria, where she was a student in the 1920s. Rivera was already at the forefront of Mexican art and a socialist; his commission at the school was the first of many semipropagandistic murals on public buildings that he was to execute over three decades. He had already fathered children by two Russian women in Europe, and in 1922 married Lupe Marín in Mexico. She bore him two more children before their marriage broke up in 1928.

Kahlo was born in Coyoacán in 1907 to a Hungarian-Jewish father and an Oaxacan mother. She contracted polio at age six, which left her right leg permanently thinner than her left. In 1925 she was horribly injured in a trolley accident which broke her back, right leg, collarbone, pelvis and ribs. She made a miraculous recovery but suffered much pain thereafter and underwent many operations to try to alleviate it. It was during convalescence that she began painting. Pain – physical and emotional – was to be a dominating theme of her art.

Kahlo and Rivera both moved in left-wing artistic circles and met again in 1928; they married the following year. The liaison, described as 'a union between an elephant and a dove,' was always a passionate love-hate affair. Rivera wrote: 'If I ever loved a woman, the more I loved her, the more I wanted to hurt her. Frida was only the most obvious victim of this disgusting trait.' Both had extramarital affairs.

In 1934, after a spell in the USA, the pair moved into a new home in San Ángel (see p100), with separate houses linked by an aerial walkway. After Kahlo discovered that Rivera had had an affair with her sister Cristina, she divorced him in 1939, but they remarried the following year. She moved back into her childhood home, the Casa Azul (Blue House; p96), in Coyoacán and he stayed at San Ángel – a state of affairs that continued for the rest of their lives, though their relationship endured, too. Kahlo remained Rivera's most trusted critic, and Rivera was Kahlo's biggest fan.

Despite the worldwide wave of Fridamania that followed the hit biopic *Frida* in 2002, Kahlo had only one exhibition in Mexico in her lifetime, in 1953. She arrived at the opening on a stretcher. Rivera said of the exhibition, 'Anyone who attended it could not but marvel at her great talent.' She died at the Blue House the following year. Rivera called the day of her death 'the most tragic day of my life...Too late I realized that the most wonderful part of my life had been my love for Frida.'

Luis Cuevas in Mexico City's Centro Histórico was founded by, and named for, one of the leaders of this movement.

Contemporary Art

The unease and irony of postmodernism found fertile ground among Mexico's ever-questioning intelligentsia from the late 1980s. Today the city has an increasingly exciting contemporary art scene. The many privately owned galleries that have sprung up display an enormous diversity of attempts to interpret the uncertainties of the early 21st century (see p184 for listings). Some of the most progressive can be found in the Roma and Polanco districts. Contemporary Mexican artists are mostly ironic individualists who can't be categorized into movements or groups.

The best way to catch up on the art scene is to visit some of the better contemporary galleries. You can also check out the Arte Mexico website (www.arte-mexico.com, in Spanish), which has a calendar of exhibitions, information on artists and galleries, maps and more.

SCULPTURE & PUBLIC ART

The Paseo de la Reforma, based on the Champs Elysées in Paris, is lined with monuments, fountains and statues of Mexican heroes. Most prominent of these is the Monumento a la

top picks

MODERN ART MUSEUMS

- Museo de Arte Moderno (p79)
- Museo de Arte Carrillo Gil (p102)
- Museo José Luis Cuevas (p56)
- Museo Sala de Arte Público David Alfaro Siqueiros (p83)
- Laboratorio de Arte Alameda (p65)
- Museo Rufino Tamayo (p81)

Independencia (Monument to Independence; p73), affectionately known as Angelito, a gilded statue of a winged Victory set atop a 45m-high column. It's a location for demonstrations and sporting and national celebrations.

Throughout the summer of 2007, locals watched in bemusement as the Angelito was joined by an altogether more whimsical series of 'street furniture': art pieces not just to look at, but to sit on. Benches and seats are made from bronze or stone, crafted into all sorts of wonderful wacky shapes by a team of local and international sculptors. There's *Reflecto*, on the corner of Genóva and Reforma, which features a double bench, one atop another, and an upside-down seated man. On the corner of Rio Marne, US sculptor Naomi Siegmann's creation *Sientate, Estas en Tu Casa* (Sit Down, You're at Home), a conventional-looking three-piece suite including crumpled cushions, made from bronze. Others feature a two-headed sphinx, a silhouetted seated couple, and the ingenious *Semilla de Descanso* (Seed for Sitting), complete with central 'pod'.

Visit them firsthand by taking a wander down the Paseo de la Reforma's sculpture stretch, from Angelito to the *Monumento a Cuauhtémoc* (Monument to Cuauhtémoc), in the comfort of knowing that there will be plenty of seating space en route.

FOLK ART

Mexicans' artisanship and love of color, beauty, fun and tradition are expressed most ubiquitously in their myriad appealing *artesanías* (handicrafts). The highly decorative crafts that catch the eye in shops and markets today are counterparts to the splendid costumes, beautiful ceramics and elaborate jewelry used by the ancient Aztec and Maya nobility. Many modern craft techniques, designs and materials are easily traced to pre-Hispanic origins. The areas producing the most exciting crafts are still mostly those with prominent indigenous populations, in states such as Chiapas, Michoacán, Oaxaca and Puebla. Happily all these are available at many of the various craft markets and *artesanía* stores in Mexico City.

Crafts to look out for include masks and bark paintings from the southern state of Guerrero, painted lacquer ware on gourds or scented wood from the remote town of Olinaláa, polished wood carvings made into dramatic human and animal shapes from the Seri people of Sonoro,

HIDDEN MURALS

So broad was the muralist movement's canvas that it sometimes seems not a wall has gone uncovered. With murals showing up in markets, libraries, metro stations and restaurants, Chilangos naturally grow indifferent to the presence of these grandiose artistic statements in their midst. Sure, you've seen the tableaux at the Palacio Nacional and de Bellas Artes, but some lesser-known murals are worth seeking out, and tracking them down is half the fun.

- El Agua, El Origen de la Vida (*Water, Origin of Life;* Map p78; Bosque de Chapultepec; admission M$10; 10am-6pm Sat) Diego Rivera painted this series of murals, *Fuente de Tláloc,* for the inauguration of the Chapultepec water works (near Lago Menor). These were built in the 1940s to channel the waters of the Río Lerma, 62km west, into cisterns to supply the city. Experimenting with waterproof paints, Rivera covered the collection tank, sluice gates and part of the pipeline with images of amphibious beings and workers involved in the project. Though technically only open Saturdays, the guard can sometimes be persuaded to let you in, for a tip.
- Velocidad (*Speed;* Map p64; Plaza Juárez, Av Juárez; Ⓜ Bellas Artes) Originally designed for a Chrysler factory, this 1953 work by David Siqueiros represents the notion of speed through the kinetic figure of a female runner. The mosaic canvas was transplanted to the west entrance of the Plaza Juárez complex as part of the Alameda development project.
- Historia de México (*History of Mexico;* Map pp48–9; Mercado Abelardo Rodríguez, cnr República de Venezuela & Rodríguez Puebla; Ⓜ Zócalo) The large Abelardo Rodríguez public market, east of the Zócalo, became a canvas for a group of young international artists in the 1930s under the tutelage of Diego Rivera (he paid them 13.5 pesos per square meter). One of the most intriguing (and best preserved) works, created by Japanese artist Isama Noguchi, is a dynamic three-dimensional mural sculpted of cement and plaster that symbolizes the struggle against fascism. It's located in the community center, upstairs from the northeast corner of the market.
- El Perfil del Tiempo (*Profile of Time;* Map p105; Metro Copilco, Línea 3 platform; Ⓜ Copilco) As any metro rider is aware, the walls of many stations were illustrated by major artists during the 1980s. The Copilco station, at the eastern entrance to UNAM, features this work by Durango artist Guillermo Cenicero. Covering 1000 sq m – the largest of any metro mural – it surveys the history of world painting, from Spain's Altamira cave paintings to Mexico's modern masters, and also includes scenes from the conquest of Mexico.

KITSCH & RETRO COMEBACK

Whether loved or reviled, indulged or condemned, the kitsch factor is alive and well in Mexico City. Stick around a while and you may seriously want to consider trading in that Corona beer T-shirt for a NaCo one (see p127), and shift your urban chic into high gear. Cruise the shops and boutiques in Roma and Condesa to see what stylish kitsch is all about: the boutiques here sell everything from Melissa-brand jelly shoes (born in Brazil in the '80s) to shiny lacquered bags with bright floral (or similar) motifs.

More kitsch Mexican must-haves include leopard- or tiger-skin-print blankets à la Elton John, puce-pink papier-mâché dolls wearing glittering tiaras (the deliciously camp boy dolls are especially hard to find), and – a real delight if you come across them – black-velvet paintings, ideally picturing a voluptuous pinup girl or the Last Supper. Some of the folk art here falls into the kitsch-without trying category, like Día de Muertos clay figurines such as pop-up skeletons in coffins and gaudy pink-haired burlesque-style gals with cigarette holders, cleavage and heels.

As for interior design, the retro look is total at the achingly cool La Bipolar cantina (see p165), owned by Mexican heartthrob Diego Luna of *Y Tu Mamá También* fame. Ceiling lights are revealed to be neatly sliced tin buckets, walls are studded with plastic crates and the tables are good old wooden butcher blocks.

At least they don't serve you those famous Mexican beans that just can't keep still on the plate…now they really *would* give you a dose of kitsch indigestion!

handmade guitars from Paracho in Michoacán, and jewelry and metalwork from Taxco and Oaxaca.

There are several city shops where you can find excellent quality *artesanías* from various regions in Mexico (see the boxed text, p128).

DANCE

Indigenous Dance

Traditional indigenous dances are an important part of many Mexican regional fiestas. There are hundreds of them: some popular in many parts of the country, others danced only in a single town or village. Many bear traces of pre-Hispanic ritual. Some have evolved from old fertility rites. Others tell stories of Spanish origin. Nearly all require special colorful costumes, sometimes including masks or enormous feathered headdresses.

Since most people in Mexico City have left behind their country roots, such traditional acts are rare. An exception is the Conchero, a recreation of a pre-Hispanic central Mexican dance performed daily to booming drums by groups in the Zócalo. Excellent performances of traditional dances from around Mexico are staged by the *Ballet Folclórico de México* (see p180).

Latin Dance

Latin-Caribbean and South American dance and dance music – broadly described as *música afroantillana* or *música tropical* – have become highly popular in Mexico. Basically this is tropical-style ballroom dancing, with percussion, guitars and brass providing infectious rhythms. Mexico City has a dozen or more clubs and large dance halls devoted to this scene; aficionados can go to a different hall each night of the week, often featuring big-name bands and performers from the Caribbean and South America (p171).

One of the more formal, old-fashioned varieties of Latin dance is *danzón*. Originally from Cuba, *danzón* is associated particularly with the port city of Veracruz. To look the part, high heels and a dress are de rigueur for women, as is a Panama hat for men. Steps are small, movement is from the hips down, and *danzón* can be danced only to *danzón* music. If you head down to the Parque Ciudadela (Plaza de Danzón; Calle Balderas, opposite the crafts market; Ⓜ Balderas) on a Saturday afternoon, you will see the dance enacted by a lively group of locals.

Cumbia originated in Colombia but now calls Mexico City home. It also has set steps, but is livelier, more flirtatious and less structured than *danzón*; you also move the top half of your body.

Salsa developed out of the 1950s New York introduction of jazz to cha-cha-cha, rumba and *son*, brought by immigrants from Cuba and Puerto Rico. Musically it boils down to brass (with trumpet solos), piano, percussion, lead vocals and chorus – the dance is a hot one with a lot of exciting turns.

Merengue, primarily from Colombia and Venezuela, is a cumbia-salsa blend with a hopping step: the rhythm catches the shoulders, and the arms go up and down. The music is strong on maracas, and its musicians go for puffed-up sleeves.

MUSIC

In Mexico City live music may start up at any time on streets, plazas or even buses or the metro. The musicians play for a living and range from full mariachi bands to ragged lone buskers with out-of-tune guitars and sandpaper voices. Mariachi music is perhaps the most 'typical' Mexican music of all. Originating in the Guadalajara area, it features trumpeters, violinists, guitarists and a singer, often dressed in smart cowboylike costumes. Mexico City's Plaza Garibaldi is one of its main adopted homes.

Mexico has a thriving pop-music industry. Its outpourings can be heard live at fiestas, nightspots and concerts. Local CDs are available in music shops and cheap bootleg vendors. The latter are certainly cheaper (around M$15 per CD) but carry the risk that your purchases may not work. To find out about live music in Mexico City, see p170.

Rock & Hip-Hop

Due to its proximity to the USA's big Spanish-speaking market, Mexico, in particular Mexico City, is one of the most important hubs of Spanish rock and hip-hop. Talented and versatile local bands such as Café Tacuba (see the boxed text, opposite) and Maldita Vecindad have taken their music to new heights and international audiences, mixing a huge range of influences – from rock, hip-hop and ska to traditional *son*, bolero or mariachi.

Local to Monterrey but well known to Mexico City concert goers are the hip-hop twosome Plastilina Mosh (a kind of Mexican Beastie Boys), hip-hoppers Control Machete, the Britpop-like Zurdoz and metal-hip-hop band Molotov, which attracts controversy with expletive-laced lyrics in a mix of Spanish and English.

Still one of the country's most popular bands is Jaguares, mystical Def Leppard-type rockers who spearheaded the coming of age of Mexican rock in the 1980s. Then there's the more contemporary goth-glam favorite, Víctimas de Doctor Cerebro, with a new release at the end of 2007, and a consistent favorite on the US concert circuit.

Probably best known worldwide of all Mexican bands, however, is Maná, an unashamedly commercial band with British and Caribbean influences, reminiscent of the Police. Not to be forgotten also are El Tri, the grandfathers of Mexican rock (not dissimilar to the Rolling Stones), who after more than 35 years are still pumping out energetic rock and roll.

Regional Music

The deepest-rooted Mexican folk music is *son*, a broad term covering a range of styles that grew out of the fusion of indigenous, Spanish and African music. *Son* is played on guitars plus harp or violin, with witty, often improvised lyrics, usually performed for a foot-stamping dance audience. The origin of mariachi music was the *son* of Jalisco state in western Mexico. Particularly celebrated *son* musicians include violinist Juan Reynoso from the hot Río Balsas basin southwest of Mexico City; harpist La Negra Graciana from Veracruz, who plays *son* which is particularly African- and Cuban-influenced; and Los Camperos de Valles from the Huasteca region in northeast Mexico, a trio composed of a solo violinist and two guitarists who sing falsetto between soaring violin passages. The independent recording label Discos Corasón is doing much to promote *son*. One place you can buy its CDs is the Tianguis Cultural del Chopo (p123).

Ranchera is Mexico's urban 'country music.' Developed in the expanding towns and cities of the 20th century, it's melodramatic with a nostalgia for rural roots: vocalist-and-combo music, sometimes with a mariachi backing. Eugenia León, Juan Gabriel and Alejandro Fernández are among the leading contemporary *ranchera* artists.

Norteño is country ballad and dance music, originating in northern Mexico but popular countrywide. Its roots are in *corridos*, heroic ballads with the rhythms of European dances such as the polka or the waltz, which were brought to southern Texas by 19th-century German and Czech immigrants. Originally the songs were tales of Latino-Anglo strife or themes

ICONIC TACUBA

For all those whose idea of Mexican music conjures up some drunken rendition of *La Cucaracha*, Café Tacuba is a tour de force to be reckoned with. The band began humbly enough in the '90s: four friends who played rock music in the garage of a house in their upper-middle-class suburban neighborhood, Satelíte, north of the city. Fortunately the guys ditched their first long-winded name: Alicia Ya No Vive Aquí (after the '70s Martin Scorsese film) in favor of Café Tacuba, after a coffee shop near the Zócalo which opened in 1912 and had its heyday in the 1950s when it represented the traditional Pachuco music scene.

A good choice, perhaps: Café Tacuba's music is both far removed from, and intrinsically related to, traditional folk music (think DVD to good old vinyl). Their initial self-titled release was a blueprint of what was to come with its fusion of innumerable music styles, from punk and ska to electronic and hip-hop, with a healthy spicing of regional Mexican music like bolero and *ranchera*. The only similarity between some songs was lead singer Albarrán's distinctive nasal vocals. This was far more sophisticated stuff than the *rock en español* style of Ricky Martin and Enrique Iglesias, and by 1996 the cult following was crossing borders.

In 2004 the band won a Grammy for Best Latin Rock/Alternative Album for *Cuatro Caminos*, which was also featured on several Top Albums of 2003 charts, including *Rolling Stone*, the *New York Times* and *Blender Magazine*. In 2005 they performed a special show in Mexico City's Palacio de Deportes, which became the basis of their subsequent *Un Viaje* release.

More than 15 years since the days of deafening suburbia, the band has evolved to become a more challenging, mature and earnest-sounding ensemble. Their October 2007 album *Sino* they describe as being 'an extension of *Cuatro Caminos* with more guitar presence and acoustic drums.' Despite the contradiction in the title, music critics have greeted it with a thumbs-up *si*, believing it may well lead to another Grammy award and still more global recognition for the band.

from the Mexican Revolution. The gritty modern ballads known as *narco-corridos* deal with drug-runners, coyotes and other small-time crooks trying to survive amid big-time corruption and crime, and with the injustices and problems faced by Mexican immigrants in the US. The superstars of *norteño* are Los Tigres del Norte, now living in California, but who play to huge concerts on both sides of the border.

Banda is Mexican big-band music, with large brass sections. Popular since the 1970s in the hands of Sinaloa's Banda el Recodo, it exploded in popularity nationwide and, more recently, among Hispanics in the US.

An exciting talent is Oaxaca-born Lila Downs, who has an American father and a Mexican Mixtec mother. She has emerged as a passionate and original reinterpreter of traditional Mexican folk songs with a repertoire that also includes *rancheros*, boleros and jazz.

Música Tropical

Though its origins lie in the Caribbean and South America, several brands of *música tropical* or *música afroantillana* have become integral parts of the Mexican musical scene. Two types of dance music – *danzón*, originally from Cuba, and *cumbia*, from Colombia – both took deeper root in Mexico than in their original homelands. The music rests on thumping bass lines with an addition of brass, guitars, mandolins and sometimes marimbas (wooden xylophones). Some *banda* and *norteño* groups throw in a lot of *cumbia*. The leading Mexican exponents were probably Los Bukis (who split in 1995). Kumbia Kings, though based in Texas, are hugely popular in Mexico with their cumbia-rap-pop mix. Also listen out for lively Junior Klan from Tabasco.

Trova

This genre of troubadour-type folk songs has its roots in the 1960s and '70s. Typically performed by *cantautores* (singer-songwriters) with a solitary guitar, it remains popular. Nicho Hinojosa, Fernando Delgadillo and Alberto Escobar are leading artists.

Powerful and popular singers like Eugenia León, Tania Libertad and the satirical cabaret artist Astrid Hadad are sometimes categorized under *trova* but they actually range wildly over Mexican song forms – and are all well worth hearing.

LITERATURE

Mexican authors such as Carlos Fuentes, Juan Rulfo and Octavio Paz produced some of the great Spanish-language writing of the 20th century.

Fuentes, a prolific novelist and commentator born in 1928, is one of Mexico's best-known authors internationally. One of his most highly regarded novels is his first, *La Región más Transparente* (Where the Air is Clear; 1958). It traces the lives of various Mexico City dwellers through Mexico's post-revolutionary decades in a critique of the revolution's failure. *Aura* (1962), which is also set in the city, is a short, magical book with a stunning ending. Set in 2020, *La Silla del Águila* (The Eagle's Throne; 2003) again deals with political corruption and cynicism.

Octavio Paz (1914–98), poet, essayist and winner of the 1990 Nobel Prize in Literature, wrote perhaps the most probing examination of Mexico's myths and the Mexican character in *The Labyrinth of Solitude* (1950). Paz' *The Other Mexico: Critique of the Pyramid*, published in 1972 in the aftermath of the 1968 Tlatelolco massacre, assesses the lingering influence of the savage Aztec worldview.

Contemporary writer Laura Esquivel shot to fame with her novel *Like Water for Chocolate* (1989), which was adapted to film in 1993 and became a huge international hit. This book about a frustrating romance is a delight, with each chapter prefaced by a traditional Mexican recipe.

CINEMA & TELEVISION

A clutch of fine, gritty movies by young directors thrust Mexican cinema into the limelight in the 1990s and early 2000s, garnering commercial success as well as critical acclaim after decades in the doldrums. Director Alejandro González Iñárritu caught the world's eye in 2000 with *Amores Perros* (Love's a Bitch), set in Mexico City. He followed this up in 2003 with *21 Grams*, a nonlinear narrative about a car accident, starring Sean Penn. In 2006 he won Best Director for *Babel*, another tale of interwoven plots, starring Brad Pitt and Cate Blanchett. Unlike *21 Grams*, parts of this were filmed in Mexico (along with Japan, Morocco and the US).

At the time of research, *Y Tu Mamá También*, Alfonso Cuarón's 2002 tale of two teenagers from privileged Mexico City circles, remained the biggest-grossing Mexican film ever, netting US$11 million in Mexico and US$13.6 million in the US.

By 2008 Mexico was producing around 50 films a year, a considerable increase from previous years. Mexico City holds a couple of annual international film festivals (p180).

The Mexican TV market is dominated by Televisa, which operates four of the six nationwide broadcast channels: 2 (El Canal de las Estrellas), 4 (El Canal de la Ciudad), 5 (Canal 5) and 9 (Galavisión). Its rival, TV Azteca, has two main channels – Azteca Siete (7) and Azteca Trece (13). A high proportion of Mexican airtime is devoted to ads, low-budget *telenovelas* (soap operas), soccer, game shows, chat shows, variety shows, movies and comedy. Content tends towards the conservative in that nudity, graphic violence and offensive language are pretty much kept off the screen.

Better than the commercial channels are Once TV (Eleven TV), run by Mexico City's Instituto Politécnico Nacional, which broadcasts intelligent travel, documentary and interview programs and movies, and Canal 22, a culture channel from Conaculta, the National Culture & Arts Council.

Mexico City's cable network is Cablevision. Sky Mexico is the country's only satellite TV service, available in an increasing number of top-end hotel rooms with the full package of Sky TV programming (in Spanish).

English-language newspaper the *News* and several other Mexican newspapers publish full TV schedules.

ARCHITECTURE

Mexico City's architecture is wonderfully varied and the city hosts some stunning examples of several distinct styles, including pre-Hispanic, baroque, colonial and art deco. Don't forget to look up occasionally when you are walking around (always remembering to watch out for those ever-present pot holes!). The building skyline is intriguingly eclectic, particularly around the Centro Histórico with its concentration of historical buildings, including ecclesiastical architecture and palaces. Architecture and sculpture are often inextricably intertwined, with carving and molding integrated into building designs or used as features in architectural spaces. A number of buildings also feature iconic murals.

Unlike most capital cities, Mexico City is not bound up by inflexible building rules and regulations. While this lack of coordinated planning inevitably spawns some real eyesores, the largely unregulated environment encourages risk-taking, resulting in some of the world's most innovative architecture.

PRE-HISPANIC

The ancient civilizations produced some of the most spectacular architecture ever built. At sites near Mexico City such as Teotihuacán, Tula and Cacaxtla, you can still see fairly intact, large sections of pre-Hispanic cities. Their spectacular ceremonial centers, used by the religious and political elite, were designed to impress with their great stone pyramids, palaces and ball courts. Pyramids usually functioned as bases for the small shrines on their summits. Three of the biggest pyramids in the world – the Great Pyramid of Cholula near Puebla, and the Pirámide del Sol and Pirámide de la Luna at Teotihuacán – are within easy reach of Mexico City.

There were many differences in architectural style between pre-Hispanic civilizations. While Teotihuacán and Aztec buildings were relatively simple, intended to awe with their grand scale, Maya architecture paid more attention to aesthetics, with intricately patterned facades, delicate 'combs' (gridlike arrangements of stone with multiple gaps) on temple roofs, and sinuous carvings.

The Toltecs' fearsome, militaristic style of carving is exhibited at their presumed capital, Tula. Aztec sculpture reflects their society's worldview, with many carvings of skulls and complicated symbolic representations of gods. Earlier, the Olmecs of the Gulf Coast (about 1200 BC to 600 BC) had produced perhaps the most remarkable pre-Hispanic stone sculpture to be found. Most awesome are the huge 'Olmec heads,' which combine the features of human babies and jaguars.

Teotihuacán's typical *talud-tablero* building style, with alternating *talud* (sloping) and *tablero* (upright) sections, was copied by several later Mexican cultures.

What to See

Substantial remains of pre-Hispanic ceremonial centers can be seen at the Templo Mayor, off the Zócalo (p51) and elsewhere in the city at Tlatelolco (p115), Cuicuilco (p115), Tenayuca and Santa Cecilia Acatitlán (p54). But the most impressive sites in the region are outside the city at such places as Tula, Cacaxtla and, supremely, Teotihuacán. The city's Museo Nacional de Antropología (p80) has fine pre-Hispanic sculpture, plus models and full and partial replicas of buildings.

COLONIAL PERIOD

One of the Spaniards' first preoccupations was the replacement of pagan temples with Christian churches. Mexico City's cathedral (p50) stands on part of the site of the Aztecs' Teocalli, its main sacred precinct.

Many of the fine mansions, churches and plazas that today provide oases of beauty and tranquillity in Mexico City's bustle were created during the 300 years of Spanish colonial rule. Most were designed using fundamental Spanish styles, but with unique local variations. Some distinctive features include the use of adobe, arches, inner courtyards, plain wall surfaces and tile roofs.

CENTRO HISTÓRICO RECOVERS LOST SPLENDOR

Spearheaded by Carlos Slim, the city's historic centre is undergoing a total revamp. This is not just a cursory brush and scrub up. In the pilot program, 615 buildings were completely renovated and then given the final essential face-lift: their facades painted in coordinating pastel colors which, with the addition of a few strings of washing, would fit happily in the Italian Riviera.

At a cost of some M$800 million, these buildings are rapidly being transformed into affordable rental apartments, targeted towards young people involved in the arts: photographers, artists, models and publicists. It is hoped that these tenants will help create the kind of boho-chic that typifies fashionable Condesa.

An advisory board to the Historic Center Foundation comprises architects, historians, government representatives and members of the local community and the business world. Apparently, one of the main challenges has been to change people's view of the historic center as being a dangerous place to live. There's nothing like cheap rent to help sway opinion with the rents as low as M$1500, and a stylish art deco apartment available for M$3000 a month. Although there are only leases available to date, the possibility of selling the properties in the future is being analyzed.

In the meantime, there is still an awesome 9 sq km of urban dilemma to solve: trash collection, street vendors, chaotic traffic and buildings that sink at a rate of 8cm a year.

At least the funding is far from slim.

What to See

We owe to this period the lovely courtyards of such buildings as the Museo de la Secretaría de Hacienda y Crédito Público (p55), the Museo Nacional de las Culturas (p56), the Museo Franz Mayer (p65), the Palacio de Iturbide (p53) and the San Ángel Inn (p102).

RENAISSANCE

This style dominated in the 16th and early 17th centuries. Originating in Italy, it emphasized ancient Greek and Roman ideals of harmony and proportion; columns and geometric shapes like squares and circles predominated.

The usual renaissance style in Mexico was plateresque, a name derived from *platero* (silversmith), because its decoration resembled the ornamentation that went into silverwork. Plateresque was commonly used on façades, particularly church doorways, which had round arches bordered by classical columns and stone sculpture. Puebla's Templo de San Francisco and the church of the Ex-Convento Domínico de la Natividad in Tepoztlán are fine examples.

A later, more austere renaissance style was called Herreresque after Spanish architect Juan de Herrera. The Mexico City and Puebla cathedrals mingle renaissance with the later baroque style.

The influence of the Muslims, who had ruled much of Spain until the 15th century, was also carried to Mexico. The 49 domes of the Capilla Real in Cholula almost resemble a mosque.

BAROQUE

Baroque style, which reached Mexico from Spain in the early 17th century, combined renaissance influences with other elements aimed at a dramatic effect – curves, color, contrasts of light and dark and increasingly elaborate decoration. Painting and sculpture were integrated with architecture, most notably in ornate, often enormous altarpieces.

Mexican baroque reached its final form, Churrigueresque, between 1730 and 1780. Named after a Barcelona carver and architect, José Benito de Churriguera, this was characterized by riotous surface ornamentation with a characteristic 'top-heavy' effect.

Mexican indigenous artisans added profuse sculpture in stone and colored stucco to many baroque buildings, while the Arabic influence continued with the popularity of *azulejos* (colored tiles) on building exteriors.

What to See

Mexico City's more restrained baroque buildings include the Plaza de Santo Domingo (p57) and the Palacio de Iturbide (p53) in the Centro Histórico, the Templo de Santiago at Tlatelolco (p115), and the Antigua Basílica de Guadalupe (p116). The Altar de los Reyes in the Catedral

Metropolitana (p51) is an extravagant piece of baroque carving. More exuberant works include the Capilla del Rosario in the Iglesia de Santo Domingo (p57); examples outside the city include the village church of Tonantzintla near Puebla, and the Templo de la Tercera Orden de San Francisco in Cuernavaca. Outstanding Churrigueresque stone carving appears on churches such as the Sagrario Metropolitano (p51) and Templo de la Santísima (p56).

The most stunning example of tiled buildings is the appropriately named Casa de Azulejos (p54) in the Centro Histórico.

NEOCLASSIC

This style was another return to Greek and Roman ideals. In Mexico it lasted from about 1780 to 1830. Spanish-born Manuel Tolsá (1757–1816) was the most prominent neoclassical architect and sculptor. This style of architecture is principally derived from the architecture of Classical Greece, typified by narrow windows, columned porches and crisp, low-relief friezes.

What to see

Don't miss Tolsá's dome and clock tower of the Catedral Metropolitana (p50), the Palacio de Minería (p55) and the equestrian statue *El Caballito* (p70) outside the Museo Nacional de Arte.

INDEPENDENT & MODERN MEXICO

The 19th and 20th centuries saw revivals of many earlier styles, and many buildings copied French or Italian modes.

After the revolution of 1910–20, art deco appeared in buildings such as the Lotería Nacional (p70) and Frontón México. In Condesa you can still see some real gems, particularly around Parque México (p86). From the '30s, architects attempted to return to pre-Hispanic roots in the search for a national identity. This trend was known as Toltecism and many public buildings feature murals and exhibit the heaviness of Aztec or Toltec monuments. It culminated in Mexico City's UNAM university campus of the early '50s, where colorful murals (p106) cover several buildings.

Modern architects have contributed a few eye-catching and adventurous buildings, as well as a large quota of dull concrete blocks. The icon is Luis Barragán (1902–88), who was strongly influenced by Le Corbusier but also exhibited a strong Mexican aesthetic in his use of vivid colors, textures, scale, space, light and vegetation, including small interior gardens. Two big names in contemporary Mexican architecture are Ricardo Legorreta (b 1931), who has designed a slew of large buildings in bold concrete shapes and 'colonial' orangey-brown hues, and Enrique Norton (b 1954), who works on a smaller scale with a lot of glass and steel. Also fast gaining a reputation is Mauricio Rocha (b 1963), who is also an accomplished artist. His transformation of the San Pablo Ozotepec Market in 2004 helped distinguish him as a pioneer in public-works construction. Rocha had an ultralow budget to redesign the 65-stall market in a run-down part of town, and created no-frills concrete-block stalls animated by the sounds and colors of Mexican life. This is not a very safe area; if you decide to explore here, be cautious and keep your money well out of sight.

What to See

The marble Palacio de Bellas Artes (p63) is one of the finest buildings from the early 20th century. The beautiful Palacio de Correos (Central Post Office; p55) and the Museo Nacional de Arte (p55) were built in the style of Italian renaissance palaces. Luis Barragán's Mexico City home (p80) was made a Unesco World Heritage Site in 2004 and is open to the public as a tribute to his life and work. The Centro Nacional de las Artes (p97) is an example of Legorreta's more contemporary architecture, while Enrique Norton's portfolio includes the fashionable Hábita Hotel (p209).

top picks

NOTABLE BUILDINGS

- Torre Latinoamerica (p65)
- Casa de Azulejos (p54)
- Palacio de Minería (p55)
- Palacio de Bellas Artes (p63)
- Museo Nacional de Arte (p55)
- Sagrario Metropolitano (p51)

ENVIRONMENT & PLANNING

THE LAND

Mexico City is located roughly in the center of the country, about 400km from both the Pacific and Gulf of Mexico coasts. It occupies the southwestern portion of the Valle de México, a highland plateau ringed by mountains and valleys in the Cordillera Neovolcánica, the volcanic chain that runs across central Mexico from east to west. The valley is about 60km across from east to west and 30 to 40km from north to south. Flat as a griddle in the center, the city reaches right up to the surrounding hills to the north, west and south. In the east the hills are further away and the perimeter of the valley is marked by the extinct volcano Iztaccíhuatl and the very much alive Popocatépetl. Once regularly visible from the city, this pair – both of which are over 5000m high – now only can be seen on exceptionally clear days. Here and there the stumps of smaller extinct volcanoes, such as Cerro de la Estrella, rise within the city.

A combination of high altitude (2240m) and tropical latitude gives the city a pleasantly cool, often springlike climate.

Much of what is today the modern metropolis was covered by shallow lakes prior to the arrival of the Spanish conquerors, who unplugged the sealed basin to leave the marshy expanses upon which they built their capital. Only a few patches of water remain east of the city in addition to the canals of Xochimilco in the southeast.

GREEN MEXICO CITY

Environmental Damage

Mexico City is an ecological tragedy. What was once a beautiful highland valley with abundant water and forests now has some of the least breathable air on the planet and only scattered pockets of greenery. It faces the real prospect of serious water shortages in the not too distant future.

Environmental damage in the Valle de México is actually nothing new. As early as the 15th century, king Nezahualcóyotl of Texcoco, alarmed at the valley's dwindling forests, decreed tree cutting in some areas punishable by execution. During the colonial period and the 19th century, a few voices were raised against further clearing of forests on the hills around the valley. It was argued that the lack of trees was partly responsible for the floods that periodically inundated the valley. Draining the valley's lakes, however, was seen as the solution to the floods – work on this began in the 17th century and was largely completed by 1900. As a result the city suffered fierce dust storms in the 20th century. A project to recover Lago de Texcoco's waters east of the airport has somewhat alleviated the situation but airborne fecal matter from sewerless slums remains a concern in the dry winter months.

Air

The city's severe traffic and industrial pollution is intensified by the mountains that ring the Valle de México and prevent air from dispersing, and by the altitude and consequent lack of oxygen. Pollution is at its worst in the cooler months, especially from November to February, when an unpleasant phenomenon called thermal inversion is most likely to happen. Thermal inversion occurs when warmer air passing over the valley stops cooler, polluted air near ground level from rising and dispersing.

Air pollution is blamed for skin problems, nervous disorders, mental retardation, cancer and thousands of premature deaths a year among Mexico City's inhabitants. Industry accounts for some of the air pollution, but the major culprit is ozone. The main ozone producer is generally reckoned to be low-lead gasoline, introduced in 1986 to counter lead pollution, which until then was the city's worst atmospheric contaminant. The reaction between sunlight and combustion residues from low-lead gasoline produces a great deal of ozone.

In an attempt to reduce traffic pollution, many cars in the city are banned from the streets on one day each week in a program called 'Hoy No Circula' (Don't Drive Today). Furthermore, catalytic converters have been compulsory on all new cars sold in Mexico since the early 1990s. But ozone levels have remained high, since Hoy No Circula unwittingly encouraged people to

THAT SINKING FEELING

Strolling around the Centro Histórico, you can't help but notice a rather serious issue: Mexico City is sinking into the ground. The metropolitan cathedral, which appears to be tilting westward, is just the most obvious example. Notice how the facade of the Iglesia de Santa Veracruz, near the Alameda Central, slouches toward the north. That long low building on Calle San Jerónimo, east of Pino Suárez, looks like a train wreck in the making. Step inside the Iglesia de Nuestro Señora de Loreto, four blocks east of the Zócalo, and you'll feel as if you've entered a topsy-turvy funhouse. The Palacio de Bellas Artes, an early-20th-century structure, has sunk so far on its right side that you have to go downstairs to pass through what used to be a street-level entrance.

All told, the historic center has dropped some 10m over the past 100 years. But the phenomenon is not exclusive to the center. The entire city has been sinking since colonial times, when the Spaniards got the bright idea of draining the lake that filled the highland basin. The spongy subsoil that remained was hardly the best place to put the capital of Nueva España, much less to erect extremely heavy churches and palaces, whose formidable weight was invariably more than the squishy lake bed could handle. And the problem has greatly intensified over the past 50 years, as an increasingly thirsty city continues to suck water from its underground aquifers before they're adequately replenished, thus removing a crucially buoyant counterbalance to the settling subsoil. The situation is especially worrisome in the heavily populated southeastern district of Iztapalapa, which queasily rests upon what used to be the deepest part of the lake. Because they've sunk well below ground level, houses there face major flooding every rainy season.

To make matters worse, some of the historic buildings in the center are sinking unevenly, causing structural cracks and in some cases total collapse. That's because their sites were previously occupied by older buildings, which compacted the earth beneath them. A good example is the Sagrario Metropolitano, next door to the cathedral, which was built upon the site of the Aztec Templo Mayor.

New technology has addressed the problem to some extent. An ambitious project to prevent the collapse of the cathedral entails the excavation of underground shafts to remove the subsoil at certain key points. Rather than stopping the sinking process entirely, the idea is to allow the higher parts to sink to the same level as the lower ones, thus ensuring the building's structural integrity. And newly built behemoths like the Torre Mayor are anchored by piles drilled deep beneath the subsoil to the underlying bedrock and stabilized by seismic dampers.

buy or rent extra cars to get around the once-a-week prohibition. Mexico City's current mayor, Marcelo Ebrard, has sought new approaches to car-induced pollution (see Urban Planning & Development, below).

Water

Extraction of groundwater makes the city sink steadily (see above). Even so, about one-third of the city's water needs to be pumped up at great cost from the Lerma and Cutzamala valleys west and southwest of the Valle de México. Meanwhile the water table is sinking by about 1m per year.

The city uses 300L of water a day per person, much more than some cities in Europe, for instance, even though millions of slum dwellers have no running water in their homes. Inefficient use of water by industry, with very little recycling, is partly to blame.

The Valle de México's streams are among the most polluted in the world. Most wastewater, treated or not, eventually leaves the valley northward by a 50km tunnel called the Emisor Central, which leads to the Río Tula, a tributary of the badly polluted Río Pánuco, which enters the Gulf of Mexico at Tampico. The Emisor Central is not big enough to cope with the extra water brought by the rainy season, when backed-up sewage floods some low-lying parts of the valley.

Sinking ground levels break underground pipes, wasting up to a quarter of the city's water supplies and allowing contaminants to enter the supply. Contaminated water supplies spread diseases such as dysentery, typhoid and hepatitis.

URBAN PLANNING & DEVELOPMENT

It may be hard to resist the notion that applying green initiatives to Mexico City is nothing more than cosmetic – sort of like telling a terminal cancer patient to cut down his smoking habit…to half a pack a day.

But rather than leave the city for dead, Mayor Marcelo Ebrard is taking a serious look at how the situation can be improved. His Plan Verde, which he presented to *capitalinos* at a referendum in mid-2007, aims to bring the capital in line with urban environmental trends elsewhere in the world. Most of the measures relate to the city's persistent traffic problems. Taxis will have to switch to alternative fuels or hybrid technology. Funds will be allotted toward mass transit, and more metrobus corridors will be installed with the aim of removing thousands of polluting (not to mention recklessly driven) microbuses from the road and replacing them with low-emission vehicles along dedicated lanes. The bike-riding mayor also wants to see 300km of bicycle lanes installed for two-wheeled commuters. Water is another major concern. The new vision entails the construction of hundreds of wells to capture rainwater as an alternative to sucking it out of the city's aquifers. Other measures aim to streamline the unwieldy trash-collection system and clear the air of unhealthy particulate matter.

Should all these goals be achieved within the 15-year period allotted for the plan, Mexico City's future may brighten considerably. But difficulties may arise due to the current administration's uneasy relationship with federal authorities, who may choose to withhold crucial financing.

GOVERNMENT & POLITICS

Mexico is a federal republic of 31 *estados* (states) and one federal district, with the states further divided into 2394 *municipios* (municipalities).

One of Mexico City's problems is that its governmental system was designed for a place a fraction of its current size. No-one foresaw, back in 1854 when the Distrito Federal was given its present 1500-sq-km limits, that the city would burst these bounds. Yet as early as the 1930s the city started to spread into the neighboring state of México. Today 28 of the state of México's 120 *municipios* are wholly or partly within the city's sprawl. The DF and the state of México are run by completely different administrations – not exactly ideal conditions for planning the megalopolis that straddles their boundaries.

The state of México, with its capital at Toluca, west of Mexico City, is just like the other 30 Mexican states in electing its own governor and Cámara de Diputados (Chamber of Deputies). The DF, however, being the nation's capital, has long been treated as a special case. Back in 1917 it was decided that its governor should be appointed by Mexico's president instead of elected. In 1928, all elected local governmental bodies in the DF were abolished, and the district was placed under the direct control of the national president and his chosen *regente* (governor). The bureaucracy in charge of the city, the Departamento del Distrito Federal, became a department of the national executive government, answerable to the national president.

Things changed radically when President Zedillo opened the post of DF governor – henceforth known as *jefe de gobierno* (head of government) or *alcalde* (mayor) – to popular elections in 1997. The DF mayor has the right to choose the city's police chief and *procurador de justicia* (attorney general), posts that had previously been of the president's choosing. Nevertheless the federal congress still had to approve any debt issues by the DF and retained the exclusive right to impeach the DF head of government. Also since 1997, citizens of the DF have elected local delegates to a legislature, the Asamblea Legislativa del Distrito Federal (ALDF), which meets in the old Cámara de Diputados building at Donceles and Allende in the Centro Histórico. Like the mayoralty, the ALDF has been dominated by members of the left-leaning PRD since its inception.

Administratively, the Distrito Federal is subdivided into 16 *delegaciones* (boroughs). Since 2000, the leaders of the *delegaciones* have been directly elected by their citizenry, making these administrative divisions roughly equivalent to the *municipios* of the 31 other Mexican states.

OPENING MOVES

When National Action Party (PAN) candidate Vicente Fox was elected president of Mexico in 2000, breaking the PRI's hold on the presidency after an uninterrupted 70 years in power, it seemed to herald a new era of openness in the country. To a great extent, that promise went unfulfilled – mainly due to Fox's ineffectiveness as a leader and his inability to enact reforms in an opposition-dominated Congress – but the country was unquestionably moving in a more democratic direction.

Three years prior to Fox's election, the Distrito Federal was permitted for the first time to elect its own head of government, after being ruled by regents appointed directly by the federal government since 1928. The winner was Cuauhtémoc Cárdenas of the center-left PRD party, who later lost his presidential bid against Fox. Another PRD candidate, Andrés Manuel López Obrador, was elected mayor of Mexico City in 2000, a post he held until 2005, when he too made a run for the presidency.

Capitalinos overwhelmingly approved of López Obrador's performance as city leader. His initiatives included an ambitious makeover of the Centro Histórico (financed in part by Carlos Slim) and the construction of an overpass for the city's ring road. His efforts to collect the revenues traditionally lost to the city government (due to tax evasion and embezzlement by departmental offices) enabled the government to pay off city debts, build schools and hospitals, invest in overdue repairs of the city's water system and provide stipends for senior citizens and people with disabilities. Such spending sprees got the mayor labeled as a populist by his detractors but the majority of Chilangos felt that they were actually getting what was due them for a change.

When López Obrador ran for president of Mexico in July 2006, he continued to receive support from Mexico City, gaining 80% of the DF's votes. But it was not enough to win him the election. In a highly controversial race, PAN candidate Felipe Calderón emerged victorious by the slightest of margins (see the boxed text, below). Born in Morelia, Michoacán, and educated at Harvard University, Felipe Calderón is a longtime PAN stalwart and served in Vicente Fox's cabinet as energy secretary. Consistent with his party's traditional Catholic image, he is socially conservative – he opposes abortion, euthanasia and gay marriage – while economically he is more of a free-market advocate than was his predecessor.

Meanwhile, PRD candidate Marcelo Ebrard won a sweeping victory in Mexico City's mayoral elections of 2006, consolidating his party's grip on the city government. The PRD triumphed in all but one of the city's 16 delegations, Miguel Hidalgo, which includes the prosperous Polanco neighborhood. Also registering an overwhelming takeover of the Federal District's legislative assembly, the PRD seized the day, passing a flood of progressive initiatives. These included the

AN OPEN WOUND

Echoing the US presidential elections of 2000, Mexico had its own cliff-hanger race in July 2006, with similar accusations of an unfair outcome being hurled. But unlike Al Gore, who acknowledged the decision and (momentarily) left the picture, the loser of Mexico's election, Andrés Manuel López Obrador, refused to accept the result and waged a highly visible postelectoral campaign to discredit what he claimed had been a fraudulent victory.

For the first six years of the millennium, AMLO (as he is commonly called) distinguished himself as possibly Mexico City's most popular mayor in modern history, and when he left his post to run for president, he was widely predicted to win by a landslide.

As it turned out, his opponent, Felipe Calderón of the PAN, was declared the winner by a razor-thin margin: around half a percentage point. López Obrador cried foul, claiming widespread ballot-stuffing and behind-the-scenes maneuvering to wrest away what he was calling a substantial victory. Such practices were supposed to have been rendered obsolete since the establishment in the 1990s of a new supposedly impartial electoral watchdog agency, the Instituto Federal Electoral (IFE). But the head of the IFE, Luis Carlos Ugalde, was widely seen as politically linked to the PAN candidate, and after Calderón's victory was announced, López Obrador demanded a recount. Ugalde refused, saying there was not sufficient evidence of wrongdoing to warrant a recount, whereupon as many as 100,000 of AMLO's supporters reacted by marching in protest to the Zócalo.

Calderón was sworn in regardless, despite attempts by PRD legislators to physically block the candidate from assuming the post at the Cámara de Diputados (Chamber of Deputies); they were restrained by soldiers. Refusing to back down, the PRD contingent camped out on Paseo de la Reforma to express their discontent, blocking traffic along that major artery for months, but to no avail. After they finally decamped, AMLO continued to claim he was the country's legitimately elected leader and established his own presidential headquarters in Colonia Roma. The candidate even delivered his own state-of-the-union address in parallel with Calderón's. Such dramatic tactics added fuel to his critics' accusations of AMLO's messianic streak, and even some of his most faithful supporters fear that his postelectoral campaign may have irreversibly damaged the candidate's political profile.

But many still doubt the legitimacy of the 2006 presidential election. As if to underline the sense that the outcome was still unresolved and remained an open wound, a documentary film about the process, *Fraude! México 2006*, shown in cinemas in late 2007, was a runaway hit in the capital.

sanctioning of gay unions and the legalization of abortion and euthanasia, all of which were vehemently protested by the conservative PAN, who is pushing for constitutional amendments to reverse the PRD initiatives.

A longtime figure in the DF administration, Marcelo Ebrard served as López Obrador's police chief until he was dismissed by President Fox for choosing not to protect two federal narcotics agents when an angry mob in an outlying area lynched the pair. The incident was a particularly horrendous example of the failure of the municipal and federal entities to cooperate within the city's boundaries. Ebrard's election was thus not a hopeful sign for the future of DF–federal relations. And indeed, he has routinely declined to attend summits with federal officials, ignoring President Calderón's overtures for reconciliation. He seems intent on showing that he's unwilling to accept the president's authority.

Ebrard's public-approval ratings have been strong, if not as overwhelming as AMLO's. Although Ebrard was a staunch supporter during his former boss's widely publicized protests over the allegedly fraudulent outcome of the presidential election, he very soon began to distance himself from AMLO's style of leadership. While López Obrador strove to restore Mexico City's greatness through highly visible public works projects such as the beautification of the Zócalo area, Ebrard has demonstrated an interest in bringing the city in line with current urban trends. The new mayor seems less interested in currying favor with the city's poorer sectors than in uprooting crime, as demonstrated by his decision to bulldoze blighted tenements in the drug-plagued Tepito and Buenos Aires districts. He also seeks to update some of the city's more regressive behaviors by adopting trends in urban design that he's picked up at the conferences in foreign cities he likes to attend. Thus, drivers who've accumulated too many violations can no longer automatically renew their licenses, surveillance cameras have been installed on freeways, and campaigns have been waged to get drivers to wear seatbelts and to remove illegally parked cars. While AMLO's initiatives may have been more tangible, Ebrard's forward-looking efforts may have longer-lasting effects. He tends not to inspire the sort of fervor demonstrated by AMLO's followers and may have alienated himself from the indigenous population by marrying a white soap-opera star in a high-profile ceremony.

NEIGHBORHOODS

top picks

- **National Anthropology Museum** (p80) Superb showcase for the nation's indigenous legacy.
- **Xochimilco** (p113) Ancient network of canals plied by festive flowery *trajineras* (gondolas).
- **Bosque de Chapultepec** (p77) Mexico City's principal park, crowned by the former emperor's castle.
- **Templo Mayor** (p51) Legendary ceremonial precinct of the Aztec empire.
- **Museo Casa de Frida Kahlo** (p96) Blue-hued home of the country's most famous tortured artist.
- **Centro Histórico** (p46) Mexico City's historic core, with four centuries of architectural gems on display.
- **Palacio de Bellas Artes** (p63) Belle époque opera house graced with the works of Mexico's leading muralists.
- **Zócalo** (p46) The thumping heart of the city and the nation.
- **Colonia Condesa** (p86) Trendy, tree-lined neighborhood.
- **Basilica de Guadalupe** (p116) Magnet for millions, site of a Christian miracle atop a pre-Hispanic shrine.

What's your recommendation? www.lonelyplanet.com/mexico-city

NEIGHBORHOODS

The Mancha Urbana, or 'urban stain,' as the metropolitan area is often referred to, spreads across the ancient bed of the Lago de Texcoco and beyond. Encompassing approximately 1500 sq km of the Distrito Federal and another 3200 sq km of the neighboring state of México to the north, Mexico City comprises hundreds of *colonias* (neighborhoods). Though this vast urban expanse is daunting at first, most of what's important to the majority of visitors lies in a relatively limited, well-defined and easily traversed central area.

The historic heart of the city is the wide plaza known as El Zócalo, surrounded by the Palacio Nacional (the presidential palace), the cathedral and the excavated site of the Templo Mayor, which is the main temple of Aztec Tenochtitlán. The Zócalo and the surrounding neighborhood are known as the Centro Histórico (Historic Center). Full of notable old buildings, interesting museums and other sights, it's where most visitors begin their explorations. Conveniently, there are loads of economical hotels and restaurants north, west and south of the Zócalo.

Eight blocks west of the Zócalo – and linked to it by Calles Madero and 5 de Mayo – lies the verdant park called the Alameda Central. On the east side of the Alameda stands the magnificent Palacio de Bellas Artes. The landmark Torre Latinoamericana (Latin American Tower) pierces the sky a block south of Bellas Artes, beside one of the city's main north–south arterial roads, the Eje Central Lázaro Cárdenas.

Some 750m west of the Alameda, across Paseo de la Reforma, is Plaza de la República, marked by the somber, copper-domed Monumento a la Revolución. This is a fairly quiet, mostly residential area with many budget and midrange hotels.

Mexico City's grandest boulevard, Paseo de la Reforma, skirts the Alameda Central's west side, tracing a northeastward diagonal across the city's heart. Major hotels, embassies, office buildings and banks rise alongside it. Landmark *glorietas* (traffic circles) along Reforma are marked with statues, including those commemorating Christopher Columbus, Cuauhtémoc (the last Aztec emperor; at the intersection with Av Insurgentes), and Mexican independence (the Monumento a la Independencia, or El Ángel).

The independence monument marks the northern edge of the Zona Rosa (Pink Zone), a shopping, eating, hotel and nightlife district bounded by Av Insurgentes to the east and Av Chapultepec to the south. North of Paseo de la Reforma is Colonia Cuauhtémoc, a quieter residential zone where many expats live.

South of the Zona Rosa across Av Chapultepec is Colonia Roma, a lower-key, more bohemian section of town with lots of cafés, galleries and early-20th-century, Parisian-influenced architecture. Roma makes a good, relatively central base with a range of lodgings to choose from.

West of the Zona Rosa, Paseo de la Reforma traverses Bosque de Chapultepec, generally known to gringos as Chapultepec Park. A large expanse of trees, gardens and lakes, it is Mexico City's 'lungs,' and holds many of the city's major museums, including the renowned Museo Nacional de Antropología and the Museo Nacional de Historia.

Two important neighborhoods flank the Bosque. To the north is Polanco, an affluent zone where many countries have their embassies and internationally acclaimed chefs work their magic at some of the city's most prestigious restaurants. A cluster of top-end hotels stands on the neighborhood's southern edge opposite the Auditorio Nacional, the main concert hall. To the south and east of Chapultepec Park, Colonia Condesa is a delightful residential enclave that's been reborn as a chic restaurant and nightlife destination.

Av Insurgentes, the city's major north–south axis, intersects with Paseo de la Reforma, connecting it to points of interest in both directions. Now plied by the metrobus, a rapid transit option that runs along a dedicated lane, the avenue extends almost 30km, straddled by mostly middle-class areas along the way. About 6½km north of Centro Histórico via Insurgentes stands the Basílica de Guadalupe, Mexico's most revered shrine. About 9km south of El Ángel are the atmospheric former colonial villages of San Ángel and Coyoacán. Immediately south of San Ángel spreads the Ciudad Universitaria, the vast campus of the national university, aka UNAM. In the far southeast of the city are the canals and gardens of Xochimilco.

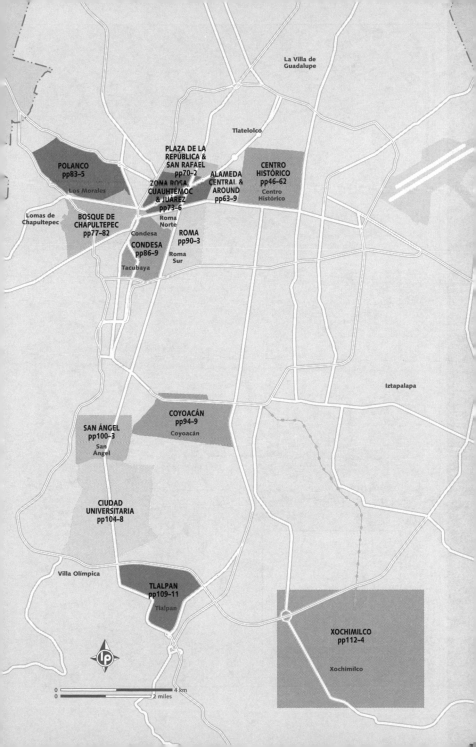

La Villa de
Guadalupe

Tlatelolco

POLANCO
pp83–5

Los Morales

PLAZA DE LA
REPÚBLICA &
SAN RAFAEL
pp70–2

ZONA ROSA,
CUAUHTÉMOC
& JUÁREZ
pp73–6

ALAMEDA
CENTRAL &
AROUND
pp63–9

CENTRO
HISTÓRICO
pp46–62

Centro
Histórico

Lomas de
Chapultepec

BOSQUE DE
CHAPULTEPEC
pp77–82

Roma
Norte

Condesa

ROMA
pp90–3

CONDESA
pp86–9

Roma
Sur

Tacubaya

Iztapalapa

SAN ÁNGEL
pp100–3

San
Ángel

COYOACÁN
pp94–9

Coyoacán

CIUDAD
UNIVERSITARIA
pp104–8

Villa Olímpica

TLALPAN
pp109–11

Tlalpan

XOCHIMILCO
pp112–4

Xochimilco

LP

0 ——————— 4 km
0 ——————— 2 miles

MEXICO CITY

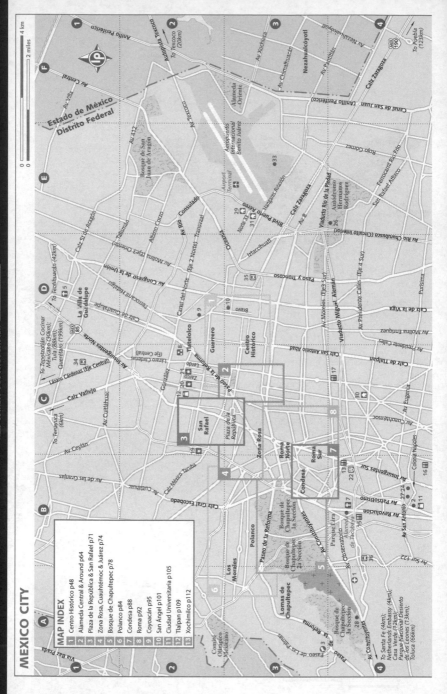

MAP INDEX

1 Centro Histórico p48
2 Alameda Central & Around p64
3 Plaza de la República & San Rafael p71
4 Zona Rosa, Cuauhtémoc & Juárez p74
5 Bosque de Chapultepec p78
6 Polanco p84
7 Condesa p88
8 Roma p92
9 Coyoacán p95
10 San Ángel p101
11 Ciudad Universitaria p105
12 Tlalpan p109
13 Xochimilco p112

EATING 🍴	(pp131–58)
Bar Montejo...................	13 B4
Centro Culinario Ambrosia.	14 B6
El Borrego Viudo............	15 B4
Fonda Margarita............	16 B4
Pozolería Tixtla.............	17 C4

NIGHTLIFE ★	(pp167–76)
California Dancing Club....	18 C5
El Balcón Huasteco........	19 C2
La Casa de Paquita del Barrio...	20 C2
Salón Los Ángeles..........	21 C2

ARTS 🎭	(pp177–86)
Centro Cultural Universitario	(see 8)
Tlatelolco....................	22 B4
Teatro Polyforum Siqueiras.	

SPORTS & ACTIVITIES	(pp187–93)
Estadio Azteca..............	23 C7
Estadio Azul................	24 B4
Estadio Olímpico............	25 B6
Foro Sol....................	26 E4
Monumental Plaza México...	27 B4
Rancho del Charro..........	28 A4

SLEEPING 🛏	(pp199–212)
Fiesta Inn..................	29 E3
Hostal Cactus..............	30 C4
Hotel Aeropuerto...........	31 E3
Ramada Aeropuerto México..	(see 31)

TRANSPORT	(pp245–50)
Embarcadero Cuemanco.....	32 D7
Terminal 2.................	33 E3
Terminal Norte.............	34 C1
Terminal Oriente (TAPO)....	35 D3
Terminal Poniente..........	36 B4

INFORMATION	(see 5)
Basílica de Guadalupe......	1 A4
Hospital ABC...............	2 B4
INEGI.....................	3 A3
Italian Embassy............	

SIGHTS	(pp39–117)
Anáhuacalli...............	4 C6
Basílica de Guadalupe......	5 D1
Cuicuilco..................	6 B7
Iglesia de Candelaria......	7 B4
Plaza de las Tres Culturas..	8 C2
Santa Muerte Altar........	9 D2
Santuario Nacional de la Santa	
Muerte..................	10 D3

SHOPPING 🛍	(pp119–30)
Fonart....................	11 B4
Tianguis Cultural del Chopo..	12 C2

ITINERARY BUILDER

You could spend weeks getting to know all the magnificent architecture, archaeological sites, murals, museums, markets, nightspots and taco stands this multifaceted capital has to offer. Particularly in the Centro Histórico, every block is worthy of extended exploration. Think of this handy tool as a way to scratch the surface.

AREA	ACTIVITIES	Sights	Eating
	Centro Histórico	Templo Mayor (p51) Catedral Metropolitana (p50) Museo del Estanquillo (p53)	El Cardenal (p135) Los Girasoles (p136) Hostería de Santo Domingo (p136)
	Alameda Central & Around	Palacio de Bellas Artes (p63) Museo de Arte Popular (p67) Museo Mural Diego Rivera (p66)	El Cuadrilátero (p140) Churrería El Moro (p138) El Regiomontano (p139)
	Plaza de la República & San Rafael	Monumento a la Revolución (p70) Museo Nacional de la Revolución (p70) Museo Nacional de San Carlos (p70)	Boca del Río (p140) El Mixteco (p140) El Califa de León (p140)
	Zona Rosa & Cuauhtémoc	Paseo de la Reforma (p73) Monumento a la Independencia (p73)	Tezka (p141) Fonda El Refugio (p141) U Rae Ok (p142)
	Bosque de Chapultepec & Polanco	Museo Nacional de Antropología (p80) Castillo de Chapultepec (p77) Zoológico de Chapultepec (p79)	Águila Y Sol (p144) Pujol (p145) Izote (p146)
	Condesa & Roma	Parque México (p86) Casa del Poeta Ramón López Velarde (p90) Centro de Cultura Casa Lamm (p184)	Hip Kitchen (p148) Ixchel (p150) Tierra de Vinos (p151)
	Coyoacán & San Ángel	Museo Frida Kahlo (p96) Ex-Convento de Churubusco (p97) Museo Casa Estudio Diego Rivera y Frida Kahlo (p100)	Los Danzantes (p152) Taberna De León (p154) Saks (p154)
	Ciudad Universitaria, Cuicuilco & Tlalpan	UNAM Campus (p104) Cuicuilco (p115) Capilla de las Capuchinas Sacramentarias (p109)	Antigua Hacienda de Tlalpan (p155) Azul Y Oro (p156) Rayuela (p156)

HOW TO USE THIS TABLE

The table below allows you to plan a day's worth of activities in any area of the city. Simply select which area you wish to explore, and then mix and match from the corresponding listings to build your day. The first item in each cell represents a well-known highlight of the area, while the other items are more off-the-beaten-track gems.

Drinking & Nightlife	Shopping
La Ópera Bar (p161) Salón Corona (p161) Pasagüero (p173)	Museo de Arte Popular (p122) Palacio de Las Máscaras (p121) Arte Mexicano Para El Mundo (p121)
La Casa de Paquita La Del Barrio (p173)	Centro de Artesaniás La Ciudadela (p123) Fonart (p122) La Europea (p123)
Cafetería Gabi's (p162) Bar Milán (p168) Papa Beto (p174)	Mercado Insurgentes (p123) Plaza Del Ángel (p124) Miniaturas Felguérez (p125)
Big Red (p163) Momma (p170) Área (p168)	Av Presidente Masaryk (p125) Pasaje Polanco (p126) La Divina (p126)
La Botica (p163) Condesa DF (p169) Mestizo Lounge (p164)	Naco Miscelánea (p127) Milagro (p127) Chic By Accident (p128)
La Bipolar (p165) El Hijo Del Cuervo (p169) Altavista 154 (p175)	Casa Del Coleccionista (p129) Bazar Sábado (p123) Plaza Loreto (p130)
La Jalisciense (p165) Los Girasoles (p136) Hostería de Santo Domingo (p136)	

CENTRO HISTÓRICO

Shopping p120; Eating p135; Drinking p160; Sleeping p200

The area defined as the Centro Histórico focuses on the large downtown plaza known as El Zócalo (Plaza de la Constitución) and stretches for several blocks in all directions from there. To the west it reaches almost as far as the Alameda Central. Packed with magnificent buildings and absorbing museums, it is the obvious place to start your explorations of the city. More than 1500 of its buildings are classified as historic or artistic monuments and it is on the Unesco World Heritage list. It also vibrates with modern-day street life and nightlife, and is a convenient area to stay in, with a range of hotels in all price categories except the very highest.

The 34-block area of the Centro Histórico approximates Mexico City's pre-20th-century extents. It was in this spot that the Aztecs founded their capital, Tenochtitlán, in 1325, when the wandering tribe sighted the prophesied vision: an eagle perched upon a cactus devouring a snake (a scene enshrined in a diorama that stands on the east side of the DF government building on Pino Suárez). As it happened, the scene unfolded on a small island in the middle of a lake, and the Aztecs were obliged to build their city in this unlikely setting. The causeways they built to connect the island to the mainland remain in use today as major thoroughfares, including Tacuba and Pino Suárez.

After the Spaniards destroyed the Aztec capital, the lake was drained and the new city was superimposed on the Aztec ruins. Many of the early structures were built of *tezontle*, a blood-red volcanic stone still in evidence around the Centro. The early Spanish city was dominated by the vast monastic complexes erected by the Franciscans, Augustinians and other evangelizing orders. Within a century of the city's construction, they had installed more than 40 of these monasteries and convents, along with hospitals and educational institutions.

Following independence, reforms on the ecclesiastical hegemony were carried out with a vengeance. The vast monastic complexes were carved up to make way for new streets, or completely demolished. Fortunes made during the late-19th-century dictatorship of Porfirio Díaz fueled a construction boom, and more colonial gems were torn down to be replaced by Parisian-style mansions. Following the Revolution, new neighborhoods were laid out to accommodate an emerging middle class, and the Centro fell into decline. The relocating of the national university to the DF's southern edge in the 1950s was a further blow to the Centro's vitality. By the 1980s much of the Centro had become very run-down, with many of its former mansions turned into overcrowded housing for the poor or simply abandoned.

Starting in 2000, under the administration of Mayor Andrés Manuel López Obrador, capital was poured into upgrading the image and infrastructure of the Centro. Streets were repaved, buildings refurbished, lighting and traffic flow improved and security bolstered. The campaign is ongoing, and under Mayor Marcelo Ebrard, more museums, restaurants and clubs have moved into the newly renovated structures, and festivals and cultural events are staged in the plazas, spurring a real renaissance. In spring, the Festival del Centro Histórico turns the whole area into a venue for special performances, exhibitions and conferences with plenty of international guests. Ebrard has also pushed to clear the Centro of the thousands of 'informal' vendors who set up stalls along the streets and sidewalks. So far, this initiative has been effective, though its success is of course dependent on the availability of alternative employment for the vendors.

Although most of the improvements have been made in the area west of the Zócalo, the unimproved portions remain equally worthy of exploration. We can only suggest some of the places to visit, but almost anywhere you poke around you're bound to make discoveries. The Centro is like a giant historical jigsaw puzzle. What is on display today are fragments of overarching themes which have been dismantled and repurposed over the centuries.

ZÓCALO

EL ZÓCALO Map pp48–9
Ⓜ Zócalo

The heart of Mexico City is the Plaza de la Constitución, more widely known as the Zócalo, meaning 'base.' City residents gave it this nickname in the 19th century, when plans for a major monument to independence went unrealized, leaving only the pedestal. Measuring more than 220m from north to south and 240m from east to west, the Zócalo is one of the world's largest city squares.

The ceremonial center of Aztec Teno-chtitlán, known as the Teocalli, lay immediately northeast of the Zócalo. In the 1520s Cortés paved the plaza with stones from the ruined Teocalli and other Aztec buildings. The Inquisition performed its first auto-da-fe here in 1574. In the 18th century, the Zócalo was given over to a maze of market stalls until it was dismantled by Santa Anna who placed the unfinished independence monument in its center. Under Emperor Maximilian's reign, the square was redesigned as a European-style garden with tree-lined paths and a gazebo for military-band recitals, but these items were removed in the next century to leave it in its current open state.

Today, the Zócalo is home to Mexico City's powers-that-be. On its east side is the Palacio Nacional, on the north the Catedral Metropolitana, and on the south the offices of the Distrito Federal government. Jewelry shops and extravagant hotels line the arcade known as the Portal de Mercaderes on the plaza's west side, once the domain of silversmiths.

The huge Mexican flag flying in the middle of the Zócalo is ceremonially removed from the Palacio Nacional and raised at 8am by soldiers of the Mexican army, then lowered at 6pm.

PALACIO NACIONAL Map pp48–9

☎ 5528-1252; Plaza de la Constitución; admission free, ID required; ⏲ 9am-5pm; Ⓜ Zócalo
Home to the offices of the president of Mexico, the Federal Treasury and dramatic murals by Diego Rivera, the National Palace fills the entire east side of the Zócalo.

The first palace on this spot was built by Aztec emperor Moctezuma II in the early 16th century. Cortés destroyed the palace in 1521, rebuilding it as a fortress with three interior courtyards. In 1562 the crown bought the palace from Cortés' family to house the viceroys of Nueva España. Destroyed during riots in 1692, it was rebuilt and remained the vice-regal residence until Mexican independence.

As you face the palace you will see three portals. On the right (south) is the guarded entrance for the president (though in fact he rarely makes an appearance here). The north (left) entrance is for Federal Treasury employees. High above the center door hangs the Campana de Dolores, the bell rung in the town of Dolores Hidalgo by Padre

Miguel Hidalgo in 1810 at the start of the Mexican War of Independence. From the balcony underneath it, the president delivers the *grito* (shout) – *Viva México!* – on September 15 to commemorate independence.

Enter the palace through the center door. The Diego Rivera murals above the main staircase were painted between 1929 and 1935. The main, largest work here is one of Rivera's masterpieces, *México a Través de los Siglos* (Mexico Through the Centuries), which shows just about every major event and personage in modern Mexican history from Cortés' conquest of the Aztecs at bottom center to the Mexican Revolution at top center. Between these two is the eagle-on-cactus symbol of Aztec Teno-chtitlán, which figures even today on the Mexican national flag. Portrayed on the right wall of the stairs is the ancient god Quetzalcóatl, as an antecedent to the Spanish-influenced centuries, along with other aspects of pre-Hispanic belief and life. On the left wall Karl Marx presides over what Rivera no doubt believed to be the logical outcome of the colonial and bourgeois eras, La Lucha de Clases (Class War).

The unfinished series of frescoes around the walkway level at the top of the staircase was painted by Rivera between 1945 and 1951. They show a sequence of pre-Hispanic cultures – Tenochtitlán, then the Tarascos of Michoacán, the Zapotecs and Mixtecs of Oaxaca, the peoples of Veracruz, and the Huastecs of the northeast. The Huastec panel emphasizes maize-growing and is followed by panels on two other plants of great importance in pre-Hispanic Mexico: the cacao (source of chocolate) and maguey (from which the drink *pulque* was made). Finally we see the arrival of Cortés – portrayed as a grotesque, knobbly-kneed simpleton – in Veracruz in 1519.

Also located on this level is the Recinto Parlamentario, a reconstructed version of the original Chamber of Deputies that was destroyed in an 1872 blaze. On display is a copy of the constitution, passed in this legislative rotunda back in 1857.

On the palace's north side is the Recinto de Homenaje a Benito Juárez (Place of Homage to Benito Juárez). Juárez, one of Mexico's most respected heroes, was born into poverty in the state of Oaxaca, but rose to lead the reform movement in the 1850s and the fight against the French invaders in the 1860s. He served as president until his death in

CENTRO HISTÓRICO

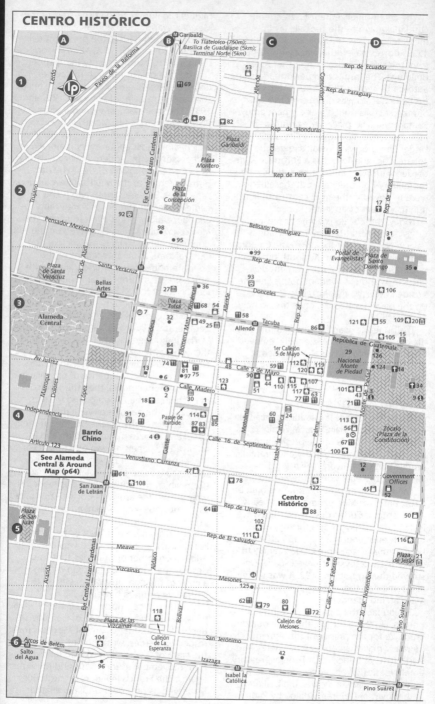

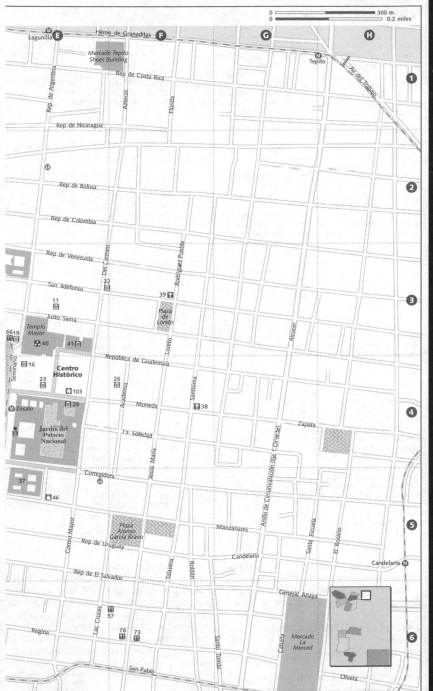

0 — 300 m
0 — 0.2 miles

Lagunilla

Héroe de Granaditas

Tepito

Av del Trabajo

Mercado Tepito
Shoes Building

Rep de Costa Rica

Rep de Argentina

Aztecas

Florida

Rep de Nicaragua

Rep de Bolivia

Rep de Colombia

Del Carmen

Rodríguez Puebla

Rep de Venezuela

San Ildefonso

22

39

11

Justo Sierra

Plaza
de
Loreto

Templo
Mayor

66 19

40

41

Loreto

Alcocer

16

Seminario

República de Guatemala

Centro
Histórico

23

26

Academia

Santísima

103

Moneda

38

Zócalo

28

La Soledad

Jesús María

Zapata

Jardín del
Palacio
Nacional

33

37

Corregidora

Anillo de Circunvalación (Eje 1 Oriente)

Santa Escuela

El Rosario

46

Correo Mayor

Plaza
Alonso
García Bravo

Manzanares

Rep de Uruguay

Talavera

Roldán

Candelaria

Candelaria

Rep de El Salvador

General Anaya

Las Cruces

57

Regina

76

73

San Jerónimo

Cabaña

Mercado
La
Merced

San Pablo

Olvera

49

CENTRO HISTÓRICO

1872. This exhibit includes various personal effects and displays on his life and times.

Beyond the main patio are botanical gardens containing plants from around Mexico.

CATEDRAL METROPOLITANA

Map pp48–9

☎ 5510-0440; admission free; ⏰ 7:30am-8pm; Ⓜ Zócalo

Although construction of the Metropolitan Cathedral began in 1573, it remained a work in progress throughout the entire colonial period. This explains the mélange of architectural styles on display, as each successive construction stage reflected the modes of the era. To complicate matters, due to the cathedral's strategic placement right on top of the ruins of the Aztec temple complex, the massive building has been sinking unevenly since its construction, resulting in fissures and cracks in the structure.

With a five-nave basilica design of vaults on semicircular arches, the cathedral was built to resemble the one in Seville. The baroque portals facing the Zócalo, built in the 17th century, have two levels of columns and marble panels with bas-reliefs. The central panel shows the Assumption of the Virgin Mary, to whom the cathedral is dedicated. The upper levels of the towers, with unique bell-shaped tops, were added in the late 18th century. The exterior was completed in 1813, when architect Manuel Tolsá added the clock tower – topped by statues of Faith, Hope and Charity – and a great central dome.

The first thing you notice upon entering from the Zócalo is the elaborately carved and gilded Altar de Perdón (Altar of Pardon). Invariably there is a line of worshippers at the foot of the Señor del Veneno (Lord of the Poison), the dusky Christ figure on the right. Legend has it that the figure attained its color when it miraculously absorbed a dose of poison through its feet from the lips of a clergyman, to whom an enemy had administered the lethal substance.

The cathedral's chief artistic treasure is the gilded 18th-century Altar de los Reyes (Altar of the Kings), behind the main altar. It's a high point of Churrigueresque style. The two side naves are lined with 14 richly decorated chapels. At the southwest corner, the Capilla de los Santos Ángeles y Arcángeles (Chapel of the Holy Angels and Archangels) is another example of baroque sculpture and painting, with altarpieces embellished by the 18th-century painter Juan Correa.

Also worthy of admiration are the intricately carved late-17th-century wooden choir stalls in the central nave and the sacristy, the first component of the cathedral to be built, with a pair of enormous painted panels. La Asunción de la Virgen, by Correa, depicts the ascension of Mary, while La Mujer del Apocalípsis, by Cristóbal de Villal-

pando, portrays the apocalyptic vision of St John the Apostle.

A M$10 donation is requested to enter the sacristy or choir, where authorized guides provide commentary. You can climb the bell tower (admission M$12; 10:30am-12:30pm & 3-6pm). Sunday at noon, Mass is conducted by the archbishop of Mexico.

Adjoining the east side of the cathedral is the 18th-century Sagrario Metropolitano (Map pp48–9; 7:30am-7:30pm). Originally built to house the archives and vestments of the archbishop, it is now the city's main parish church. Its front entrance and mirror-image eastern portal are superb examples of the ultradecorative Churrigueresque style.

You may well wonder what those guys are doing sitting on the ground on the west side of the cathedral, with tool bags at their feet and cardboard signs in front of them. They're plumbers, painters, bricklayers and electricians, and they're just looking to make an honest peso. Their signs announce their trades to potential customers seeking home improvements.

TEMPLO MAYOR Map pp48–9

5542-4943; www.conaculta.gob.mx/templo mayor; Seminario 8; admission incl entry to Museo del Templo Mayor M$45, Sun free; 9am-5pm Tue-Sun

The Teocalli of Tenochtitlán, demolished by the Spaniards in the 1520s, stood on the site of the cathedral and the blocks to its north and east. It wasn't until 1978, after electricity workers happened on an eight-ton stone-disc carving of the Aztec goddess Coyolxauhqui, that the decision was taken to demolish a block of colonial buildings and excavate the Templo Mayor. The temple is thought to be on the exact spot where the Aztecs saw their symbolic eagle, perching on a cactus with a snake in its beak – the symbol of Mexico today. In Aztec belief this was, literally, the center of the universe.

FILLING IN THE SQUARE

It is the very emptiness of the Zócalo that allows it to be adapted and rearranged for multiple uses. It has variously served as a forum for mass protests and a campground for demonstrators, a free concert venue, a great dance hall, a human chessboard, a stage for military marches on Independence day and a gallery of spooky altars for Día de Muertos (Day of the Dead) in November. Café Tacuba and Manu Chao have played before crowds of 200,000 fans in the Zócalo. It became an extension of the cathedral's atrium when Pope John Paul II conducted mass here. It's even been a canvas for photo artist Spencer Tunick, who filled the square with 18,000 nude Mexicans in May 2007 (a record for Tunick, who has staged similar photo shoots in cities around the world). The buildings around the square are often decorated with holiday iconography.

MODERN DANCE

As you emerge from Metro Zócalo onto the vast central plaza, you'll invariably hear the booming of drums from the direction of the cathedral – the Aztec dancers are doing their thing. Wearing snakeskin loincloths, elaborately feathered headdresses and shell ankle bracelets, they move in a circle and chant in Náhuatl in what appears to be a display of pre-Hispanic aerobics. At the center, engulfed in a cloud of fragrant copal smoke, drummers bang on the conga-like *huehuetl* and the barrel-shaped, slitted *teponzantli*.

Variously known as Concheros, Danzantes Aztecas or Danza Chichimeca, the ritual is performed daily near the Templo Mayor, often throbbing on for hours without pause. It is meant to evoke the Mexica *mitote*, a frenzied ceremony performed by pre-Conquest Mexicans at harvest times. Yet scant evidence exists that their moves bear any resemblance to those of their forebears. Prohibited by the Spanish colonists from performing their dances or using the *huehuetl*, indigenous Mexicans fused elements of Christian worship into their rituals, dancing in the atriums of churches and playing mandolinlike instruments backed by a *concha* (armadillo shell; from whence the name Concheros derives).

Today's Zócalo dancers, however, reject any association with Christianity, seeking instead a purer connection to their pre-Hispanic roots. Critics mock their representation of a sacred yet unknowable past as a pastiche of New Age nonsense. Yet this celebration of Mexican heritage appears to be developing into a movement, as it's embraced by more and more young Mexicans seeking a continuity with their past, many of whom you'll see gyrating along in their street clothes. Stranger still, the dance craze is being taken up by the descendants of the conquistadors, as roots-minded youth in Madrid go Aztec.

Like other sacred buildings in Tenochtitlán, the temple, begun in 1325, was enlarged several times, with each rebuilding accompanied by the sacrifice of captured warriors. In 1487 these rituals were performed at a frenzied pace to rededicate the temple after one major reconstruction. By some estimates, as many as 20,000 sacrificial victims went under the blade in one ghastly four-day ceremony.

What we see today are sections of the temple's different phases. (Little is left of the seventh and last version seen by the Spanish conquistadors, built around 1500.) At the center is a platform dating from about 1400; on its southern half, a sacrificial stone stands in front of a shrine to Huizilopochtli, the Aztec war god. On the northern half is a *chac-mool* (a Maya reclining figure that served as a messenger to the gods) before a shrine to the water god, Tláloc. By the time the Spanish arrived, a 40m-high double pyramid towered above this spot, with steep twin stairways climbing to shrines of the two gods.

Elsewhere in the site, don't miss the stone replica of a tzompantli (skull-display rack), carved with 240 stone skulls, or the 15th-century Recinto de los Guerreros Águila (Sanctuary of the Eagle Warriors, an elite band of Aztec fighters), decorated with colored bas-reliefs of military processions.

As you approach the museum, notice the large-scale quotations chiseled on its west walls. These are awestruck descriptions of Tenochtitlán from three of its earliest European visitors – Hernán Cortés, Bernál Díaz del Castillo and Motolinía.

The Museo del Templo Mayor houses artifacts from the site and gives a good overview of Aztec civilization, including *chinampa* agriculture, systems of government and trade, and beliefs, wars and sacrifices. Pride of place is given to the great wheel-like stone of Coyolxauhqui (She of Bells on her Cheek, the Aztec goddess of the moon), best viewed from the top floor vantage point. On the stone, Coyolxauhqui is shown decapitated. According to Aztec mythology, she led her 400 siblings in an attack against her pregnant mother, Coatlicue. But before they could do so, Coatlicue bore Huizilopochtli (god of war) who hacked Coyolxauhqui to pieces, hurling her head into the sky where it became the moon. Other outstanding exhibits include full-size terracotta eagle warriors.

The entrance to the temple site and museum is east of the cathedral, across the hectic Plaza Templo Mayor, with its model of Tenochtitlán. On the temple site, explanatory text is accompanied by quality English translations, but no translations are provided inside the museum. Alternatively, rent a recorded audio-guide inside the museum, available in English (M$50), or hire one of the authorized tour guides (with Sectur ID, M$250) by the entrance.

GALERÍA DE NUESTRA COCINA DUQUE DE HERDEZ Map pp48–9

☎ 5522-8860; www.fundacionherdez.com.mx; Seminario 18; admission M$5; ⏰ 10am-5pm Tue-Sat; Ⓜ Zócalo

This modest museum, sponsored by Mexican canned-food giant Herdez, follows the history of the country's renowned cuisine. You'll find out what Mexicans were eating before the Spanish conquest and how the two traditions fused to yield all those wonderful tacos, tamales and salsas. Probably the most useful feature is the gastronomic library downstairs.

MUSEO ARCHIVO DE LA FOTOGRAFÍA Map pp48–9

☎ 2616-7057; www.maf.df.gob.mx; República de Guatemala 34; admission free; ⏰ 10am-6pm Tue-Sun; Ⓜ Zócalo

Inaugurated in November 2007, the photographic archive museum occupies the 16th-century Casa de Ajaracas, which was completely renovated for the purpose. The museum draws from a century's worth of images taken for the *Gaceta Oficial del Distrito Federal* – the DF public record – to document the capital's development and preserve the memory of its streets, plazas, buildings and people.

ANTIGUO PALACIO DEL AYUNTAMIENTO Map pp48–9

☎ 5662-7680; www.df.gob.mx; Plaza de la Constitución 7; admission free; ⏰ 10am-6pm; Ⓜ Zócalo

The two buildings on the south side of the Zócalo may look similar with their stately arcades and handsome carved window frames, but the Ayuntamiento (the one on the right) predates its twin by over 400 years. The mayor has his office there, while various city departments occupy the east building. Recently restored and opened for public viewing, the grand Salón de Cabildos, on the upper level of the Ayuntamiento, was the place where the city council traditionally convened to settle local disputes. The entry hall contains a gallery of portraits of all 62 Spanish viceroys.

WEST OF THE ZÓCALO

NACIONAL MONTE DE PIEDAD Map pp48–9

Monte de Piedad 7; ⏰ 8:30am-6pm Mon-Fri, to 1pm Sat; Ⓜ Zócalo

Facing the west side of the cathedral is Mexico's national pawnshop, founded in 1774 by silver magnate Pedro Romero de Terreros. The site was once occupied by the Palacio de Axayacatl, where Cortés and his companions were first lodged by Moctezuma II in 1519. Cortés installed the original colonial headquarters over the ruins of his host's palace. People pawn their jewelry and other possessions in the central hall for loans at 12% interest. Unclaimed items are sold in shops off the central passageway.

MUSEO DEL ESTANQUILLO Map pp48–9

☎ 5521-3052; www.museodelestanquillo.com.mx; Isabel la Católica 26; admission free; ⏰ 10am-6pm Wed-Mon; Ⓜ Allende

The 'corner shop' museum contains the vast pop-culture collection amassed over the decades by DF essayist, commentator and pack rat Carlos Monsiváis. Housed in a magnificent neoclassical building which was an important jewelry store in the early 20th century, the museum illustrates various phases in the capital's development through numerous photos, paintings, daguerreotypes, board games, movie posters, illustrated sheets of verse, comic strips and so on from the collection. Taken together, these objects culled from the city's flea markets, rare book stores and antique shops add up to a vivid people's history of Mexico City.

PALACIO DE ITURBIDE Map pp48–9

☎ 1226-0011; Madero 17; admission free; ⏰ 10am-7pm Wed-Mon; Ⓜ Allende

West of Bolívar, you'll encounter the baroque facade of the late-18th-century Palacio de Iturbide. Built for colonial nobility, in 1821 it became the residence of General Agustín Iturbide, a hero of the Mexican struggle for independence. To the cheers

NEW FINDS

Ongoing excavation continues to turn up major pieces in the vicinity of the Templo Mayor. Just west of the temple, a monolithic stone carved with the image of Tlaltecuhtli, the goddess of earth fertility, was unearthed in a fractured state in October 2006. Archaeologists believe the stone marks the tomb of Ahuízotl, the Aztec *tlatoani* (emperor), who immediately preceded Moctezuma II and whose military conquests greatly expanded Aztec domains. Excavation of the tomb was proceeding as this was being written.

WORTH THE TRIP

Tenayuca & Santa Cecilia

These two sites of lesser Aztec ruins in Estado de México, north of the DF line, might appeal not only to archaeology enthusiasts but also to anyone who enjoys discovering calm and beautiful nooks amid the modern urban sprawl. You can visit both in a half-day trip from the city center.

Settled by Chichimecs in about the 13th century, Tenayuca (☎ 5391-0780; Tizoc & Calle Quetzalcóatl; admission M$34, free Sun; ☉ 10am-5pm) was later ruled by the Aztecs, and the double-staircase pyramid they left is a smaller version of the now-ruined one that stood in the Templo Mayor. As at the Templo Mayor, each staircase was topped by a temple – one dedicated to the water god Tláloc, the other probably dedicated to the Aztec tribal god Huizilopochtli. Striking serpent sculptures, possibly pre-Aztec, surround three sides of its base (imagine what they looked like when they were painted bright red, yellow and green!). If you just want to admire the pyramid there's no need to go in, other than to visit the small museum and read the explanatory signs, since the site is perfectly visible from the outside.

Santa Cecilia Acatitlán (admission M$34, free Sun; ☉ 10am-5pm Tue-Sun), 2km north of Tenayuca, is a small but fine pyramid topped with a temple (both reconstructed) dedicated to the gods Tláloc and Huizilopochtli. It stands in pleasant, leafy grounds behind the pretty, 16th-century Parroquia Santa Cecilia, some of whose stone came from the original pyramid. Access to the pyramid is through the Museo Hurtado, with a small collection of pre-Hispanic sculpture.

Tenayuca is 11km north-northwest of the Zócalo. To get there you can take a northbound 'Tenayuca' pesero on the Eje Central Lázaro Cárdenas at Donceles (one block north of the Palacio de Bellas Artes), or from the Plaza de las Tres Culturas. You need to get off at the intersection of Av Acueducto de Tenayuca and Cuauhtémoc, half an hour from the Bellas Artes in moderate traffic (there are traffic signals at the corner; if in doubt ask the driver or fellow passengers for the *pirámide de Tenayuca*). Walk north (to the right) along Cuauhtémoc and you'll see the pyramid beside a park after a couple of blocks.

You can reach Santa Cecilia by taking a pesero that's headed north up Carretera Tenayuca Santa Cecilia, north of the Tenayuca pyramid. Get off at Calle Pirámide de Tula and walk a few blocks east to the church. You'll probably need to ask for directions – the people at Tenayuca will get you started.

of a rent-a-crowd, Iturbide was proclaimed Emperor Agustín I here in 1822. (He abdicated less than a year later, after General Santa Anna announced the birth of the republic.) Acquired and restored by Banamex bank in 1965, the palace now functions as the Palacio de Cultura Banamex, with exhibits drawn from the bank's vast Mexican art collection, as well as contemporary Mexican handicrafts. Some of the palace's original salons are displayed on the upper level, along with exhibits on its eventful history. Free guided tours are offered (in Spanish) at noon, 2pm and 4pm.

CASA DE AZULEJOS Map pp48–9

☎ 5512-9820; Madero 4; ☉ 7am-1am; Ⓜ Allende

A block east toward the Zócalo stands one of the city's gems, the Casa de Azulejos. Dating from 1596, it was built for the Condes (Counts) del Valle de Orizaba. Although the superb tile work that has adorned the outside walls since the 18th century is Spanish and Moorish in style, most of the tiles were actually produced in China and shipped to Mexico on the Manila *naos* (Spanish galleons used up to the early

19th century). The building now houses a Sanborns restaurant in a covered courtyard around a Moorish fountain. The staircase has a 1925 mural by Orozco.

IGLESIA DEL CONVENTO DE SAN FRANCISCO Map pp48–9

Madero 7; admission free; ☉ 7:30am-9pm

The temple is just a remnant of the vast Franciscan monastery erected in the early 16th century over the site of Moctezuma's private zoo. In its heyday it extended two blocks south and east, and its atrium could hold 60,000 worshippers. The monastic complex was divvied up under the post-Independence Reform Laws, then returned to the Franciscan order, in a deplorable state, in 1949, and was subsequently restored. The entrance is reached through a broad atrium, where art exhibitions are held; the elaborately carved doorway is a shining example of 18th-century baroque.

PLAZA TOLSÁ Map pp48–9

Several blocks west of the Zócalo is this handsome square, named after the illustrious late-18th-century sculptor and architect who completed the Catedral Metropolitana.

Manuel Tolsá also created the bronze equestrian statue of the Spanish king Carlos IV (who reigned from 1788 to 1808), which is the plaza's centerpiece. It originally stood in the Zócalo, then on Paseo de la Reforma, before being moved here in 1979 ('as a work of art,' a chiseled plaque emphasizes).

MUSEO NACIONAL DE ARTE Map pp48–9

☎ 5130-3400; www.munal.com.mx, in Spanish; Tacuba 8; admission M$30, Sun free; ☻ 10:30am-5:30pm Tue-Sun; Ⓜ Bellas Artes
Built around 1900 in the style of an Italian renaissance palace, the National Art Museum holds collections representing every school of Mexican art until the early 20th century. A highlight is the work of José María Velasco, depicting the Valle de México in the late 19th century, with Guadalupe and Chapultepec far outside the city.

PALACIO DE MINERÍA Map pp48–9

☎ 5623-2982; Tacuba 5; admission M$25; ☻ tours 10am-3pm Sat & Sun; Ⓜ Bellas Artes
Opposite the national art museum is the Palace of Mining, where mining engineers were trained in the 19th century. Today it houses a branch of the national university's engineering department. A neoclassical masterpiece, the palace was designed by Tolsá and built between 1797 and 1813. Visits are by guided tour only. There's a small museum (admission M$10; ☻ 10am-6pm Wed-Sun) on the illustrious architect's life and work.

SENADO DE LA REPÚBLICA Map pp48–9

☎ 5130-2200; Xicoténcatl 9
The upper house of Mexico's federal congress, the Cámara de Senadores, meets in a building on the east side of the Museo Nacional de Arte. It's usually in session from September to December. The Distrito Federal's elected assembly, the Asamblea Legislativa del Distrito Federal (ALDF), uses the old Cámara de Diputados building around the corner on Donceles and Allende. The Cámara de Diputados itself, the lower house of the federal congress, now uses the modern Palacio Legislativo on Av Congreso de la Unión, about 2km east of the Zócalo. It, too, is in session from September to December.

PALACIO POSTAL Map pp48–9

☎ 5521-1408; Tacuba 1; Ⓜ Bellas Artes
More than just Mexico City's central post office, this early-20th-century palace is an architectural stunner. Across Eje Central from the Palacio de Bellas Artes, it was designed in Italian renaissance style by that structure's original architect, Adamo Boari. The beige stone facade features baroque columns and carved filigree around the windows; inside, the bronze railings on the monumental staircase were cast in Florence. Philatelists can ogle the rare Mexican stamps in the first-floor postal museum (admission free; ☻ 10am-5:30pm Mon-Fri, to 1:30pm Sat), while even noncollectors might enjoy the mural depicting a Tarascan farmer, which is a mosaic of more than 48,234 stamps postmarked between 1890 and 1934.

MUSEO INTERACTIVO DE ECONOMÍA Map pp48–9

☎ 5130-4600; www.mide.org.mx; Tacuba 17; adult/child M$45/35; ☻ 9am-6pm Tue-Sun; Ⓜ Allende
Housed in the former hospital of the Bethlehemites (the only religious order to be established in the Americas), this sprawling 18th-century structure has since 2006 been the unlikely home of a museum devoted to economics. A slew of hands-on exhibits are aimed at breaking down economic concepts and demonstrating how every Mexican affects and is affected by these principles. Visitors can start a corporation, chart their investments or design their own currency. For coin connoisseurs, the highlight is the Banco de México's numismatic collection. Unfortunately, only a few of the exhibits provide English text.

EAST OF THE ZÓCALO

MUSEO DE LA SECRETARÍA DE HACIENDA Y CRÉDITO PÚBLICO Map pp48–9

☎ 9158-1245; Moneda 4; admission M$8, Sun free; ☻ 10am-6pm Tue-Sun; Ⓜ Zócalo
The Museum of the Finance Secretariat shows off its vast collection of Mexican art, much of it contributed by painters and sculptors in lieu of paying taxes. The former colonial archbishop's palace also hosts a full program of cultural events (many free), from puppet shows to chamber-music recitals.

TRANSPORTATION: CENTRO HISTÓRICO

- Metro – the Zócalo station (Línea 2) exits right onto the central plaza. Metro Allende, one stop west on Línea 2, is best for points west of the Zócalo along Madero, Av 5 de Mayo and Tacuba (note: there's no transfer between eastbound and westbound sides of the platform at this station). Metro Isabel La Católica (Línea 1) and Pino Suárez (Línea 1 & 2) are on the south side of the Centro Histórico, at the bottom of the streets of the same name. Metro San Juan de Letrán (Línea 8) and Salto del Agua (Líneas 1 & 8) access the Centro from the west, along the north–south thoroughfare Eje Central Lázaro Cárdenas.
- Trolleybus – 'Autobuses del Sur' and 'Autobuses del Norte' trolleybuses run south and north, respectively, along Eje Central Lázaro Cárdenas, which skirts the west side of the Centro Histórico.
- Bus – though it's often faster to walk, pesero routes ply most of the streets crisscrossing the Centro grid, including Bolívar (southbound) and Isabel La Católica (northbound).
- Bicycle – free bike loans are offered 9am to 6pm daily, from a module on the west side of the Catedral Metropolitana. Leave a passport or driver's license for two hours of riding time.

MUSEO NACIONAL DE LAS CULTURAS Map pp48–9
☎ 5512-7452; Moneda 13; admission free; ◷ 9:30am-6pm Tue-Sat, 10am-5pm Sun; Ⓜ Zócalo

Constructed in 1567 as the colonial mint, the museum features ethnographic displays on the dress and handicrafts of the world's cultures. At least as interesting is the Rufino Tamayo mural in the entryway, entitled *La Revolución*. An atypically realistic canvas for the artist, it depicts the downfall of the Porfirio Díaz regime.

MUSEO JOSÉ LUIS CUEVAS Map pp48–9
☎ 5522-0156; www.museojoseluiscuevas.com.mx; Academia 13; admission M$20, Sun free; ◷ 10am-5:30pm Tue-Sun; Ⓜ Zócalo

A haven for Mexico's fringe art scene, the museum showcases the works of Cuevas, a leader of the 1950s Ruptura movement which broke with the politicized art of the postrevolutionary regime. Cuevas' *La Giganta*, an 8m-high bronze figure with male and female features, dominates the central patio, while the Sala de Arte Erótico is an intriguing gallery of the artist's sexual themes.

TEMPLO DE LA SANTÍSIMA Map pp48–9
☎ 5522-2215; cnr Zapata & Santísima; admission free; ◷ 7am-1:30pm & 5-8pm

The profusion of ornamental sculpture on the facade – including ghostly busts of the 12 apostles and a representation of Christ with his head in God's lap – is the main reason to visit the Church of the Holy Sacrament, three blocks east of the Museo Nacional de las Culturas. Most of the carving was done by Lorenzo Rodríguez between 1755 and 1783.

ANTIGUO COLEGIO DE SAN ILDEFONSO Map pp48–9
☎ 5702-6378; www.sanildefonso.org.mx, in Spanish; Justo Sierra 16; admission M$45, Tue free; ◷ 10am-5:30pm Tue-Sun; Ⓜ Zócalo

Built in the 16th century as a Jesuit college, this remarkable building was later turned into a prestigious teacher-training institute. In the 1920s, Diego Rivera, José Clemente Orozco, David Alfaro Siqueiros and others were brought in to do murals. Most of the work on the main patio is by Orozco; check out the portrait of Cortés and La Malinche, his mistress, underneath the staircase. The amphitheater, off the lobby, holds Rivera's first mural, *La Creación*, commissioned by education minister José Vasconcelos upon Rivera's return from Europe in 1923. Mural tours (in Spanish) are given at noon and 4pm. Nowadays, the San Ildefonso hosts outstanding temporary exhibitions, as well as the Filmoteca of the national university.

MUSEO DE LA LUZ Map pp48–9
☎ 5702-3183; Del Carmen 31; admission M$20; ◷ 9am-4pm Mon-Fri, 10am-5pm Sat & Sun; Ⓜ Zócalo

The 'museum of light' occupies the former monastery of San Pedro and San Pablo, one of the Centro's most ancient structures. Kids will enjoy the array of interactive exhibits here, including optical illusions, one-way mirrors and kaleidoscopes, designed to demonstrate various optical principles (though only readers of Spanish will be illuminated by the accompanying explanations). At the rear of the museum are all kinds of devices to test your eyesight, and an optometrist performs eye exams for just M$25.

TEMPLO DE NUESTRA SEÑORA DE LORETO Map pp48–9

cnr San Ildefonso & Rodríguez Puebla; noon for midday mass

Noticeably sagging toward the east, this extraordinary church stands upon the site of an earlier chapel that housed a replica of Our Lady of Loreto brought from Italy by a Jesuit priest in 1675. The current church was completed in 1816 with the obligatory neoclassical facade of the period. It promptly started sinking into the ground but fortunately stopped a few years later. Inside, the sinking effect makes you feel like you're in a topsy-turvy funhouse. A magnificent cupola, ringed at the base by stained-glass images, crowns an unusual four-lobed cross with semicircular chapels in the lobes. After the 1985 earthquake the building was raided of its treasures, and the murals that covered the underside of the cupola were allowed to deteriorate.

NORTH OF THE ZÓCALO

CENTRO CULTURAL DE ESPAÑA

Map pp48–9

5521-1925; www.ccemx.org; República de Guatemala 18; admission free; 10am-8pm Tue & Wed, to 11pm Thu-Sat, to 4pm Sun; Zócalo

One of the more happening spaces in the Centro, the Spanish Cultural Center has various cutting-edge exhibitions going on at once, plus frequent shows by Spanish performers. The splendidly restored building, which conquistador Hernán Cortés once awarded to his butler, has a rooftop terrace for tapas-munching and, on weekends, late-night DJ sessions (see p175).

MUSEO DE LA CARICATURA Map pp48–9

5702-9256; Donceles 99; admission M$20; 10am-6pm; Zócalo

Mexico boasts a rich tradition of cartooning. Save for an eight-year period during the Porfirio Díaz regime when the dictator banned their publication, Mexican political cartoons have targeted the country's leaders since the early 19th century. And as a glance at many daily newspapers shows, the art of scathingly political caricatures is very much alive and well.

Housed in an 18th-century building that was originally an annex to the Jesuit college of San Ildefonso, the Museum of Cartooning displays the works of Mexico's most prominent cartoonists from a collection of some 1500 original panels. These date from 1826, when Italian Claudio Linati published the country's first political cartoon, entitled 'Tyranny,' in his newspaper the *Iris*. A browse through the collection provides an amusing take on Mexican political history. Prominently featured are the works of José Guadalupe Posada, whose instantly recognizable skeletal figures illustrated newspapers and sheet music in the early 1900s. His Calavera de Catarina, a female skeleton wearing a broad-brimmed frilly hat, has become a Día de Muertos (Day of the Dead) icon, though originally it was a satiric barb against the typically aristocratic characters who sashayed through the capital prior to the revolution.

PLAZA DE SANTO DOMINGO

Map pp48–9

Two blocks north of the Zócalo is this smaller, less formal plaza. The printers who work beneath the Portal de Evangelistas, along its west side, are descendants of the scribes who did the paperwork for merchants using the customs building (now the Education Ministry) across the square. The maroon stone Iglesia de Santo Domingo was at the time of its construction in 1736 a more formidable temple than the Catedral. The three-tiered facade deserves a close look: statues of St Francis and St Augustine stand in the niches alongside the doorway. The middle panel shows St Dominic de Guzmán receiving a staff and the Epistles from St Peter and St Paul, respectively; the dove above them represents the Holy Spirit. At the top is a bas-relief of the Assumption of the Virgin Mary.

Opposite the church, the 18th-century Palacio de la Inquisición was headquarters of the Holy Inquisition in Mexico until Spain decreed its closure in 1812. Its official shield can be seen at the top of the facade.

SECRETARÍA DE EDUCACIÓN PÚBLICA

Map pp48–9

3003-1000; República de Brasil 31; admission free; 9am-6pm Mon-Fri; Zócalo

In the 1920s the postrevolution education minister, José Vasconcelos, commissioned talented young artists – among them Diego Rivera, David Alfaro Siqueiros and José Clemente Orozco – to decorate numerous public buildings with dramatic, large-scale

DEATH'S NEW FACE

Garbed in a sequined white gown, wearing a wig of dark tresses and clutching a scythe in her bony hand, the skeletal figure bears an eerie resemblance to Mrs Bates from the film *Psycho*. Santa Muerte (St Death), as she is known, is the object of a fast-growing cult in Mexico, particularly in the rough Barrio Tepito, where the principal altar (Map pp42–3; Ⓜ Tepito) stands on Alfarería north of Mineros. Possibly rooted in pre-Hispanic ritual, Santa Muerte has been linked to Mictlantecuhtli, the Mexican god of death.

On the first day of each month, as many as 5000 followers line up at the Tepito altar to express their devotion and leave candles, bottles of tequila and other tokens of their affection. The proceedings are overseen by the cheerful, aproned 'Doña Queta' Romero, who built the shrine herself back in 2001.

At the saint's official home 1km south of the shrine, however, she is nowhere to be seen. Instead, the Santuario Nacional de la Santa Muerte (National Sanctuary of St Death; (Map pp42–3; ☎ 5702-8607; Bravo 35; ☯ 10am-6pm Tue-Fri, 11am-6pm Sun; Ⓜ Morelos) has a new figure of worship: a tall, winged woman with a ghostly pale complexion (though like her predecessor, she bears a scythe). In August 2007, the church substituted this ethereal Angel of St Death, because, as its bishop explained, Santa Muerte had become associated with drug runners, Satanists and other bad elements – an image, he claimed, that runs counter to her nature.

Some attribute the image change to other factors. The saint's popularity, especially among the lower echelons of society, is feared to be rivaling that of the Virgin of Guadalupe, and the Roman Catholic Church has harshly denounced the cult. The Traditional Catholic Mex-USA Church, the cross-border sect's official title, had recently lost its recognition (and associated tax benefits) by Mexico's Board of Religious Associations and is petitioning to regain its former status. But if the new lite version of Santa Muerte is in fact the church's attempt to demonstrate a more wholesome mission, it runs the risk of losing its more fervent devotees to keepers of the flame like Doña Queta.

While the altar and sanctuary are open to the public, travelers should be aware that the Tepito neighborhood is notorious among Mexicans as a scene of criminal activity and that church members may not welcome the scrutiny of curious onlookers.

murals conveying a new sense of Mexico's past and future. One was the former monastery that housed the newly established Education Ministry. The entrance is on the east side of Plaza de Santo Domingo.

The two front courtyards (on the opposite side of the building from the entrance) are lined with 120 fresco panels painted by Diego Rivera in the 1920s. Together they form a tableau of 'the very life of the people,' in the artist's words. Each courtyard is thematically distinct: the one nearest the República de Argentina entrance deals with labor, industry and agriculture, and the top floor holds portraits of Mexican heroes. The second courtyard depicts traditions and festivals. On its top level is a series on capitalist decadence and proletarian and agrarian revolution, underneath a continuous red banner emblazoned with a Mexican *corrido* (folk song). The likeness of Frida Kahlo appears in the first panel, as an arsenal worker.

SOUTH OF THE ZÓCALO

SUPREMA CORTE DE JUSTICIA
Map pp48–9

Pino Suárez 2; admission free, ID required; ☯ 9am-5pm Mon-Fri; Ⓜ Zócalo

More Orozco murals are inside the Supreme Court Building, just south of the Zócalo. In 1940, the artist painted four panels around the first level of the central stairway, two of which deal with the theme of justice. A more contemporary take on the same subject, *Los Siete Crímenes Mayores* (*The Seven Worst Crimes*), by *defeño* (DF native) Rafael Cauduro, unfolds over the three levels of the building's southwest stairwell. Executed in his hyperrealist style, the series catalogues the horrors of state-sponsored crimes against the populace, including the ever-relevant torture-induced confession. Cauduro's mural is one of four justice-related works recently commissioned by the Supreme Court for each of the building's corner stairwells. The other three are by Luis Nishizawa, Leopoldo Flores and Ismael Ramos.

MUSEO DE LA CIUDAD DE MÉXICO
Map pp48–9

☎ 5542-0083; Pino Suárez 30; admission M$20, Wed free; ☯ 10am-6pm Tue-Sun; Ⓜ Pino Suárez
For a good overview of the megalopolis, visit the Museum of Mexico City. The innovative permanent exhibit, 'It All Fits in a Basin,' presents a concise history of the city with models and maps; one room is devoted to

the Zócalo and its role as a stage for social movements. Upstairs is the former studio of Joaquín Clausell, considered Mexico's foremost impressionist. He used the four walls of the windowless room as a sketchbook during the three decades he worked there until his death in 1935. The result is an insanely detailed mural consisting of hundreds of small canvasses, full of people, animals, bucolic landscapes, religious motifs – whatever was on his mind.

UNIVERSIDAD DEL CLAUSTRO DE SOR JUANA Map pp48 9

☎ 5130-3336; www.ucsj.edu.mx; Izazaga 92; admission free; ⊙ 7am-8pm Mon-Fri, to 3pm Sat; Ⓜ Isabel la Católica

Considered the greatest Spanish-language poet of the 17th century, Sister Juana Inés de la Cruz composed many of her sonnets in the former convent of San Jerónimo, today the University of the Cloister of Sor Juana. Its magnificent two-level cloister, dating from 1585, now buzzes with students of gastronomy, literature and philosophy. To the east is the painstakingly restored Iglesia de San Jerónimo containing Sor Juana's tomb and a 1750 portrait of the poet. The series of tiled niches on its south wall is what remains of the confessionals. The adjacent Museo de la Indumentaria Mexicana (admission free; ⊙ 10am-5pm Mon-Fri) displays regional outfits from around Mexico.

The university also hosts a dynamic range of cultural activities, including films, plays, book presentations and conferences.

GILT TRIP
Walking Tour

1 Metro Pino Suárez Before exiting the station, take the corridor that links lines 1 and 2 (look for the 'Correspondencia' sign) to find the shrine to Ehécatl, the Aztec god of the wind (p62). Dating from 1400, the circular structure is one of the numerous pre-Hispanic pieces unearthed during the excavations for the metro.

2 Museo de la Ciudad de México To exit the station, look for the blue 'Salida' sign near the shrine. You'll emerge onto a frenetic plaza with a large market building. At the nearest intersection, cross Av Izazaga, and head north along Pino Suárez. At República de El Salvador, you'll find another pre-

Hispanic fragment, a set of serpent's teeth embedded into the Mexico City Museum (opposite). The museum, by the way, presents a compelling overview of the city.

To exit the station, look for the blue 'Salida' sign near the shrine. You'll emerge onto a frenetic plaza with a large market building. At the nearest intersection, cross Av Izazaga, and head north along Pino Suárez.

3 Templo de Jesús Nazareno Diagonally opposite the museum, across Pino Suárez, is the Templo de Jesús, where conquistador *número uno*, Hernán Cortés, is entombed. Note the incongruously anticlerical mural by Orozco over the church's choir section.

4 Hospital de Jesús Continue west on República de El Salvador past the rear of the church. Take the first left, through the hospital garage. Behind the modern exterior is the superb double patio of the original hospital established by Cortés in 1524. This is supposedly where the conquistador first met Moctezuma II, a scene depicted in a mural on the upper level.

5 Calle 20 de Noviembre Turn right (north) on 20 de Noviembre, a busy shopping thoroughfare. Two blocks up stand the original Palacio de Hierro and Liverpool department stores, dating from the 1920s and '30s. The two upscale stores have since branched across the DF and beyond.

6 El Zócalo Proceed up to El Zócalo (p46), entering the broad plaza between the twin buildings of the city government (p53). Go left, through the stately arcade of the Ayuntamiento, emerging opposite the Gran Hotel de la Ciudad (p200), a French art nouveau structure from the gilded age before the Revolution.

7 Portal de Mercaderes Cross Calle 5 de Febrero and proceed along the plaza's western side, through the Portal de Mercaderes. Dating from the 1600s, the arched passageway was once lined with silversmiths' workshops; today it fronts a number of jewelry stalls. At the north end is another longstanding Zócalo luxury hotel, the Majestic (p200).

8 Calle Madero Next, turn left onto Calle Madero. This stately avenue boasts a veritable catalogue of architectural styles interspersed with opticians and jewelers. At the second corner is the Edificio Esmeralda, a fine example

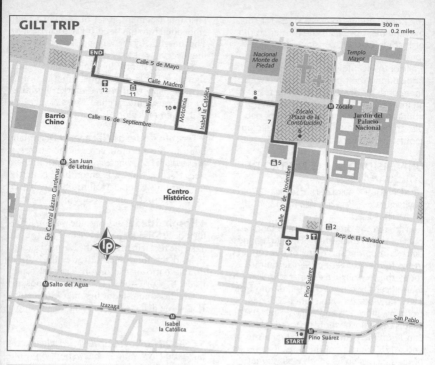

GILT TRIP

END

Calle 5 de Mayo

Calle Madero

Nacional Monte de Piedad

Templo Mayor

12

11

Barrio Chino

Calle 16 de Septiembre

10

9

Motolinía

Isabel la Católica

Bolívar

8

7

Zócalo (Plaza de la Constitución)

6

Zócalo

Jardín del Palacio Nacional

San Juan de Letrán

Eje Central Lázaro Cárdenas

Centro Histórico

Calle 20 de Noviembre

5

2

3

4

Rep de El Salvador

Salto del Agua

Izazaga

Isabel la Católica

Pino Suárez

San Pablo

1

START

Pino Suárez

0   300 m
0   0.2 miles

WALK FACTS

Start Metro Pino Suárez
End Casa de los Azulejos
Distance 1.7km
Duration 1½ hours
Fuel stops Numerous

of the Parisian mode favored by the city's early-20th-century moguls. Above a Mixup record store is the Museo del Estanquillo (p53).

9 Calle Isabel la Católica Turn left on Isabel la Católica. On your right, across the street, is the Casino Español (p136), built by Spanish immigrants as a social hall in 1903; on your left, the Casa del Conde de Miravalle, former home of a 16th-century silver baron. Its beautifully restored patio makes a nice respite from the crowds.

10 Calle Motolinía Turn right at the corner, Calle 16 de Septiembre, past the Casa Boker, a hardware store started by German immigrants in 1865. Go right on Motolinía, a pedestrian thoroughfare with a few popular cantinas and greasy spoons specializing in

turkey sandwiches. Back at Madero, a lion's head on your left marks the water level during the great flood of 1629.

11 Gandhi and Iturbide Continue west along Madero. Stop into the new Gandhi bookstore (Madero 32), across the street, with two levels of literature and music to browse. Half a block past Bolívar, on your left, the Palacio de Iturbide (p53) displays handicrafts from the Banamex collection behind its sumptuous facade.

12 Casa de los Azulejos On the next block west, the Iglesia de San Francisco (p54) is a remnant of the vast Franciscan monastery built over the site of Moctezuma's private zoo in the 16th century. Conclude the tour with refreshments at the Sanborns branch opposite, inside the magnificent House of Tiles (p54).

EASTERN LOOP
Walking Tour

1 Catedral Metropolitana Start at the massive Mexico City cathedral. (Alternatively, you can rent a bicycle at the Plaza del Empedradillo, on the church's west side.) You might pick up a bargain at the Nacional Monte de Piedad (Map p53), the national pawn shop, just across the way.

2 Plaza de Santo Domingo Take República de Brasil north two blocks to reach the Plaza de Santo Domingo (p57). On your left, printers ply their trade beneath the Portal de Evangelistas. On the right, the Secretaría de Educación Pública (p57) houses Diego Rivera's epic series of murals on Mexican life and culture.

3 Museo de la Luz From the top end of the plaza, take República de Venezuela two blocks east. Across Calle Del Carmen, the building on your right is the ancient Templo de San Pedro y San Pablo, which today houses the interactive Museum of Light (p56) (entrance one block south).

4 Mercado Abelardo Rodríguez Half a block east, the tall arcade on the left fronts the Teatro del Pueblo – inside, the theater is decorated with a startling combination of art deco and indigenous motifs. Enter the adjacent Mercado Abelardo Rodríguez (p26) to admire the numerous murals painted by Rivera's students in the 1920s.

5 Templo de Nuestra Señora de Loreto Turn right at the corner (Rodríguez Puebla). One block south, the Templo de Nuestra Señora de Loreto (p57) has a remarkable dome, best viewed from inside. Across the eponymous plaza on Justo Sierra is Mexico City's first synagogue, built by the Syrian Jews who formerly populated this zone. Look for the Star of David over the doorway.

6 Templo de la Santísima Trinidad Follow Loreto one block south to República de Guatemala, turn left, then go right on Santísima. The below street level walkway here follows the course of an earlier waterway used to ferry produce from the southern community of Xochimilco. On the next corner is the hyperbaroque Templo de la Santísima Trinidad (p56).

WALK FACTS

Start Catedral Metropolitana
End Plaza del Templo Mayor
Distance 2.2km
Duration 2½ hours
Fuel stop Carnitas 'Don One' inside Mercado Abelardo Rodríguez

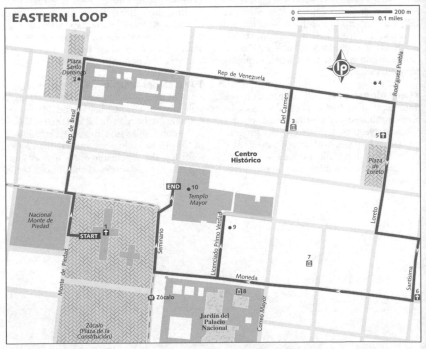

EASTERN LOOP

0 — 200 m
0 — 0.1 miles

METRO ACTIVE

As if there weren't enough to see *above* ground in this encyclopedia of a city, a number of the capital's metro stations give you something to look at while waiting for a train or transferring to another line. When planning your next excursion, be sure to include some of the following attractions en route.

- **Metro Pino Suárez (Líneas 1 & 2)** Unearthed in 1967 during excavations to install metro Line 2, the Templo de Ehécatl dates from the origins of Aztec Tenochtitlán. The circular shrine was devoted to the god of the wind. Look for it in an open-air section of the transfer corridor between Lines 1 and 2.
- **Metro Zócalo (Línea 2)** Models inside the station's busy main corridor show Mexico City's central precinct at three different periods in its history: before the Conquest, with the Templo Mayor standing prominently at the front of the ceremonial center; before independence, with the equestrian statue of Spain's King Carlos IV; and in the early 1900s, with streetcars running around the square when it still had trees and gardens.
- **Metro La Raza (Líneas 3 & 5)** The long hike between Lines 3 and 5 becomes an educational field trip as you traverse a Tunnel of Science. The corridor is lined with large-format photos that span the focal spectrum from planetary phenomena to single-celled organisms. About midway, there's a planetarium.
- **Metro Bellas Artes (Líneas 2 & 8)** French artist Jean Paul Chambas' colorful murals for the Line 8 corridor present his affectionate vision of Mexico with a strong dose of magical realism. The artist himself appears in the first panel, sipping *mezcal* (tequilalike drink) and contemplating a pair of masks from Teotihuacán.
- **Metro Auditorio (Línea 7)** At the top of the escalators is a permanent exhibit on the metros of the world, with a different panel for each city.
- **Metro Insurgentes (Línea 1)** *Defeño* (DF native) painter Rafael Cauduro executed two murals for the Zona Rosa's principal station, one interpreting the London Underground and the other the Parisian Metro. Executed in the artist's typically multilayered realist style, these paintings may give riders the fleeting illusion that they're waiting on the platform in those European capitals.

7 Museo José Luis Cuevas Now head west on Zapata, which becomes Moneda. Two blocks along, on your left, stands the Academia de San Carlos, where Mexico's 19th-century painters and sculptors learned their skills. Strike half a block north on Academia to stand face-to-ankle with modern Mexican artist José Luis Cuevas' imposing 8m woman (p56).

8 Calle Moneda Return to Moneda and continue west. This historic corridor has long been dominated by 'informal' vendors until a major sweep by the current city government. Just past Correo Mayor on your left is the building that Calle Moneda was named for, the old colonial mint, now an ethnographic museum (p56).

9 Licenciado Primo Verdad A bit further west, the building at the corner of Licenciado Primo Verdad housed the Americas' first printing press. Behind it, the ancient convent of Santa Teresa de Ávila is now a space for cutting-edge art. Across the way, the former archbishop's palace (p55) is a showcase for the tax bureau's vast art collection.

10 Plaza del Templo Mayor Continue west along Moneda, keeping the Palacio Nacional's wall to your left. Just before the Zócalo, the building on the right-hand side marks the site of the continent's first university, established in 1551 (it was relocated south in the 1940s). Celebrate the conclusion of the tour by joining the Aztec dancers at the Plaza del Templo Mayor (p52).

ALAMEDA CENTRAL & AROUND

Shopping p122; Eating p139; Sleeping p203

Emblematic of the downtown renaissance, the green rectangle just west of the Centro Histórico holds a vital place in Mexico City's cultural life. Surrounded by historically significant buildings, the Alameda Central has been a leisurely strolling ground for the capital's denizens for over four centuries. Indelibly linked with the city's long, tumultuous history, the park became the stage for one of Diego Rivera's most imaginative tableaux, a mural populated with a cast of Mexican notables that is today enshrined in its own museum on the park's west side. Anchoring the opposite end is the shimmering Fine Arts Palace, an art nouveau masterpiece which continues to attract opera- and theater-goers more than a century after its completion. On the park's north side, the sunken Plaza de Santa Veracruz features a couple of superb museums housing collections of colonial and modern art.

The Alameda Central has also been the focus of ambitious redevelopment over the past decade. In particular, the high-rise towers on the Plaza Juárez and the Sheraton Centro Histórico have transformed the look of the zone south of the park, much of which was destroyed in the 1985 earthquake. Behind the Sheraton stands the recently opened Museo de Arte Popular, a compendium of folk-art styles within an innovatively restored art deco building dating from the 1920s.

Largely unaffected by the development wave, the streets south of the Alameda remain a chaotic hodgepodge of shops, markets, hotels and eateries. Immediately west of this zone is La Ciudadela, a former factory and prison that today houses the national library and an excellent photography museum; nearby you'll find a sprawling crafts market that's an obligatory stop for souvenir shoppers.

Metro stations Bellas Artes and Hidalgo are located on the Alameda's east and west sides, respectively.

ALAMEDA CENTRAL Map p64

Created in the late 1500s by mandate of then-viceroy Luis de Velasco, the Alameda took its name from the *álamos* (poplars) planted over its rectangular expanse. By the late 19th century, the park was lit by gas lamps and graced with European-style statuary and a bandstand – it became the place to be seen for the city's elite. Today the Alameda is a popular refuge, particularly on Sundays, when families stroll its broad pathways and gather for open-air concerts.

On the south side of the Alameda, facing Av Juárez, is the Hemiciclo a Juárez, a gleaming white semicircle of marble columns around a regally seated statue of Benito Juárez (1806–72). Born a poor Zapotec villager in the state of Oaxaca, Juárez – one of Mexico's most respected heroes – rose to become national president and conquer the armies of Maximilian of Hapsburg.

PALACIO DE BELLAS ARTES Map p64

☎ 5130-0900; Av Juárez & Eje Central Lázaro Cárdenas; admission M$35, Sun free; ☽ 10am-6pm Tue-Sun; Ⓜ Bellas Artes

Dominating the east end of the Alameda is the splendid white-marble Palace of Fine Arts, a concert hall and arts center commis-

sioned by President Porfirio Díaz. Construction began in 1905 under Italian architect Adamo Boari, who favored neoclassical and art nouveau styles. The project became more complicated than anticipated as the heavy marble shell sank into the spongy subsoil, and then the Revolution intervened. Work was halted and Boari returned to Italy. Architect Federico Mariscal eventually finished the interior in the 1930s, using the more modern art deco style.

One of Mariscal's achievements was to incorporate pre-Hispanic motifs into the structure. Notice, for example, the serpents' heads set atop the window arches on the lower level. Inside, check out the Maya Chac masks atop the vertical light panels, a feature borrowed from the temples of Uxmal.

Immense murals dominate the upper floors. On the 2nd floor are two early-1950s works by Rufino Tamayo: *México de Hoy* (Mexico Today) and *Nacimiento de la Nacionalidad* (Birth of Nationality), a symbolic depiction of the creation of the mestizo (person of mixed indigenous and European ancestry) identity.

At the west end of the 3rd floor is Diego Rivera's famous *El Hombre En El Cruce de Caminos* (Man at the Crossroads), originally

ALAMEDA CENTRAL & AROUND

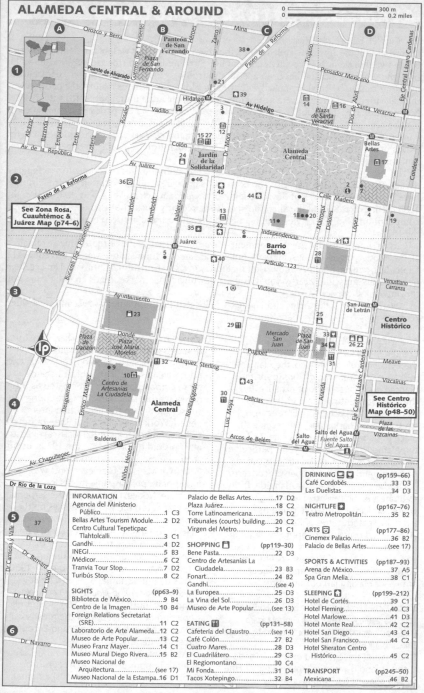

commissioned for New York's Rockefeller Center. The Rockefellers had the original destroyed because of its anticapitalist themes, but Rivera recreated it here in 1934. Capitalism, accompanied by war, is shown on the left; socialism, with health and peace, on the right.

On the north side are David Alfaro Siqueiros' three-part *La Nueva Democracia* (New Democracy) and Rivera's four-part *Carnaval de la Vida Mexicana* (Carnival of Mexican Life); to the east is José Clemente Orozco's eye-catching *La Katharsis* (Catharsis), depicting the conflict between humankind's 'social' and 'natural' aspects.

The 4th-floor Museo Nacional de Arquitectura (admission M$30, Sun free; ☼ 10am-5:30pm Tue-Sun) features changing exhibits on contemporary architecture.

The Bellas Artes theater (only available for viewing at performances) is itself an architectural gem, with a stained-glass curtain depicting the Valle de México. Based on a design by Mexican painter Gerardo Murillo (aka Dr Atl), it was assembled by New York jeweler Tiffany & Co from almost a million pieces of colored glass. A 55m mural over the proscenium arch studded with mythological figures offers audiences plenty to look at during slow-paced performances.

In addition, the palace stages outstanding temporary art exhibitions and the *Ballet Folclórico de México* (see p180). A worthwhile bookstore and an elegant café are on the premises, too.

TORRE LATINOAMERICANA Map p64

☎ 5518-7423; Eje Central Lázaro Cárdenas 2; adult/child M$50/40; ☼ 9am-10pm; Ⓜ Bellas Artes

A landmark for disoriented visitors since 1956, the Torre Latinoamericana was Latin America's tallest building when constructed. (Today it's Mexico City's fifth tallest.) Thanks to the deep-seated pylons that anchor the building, it has withstood several major earthquakes. In 2002 it was acquired by Mexican mogul Carlos Slim. Views from the 44th-floor observation deck are spectacular, smog permitting.

MUSEO FRANZ MAYER Map p64

☎ 5518-2266; www.franzmayer.org.mx; Hidalgo 45; admission M$35, Tue free; ☼ 10am-5pm Tue & Thu-Sun, to 7pm Wed; Ⓜ Bellas Artes

Housed in the old hospice of the San Juan de Dios order, which under the brief reign

TRANSPORTATION: ALAMEDA CENTRAL

- Metro – Bellas Artes (Líneas 2 & 8) and Hidalgo (Líneas 2 & 3) stations are at the northeast and northwest corners of the Alameda respectively.
- Bus – peseros along Paseo de La Reforma stop at Metro Hidalgo, on the northwest side of the Alameda, on their way to and from the Zona Rosa and Bosque de Chapultepec.
- Trolleybus – 'Autobuses del Sur' and 'Autobuses del Norte' trolleybuses run south and north, respectively, along Eje Central Lázaro Cárdenas.

of Maximilian became a halfway house for prostitutes, the museum is the fruit of the efforts of Franz Mayer, born in Mannheim, Germany, in 1882. Prospering as a financier in his adopted Mexico, Mayer amassed the collection of Mexican silver, textiles, ceramics and furniture masterpieces that is now on display. The exhibit halls open off a superb colonial patio; along its west side is a suite of rooms decorated with antique furnishings, on the north side is the Cloister Café.

The museum takes up the west side of the Plaza de Santa Veracruz, a sunken square north of the Alameda across Av Hidalgo. It's named for the slanting structure on the opposite side, the Iglesia de la Santa Veracruz. Elaborately carved pillars flank the doorway of the harmonious 18th-century church. Inside is the tomb of neoclassical architect and sculptor Manuel Tolsá.

MUSEO NACIONAL DE LA ESTAMPA Map p64

☎ 5521-2244; Av Hidalgo 39; admission M$10, Sun free; ☼ 10am-5:45pm Tue-Sun

Adjacent to the Iglesia de Santa Veracruz is the National Print Museum. Devoted to the graphic arts, it stages compelling thematic exhibits from the National Fine Arts Institute's collection of over 10,000 prints, lithographs and engravings, as well as the tools of these techniques.

LABORATORIO DE ARTE ALAMEDA Map p64

☎ 5510-2793; www.artealameda.inba.gob.mx; Dr Mora 7; admission M$15, Sun free; ☼ 9am-5pm Tue-Sun; Ⓜ Hidalgo

As with many museums in the Centro Histórico, the building that contains the

WORTH THE TRIP

Santa María La Ribera

One of the first residential zones to be constructed outside the city center, Santa María La Ribera, northwest of the Alameda Central, possesses a distinct neighborhood character. Though a bit rough around the edges, the neighborhood provides refreshing glimpses of Chilango everyday life. Strolling the streets, you'll hear the knife grinder's whistle and the singsong banter of workmen, get whiffs of *pulque* mingled with propane, and see schoolgirls in plaid skirts hopping along cracked sidewalks past walls of peeling posters.

Streets bearing names of literary and artistic figures like Salvador Díaz Mirón, Jaime Torres Bodet and Dr Atl are lined with a mishmash of architectural styles. Check out, for example, the house at Santa María La Ribera 182, which has an exquisite stained-glass bay window, adjacent to a hideous apartment building with purple painted window panes.

The remarkably calm center of the neighborhood, the expansive Alameda de Santa María, covers an entire city block. At its center is the almost surreal Kiosco Morisco, an arabesque, iron-framed rotunda ringed by Moorish archways and capped by a glass dome. It was the Mexico pavilion at the New Orleans World Expo of 1885, and was placed here for the independence centennial celebration of 1910.

Most of the neighborhood's modest attractions are on the Alameda's perimeter: a Russian diner (p157), a few cafés, a lively cantina and the Museo de Geología (☎ 5547-3900; Jaime Torres Bodet 176; M$15; ☽ 10am-4:30pm Tue-Sun). Built around 1904, it was the national university's geological institute until UNAM moved south. More compelling perhaps than the cases of rocks and minerals is the cast-iron art nouveau staircase in the entryway beneath a translucent oval dome. A couple of blocks west of the Alameda is the Mercado Sabino, the zone's busy market, with aisle after aisle of neatly arranged food and produce.

Santa María's most impressive structure, with its two prominent spires, is the Museo Universitario del Chopo (☎ 5546-5484; www.chopo.unam.mx; Enrique González Martínez 10; M San Cosme), four blocks south of the Alameda. Forged of iron in Dusseldorf around the turn of the 20th century, the building was brought over in pieces and assembled in Mexico City to serve as a pavilion for trade fairs. UNAM took over the historic building in 1975 and made it into a center for on-the-fringe artistic currents. At the time of research, the museum was closed for renovations.

Metro San Cosme is four blocks south of the Alameda de Santa María; slightly closer is Metro Buenavista (or metrobus Buenavista), three blocks east of the plaza.

Alameda Art Laboratory is as interesting as its contents. The former church is just a fragment of the 17th-century Convento de San Diego which was dismantled under the postindependence reform laws. As the museum's name suggests, it hosts installations by leading experimental artists from Mexico and abroad, with an emphasis on current electronic, virtual and interactive media. They could not have asked for a grander exhibition space.

MUSEO MURAL DIEGO RIVERA Map p64

☎ 5510-2329; cnr Balderas & Colón; admission M$15, Sun free; ☽ 10am-6pm Tue-Sun; M Hidalgo
Among Diego Rivera's most famous works is *Sueño de una Tarde Dominical en la Alameda* (Dream of a Sunday Afternoon in the Alameda), painted in 1947. In the 15m-long by 4m-high mural, the artist imagined many of the figures who walked in the city from colonial times onward, among them Cortés, Juárez, Emperor Maximilian, Porfirio Díaz, and Francisco Madero and his nemesis, General Victo-riano Huerta. All are grouped around a *Catarina* (skeleton in prerevolutionary women's garb). Rivera himself, as a pugfaced child, and Frida Kahlo stand beside the skeleton. Charts identify all the characters. Just west of the Alameda, this Diego Rivera Mural Museum was built in 1986 to house the mural, after its original location, the Hotel del Prado, was wrecked by the 1985 earthquake.

JARDÍN DE LA SOLIDARIDAD Map p64

The little parklike plaza in front of the Museo Mural Diego Rivera is the Solidarity Garden, created in 1986 on the site of the old Hotel Regis to commemorate the struggle of Mexico City's residents to rebuild their city after the earthquake of 1985. People gather here to play and watch open-air chess.

PLAZA JUÁREZ Map p64

Av Juárez & Dolores 11
Representing the new face of the zone, this modern plaza is across the way from the Alameda's Hemiciclo a Juárez, a semicircle

of marble columns dedicated to post-independence president Benito Juárez, and behind the fully restored Templo de Corpus Christi, which now holds the DF's archives. The plaza's centerpiece is a pair of Tetris-block towers by leading Mexican architect Ricardo Legorreta: the 24-story Foreign Relations Secretariat building and the 23-story Tribunales (courts) building. Fronting these monoliths is some interesting art, including a bronze aviary by Mexican sculptor Juan Soriano and, near the west entrance, a David Alfaro Siqueiros mosaic entitled *Velocidad* (Speed), originally designed for a Chrysler factory. Perhaps the most arresting piece, though, is a set of 1034 reddish pyramids in a broad pool, a collaboration between Legorreta and Spanish artist Vicente Rojo. The plaza also hosts some excellent photo exhibits.

MUSEO DE ARTE POPULAR Map p64

☎ 5510 2201; www.map.org.mx; Revillagigedo 11; admission free; ☉ 10am-5pm Tue-Sun, to 9pm Thu; Ⓜ Juárez

Opened in 2006, the Museo de Arte Popular is a major showcase for Mexico's folk arts and traditions. Contemporary crafts from all over Mexico are thematically displayed on the museum's three levels, including pottery from Michoacán, carnival masks from Chiapas, *alebrijes* (fanciful animal figures) from Oaxaca and trees of life from Puebla. There are also beaded textiles, fantastic headdresses and votive paintings, along with videos of indigenous festivities. The museum occupies the former fire department headquarters, itself an outstanding example of 1920s art deco by architect Vicente Mendiola, with a skylight over the interior patio. Not surprisingly, the ground-level shop is an excellent place to look for quality handicrafts.

VIRGEN DEL METRO Map p64

Cnr Paseo de la Reforma & Zarco

Housed in a small tiled shrine is this evidence of a recent miracle. Metro riders in June 1997 noticed that a water leak in Hidalgo station had formed a stain in the likeness of the Virgin of Guadalupe. Following the discovery, thousands flocked to witness the miraculous image. The stone section was removed and encased in glass at the Zarco entrance to metro Hidalgo.

BIBLIOTECA DE MÉXICO Map p64

☎ 9172-4730; Plaza de la Ciudadela 4; ☉ 8:30am-7:30pm; Ⓜ Balderas

The formidable compound now known as 'The Citadel' started off as a tobacco factory in the late 18th century. Later it was converted to an armory and a political prison, but it is best known as the scene of the Decena Trágica (Tragic Ten Days), the coup that brought down the Madero government in 1913. Today it is home to the National Library, with holdings of over 260,000 volumes and a good periodicals collection. The central halls are given over to art exhibits.

CENTRO DE LA IMAGEN Map p64

☎ 9172-4724; centrodelaimagen.conaculta.gob .mx, in Spanish; admission free; ☉ 11am-6pm Tue-Sun; Ⓜ Balderas

At the Balderas entrance to La Ciudadela is the city's photography museum. The innovatively curated space stages compelling exhibitions, often focusing on documentary views of Mexican life by some of the country's sharpest observers. Pick up a copy of *Luna Córnea*, the photography journal published by the center, at the excellent bookstore.

DREAM OF AN AFTERNOON IN (& AROUND) THE ALAMEDA
Walking Tour

1 Sears Café Start things off with coffee on the Sears building's 8th-floor terrace, with stunning views of the Palacio de Bellas Artes (p63) across the way. The café makes a particularly good vantage to admire the palace's onyx-paned triple dome, crowned by the proverbial eagle devouring a snake.

2 Alameda Down on the ground, cross Av Juárez and join the crowds milling about the broad plaza that fronts the Palacio. Look for the tourism module at the Alameda's southeast corner, and enter the park. The fountain here, with water-spouting cherubs around its central pedestal, is often the backdrop for some performance event.

3 Park ramble Make your way up the diagonal path to the modestly attired Venus, then turn right (north). You may run into some horse-riding *charros* (cowboys); they're police on patrol. Continue past a Madonna statue and a fountain with a pair of water carriers, finally emerging on Av Hidalgo.

4 Plaza de Santa Veracruz Cross Hidalgo to enter the Plaza de Santa Veracruz, the sunken square named for the sinking church on the right. Art aficionados can survey the collection of the adjacent Museo Nacional de la Estampa (p65) or the treasure trove of colonial masterworks at the Museo Franz Mayer (p65) across the plaza.

5 Hotel de Cortés Proceed west along Hidalgo. At the end of the next block, pop into the Hotel de Cortés (p203) for a peek at the tranquil courtyard, once part of a hospice for Augustinian missionaries. The front bar

makes a suitably colonial setting for a tequila and sangrita break.

6 Dr Mora Recross Av Hidalgo and walk down the west side of Dr Mora, alongside the Alameda. Ponder conceptual art at the Laboratorio Arte Alameda (p65), inside the former San Diego monastery. Around the corner, the Museo Mural Diego Rivera (p66) displays the artist's hallucinatory vision of the nearby park.

7 Sheraton Centro Histórico Continue around the Alameda. The black monolith across Av Juárez is the Sheraton hotel (p203), whose opening in 2004 heralded an ambitious redevelopment of the zone which is still going on. Just beyond the hotel, cross Juárez and proceed down Revillagigedo.

8 Museo de Arte Popular At the next corner, Independencia, stands the recently inaugurated Museo de Arte Popular (p67), an art deco gem that once housed the fire station. Note the pair of Olmec masks embedded into the base at the corner. Don't miss the museum's outstanding collection of folk art.

WALK FACTS

Start Sears building
End Metro Balderas
Distance 2km
Duration 2½ hours
Fuel stop Cloister Café in Museo Franz Mayer

DREAM OF AN AFTERNOON IN (& AROUND) THE ALAMEDA

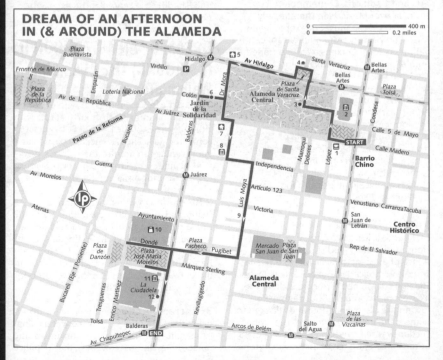

9 Calle Luis Moya Head east on Independencia, then south down the next block over, Luis Moya. Dozens of lighting and plumbing wholesalers line this busy shopping corridor. Just past Ayuntamiento stop into *lucha libre* (wrestling) shrine El Cuadrilátero (p140) to admire its gallery of wrestlers' masks or chomp a giant *torta* (Mexican-style sandwich in a bread roll).

10 Mercado de la Ciudadela Turn right at Pugibet. A block past the modest Plaza Pacheco, you reach Balderas. Pick up that beaded mask or painted armadillo at the Mercado de Ciudadela, across the way. If it's a Saturday, you can learn a few dance steps at the Plaza de Danzón, southwest of the market.

11 La Ciudadela Proceed down Balderas to the Ciudadela building, a former cigar factory that now contains the Biblioteca de México, the national library (p67), swarming with students during the school term. Nearer to Balderas is the entrance to the excellent Centro de la Imagen (p67), a space for photographic art.

12 Book market Prowl through the booksellers' stalls along the next stretch of Balderas, which skirts the east side of the Ciudadela building. Some of these vendors do a brisk trade in textbooks; others hawk political manifestos, used magazines and comic books. At the bottom of the market, board the metro to your next destination.

PLAZA DE LA REPÚBLICA & SAN RAFAEL

Eating p140; Sleeping p204

The Plaza de la República is dominated by the vaguely Stalinist domed Monumento a la Revolución. The site of demonstrations, military displays and the odd rock show, the square is the somber centerpiece of the otherwise cheerfully scruffy Tabacalera. Named after the tobacco industry that once thrived here, the zone is dotted with low-cost lodgings, cafés and cantinas.

Erected in the 1880s, Colonia San Rafael was one of the earliest residential districts for the affluent seeking greener pastures. Their elegant private lodgings line Sadi Carnot, Serapio Rendón and Rosas Moreno, all of which run into Ribera de San Cosme, the hectic thoroughfare that forms the neighborhood's northern border. Street vendors have established semipermanent stalls along this avenue's length, leaving pedestrians a thread's-width strip of sidewalk.

MONUMENTO A LA REVOLUCIÓN
Map p71
Plaza de la República
Begun in the 1900s under Porfirio Díaz, this monument was originally meant to be a meeting chamber for legislators. But construction (not to mention Díaz' presidency) was interrupted by the Revolution. The structure was modified and given a new role in the 1930s: the tombs of the revolutionary and postrevolutionary heroes are inside its wide pillars.

MUSEO NACIONAL DE LA REVOLUCIÓN Map p71
☎ 5546-2115; Plaza de la República; admission M$15, Sun free; ☷ 9am-5pm Tue-Sun; Ⓜ Revolución
Underlying the monument, this museum covers an 80-year period, from the implementation of the constitution guaranteeing human rights in 1857 to the installation of the postrevolutionary government in 1920. Explanatory text is in Spanish only. Enter from the northeast quarter of the plaza.

MUSEO NACIONAL DE SAN CARLOS
Map p71
☎ 5566-8342; Puente de Alvarado 50; admission M$25, Mon free; ☷ 10am-6pm Wed-Mon; Ⓜ Revolución
The museum hosts a formidable collection of European art from the 16th century to the early 20th century, including works by Rubens, Van Dyck and Goya. This former mansion of the Conde de Buenavista later became home to Alamo victor Santa Anna, and subsequently served as a cigar factory, a lottery headquarters and a school before being reborn as a museum in 1968.

IGLESIA Y PANTEÓN DE SAN FERNANDO Map p71
Avs Hidalgo & Guerrero; admission free; ☷ 9am-3pm Tue-Fri, to 5pm Sat; Ⓜ Hidalgo
At the top of the Plaza de San Fernando stands the handsome 18th-century church of the same saint, with baroque carved doors and an impressive altar. Next door is the Panteón de San Fernando, a cemetery containing the tombs of illustrious 19th-century Mexicans such as Benito Juárez, Vicente Guerrero and Ignacio Zaragoza.

LOTERÍA NACIONAL Map p71
☎ 5140-7000; Plaza de la Reforma 1; admission free; Ⓜ Hidalgo
Mexico's lottery is a national passion, and the art deco tower on the west side of Paseo de la Reforma is the game's headquarters. Almost any Sunday, Tuesday or Friday after 7:30pm, you can take a seat in the auditorium to watch the *sorteo* (the ceremony of picking the winning numbers) at 8pm. Numbered wooden balls are plucked from cages by uniformed pages who announce the winning numbers and amounts.

EL CABALLITO Map p71
A couple of blocks west of the Alameda Central is El Caballito, a bright yellow horse's

TRANSPORTATION: PLAZA DE LA REPÚBLICA & SAN RAFAEL

- Metro – Línea 2 stops north of Plaza de la República (Revolución) and San Rafael (San Cosme).
- Metrobus – the Tabacalera station on Av Insurgentes is 100m west of Plaza de la República.
- Bus – any pesero running along Paseo de la Reforma en route to the Alameda Central or Bosque de Chapultepec stops at the Monumento a Cristóbal Colón.

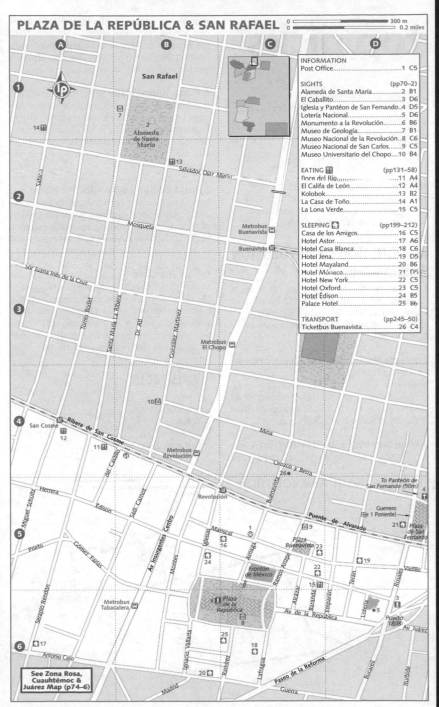

0 | 300 m
0 | 0.2 miles

INFORMATION
Post Office.................................1 C5

SIGHTS (pp70–2)
Alameda de Santa María................2 B1
El Caballito....................................3 D6
Iglesia y Pantéon de San Fernando..4 D5
Lotería Nacional...........................5 D6
Monumento a la Revolución.........6 B6
Museo de Geología.......................7 B1
Museo Nacional de la Revolución..8 C6
Museo Nacional de San Carlos......9 C5
Museo Universitario del Chopo....10 B4

EATING (pp131–58)
Boca del Río.................................11 A4
El Califa de León.........................12 A4
Kolobok..13 B2
La Casa de Toño..........................14 A1
La Lona Verde..............................15 C5

SLEEPING (pp199–212)
Casa de los Amigos.....................16 C5
Hotel Astor..................................17 A6
Hotel Casa Blanca.......................18 C6
Hotel Jena...................................19 D5
Hotel Mayaland..........................20 B6
Hotel Mónaco..............................21 D5
Hotel New York...........................22 C5
Hotel Oxford...............................23 C5
Hotel Édison................................24 B5
Palace Hotel................................25 B6

TRANSPORT (pp245–50)
Ticketbus Buenavista..................26 C4

top picks

IT'S FREE

- Bosque de Chapultepec (p77)
- Diego Rivera murals at Secretaría de Educación Pública (p57)
- Museo del Estanquillo (p53)
- Museo de Arte Popular (p67)
- Most museums on Sunday

head by the sculptor Sebastián. It commemorates another equestrian sculpture that stood here for 127 years and today fronts the Museo Nacional de Arte (p55).

WALKIN' 'BOUT A REVOLUTION
Walking Tour

1 El Caballito The tour takes off from El Caballito, which marks the old location of a traditional statue of Spain's King Carlos V on horseback which has been relocated to the Plaza Tolsá (p54).

2 Lotería Nacional Cross Rosales to the National Lottery building (p70); its stature reflects the institution's importance in the lives of ordinary Mexicans. Look west (left) down Av de la República to see the imposing copper dome of the Monument to the Revolution.

3 Monumento a la Revolución Once you've paid your respects to the heroes com-

memorated here, visit the Museo de la Revolución (p70), underneath the plaza's east side. Note the Frontón de México building immediately north of the plaza. This now-abandoned palace used to host jai alai (court game) matches.

4 Plaza Buenavista Skirt the right side of this building, and head north on Ramos Arizpe. In one short block you reach the sleepy Plaza Buenavista, a showcase for abstract topiary, behind the Museo Nacional de San Carlos (p70). (The entrance is around the corner on Puente de Alvarado.)

5 Plaza de San Fernando Two blocks east is the Plaza de San Fernando, with fountains and neatly tended gardens, below the church of the same name. Next to the church entrance is the San Fernando graveyard (p70), where Benito Juárez and other illustrious Mexicans lie.

6 San Hipólito Proceed east through the arcade that flanks the Panteón. A block past the cemetery, turn right onto Zarco. Note the oddly turned towers of San Hipólito church on your right. A nearby shrine contains the Virgen del Metro, the Virgin's image miraculously engraved in a slab of subway platform.

WALK FACTS

Start El Caballito
End Virgen del Metro
Distance 1.7km
Duration 1½ hours
Fuel stop Café Quetzal

WALKIN' 'BOUT A REVOLUTION

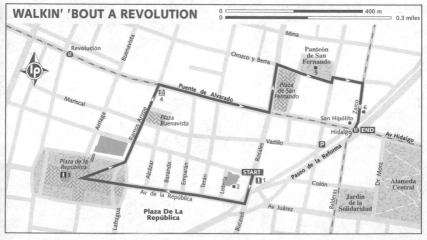

ZONA ROSA, CUAUHTÉMOC & JUÁREZ

Shopping p124; Eating p140; Drinking p162; Sleeping p206

Wedged between Paseo de la Reforma and Av Chapultepec, the 'Pink Zone' was developed as an international playground and shopping district during the 1950s, when it enjoyed a cosmopolitan panache. After the installation of the metro station on its southern edge in 1969, the area fell into decline. What remains after decades of haphazard redevelopment is a hodgepodge of touristy boutiques strip clubs, discos and fast-food franchises. People-watching from its sidewalk cafés reveals a higher degree of diversity than elsewhere: it's the city's principal gay and lesbian district and an expat haven, with a significant Korean population. Recently, the Ebrard administration has been busy renewing the Génova pedestrian mall in an attempt to put the zone back in the pink.

PASEO DE LA REFORMA Map pp74–5

Originally laid out by Emperor Maximilian of Hapsburg to connect his castle on Chapultepec Hill with the old city center, Mexico City's main boulevard links a series of monumental *glorietas* (traffic circles) on its way from the Bosque to the Alameda Central. The López Obrador administration undertook a thorough restoration of Reforma, paving the broad esplanades with mosaic cobblestones and planting attractive gardens along its length.

MONUMENTO A LA INDEPENDENCIA
Map pp74–5

Admission free; ☉ **10am-6pm;** Ⓜ **Insurgentes**
On the northwest flank of the Zona Rosa stands the symbol of Mexico City, the

---

top picks

FOR CHILDREN

- Chapultepec Zoo (p79)
- Papalote Museo del Niño (p81)
- La Feria (p81)
- Xochimilco Canals (p113)
- Torre Latinoamericana (p65)

Monument to Independence. Known as 'El Ángel' (The Angel), this gilded statue of Victory on a 45m pillar was sculpted for the independence centennial of 1910, just as the Mexican Revolution got under way. The female figures around the base portray Law, Justice, War and Peace; the male ones represent Mexican independence heroes. Inside the monument are the remains of Miguel Hidalgo, Ignacio Allende, José María Morelos and nine other notables.

LA DIANA CAZADORA Map pp74–5

At Reforma's intersection with Sevilla is the monument commonly known as La Diana Cazadora (Diana the Huntress), a 1942 bronze sculpture actually meant to represent the Archer of the North Star. The League of Decency under the Ávila Camacho administration had the sculptor add a loincloth to the female figure, which wasn't removed until 1966.

TORRE MAYOR Map pp74–5

☎ 5283-8000; www.torremayor.com.mx; Paseo de la Reforma 505; Ⓜ Sevilla
A 2003 addition to the Mexico City skyline, the Torre Mayor stands like a solitary sentinel

---

TRANSPORTATION: ZONA ROSA, CUAUHTÉMOC & JUÁREZ

- Metro – Insurgentes station (Línea 1) marks the southern edge of the Zona Rosa at Av Chapultepec, 500m south of Reforma. Metro Sevilla and Cuauhtémoc, on the same line, are on the west and east ends of the zone, respectively.
- Bus – any pesero along Paseo de la Reforma stops at the Ángel monument, between the Zona Rosa and Cuauhtémoc neighborhoods, en route to the Alameda Central or Bosque de Chapultepec.
- Metrobus – north- and southbound metrobus lines (which are labeled 'Indios Verdes' and 'Dr Gálvez', respectively) have stations above the big Insurgentes roundabout, which provides access to the Zona Rosa via the Calle Génova exit. Another convenient metrobus station, Hamburgo, is situated on the east end of the Zona Rosa.

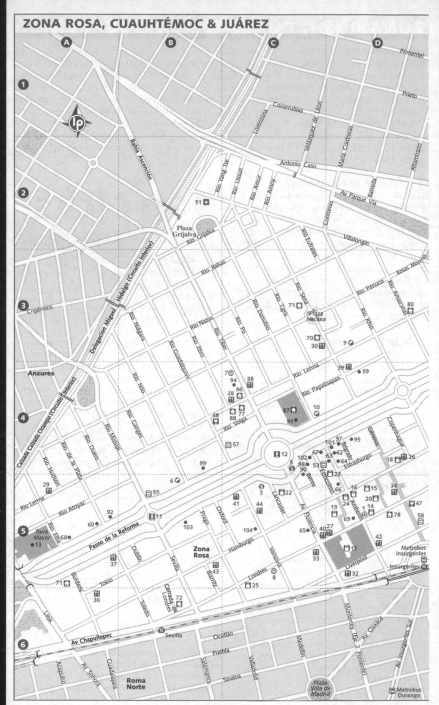

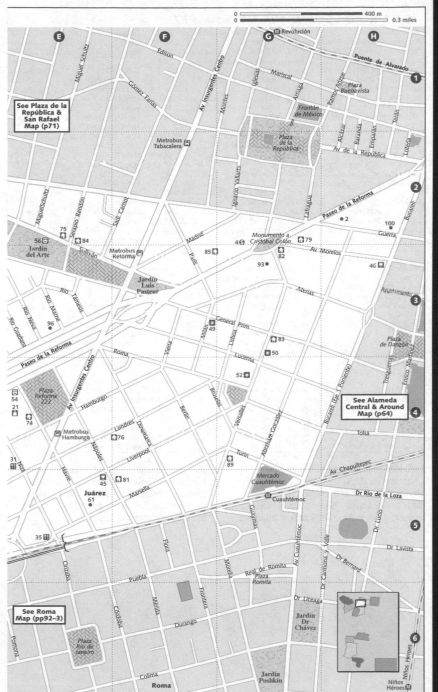

0   400 m
0   0.3 miles

Ⓜ Revolución

Puente de Alvarado

Edison

Iglesias

Mariscal

Ramos Arizpe

Plaza
Buenavista

Arriaga

Miguel Schultz

Gómez Farías

Av Insurgentes Centro

Montes

Alcázar

Barrida

Empáran

Terán

Lotería

See Plaza de la
República &
San Rafael
Map (p71)

Frontón
de México

Metrobus
Tabacalera

Plaza
de la
República

Ignacio Vallarta

Av de la República

Paseo de la Reforma

Bucareli

● 2

100 ●
Guerra

Miguel Schultz

Serapio Rendón

Sur Carnot

Madrid

Monumento a
Cristóbal Colón

4 🚇

79

82

56 🏨
84

Jardín
del Arte

Sullivan

Metrobus
Reforma

Park

85 🏨

93 ●

Av Morelos

46 🏨

Río Tíber

Río Marne

Río Neva

Río Guadiana

96 ●

Jardín
Luis
Pasteur

Atenas

Ayuntamiento

Plaza
de Danzón

General Prim

49

Milán

Lisboa

83

50

Río Tamesis

Paseo de la Reforma

Roma

Viena

Lucerna

52

Versalles

Enrico Martinez

Tresguerras

Plaza
Reforma
222

54
21

74

Av Insurgentes Centro

Hamburgo

Bruselas

Berlín

Abraham González

See Alameda
Central & Around
Map (p64)

Bucareli (Eje 1 Poniente)

Metrobus
Hamburgo

76

Londres

Dinamarca

Liverpool

Turín

89

Tolsá

31

Nita

Havre

Napoles

Mercado
Cuauhtémoc

Av Chapultepec

45

81

Marsella

Juárez
61 ●

Cuauhtémoc

Ⓜ Cuauhtémoc

Dr Río de la Loza

Dr Lucio

35

Oaxaca

Flora

Morelia

Av Cuauhtémoc

Dr Carmona y Valle

Dr Bernard

Dr Lavista

Puebla

Córdoba

Mérida

Frontera

Real de Romita
Plaza
Romita

Dr Liceaga

See Roma
Map (pp92–3)

Durango

Dr
Jardín
Dr
Chávez

Pomona

Plaza
Río de
Janeiro

Colima

Jardín
Pushkin

Niños Héroes

Roma

Niños
Héroes Ⓜ

ZONA ROSA, CUAUHTÉMOC & JUÁREZ

before the lion's gate of Bosque de Chapultepec. Designed by the Canadian architect Heberhard Zeidler, the green-glass tower soars 225m above Mexico City, making it Latin America's tallest building.

The earthquake-resistant structure is anchored below by 98 seismic shock absorbers. Unfortunately, the observation deck on the building's top tower was shut in 2006, with no explanation.

BOSQUE DE CHAPULTEPEC

Eating p143; Sleeping p208

Chapultepec (Náhuatl for 'Hill of Grasshoppers') served as a refuge for the wandering Aztecs before becoming a summer residence for their noble class. It was the nearest freshwater supply for Tenochtitlán, and in the 15th century, Nezahualcóyotl, ruler of nearby Texcoco, oversaw the construction of an aqueduct to channel its waters over Lago de Texcoco to the pre-Hispanic capital.

Today Mexico City's largest park, the Bosque de Chapultepec covers more than 4 sq km and has lakes, a zoo and several excellent museums. It also remains an abode of Mexico's high and mighty, hosting the current presidential residence, Los Pinos (Map p78), and a former imperial palace, the Castillo de Chapultepec (Chapultepec Castle).

Sunday is the park's big day as vendors line its main paths, and throngs of families come to picnic, navigate the big lake on rowboats and crowd into the museums. It is divided into two main sections by two major north–south roads: Calz Chivatito and the Anillo Periférico. Most of the major attractions are in or near the eastern 1a Sección (First Section; Map p78; 5am-5pm Tue-Sun), while a large amusement park and a children's museum dominate the 2a Sección.

A pair of bronze lions overlooks the main gate at Paseo de la Reforma and Lieja, across from the Torre Mayor building. Other access points are opposite the Museo Nacional de Antropología and by metro Chapultepec. The fence along Paseo de la Reforma serves as the Galería Abierta de las Rejas de Chapultepec, an outdoor photo gallery that extends from the zoo entrance to the Rufino Tamayo museum.

MONUMENTO A LOS NIÑOS HÉROES
Map p78

The six marble columns marking the eastern entrance to the park, near Chapultepec metro, commemorate the 'boy heroes,' six brave cadets who perished in battle. On September 13, 1847, more than 8000 American troops stormed Chapultepec Castle, which then housed the national military academy. Mexican General Santa Anna retreated before the onslaught, excusing the cadets from fighting, but the youths, aged 13 to 20, chose to defend the castle. Legend has it that one of them, Juan Escutia, wrapped himself in a Mexican flag and leapt to his death rather than surrender.

CASTILLO DE CHAPULTEPEC Map p78

☎ 5061-9200; www.castillodechapultepec.inah
.gob.mx; adult/child under 13 M$45/free, Sun free;
9am-5pm Tue-Sun; M Chapultepec

A visible reminder of Mexico's bygone aristocracy, the 'castle' that stands atop Chapultepec Hill was begun in 1785 but not completed until after independence, when it became the national military academy. When Emperor Maximilian and Empress Carlota arrived in 1864, they refurbished it as their residence. The castle became home to Mexico's presidents until 1939, when President Lázaro Cárdenas converted it into the Museo Nacional de Historia (National History Museum).

Historical exhibits chronicle the period from the rise of colonial Nueva España to the Mexican Revolution. In addition to displaying such iconic objects as the sword wielded by José María Morelos in the Siege of Cuautla and the Virgin of Guadalupe banner borne by Miguel Hidalgo in his march for independence, the museum features a number of dramatic interpretations of Mexican history by leading muralists. These include Juan O'Gorman's panoramic *Retablo de la Independencia* (Panel of Independence) in room 6, and David Alfaro Siqueiros' *Del Porfiriato a la Revolución* (From Porfirism to the Revolution) alongside the main staircase. Explanatory text is not translated into English.

The east end of the castle preserves the palace occupied by Maximilian and Carlota, with sumptuously furnished salons opening on an exterior deck with sweeping city views. On the upper floor, Porfirio Díaz' opulent rooms surround a lovely patio where a tower marks the top of Chapultepec Hill, 45m above street level.

To reach the castle, follow the road that curves up the hill behind the Monumento a los Niños Héroes. Alternatively, a little road-train (M$10 round-trip) runs up every 15 minutes while the castle is open.

Back at ground level, follow the south side of the hill's base to find a formidable monument to Mexico's WWII veterans on

BOSQUE DE CHAPULTEPEC

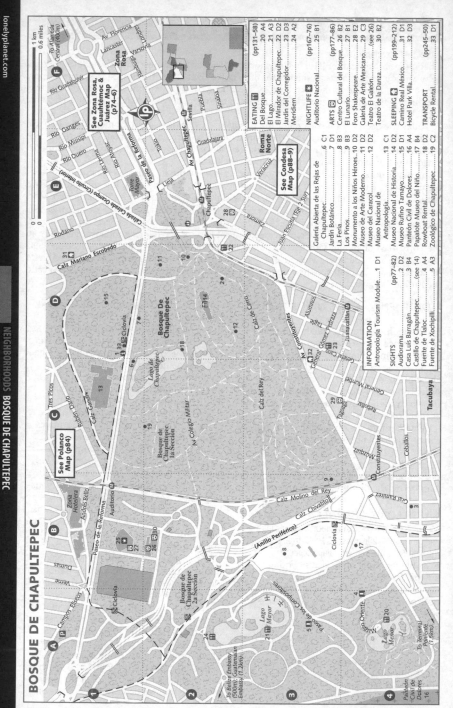

INFORMATION	
Antropología Tourism Module.....1	D1

SIGHTS	(pp77–82)
Audiorama.................................2	D2
Casa Luis Barragán....................3	B4
Castillo de Chapultepec.......(see 14)	
Fuente de Tláloc.........................4	A4
Fuente de Xochipilli....................5	A3
Galería Abierta de las Rejas de	
Chapultepec............................6	C1
Jardín Botánico..........................7	D1
La Feria....................................8	B3
Los Pinos..................................9	B3
Monumento a los Niños Héroes..10	D2
Museo de Arte Moderno............11	D2
Museo del Caracol....................12	D2
Museo Nacional de	
Antropología..........................13	C1
Museo Nacional de Historia.......14	D2
Museo Rufino Tamayo...............15	D1
Panteón Civil de Dolores...........16	A4
Papalote Museo del Niño...........17	B4
Rowboat Rental........................18	D2
Zoológico de Chapultepec.........19	C2

EATING ⑪	(pp131–58)
Del Bosque..............................20	A4
El Lago....................................21	A3
El Mirador de Chapultepec.........22	D2
Jardín del Corregidor................23	D3
Meridiem.................................24	A2

NIGHTLIFE ★	(pp167–76)
Auditorio Nacional....................25	B1

ARTS ⓒ	(pp177–86)
Centro Cultural del Bosque........26	B2
El Lunario................................27	B1
Foro Shakespeare.....................28	E2
Galería de Arte Mexicano...........29	C3
Teatro El Galeón.................(see 26)	
Teatro de la Danza....................30	B2

SLEEPING ⓗ	(pp245–50)
Camino Real México..................31	D1
Hotel Park Villa........................32	D3

TRANSPORT	
Bicycle Rental..........................33	D1

See Zona Rosa, Cuauhtémoc & Juárez Map (p74–6)

See Condesa Map (p88–9)

See Polanco Map (p84)

0   1 km
0   0.6 miles

TRANSPORTATION: BOSQUE DE CHAPULTEPEC

- Metro – Chapultepec metro station (Línea 1) is at the east end of the Bosque de Chapultepec, near the Monumento a los Niños Héroes and Castillo de Chapultepec. Auditorio metro station (Línea 7) is on the north side of the park, in front of the Auditorio Nacional and 500m west of the Museo Nacional de Antropología. The park can also be accessed from the south side at Constituyentes station (Liñea 7).
- Bus – from anywhere on Paseo de la Reforma west of the Alameda Central, buses saying 'Metro Chapultepec' reach Chapultepec metro station, while 'Metro Auditorio' buses pass right outside the Museo Nacional de Antropología. Returning downtown, any 'Metro Hidalgo/La Villa', 'Alameda' or 'Garibaldi' bus, from either metro Chapultepec or heading east on Reforma, follows Reforma at least as far as metro Hidalgo. To get to the 2a Sección and La Feria, take the 'Paradero' exit from metro Chapultepec and catch a 'Feria' bus at the top of the stairs. These depart continuously and travel nonstop to the 2a Sección (Second Section), dropping off riders at the Papalote Museo del Niño and La Feria.
- Bicycle – rent bikes from a module on Paseo de la Reforma, just outside the Museo de la Antropología (8am–6pm; per hr M$50, per day M$150). A *ciclovía* (bicycle path) runs through the park's 2a Sección, with access from the west side of Polanco.

your right. On the left side of the monument, enter the Audiorama, a pebbly garden where you can kick back on body-contoured benches and enjoy opera or classical in septophonic sound.

JARDÍN BOTÁNICO Map p78
☎ 5553-8114; admission free; ⏰ 10am-4pm;
🚇 Auditorio

Gardening is an ancient pastime in this part of the world – Nezahualcóyotl was planting cypresses here six centuries ago for their sheer aesthetic value – and the recently opened Botanical Garden, 300m east of the anthropology museum, carries the tradition forward. Highlighting Mexico's plant diversity, the 4-hectare complex is divided into sections that reflect the country's varied climate zones, with a special emphasis on the plants and trees of central Mexico. Still in a nascent stage, the garden features a desertlike patch of diminutive cacti and a greenhouse full of rare orchids, with over 150 varieties on display.

MUSEO DEL CARACOL Map p78
☎ 5061-9241; admission M$48; ⏰ 9am-4:15pm
Tue-Sun; Ⓜ Chapultepec

A short distance down the road from the Castillo, this 'gallery of history' traces the origins of Mexico's present-day institutions, identity and values through a series of audio-enhanced dioramas re-enacting key moments in the country's struggle for liberty. The museum is shaped like a snail shell, with its 12 exhibit halls spiraling downward. Along the way you'll see the cry for independence at Dolores Hidalgo, the

May 5 battle of Puebla, the execution of Maximillian, and the triumphant entrance of Madero into Mexico City. The tour ends at a circular hall which contains only one item – a replica of the 1917 Constitution of Mexico.

MUSEO DE ARTE MODERNO Map p78
☎ 5211-8331; cnr Paseo de la Reforma & Gandhi;
admission M$20, Sun free; ⏰ 10am-5:30pm Tue-Sun; Ⓜ Chapultepec

The Museum of Modern Art exhibits work by noteworthy 20th-century Mexican artists. The main building consists of four skylit rotundas, housing canvasses by Dr Atl, Rivera, Siqueiros, Orozco, Kahlo, Tamayo and O'Gorman, among others. *Las Dos Fridas*, possibly Frida Kahlo's most well-known painting, is in the Sala Xavier Villarrutia. Temporary exhibitions feature prominent Mexican and foreign artists. Just northwest of the Monumento a los Niños Héroes (access is via Paseo de la Reforma), the museum has a pleasant café beside a sculpture garden.

ZOOLÓGICO DE CHAPULTEPEC
Map p78
☎ 5553-6263; www.chapultepec.df.gob.mx; admission free; ⏰ 9am-4:30pm Tue-Sun; Ⓜ Auditorio

The Chapultepec Zoo houses a wide range of the world's creatures in large open-air enclosures. The first place outside China where pandas were born in captivity, the zoo has three of these rare bears, descendants of the original pair donated by the People's Republic in 1975. Endangered Mexican species include the Mexican grey wolf and the hairless xoloitzcuintle, the only surviving dog species from pre-Hispanic times.

WORTH THE TRIP

Tacubaya

Strange as it may seem today, this working-class neighborhood south of the Bosque de Chapultepec's 2a Sección (Second Section) was a coveted locale for Mexico City's elite during the 19th century, when they maintained garden-filled estates there. Crisscrossed by rivers and standing on slightly higher ground than the center of town, it was a more salubrious, less flood-prone area in which to reside. Tacubaya's character changed irrevocably under the administration of President Adolfo Ruíz Cortines in the 1950s, when the rivers were overlaid by major highways, slicing the neighborhood into isolated fragments. Urban explorers should enjoy picking up the pieces of its illustrious past.

Just south of the Bosque across Av Constituyentes, the Casa Luis Barragán (Map p78; ☎ 5272-4945; www.casa luisbarragan.org; Ramírez 14; admission M$100; ☾ 10am-2pm & 4-6pm by guided tour only; Ⓜ Constituyentes) was the home of internationally prominent Mexican architect Luis Barragán from 1948 until his death 40 years later. With its purposely circuitous passageways, seamless integration of outdoor and indoor spaces and bold swathes of Mexican folk tones, the building was designated a Unesco World Heritage Site in 2004 'as a masterpiece of human creative genius.'

One of Tacubaya's lavish 19th-century estates remains open to the public as the Parque Lira. Studded with fountains and crisscrossed by sloping paths, it's a favorite Sunday strolling place for neighborhood families and sweethearts. The Casa de la Bola (Map pp42–3; ☎ 5515-8825; admission M$20; Av Parque Lira 136; ☾ 11am-5pm Sun), on the park's east side, was occupied by Mexican gentry from the 1600s until the 1940s, when its last resident, Don Antonio Haghenbeck, chose to restore it as a museum. Each of the interconnected upper-floor rooms is a showcase for Mexican aristocratic tastes, with beautiful painted ceilings, ebony-inlay furniture, alabaster vases, European tapestries and so on. The idyllic rear gardens are interlaced with paths through tropical foliage.

Southeast of the park, past the chaotic zone of Metro Tacubaya, you come to the Alameda de Tacubaya. This city plaza once formed part of the atrium of the Iglesia de Candelaria, though the two are now separated by the major southbound artery Av Revolución. The single-nave church has been in continuous use since the 16th century, when it was built atop the pre-Hispanic temple of Cihuacoatl by the Dominican order.

Part of Chapultepec forest was given over to a bird sanctuary back during Moctezuma's reign; today, parrots, macaws, toucans, flamingos and other Mexican species swoop around the Aviario Moctezuma (only 20 visitors allowed in at a time).

There are various fast-food franchises on the premises.

MUSEO NACIONAL DE ANTROPOLOGÍA Map p78

☎ 5553-6381; www.mna.inah.gob.mx; cnr Paseo de la Reforma & Gandhi; admission M$48; ☾ 9am-7pm Tue-Sun; Ⓜ Auditorio

The National Museum of Anthropology, among the finest of its kind, stands in an extension of the Bosque de Chapultepec.

The vast museum offers more than most people can absorb in a single visit. Concentrate on the regions you plan to visit or have visited, with a quick look at some of the other eye-catching exhibits. Everything is superbly displayed, with much explanatory text translated into English. Audioguide devices, in English, are available at the entrance (M$60).

The complex is the work of Mexican architect Pedro Ramírez Vázquez. Its long, rectangular courtyard is surrounded on three sides by two-story display halls. An immense umbrellalike stone fountain rises up from the center of the courtyard.

The 12 ground-floor salas (halls) are dedicated to pre-Hispanic Mexico. The upper level shows how Mexico's indigenous descendants live today. Here's a brief guide to the ground-floor halls, proceeding counterclockwise around the courtyard:

Culturas Indígenas de México Currently serves as a space for temporary exhibitions.

Introducción a la Antropología Introduces visitors to the field of anthropology.

Poblamiento de América Demonstrates how the hemisphere's earliest settlers got here and survived in their new environment.

Preclásico en el Altiplano Central Focuses on the pre-classic period, approximately 2300 BC to AD 100, and the transition from a nomadic hunting life to a more settled farming life in Mexico's Central Highlands.

Teotihuacán Displays models and objects from the Americas' first great and powerful state.

Los Toltecas y Su Época Covers cultures of central Mexico between about AD 650 and 1250; on display is one of the four basalt warrior columns from Tula's Temple of Tlahuizcalpantecuhtli.

Mexica Devoted to the Mexicas, aka Aztecs. Come here to see the famous sun stone, unearthed beneath the Zócalo in 1790, and other magnificent sculptures from the pantheon of Aztec deities.

Culturas de Oaxaca Displays the legacy of Oaxaca's Zapotec and Mixtec civilizations.

Culturas de la Costa del Golfo Spotlights the important civilizations along the Gulf of Mexico including the Olmec, the Totonac and the Huastec. Stone carvings include two Olmec heads weighing in at almost 20 tons.

Maya Exhibits findings from southeast Mexico, Guatemala, Belize and Honduras. A full-scale replica of the tomb of King Pakal, discovered deep in the Templo de las Inscripciones at Palenque, is breathtaking.

Culturas del Occidente Profiles cultures of western Mexico.

Culturas del Norte Covers the Casas Grandes (Paquimé) site and other cultures from northern Mexico, and traces their links with indigenous groups of the US southwest.

In a clearing about 100m in front of the museum's entrance, indigenous Totonac people perform their spectacular *voladores* rite – 'flying' from a 20m-high pole – several times a day.

MUSEO RUFINO TAMAYO Map p78
☎ 5286-6519; www.museotamayo.org, in Spanish; cnr Paseo de la Reforma & Gandhi; admission M$15, Sun free; ☒ 10am-6pm Tue-Sun; Ⓜ Auditorio
A concrete and glass structure east of the anthropology museum, the Tamayo Museum was built to house international art donated by Oaxaca-born Rufino Tamayo and his wife, Olga, to the people of Mexico. Exhibitions of modern art from around the globe alternate with thematically arranged shows from the Tamayo collection.

SEGUNDA (2ª) SECCIÓN Map p78
The second section of the Bosque de Chapultepec lies west of the Periférico. In addition to family attractions, there is a pair of upscale lake-view restaurants on the Lago Mayor and the Lago Menor.

Kids will enjoy La Feria (☎ 5230-2121; passes from M$50; ☒ 10am-6pm Tue-Fri, to 7pm Sat, to 8pm Sun; Ⓜ Constituyentes), an old-fashioned amusement park with some hair-raising rides. A 'Super Ecolín' passport (M$80) is good for all the rides except the roller coaster.

Your children won't want to leave Papalote Museo del Niño (☎ 5237-1773; www.papalote.org .mx; adult/child 2-11yr & seniors M$85/80; ☒ 9am-6pm Mon-Wed & Fri, to 11pm Thu, 10am-7pm Sat & Sun;

Ⓜ Constituyentes). At this innovative, hands-on museum, kids can put together a radio program, join an archaeological dig and try out all manner of technological gadget games. All activites are supervised. The museum also features a 3-D IMAX movie theater.

About 200m west of the Papalote, turn right to reach the Fuente de Tláloc, an oval pool containing a huge mosaic-skinned sculpture of the rain god by Diego Rivera. There's more Rivera art inside the Chapultepec waterworks, housed in a pavilion behind the fountain (p26). To the north is the beautiful Fuente de Xochipilli, dedicated to the Aztec 'flower prince,' with terraced fountains around a *talud-tablero*-style pyramid (a steep building style typical of Teotihuacán).

PANTEÓN CIVIL DE DOLORES Map p78
☒ 6am-6pm
Chapultepec's second and third sections are divided by this huge cemetery. Near its main entrance on Av Constituyentes, the Rotonda de los Hombres Ilustres (Rotunda of Illustrious Men) holds the remains of celebrated Mexicans such as the artists Diego Rivera, José Clemente Orozco and Dr Atl (Gerardo Murillo).

HILL OF THE GRASSHOPPERS
Walking Tour
1 Museo Nacional de Antropología Start in front of the National Anthropology Museum (opposite). Across from the main entrance, witness the Voladores de Papantla perform their ritual 'flying' descent from a 30m-high pole. Then stroll down the entry plaza to Paseo de la Reforma.

2 Jardín Botánico Cross Reforma to the Bosque entrance, then go left to check out the excellent open-air photo exhibit along the fence. Around 250m east, you'll find another entrance to the Botanical Garden (p79), with a greenhouse full of exotic orchids.

3 Gran Avenida Leaving the garden toward the park's interior, turn right on the Gran Avenida, which loops around this section of the Bosque. On Sunday this route becomes a major promenade for Chilango families. Off to your right is a warren of food stalls, all serving some variation on tacos and *tortas*.

4 The Lake Continue along the Gran Avenida as it cuts across Chapultepec Lake. There

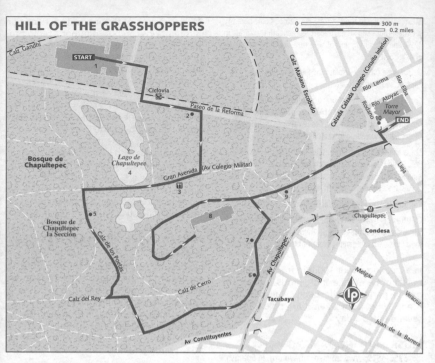

HILL OF THE GRASSHOPPERS

WALK FACTS

Start Museo Nacional de Antropología
End Torre Mayor
Distance 4.5km
Duration 3½ hours
Fuel stop Taco and *tortas* by Lago de Chapultepec

are rowboats and pedal boats for rent along the east bank. A short distance up the opposite bank, the Casa del Lago stages art exhibits and performances.

5 Poets Walk On the west end of the lake, turn left to head down the Calzada de los Poetas. Proceed beneath a tunnel of trees lined with monuments to Mexico's greatest poets. At the end of the path, look for a small sculpture of Don Quixote to your right.

6 Baños de Moctezuma Continue down to the next major path, the Calzada del Rey, and turn left. Take the first path down to your right to reach the lower section of the Gran Avenida. Another 200m on are the Baños de Moctezuma (Moctezuma's Baths), which supplied Aztec Tenochtitlán with drinking water.

7 Audiorama Just past the Baños, go left to return to the upper path. Continuing east, the monument to Mexico's WWII veterans is on your left. On its left side, enter a pebbly garden (p79) and enjoy opera in septophonic sound.

8 Chapultepec Castle Continue around the base of Chapultepec Hill. About 150m further along, board the little train up to the Castillo de Chapultepec p77. Up on the hill, you may browse the posh chambers of the former emperor's residence and enjoy incomparable views down Paseo de la Reforma.

9 Monumento a los Niños Héroes Hike back down the hill, optionally stopping in at the Museo de Caracol (p79). At the bottom make for the six tall torches that comprise the Monumento a los Niños Héroes (p77), commemorating the boy cadets who plunged to their deaths rather than surrender to gringo invaders in 1847.

10 Paseo de la Reforma Take the broad path over the Circuito Interior to the park's main gate, guarded by a pair of bronze lions. Across the way is the 59-story Torre Mayor, the city's tallest building. From here, you can take a pesero (minibus) back downtown.

POLANCO

Eating p144; Drinking p162; Sleeping p209

The affluent neighborhood of Polanco, north of Bosque de Chapultepec, arose in the 1940s as a residential alternative for a burgeoning middle class anxious to escape the overcrowded Centro. With streets named after famous writers, philosophers and scientists, the neighborhood cultivated a cosmopolitan outlook. Looking northward for architectural inspiration, builders erected many homes in the California Colonial style, a Hollywood version of Andalusian splendor with intricate carvings around doorways and windows. Polanco is traditionally considered a Jewish enclave though much of the community has moved even further west to Lomas de Chapultepec.

Today the area is known for its exclusive hotels, fine restaurants, nightlife and designer stores, with much of the retail activity along Calle Presidente Masaryk. Some of the city's most prestigious art galleries are here, including the Gallery Juan Martín (p185) and the Lourdes Sosa gallery (p185).

MUSEO SALA DE ARTE PÚBLICO DAVID ALFARO SIQUEIROS Map p84

☎ 5203-5888; www.siqueiros.inba.gob.mx; Tres Picos 29; admission M$10; ⓥ 10am-6pm Tue-Sun; Ⓜ Auditorio

One of the Big Three of Mexican muralism along with Diego Rivera and José Clemente Orozco, David Alfaro Siqueiros is recalled as much for his fiercely radical political views as for his larger-than-life paintings. An avowed anarchist, he notoriously organized an (unsuccessful) assassination attempt on the Russian revolutionary Leon Trotsky.

Shortly before his death in 1974, Siqueiros donated his Polanco residence and studio to the government for use as a museum. Fans of the iconoclastic painter will find plenty of illuminating material about his life and work here, including sketches for his mural projects, and some of his paintings, notably an unfinished homage to Vietnam. But Siqueiros' greatest works reside elsewhere, such as at the Museo Nacional de Historia (p77),

Antiguo Colegio de San Ildefonso (p56), Palacio de Bellas Artes (p63) and the campus of UNAM (p104).

A WALK ON THE CHIC SIDE
Walking Tour

1 Gandhi's Place Start at the monument to Mahatma Gandhi, behind the Museo Nacional de Antropología. Ironically, the shrine was erected by Mexican President Díaz Ordaz two years after his forces gunned down peaceful student protesters. Facing Gandhi, take the path to the left and bear right where it forks.

2 Art of Siqueiros Cross Rubén Darío and go left on Tres Picos, past the Canadian Embassy. Check out the Sala de Arte David Siqueiros (left), a space devoted to the prolific muralist. Turn right at the corner, then right again on Campos Elíseos, to the circle at Schiller.

3 Calle Schiller Head north up Schiller. As you approach the next corner, note the carved archways of the building that houses the Italian Coffee Company. It's a typical example of the California Colonial style which prevailed in the 1930s when the neighborhood was laid out. Turn left at the next block, Horacio.

4 Calle Horacio Stroll along Horacio's tree-lined central median. A block up on your left is the pretty Plaza Uruguay, a gathering place for local office workers and moms with nannies in tow. Beyond the archway at Arquímedes, the path becomes more parklike.

5 President Masaryk A block past the Spanish Embassy (another California Colonial gem), the López Quiroga gallery (☎ 5280-1710; Aristóteles 169) features works by contemporary Latin American artists. Turn left at Aristóteles and right at

---

TRANSPORTATION: POLANCO

- Metro – Metro Polanco (Línea 7), on Horacio, is smack in the center of the neighborhood. To reach the Zona Hotelera, the hotel zone on Polanco's south side, use the Auditorio station on the same line.
- Bus – 'Metro Auditorio' peseros traveling west from the Alameda access Polanco from the south (Bosque de Chapultepec) side of the neighborhood – get off at Verne, just past the Auditorio, and walk north. Another convenient pesero, labeled 'Metro Sevilla-P Masaryk', travels between Colonia Roma (Av Álvaro Obregón) and Polanco, stopping at metro Sevilla on the west end of the Zona Rosa.

POLANCO

See Bosque De
Chaputepec
Map (p78)

Bosque de
Chapultepec
La Nación

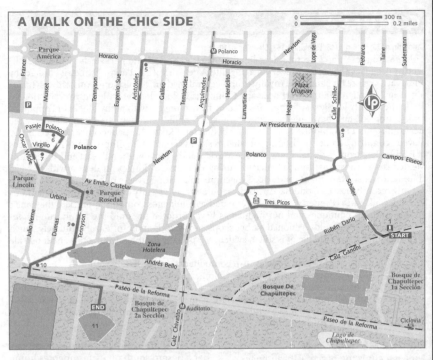

A WALK ON THE CHIC SIDE

WALK FACTS

Start Gandhi monument
End Auditorio Nacional
Distance 3km
Duration 2½ hours
Fuel stops Numerous

the next street, Av Presidente Masaryk, Polanco's '5th Avenue,' lined with exclusive shops.

6 Pasaje Polanco Turn left into the Pasaje Polanco (behind Starbucks), a courtyard shopping plaza with boutiques and benches below the white-stuccoed balconies of a residential complex. Exit left, through the trattoria, where Polanco's smart set sip Perrier and gaze lovingly at their cell phones.

7 Virgilio Go right on Julio Verne, then right again on Virgilio, a hemispheric slice of old-time Polanco with fruit markets, a candy store, a kosher deli and a few *taquerías* (taco stalls). Turn left at the next corner, Oscar Wilde.

8 Parque Rosedal A few steps later, you emerge between two parks – to the right,

Lincoln; to the left, Rosedal – which together form a long leafy mall. Cross Castelar and go left. Past a reflecting pool is a tiny gallery, La Casita, a sculpture garden and a big cage chittering with parakeets.

9 Zona Hotelera Beyond the bird cage is a major playground. Turn right to reach the lower side of the park, and proceed down Tennyson, with more fine examples of California Colonial architecture. At the bottom of the street stands the W Hotel (p209), the westernmost of four high-rise luxury lodgings.

10 Campos Elíseos Turn right on Campos Elíseos. You'll pass Calle Dumas, site of some of the city's swankiest restaurants. At the bottom of the street, check out the rock memorabilia at the beautiful mansion housing the Hard Rock Café (p173).

11 Auditorio Nacional At the west end of Campos Elíseos is a 15m obelisk dedicated to Simón Bolívar. Cross Paseo de la Reforma and turn left. About 200m further stands the massive Auditorio Nacional; check the board in front for upcoming shows. You can alight the metro here, or catch a pesero down Reforma.

85

CONDESA

Shopping p126; Eating p148; Drinking p163; Sleeping p210

Colonia Condesa's architecture, tree-lined esplanades and idyllic parks echo its early-20th-century origins as a haven for a newly emerging elite. A network of quiet narrow streets is bordered by boulevards where fat palms rise royally from a central median. Stroll along Ámsterdam, Tamaulipas or Mazatlán to admire art deco and California Colonial–style buildings. Several times a week, the usually low-key streets are invaded by busy *tianguis*, with many blocks of temporary pink-canopied stalls hawking the freshest tomatoes, chilies and mangos. Come February the jacarandas burst into bloom. Sweet-potato vendors and knife sharpeners cover the terrain by bicycle, conjuring a not-so-distant past when residents could still glimpse the twin volcanoes of Puebla state from their balconies. Parque México, at the neighborhood's east end, is certainly Mexico City's most harmonious enclave, fusing elements of European design with tropical abundance. It is a testament to Mexico's ingenuity in creating livable public spaces.

Only recently has 'La Condesa' earned its reputation as a trendy area of informal restaurants and sidewalk cafés. Property values have soared as Chilangos come to appreciate the zone's virtues, and hip boutiques and hot nightspots have sprouted up amid the family-run *fondas* (market eating stalls), old-fashioned barber shops, taco stands and cantinas. Fortunately, much of the neighborhood's old flavor is still in evidence, especially for those willing to wander outside the valet-parking zones.

Condesa's rather odd geography has two components. Immediately west of Av Insurgentes is the older section, often referred to as the Colonia Hipódromo in reference to the old racetrack that later became the Parque México. Nearer Bosque de Chapultepec is the more recently constructed grid section, where the streets are named after Mexican towns and states; the main restaurant and club zone is found here, with most of the activity at the east end of Calle Michoacán and along Av Tamaulipas.

PARQUE MÉXICO Map p88

A main focus is the peaceful, beautifully kept Parque México, full of trees, well-maintained paths, benches with cute little roofs, and signs exhorting everyone to demonstrate their ecoconsciousness and treat their *parque* nicely. Amsterdam, which runs in an oval loop one block outside the park's perimeter, was originally a horse-race track. When the track was handed over to developers in 1924, it was stipulated that a certain area inside it must be kept green – hence Parque México. Parque España, two blocks northwest, has a children's fun fair and is a bit more frenetic.

Parque México is a 500m walk north from Chilpancingo metro station, or a 1km walk south from Sevilla station – or you can get a pesero south on Av Insurgentes from Insurgentes metro station to the intersection with Calle Michoacán (there's a Woolworth store on the corner), and walk two blocks west to the park.

AV MÉXICO Map p88

A couple of art deco landmarks can be spotted on Av México, immediately northeast of Parque México. The Edificio Basurto (México 187), an aerodynamically streamlined structure from the mid-1940s, is a paragon of the style. Across the way, the Edificio Tehuacán (México 188), recently converted into the Hippodrome Hotel (p210),

TRANSPORTATION: CONDESA

- Metro – Metro Patriotismo (Línea 9) provides the easiest access: take the 'Baja California' Nte exit, turn around at the top of the stairs and cross six-lane Av Patriotismo, then proceed up Av Tamaulipas. Alternatively, metro Chapultepec (Línea 1) is the northern approach.
- Bus – peseros labeled 'Metro Tacubaya-Balderas-Escandón' travel between Condesa and Plaza San Juan in the Centro Histórico via Colonia Roma.
- Metrobus – for Parque México, get off the Av Insurgentes metrobus at the Sonora station and go two blocks west. The Campeche station puts you on the park's south side.
- Taxi – there are convenient *taxi seguro* (safe taxi) stands on Calle Michoacán at the west side of Parque México and on Vicente Suárez, next to Cafebrería El Péndulo.

features a typical deco marquee, as well as a Maya-influenced arch around the entryway.

FLIRTING WITH CONDESA
Walking Tour

1 Edificio Casas Jardines From metrobus Sonora station, walk west on Sonora, pausing before you cross Amsterdam to admire the art deco apartment building on the right. When it was built in the 1920s, the building's roof garden was considered a bold innovation. Across Amsterdam, at the Gran Vía bakery, you won't believe what they can do with Jello.

2 Art deco buildings More art deco treasures await one block west at Av México. On the right stands the barrel-shaped Edificio Berta. A few

WALK FACTS

Start Metrobus Sonora station
End Condesa DF
Distance 3.5km
Duration 2½ hours
Fuel stops Numerous

steps north on Av México is the Edificio Basurto (México 187), a modernist milestone from the mid-1940s. Ask the doorman to let you peek inside at the amazing snail-shell staircase.

3 Parque México Return to Av Sonora and cross over to Parque México. Make your way south (paralleling Av México), choosing whichever paths suit you. Originally a horse-race track (and later an auto circuit), the park is an oval of lush tropical foliage and a favored spot for neighborhood children, dog walkers and joggers.

4 El Teatro South of the duck pond is an open-air theater dating from 1928. When it's not being used for performances, the broad plaza in front is the domain of skateboarders and soccer players. La Muñeca (The Doll), the buxom jug-bearing woman facing Calle Michoacán, is the park's art deco icon.

5 Radio fountain Cross Michoacán to dip down into Parque México's southern section. Its focal point is a fountain centered on a classic deco tower which used to have a clock and a radio for open-air listening. Return to Calle Michoacán and turn left (west).

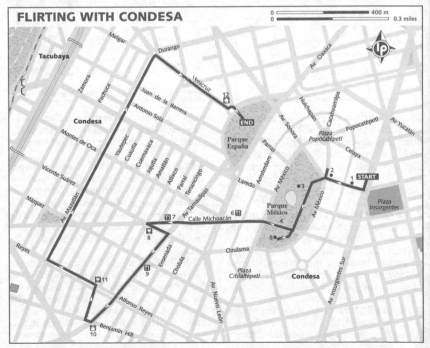

FLIRTING WITH CONDESA

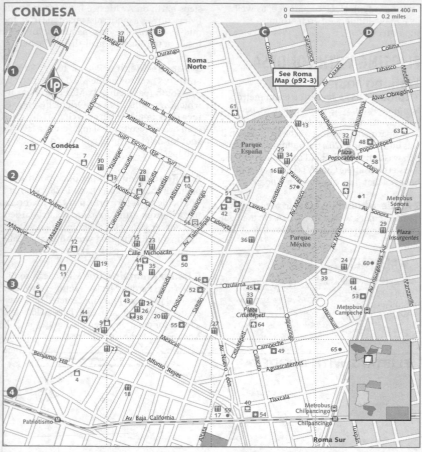

CONDESA

See Roma
Map (p92-3)

Roma
Norte

Condesa

Parque
España

Plaza
Popocatépetl

Metrobus
Sónora

Parque
México

Plaza
Insurgentes

Calle Michoacán

Ozulama

Metrobus
Campeche

Plaza
Citlaltépetl

Metrobus
Chilpancingo

Patriotismo

Roma Sur

6 Calle Michoacán For sustenance, grab a
well-stuffed taco or two at Hola (p150), on the
other side of Amsterdam. (But didn't I already cross Amsterdam? Yes, it circles Parque
México.) Continue west on Michoacán, past
Av Nuevo León to enter the heart of Colonia
Condesa's restaurant district.

7 The Restaurant Zone Crossing Tamaulipas, you'll notice the oblong market building
on your left, a throwback to a less trendy era.
On your right is a continuous row of sidewalk
tables, invariably filled with stylish Chilangos
and foreign visitors, and serviced by an army
of waiters and valet car parkers.

8 Vicente Suárez At Atlixco, cross Michoacán and double back on Vicente Suárez.
Across from the market, El Centenario (p163) is a

beautiful tiled cantina that's more than suitable
for a tequila stop. Turn right on Av Tamaulipas,
an extension of the main restaurant zone.

9 Av Tamaulipas Proceed down Tamaulipas,
optionally stopping at El Tizoncito (p150), an always
lively *taquería* at the corner with Campeche, or
at Nevería Roxy, an old-fashioned ice-cream parlor
at the corner with Alfonso Reyes. Opposite the
Roxy, across Alfonso Reyes, is the attractive
neighborhood church, Santa Rosa de Lima.

10 Bella Época A block further south is a
minaret marking the Centro Cultural Bella Época
(p126). The former cinema was recently converted into a huge, browseable bookstore with
a café and a video cinema. Leaving the Bella
Época, turn left on Benjamín Hill, then right at
the next corner, to return to Alfonso Reyes.

CONDESA

11 Alfonso Reyes Across Alfonso Reyes, just west of Amatlán, you'll spot La Botica (p163), a popular *mezcalería* where you can sample different varieties of *mezcal* from Oaxaca and Zacatecas. Continue west along Alfonso Reyes to Av Mazatlán and take a right. Stick to the palm-lined central median for this leg of the tour.

12 Av Mazatlán Five blocks up Mazatlán is the Edificio Condesa, a coveted apartment complex taking up the entire block between Mazatlán and Pachuca. Turn right at the next corner, Av Veracruz, and go three blocks east. Conclude the tour with cocktails on the roof of the Condesa DF hotel (p169), with views over Parque España, Parque México's little sister.

ROMA

Eating p150; Drinking p164; Sleeping p210

Northeast of Condesa, Colonia Roma is a bohemian enclave inhabited by artists and writers. This is where beat writers William S Burroughs and Jack Kerouac naturally gravitated during their 1950s sojourns to Mexico City. Built around the turn of the 20th century, the neighborhood is a showcase for the Parisian-influenced architecture favored by the Porfirio Díaz regime. Some of the most outstanding examples stand along Calles Colima and Tabasco. When in Roma, be sure to browse the secondhand-book stores, linger in the cafés and check out a few art galleries. A stroll down tree-lined Calle Orizaba takes you past two of the neighborhood's loveliest plazas – Río de Janeiro, with a statue of David, and Luis Cabrera, with its dancing fountains. On weekends inspect the antique market along Av Álvaro Obregón, the main thoroughfare.

Roma harbors a high proportion of the city's fashionable art galleries. The Galería Nina Menocal (p186) specializes in contemporary Latin American art, while the Centro de Cultura Casa Lamm (p184), in a handsome Porfiriato-era building, contains an excellent culturally oriented bookshop and exhibition rooms. More galleries are found on and around nearby Colima and Plaza Río de Janeiro – the Arte-México website (www.arte-mexico.com) is a good place to find out what's on where.

CASA DEL POETA RAMÓN LÓPEZ VELARDE Map pp92–3

☎ 5533-5456; Álvaro Obregón 73; admission M$5; ☻ 10am-6pm Tue-Fri, to 3pm Sat; Ⓜ Insurgentes

Composer of the lyrical paean to the nation *La Suave Pátria*, the beloved poet Ramón López Velarde resided in this building until his death in 1921. From his humble studio, you go through an armoire to embark on a journey through López Velarde's imagination. Fragments of the poet's verses are scattered around surreal sculptures, toys and dioramas.

READING ROMA
Walking Tour

1 Romita From Metro Cuauhtémoc, take the 'Av Chapultepec Sur' exit. Turn left out of the station, then left at the corner, Guaymas. Cross Puebla and turn right at the next corner. You'll enter Plaza Romita, core of the old village that gives the greater neighborhood its name.

2 Calle Morelia After inspecting the beautifully preserved little San Francisco Javier church,

THE GREEN HOUSE

Art is, by definition, a creative expression and so should not necessarily be restricted to urban galleries and museums. And, in the case of the Casa Verde (Green House; off-Map pp42–3; ☎ 5810-1445; www.lacasaverde.com.mx; Desierto de los Leones, Santa Rosa Xochiac; Ⓜ Barranca del Muerto), the reverse is the case. Located on the outskirts of the city, this bold new gallery, founded in 2005, has integrated contemporary sculpture with the natural environment in an open-air gallery that covers a hectare of lushly unspoiled natural parkland and gardens. Dramatic contemporary sculptures punctuate their surroundings like so many exclamation marks; exhibited on a series of grassy terraces and, thus, open to the elements, rather than just the air-con–cum-cigarette-smoke gallery norm.

The sculptures are well-spaced out and varied, which adds to the treasure-hunt intrigue of a visit here. New York–born Carol Miller, winner of numerous awards for her contribution to Mexican arts, has an evocative series of bold bronze figures, while Mexican-Japanese sculptor and UNAM professor Kiyoto Ota has four tantalizingly subdued pieces, all untitled and open to interpretation. Ota has also created an intriguing art structure here, entitled *Huipil*, made of rope and wood which visitors can climb and walk through.

Within Casa Verde there is a more conventional gallery, where past exhibitions have included the title *Eroticando*. No guesses as to the theme here, but the sculptures and paintings exhibited were an aesthetic, rather than lewd, delight and included the exquisite sculptures of Brazilian sculptor Flavio José de Silva.

To reach the Casa Verde, take the metro to Barranca del Muerto and catch bus 45 outside the station to Santa Rosa; the complex is around 150m walk from the last stop. The complex includes art and sculpture workshops and a cafeteria. Prior appointment, via email or phone, is unproblematic but essential and there is no charge for visitors.

which was built by Jesuits in 1530, leave the plaza via the west side (opposite the church entrance), and head to the left on Calle Morelia. After crossing Calle Colima, you'll walk alongside Jardín Pushkin, site of a major *tianguis* (street market) on Wednesdays and Sundays.

3 Av Álvaro Obregón Continue south to Av Álvaro Obregón, the neighborhood's main street. Turn right, walking along the statue-studded median. Half a block past Mérida on the left is the former home of poet Ramón Velarde, who penned *La Suave Pátria* for his beloved Mexico.

4 Parque Luis Cabrera Next, turn left onto Córdoba, head three blocks south to Zacatecas, and then turn right. Halfway up

WALK FACTS

Start Metro Cuauhtémoc
End Plaza de la Villa de Madrid
Distance 3km
Duration 2½ hours
Fuel stops Numerous

the block is the Nina Menocal Gallery (p186), specializing in Cuban sculpture. Just beyond is the lovely Parque Luis Cabrera, which features a group of dancing fountains. This was beat writer William S Burroughs' territory in the early 1950s.

5 Roma cafés Exit the park at the north end and proceed up Orizaba. Just before Álvaro Obregón on the right is La Bella Italia, a relic of 1950s Mexico City that was a setting in José Emilio Pacheco's novella *Las Batallas en el Desierto*. Across the street is the more popular Café de Carlo (p164).

6 Plaza Río de Janeiro Cross Álvaro Obregón and pop into the Casa Lamm (p184) to browse through its excellent bookstore and explore its art gallery. Continue up Orizaba to reach the Plaza Río de Janeiro and its statue of David. The reddish structure on the right is sometimes called the witch's house – a glimpse at its corner turret should explain why.

7 Calle Tabasco Head west along Durango, then turn left at Jalapa. One block down, across Colima, you'll find the headquarters of Mexico's 'legitimate government,' according to

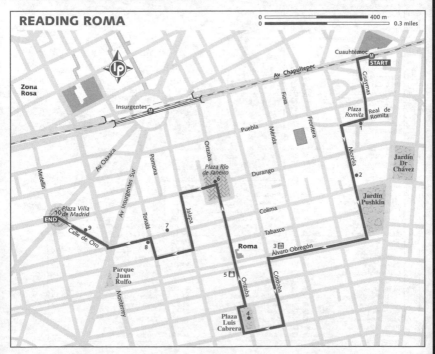

ROMA

See Zona Rosa,
Cuauhtémoc &
Juárez Map
(p74–6)

Zona
Rosa

Roma
Norte

Plaza
Villa de
Madrid

Roma

See Condesa
Map (p88–9)

Parque
México

Plaza
Insurgentes

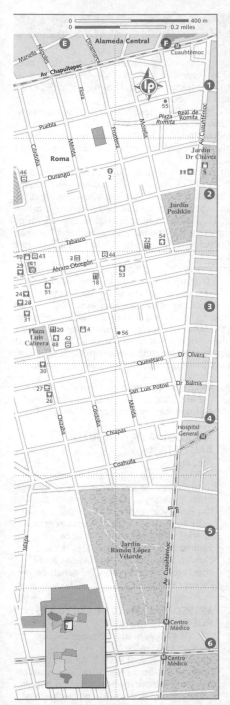

TRANSPORTATION: ROMA

- **Metro** – Metro Insurgentes (Línea 1) is a five-block walk north of Álvaro Obregón via Calle Jalapa. Exiting at the Insurgentes roundabout, take the 'Calle Jalapa' passageway on the south side (it runs alongside the doughnut shop).
- **Bus** – peseros labeled 'Metro Tacubaya-Balderas-Escandón' travel eastbound on Durango and westbound on Puebla while on their way to the Centro Histórico and Condesa respectively, 'Metro Sevilla – P Masaryk' buses go west on Álvaro Obregón to the Zona Rosa and Polanco.
- **Metrobus** – the most convenient metrobus stations are Durango and Álvaro Obregón, which are situated three and four blocks west of Calle Orizaba, respectively.
- **Taxi** – there's a taxi *sitio* on Calle Durango, a block west of Plaza Río de Janeiro.

supporters of Andrés Manuel López Obrador, who claimed fraud in the presidential election of 2006 (see the boxed text, p37). Turn right at the next corner, Tabasco, and take a moment to admire a series of well-preserved Porfiriato-era structures.

8 Roma Norte Take the next right, Tonalá. Up at the corner with Colima is the Roma branch of MUCA (p185), the national university's art gallery, which regularly hosts iconoclastic exhibits. Turn left on Colima to reach Av Insurgentes, and cross over to the bit of Roma that borders Colonia Condesa's north end.

9 Tianguis de Oro Cross Insurgentes and head up the street angling off to the right, Calle de Oro. Its single block is transformed into a busy street market on Wednesdays, Saturdays and Sundays, when you'll find steaks and snacks along the left aisle, handbags and glad rags on the others.

10 Plaza Villa de Madrid At the end of the block, Plaza Villa de Madrid sports a replica of Madrid's Cibeles fountain within its central circle. Have lunch at Contramar (p151) or one of the other fine nearby restaurants, followed by coffee or perhaps a hand-rolled cigar at the modest Café Villa de Madrid (p165).

Shopping p128; Eating p152; Drinking p165; Sleeping p212

Though part of the Distrito Federal, Coyoacán, 10km south of downtown, is often thought of as a distinct community. Once home to Leon Trotsky and Frida Kahlo (whose houses are now fascinating museums), it exudes a decidedly countercultural vibe and has traditionally been a haven for painters, writers, movie directors and other oddballs.

'Place of Coyotes' in the Náhuatl language, Coyoacán was one of a string of tribal centers on the western shore of Lake Texcoco before the Spanish conquest. It was subdued by the Aztecs soon after they defeated the neighboring Tepanecas, and later became Cortés' base after the fall of Tenochtitlán. The neighborhood's principal plazas – Hidalgo and La Conchita – were built over indigenous ceremonial centers.

Coyoacán has been a cultural hotspot since at least the early 1900s, when poet Francisco Sosa organized a series of soirees there that attracted some of the country's leading literary lights. During the 1920s, Frida Kahlo's house and the Ex-Convento de Churubusco hosted some of the earliest Schools of Open-Air Painting, a program supported by the postrevolutionary education ministry to train young artists of modest means. The Estudios Churubusco Azteca, which forms part of the Centro Nacional de las Artes complex at the east end of the neighborhood, has been the center of the Mexican movie industry for the past 60 years, and the Cineteca Nacional, just north, is the city's premier venue for art films.

Only in recent decades has urban sprawl overtaken the outlying village, and Coyoacán retains its restful identity, with narrow colonial-era streets, plazas, cafés and a lively atmosphere. On weekends, assorted musicians, mimes and crafts markets draw large but relaxed crowds from all walks of life to the festive double square at the center of the neighborhood, anchored by the massive San Juan Bautista temple. From there, walkers will find no shortage of splendid destinations to make for. North of the plazas stands one of the capital's most colorful markets and the main residential zone, permeated by the spirit of Frida. To the west, linked by quaint Av Francisco Sosa, are the Viveros de Coyoacán, the city's principal tree nurseries; to the east, the superb Franciscan monastery of Churubusco, housing an excellent historical museum.

There's a helpful tourist information office (☎ 5-659-2256, ext 181; Plaza Hidalgo 1; ☯ 9am-8pm) in the Casa de Cortés.

PLAZA HIDALGO & JARDÍN DEL CENTENARIO Map p95
Plaza Hidalgo & Jardín del Centenario; Ⓜ Viveros
The focus of Coyoacán life and the scene of most of the area's weekend fun are its twin central plazas. The eastern Plaza Hidalgo has a statue of Miguel Hidalgo; the western Jardín del Centenario is surrounded by attractive cafés and centers on a fountain with a coyote sculpture, which is a symbol of Coyoacán. The two plazas are divided by Calle Carrillo Puerto.

The Coyoacán tourist office is housed in the former Coyoacán Ayuntamiento (Town Hall), also called the Casa de Cortés, on the north side of Plaza Hidalgo. It's said that on this spot the Spanish tortured the defeated Aztec king Cuauhtémoc to try to make him reveal the whereabouts of treasure. The existing 18th-century building was the headquarters of the Marquesado del Valle de Oaxaca, the Cortés family's lands in

Mexico, which included Coyoacán. Above the entrance is the coat of arms bestowed on Coyoacán by King Carlos IV of Spain.

PARROQUIA DE SAN JUAN BAUTISTA Map p95
Plaza Hidalgo
This single-nave church and its adjacent former monastery dominate the east side of Plaza Hidalgo. First erected in 1592 by the Franciscan order, the Parroquia de San Juan Bautista has a lavishly ornamented interior, with painted scenes all over the vaulted ceiling. Be sure to inspect the cloister, featuring Tuscan columns and a checkerboard of carved relief panels on the corner ceilings.

MUSEO NACIONAL DE CULTURAS POPULARES Map p95
☎ 5554-8968; Av Hidalgo 289; admission free; ☯ 10am-6pm Tue-Sun
Half a block east of Plaza Hidalgo is the National Museum of Popular Culture, which has good temporary exhibitions on popular culture, indigenous crafts and celebrations

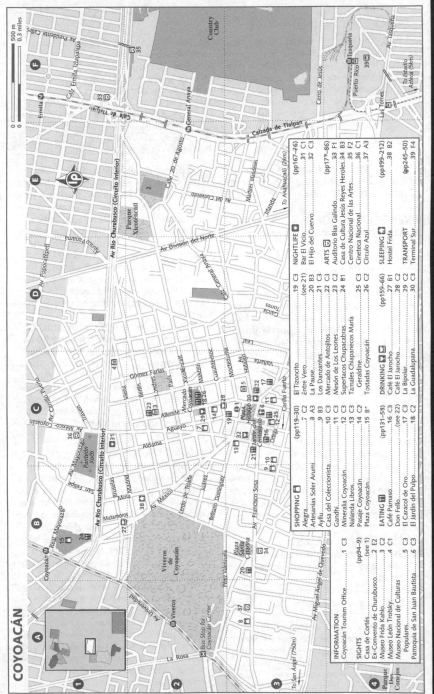

COYOACÁN

500 m
0.3 miles

lonelyplanet.com

INFORMATION
Coyoacán Tourism Office....................1 C3

SIGHTS (pp94–9)
Casa de Cortés..............................(see 1)
Ex-Convento de Churubusco..............2 E2
Museo Frida Kahlo...........................3 C1
Museo León Trotsky.........................4 C1
Museo Nacional de Culturas
  Populares...................................5 C3
Parroquia de San Juan Bautista........6 C3

SHOPPING (pp119–30)
Alegra...7 C2
Artesanías Soler Arumi......................8 A3
Ayllu..9 B3
Casa del Coleccionista....................10 C3
Gandhi...11 C3
Mineralia Coyoacán.......................12 C3
Nalanda Libros..............................13 C3
Pasaje Coyoacán...........................14 C2
Plaza Coyoacán.............................15 B*

EATING (pp131–58)
Café Parnaso.................................16 C3
Don Fello.....................................(see 22)
El Caracol de Oro..........................17 C3
El Jardín del Pulpo.........................18 C2

El Tizoncito..................................19 C3
Entre Vero...................................(see 21)
La Pause......................................20 B3
Los Danzantes..............................21 C3
Mercado de Antojitos.....................22 C3
Mesón de Los Leones.....................23 C3
Supertacos Chupacabras..................24 B1
Tamales Chiapanecos María
  Geraldine..................................25 C3
Tostadas Coyoacán........................26 C2

DRINKING (pp159–66)
Café El Jarocho..............................27 B1
Café El Jarocho..............................28 C2
La Bipolar....................................29 C2
La Guadalupana.............................30 C3

NIGHTLIFE (pp167–76)
Bar El Vicio...................................31 C1
El Hijo del Cuervo..........................32 C3

ARTS (pp17*–86)
Auditorio Blas Galindo....................33 F1
Casa de Cultura Jesús Reyes Heroles..34 B3
Centro Nacional de las Artes............35 F2
Cineteca Nacional..........................36 C1
Círculo Azul.................................37 A3

SLEEPING (pp199–212)
Hostel Frida..................................38 B2

TRANSPORT (pp245–50)
Terminal Sur.................................39 F4

TRANSPORTATION: COYOACÁN

- Metro – the nearest metro stations are Viveros and Coyoácan (Línea 3) and General Anaya (Línea 2), all 1.5km to 2km from Plaza Hidalgo. If you don't fancy a hike, catch one of the suggested peseros (below).
- Bus – from metro Viveros, walk south (left, if you're facing Av Universidad) to Peréz Valenzuela, cross and catch an eastbound 'M(etro) Gral Anaya' pesero to Allende. From the Coyoácan station take a 'Coyoácan' pesero going southeast on Av México. From metro General Anaya, take the exit off the southbound platform and catch an RTP bus labeled 'Centro Coyoácan.' (The last option is best for the Ex-Convento de Churubusco.) Returning, 'Metro Viveros' peseros go west on Malitzin; 'Metro Coyoácan' and 'Metro Gral Anaya' peseros depart from the west side of Plaza Hidalgo. San Ángel-bound peseros and buses head west on Av de Quevedo, five blocks south of Plaza Hidalgo.

in its various courtyards and galleries. Past exhibits have covered *lucha libre, nacimientos* (nativity models) and circuses.

VIVEROS DE COYOACÁN Map p95

☎ 5554-1851; admission free; ☺ 6am-6pm; Ⓜ Viveros

A pleasant approach is via the Viveros de Coyoácan, the principal nurseries for Mexico City's parks and gardens. The 390,000-sq-meter swath of greenery, 1km north of central Coyoácan, is popular with joggers and perfect for a stroll, but watch out for belligerent squirrels! From metro Viveros, walk south along Av Universidad and take the first left, Av Progreso; or enter on Av México near Calle Madrid.

CASA DE CULTURA JESÚS REYES HEROLES Map p95

☎ 5658-5281; Francisco Sosa 202; ☺ 8am-8pm; Ⓜ Viveros

Across the street from the tranquil Plaza Santa Catarina, the Casa de Cultura Jesús Reyes Heroles is an old colonial estate hosting book presentations, dance classes and so on (see p181). Take a wander round the grounds, where yuccas and jacarandas spring from carefully tended gardens.

MUSEO FRIDA KAHLO Map p95

☎ 5554-5999; www.museofridakahlo.org; Londres 247; admission M$45; ☺ 10am-6pm Tue-Sun; Ⓜ Coyoácan

Iconic Mexican artist Frida Kahlo was born, lived and died in the 'Blue House,' six blocks north of Plaza Hidalgo.

Almost every visitor to Mexico City makes a pilgrimage here to gain a deeper understanding of the painter (and maybe to pick up a Frida handbag). Built by her father Guillermo three years before Frida's birth, the house is littered with mementos

and personal belongings that evoke her long, often tempestuous relationship with husband Diego Rivera and the leftist intellectual circle they often entertained here.

Kitchen implements, jewelry, outfits, books and other objects from the artist's everyday life are interspersed with art, photos and letters, as well as a variety of pre-Hispanic art and Mexican crafts. The collection was greatly expanded in 2007 upon the discovery of a cache of previously unseen items that had been stashed in the attic.

Kahlo's art expresses the anguish of her existence as well as her flirtation with socialist icons: portraits of Lenin and Mao hang around her bed, and in the upstairs studio an unfinished portrait of Stalin stands before a poignantly positioned wheelchair. In another painting, *Retrato de la Familia* (Family Portrait), the artist's Hungarian-Oaxacan roots are fancifully entangled.

MUSEO LÉON TROTSKY Map p95

☎ 5658-8732; Río Churubusco 410; admission M$30; ☺ 10am-5pm Tue-Sun; Ⓜ Coyoácan

Having come second to Stalin in the power struggle in the Soviet Union, Trotsky was expelled in 1929 and condemned to death in absentia. In 1937 he found refuge in Mexico. At first Trotsky and his wife, Natalia, lived in Frida Kahlo's Blue House, but after falling out with Kahlo and Rivera they moved a few streets northeast, to Viena 45.

The Trotsky home remains much as it was on the day when a Stalin agent, a Catalan named Ramón Mercader, finally caught up with the revolutionary and smashed an ice pick into his skull. Memorabilia and biographical notes are displayed in buildings off the patio, where a tomb engraved with a hammer and sickle contains the Trotskys' ashes.

The main entrance is at the rear of the old residence, facing the Circuito Interior.

EX-CONVENTO DE CHURUBUSCO
Map p95

☎ 5604-0699; cnr Calle 20 de Agosto & Anaya; admission M$39, Sun free; ☽ 9am-6pm Tue-Sun; Ⓜ General Anaya

Scene of a historic military defeat, the 17th-century former Monastery of Churubusco, now a museum, stands within peaceful wooded grounds, 1.5km northeast of Plaza Hidalgo.

On August 20, 1847, Mexican troops defended the monastery against US forces in a dispute over the US annexation of Texas. The Mexicans fought until they ran out of ammunition and were beaten only after hand-to-hand fighting.

The US invasion was but one example in a long history of foreign intervention, as compellingly demonstrated by the National Interventions Museum inside the former *convento*. Displays include an American map showing operations in 1847, and material on the French occupation of the 1860s and the plot by US ambassador Henry Lane Wilson to bring down the Madero government in 1913. (None of the explanatory text is translated into English.)

The superbly restored exhibit rooms, bordered by original frescoes, surround a small cloister where numbered stations provided instructions for meditating monks. Leaving the museum, you may wander amid the monastery's old orchard, which now holds wonderful gardens.

To reach Churubusco, catch an eastbound 'M(etro) Gral Anaya' pesero or bus on Xicoténcatl at Allende, a few blocks north of Plaza Hidalgo. Alternatively, walk 500m west from the General Anaya metro station.

top picks

ON SUNDAY

- Cycling (p188) on Paseo de la Reforma
- Museo Nacional de Antropología (p80)
- Coyoacán's Plaza Hidalgo (p94)
- Xochimilco (p113)
- Catedral Metropolitana (p50) hosts mass by the Archbishop

CENTRO NACIONAL DE LAS ARTES
Map p95

☎ 4155-0000; www.cenart.gob.mx in Spanish; Río Churubusco 79; Ⓜ General Anaya

The National Arts Center, just east of Calzada de Tlalpan, is a modern hothouse of the arts. It's home to the Auditorio Blas Galindo (p178), the Teatro de las Artes and two other theaters, the national music conservatory and the schools of theater, dance, cinema, painting, sculpture and engraving. Even if you're not here for a performance, it's still interesting to stroll through the grounds amid the modern architecture and browse the center's excellent bookshop and art materials shop.

ANAHUACALLI Map p95

☎ 5617-4310; www.anahuacallimuseo.org; Calle del Museo 150; admission M$45; ☽ 10am-6pm Tue-Sun

Designed by Diego Rivera to house his collection of pre-Hispanic art, this museum, 3.5km south of Coyoacán, is a fortresslike building made of dark volcanic stone. It incorporates stylistic features from many pre-Hispanic cultures. An inscription over the door reads: 'To return to the people the artistic inheritance I was able to redeem from their ancestors.' If the air is

THROW A PESO IN THE HAT

Dressed in khaki uniforms, they stand on street corners, in front of theaters, at busy traffic intersections – anywhere that people congregate. They work in pairs: the organ grinder and the tip collector, who extends an upturned cap at any pedestrian or driver in sight. The music-maker cranks the handle of a varnished wooden box, manufactured in Berlin in the late 19th century, to produce a carnivalesque string of tunes that echo Mexico's distant past. The jukeboxes of their era, these 'organs' generally play eight tunes of a minute each. Though some passersby consider them a mere annoyance, the 100 or so organ grinders who work the city are actually heirs to a tradition dating back to before the Revolution. Brought over by Italian immigrants who earned their living as itinerant carnival performers, the instrument became fashionable during the Porfirio Díaz regime. Later the old European ditties were replaced by Mexican tunes. If you'd like to see the tradition continue, drop a few pesos in the hat.

clear, the view over the city from the roof is great.

The House of Anáhuac (Aztec name for the Valle de México) also contains one of Rivera's studios and some of his work, including a study for *Man at the Crossroads*, the mural that was commissioned for the Rockefeller Center in 1934. In November elaborate Día de Muertos offerings pay homage to the painter.

The entry fee includes admission to the Frida Kahlo house (p96).

To get to Anahuacalli, take the Tren Ligero (from metro Tasqueña) to the Xotepingo station. Exit on the west side and walk 200m to División del Norte; cross and continue 600m along Calle del Museo.

FRIDA'S NEIGHBORHOOD
Walking Tour

1 Viveros de Coyoacán Exit metro Viveros onto Av Universidad, a major thoroughfare that skirts Viveros de Coyoacán (p96), which serves as the nursery for many of the DF's public gardens. Facing the fence, go right (south), walk 400m to the corner and turn left. The

WALK FACTS

Start Metro Viveros
End Café El Jarocho
Distance 3.7km
Duration 2½ hours
Fuel stops Numerous

entrance is a short distance down on your left. Enter the park, go straight ahead and take the second right (Olmos). Follow this broad path east, through the park, exploring the intersecting paths named after the kinds of trees along them. About 500m along, turn right, through the playground, to exit the park.

2 Plaza Santa Catarina Cross Av Pérez Valenzuela, go right and look for Calle Torresco – more an alley than a street. This bends right at a school, then puts you on the lovely Plaza Santa Catarina. On the far end is the modest, mustard-colored church that gives the plaza its name.

3 Casa de Cultura Jesús Reyes Héroles Cross the street that borders the plaza and stop into the Casa de Cultura Jesús Reyes Heroles (p181), a colonial complex hosting book presentations, dance classes and so on. Take a wander round the carefully tended gardens and bask in the tranquillity at the open-air café.

4 Francisco Sosa Leaving the Casa, head right and down Francisco Sosa. Named for the poet and journalist who organized literary soirees here in the early 1900s, the tree-lined street is flanked by fine colonial buildings and dotted with cafés, notably the one inside the Italian Cultural Center at number 77.

5 Jardín del Centenario About 700m east of the Plaza Santa Catarina, pass through a double-arched gate to enter the Jardín del Centenario, with Coyoacán's iconic coyotes frolicking in its central fountain and lively cafés around the

FRIDA'S NEIGHBORHOOD

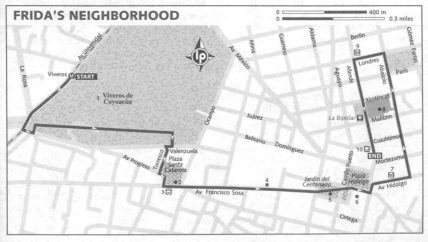

perimeter. If it's the weekend, wander through a maze of stalls hawking hippie accessories.

6 Plaza Hidalgo Proceed across Calle Carrillo Puerto to the adjacent Plaza Hidalgo, a sprawling cobblestoned square with an invariably festive atmosphere. Directly ahead stands which has a flamboyant interior. To the left is the Casa de Cortés (p94), now housing Coyoacán's delegational offices.

7 Museo de Culturas Populares Go around the left side of San Juan Bautista and cross over to the classic cantina, La Guadalupana (p165). Go left, then turn right at the corner, Av Hidalgo. Half a block east is the Museo de Culturas Populares (p94), which has compelling exhibits on home-grown arts and customs.

8 Mercado de Coyoacán Go left at the next corner, Abasolo, and walk north three blocks. On your left is the Mercado de Coyoacán,

one of Mexico City's most inviting covered markets. It's densely packed with vendors of quality produce, *moles* (sauces), piñatas, basketry etc, as well as the terrific Tostadas Coyoacán (p156).

9 Casa Azul Continue another couple of blocks north and turn left on Londres. On the next corner, you'll find the famous Blue House, where artist Frida Kahlo was born and lived for many years, now housing the Museo Frida Kahlo (p96). Afterwards, head back down to the center via Allende.

10 El Jarocho A block below the market join the crowds lining up for cappuccino and doughnuts at popular Café El Jarocho (p165), an obligatory stop on any Coyoacán visit. Alternatively, knock back a few mescals at La Bipolar (p165), the popular new cantina and guardian of Mexican kitsch, half a block west of the market on Malintzin.

Shopping p129; Eating p153

Settled by the Dominican order soon after the Spanish conquest, San Ángel, 12km southwest of the center, maintains its colonial splendor despite being engulfed by the metropolis. It's most often associated with the big Saturday crafts market held alongside the Plaza San Jacinto. Though the main approach via Av Insurgentes is typically chaotic, wander westward to experience the old village's cobblestoned soul, a tranquil enclave of colonial mansions with massive wooden doors, pots of geraniums behind window grills and bougainvillea spilling over stone walls.

The two main roads through San Ángel are Av Insurgentes Sur, which runs north–south through the eastern side of the suburb, and Av Revolución, which parallels Insurgentes about 200m to the west.

On weekends, tourist information is available at a module (Map p101; ☺ 10am-6pm Sat & Sun) on the Plaza San Jacinto.

TEMPLO Y MUSEO DE EL CARMEN
Map p101

☎ 5616-2816; Av Revolución 4; admission M$39, Sun free; ☺ 10am-5pm Tue-Sun

A storehouse of magnificent sacred art, this museum occupies a former school run by the Carmelite order, adjacent to their 17th-century Templo de El Carmen. (The village was named for their patron saint, San Ángelo Mártir.) The collection includes eight oils by Mexican master Cristóbal Villalpando; equally splendid are the polychrome and gilt designs on the ceilings. The big draw, however, are the dozen mummies in the crypt. Thought to be the bodies of 17th-century benefactors of the order, they were uncovered during the revolution by Zapatistas looking for buried treasure.

PLAZA SAN JACINTO Map p101

🚇 Metrobus La Bombilla

Every Saturday the Bazar Sábado (p123) brings a festive atmosphere, masses of color, and crowds of people to San Ángel's pretty little Plaza San Jacinto.

The main building of the Bazar Sábado is Plaza San Jacinto 11, on the north side of the square. This house served as quarters

for invading forces from the US in 1847 and from France in 1863. A plaque on one of the buildings on the west side of the plaza, however, commemorates 71 soldiers of the Irish Battalion of St Patrick who were hung after helping the Mexicans resist the US invasion. The Irish were originally fighting in the American forces but thought the US cause was so unjust that they switched sides.

Midway along the plaza's north side, look for the elaborate fountain inside the courtyard Museo Casa del Risco (☎ 5616-2711; Plaza San Jacinto 15; admission free; ☺ 10am-5pm Tue-Sun; Ⓜ Miguel Angel de Quevedo), a mad mosaic of Talavera tile and Chinese porcelain. Upstairs is a treasure trove of Mexican baroque and medieval European paintings.

About 50m west of the plaza is the 16th-century Iglesia de San Jacinto and its peaceful gardens.

MUSEO CASA ESTUDIO DIEGO RIVERA Y FRIDA KAHLO Map p101

☎ 5550-1518; Diego Rivera 2, cnr Av Altavista; admission M$10, Sun free; ☺ 10am-6pm Tue-Sun

If you saw the movie Frida, you'll recognize the Diego Rivera & Frida Kahlo Studio Museum, 1km northwest of Plaza San Jacinto.

TRANSPORTATION: SAN ÁNGEL

- Metro – from Metro Miguel Ángel de Quevedo (Línea 3), walk or catch a 'San Ángel' pesero (minibus) 1km west to Plaza San Jacinto. From Metro Barranca del Muerto, catch any pesero 1.5km south along Av Revolución.
- Metrobus – the easiest option: from the La Bombilla station of the Av Insurgentes metrobus, it's a 500m walk west along Av de la Paz to Plaza San Jacinto.
- Bus – to Coyoacán, get a 'M(etro) Tasqueña' pesero or bus going east on Miguel Ángel de Quevedo; it will take you to the corner of Carrillo Puerto (2.5km), a five-block walk north to the Jardín del Centenario.
- Taxi – there's a sitio (taxi stand) on the east side of Plaza San Jacinto.

SAN ÁNGEL

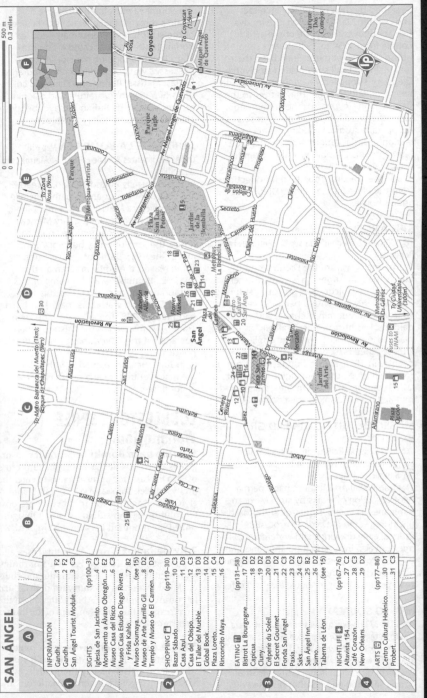

INFORMATION
Gandhi..................................1 F2
Gandhi..................................2 F2
San Ángel Tourist Module.......3 C3

SIGHTS   (pp100–3)
Iglesia de San Jacinto.............4 C3
Monumento a Álvaro Obregón...5 E2
Museo Casa del Risco............6 C3
Museo Casa Estudio Diego Rivera
  y Frida Kahlo........................7 B2
Museo Soumaya.............(see 15)
Museo de Arte Carrillo Gil.......8 D2
Templo y Museo de El Carmen...9 D3

SHOPPING 🛍   (pp119–30)
Bazar Sábado........................10 C3
Casa Azul.............................11 C3
Casa del Obispo....................12 C3
El Taller del Mueble...............13 D3
Global Book..........................14 D2
Plaza Loreto.........................15 C4
Rinconcito Maya...................16 C3

EATING 🍴   (pp131–58)
Bistrot La Bourgogne.............17 D2
Capicúa..............................18 D2
Cluny..................................19 D2
Crêperie du Soleil..................20 D3
El Secret Gourmet.................21 D2
Fonda San Ángel....................22 D2
Paxia...................................23 D2
Saks....................................24 D2
San Ángel Inn.......................25 B2
Sumo...................................26 D2
Taberna de León.............(see 15)

NIGHTLIFE ★   (pp167–76)
Altavista 154........................27 C2
Café Corazón.......................28 D2
New Orleans.........................29 D2

ARTS 🎭   (pp177–86)
Centro Cultural Helénico.........30 D1
Probert................................31 C3

Designed by their friend, the architect and painter Juan O'Gorman, the innovative abode was the home of the artistic couple from 1934 to 1940, with a separate house for each of them. Frida lived there for five years until she decided to divorce Diego for supposedly having an affair with her sister, and took her things over to the Casa Azul in Coyoacán. (They remarried soon afterward.) Rivera's house preserves his upstairs studio, including Rivera's collection of Judas effigies. Frida's (the blue one) contains changing exhibits from the memorabilia archives.

See the Walking Tour (right) for directions from the Plaza San Jacinto to Diego and Frida's houses.

SAN ÁNGEL INN Map p101

☎ 5616-1402; Diego Rivera 50; 🚍 Metrobus La Bombilla

Across the way from the Diego–Frida home, the San Ángel Inn is in the former Hacienda de Goicoechea, an 18th-century *pulque* plantation with a beautiful verdant courtyard, a fountain, a chapel and colonial gardens. It is historically significant as the place where 'Pancho' Villa and Emiliano Zapata agreed to divide control of the country in 1914. If your budget won't run to a meal here at the prestigious restaurant (p153), you can still stroll in the gardens and perhaps have a drink in the cocktail bar.

MUSEO DE ARTE CARRILLO GIL
Map p101

☎ 5550-6289; Av Revolución 1608; admission M$15, Sun free; 🕙 10am-6pm Tue-Sun; Ⓜ Barranca del Muerto

The Carrillo Gil Art Museum has a permanent collection of works by such Mexican luminaries as Rivera, Siqueiros and Orozco (including some of Orozco's grotesque, satirical early drawings and watercolors). The museum also includes engravings and prints by Klee, Rouault, Braque and Kandinsky, plus often excellent temporary exhibits. In the basement is a pleasant bookstore and café.

MUSEO SOUMAYA Map p101

☎ 5616-3731; www.museosoumaya.com; Plaza Loreto, Altamirano 46; admission M$10, Sun & Mon free; 🕙 10:30am-6:30pm Wed, Thu & Mon, to 8:30pm Fri & Sat; 🚍 Metrobus Doctor Gálvez

Property of multibillionaire businessman Carlos Slim and named after his late wife,

the Soumaya museum houses one of the world's three major collections (70 pieces) of the sculpture of Frenchman Auguste Rodin (1840–1917). Located inside the Plaza Loreto shopping mall (p130), it also possesses work by Rodin's contemporaries Degas, Matisse, Renoir and Daumier, collections of Mexican portraiture and colonial art, and murals by Rufino Tamayo, besides staging major temporary exhibitions.

JARDÍN DE LA BOMBILLA Map p101

Cnr Av Insurgentes & Av de La Paz; 🚍 Metrobus La Bombilla

In this tropically abundant park spreading east of Av Insurgentes, paths encircle the Monumento a Álvaro Obregón, a monolithic shrine to the postrevolutionary Mexican president. The monument was built to house the revolutionary general's arm, lost in the 1915 Battle of Celaya, but for some reason the limb was cremated in 1989. 'La Bombilla' was the name of the restaurant that once occupied this spot where Obregón was assassinated during a banquet in 1928. The killer, José de León Toral, was involved in the Cristero rebellion against the government's anti-Church policies.

In July, the park explodes with color as the main venue for Feria de las Flores, a major flower festival.

COBBLESTONE SPREE
Walking Tour

1 Jardín de la Bombilla Get off the Insurgentes metrobus at 'La Bombilla' and cross over to the east side of Insurgentes to enter the pretty Jardín de la Bombilla (above). The tall, Stalinist-style monument in the middle honors postrevolutionary president Álvaro Obregón; until 1989 it housed his arm, lost in battle.

2 Av de la Paz Cross Av Insurgentes and head west along Av de la Paz, a major dining and nightlife zone with restaurants and clubs enclosed in a series of courtyard malls. Turn left on Av Revolución. About 50m down the street, explore the inner sanctum of the former Carmelite convent (p100).

3 Plaza del Carmen Cross Av Revolución and skirt the left side of the Plaza del Carmen, where local artists display their works every Saturday. To your left across Madero is the

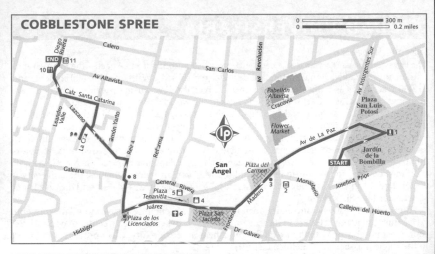

COBBLESTONE SPREE

WALK FACTS

Start Jardín de la Bombilla
End Museo Casa Estudio Diego Rivera y Frida Kahlo
Distance 1.7km
Duration 1½ hours
Fuel stops El Convento for *churros* and chocolate

Centro Cultural San Ángel, a neighborhood activity center with a theater and art exhibits.

4 Plaza San Jacinto A short walk down Madero takes you to the Plaza San Jacinto (p100), the zone's center of activity, especially on Saturdays when the weekly crafts market is open for business. About halfway along the plaza's north side, look for the insanely decorated fountain inside the Casa del Risco.

5 Plaza Tenanitla A few doors down is the Bazar Sábado building. The Saturday crafts market spills over to the smaller Plaza Tenanitla, opposite the building's west side. The rest of the week you can still find great crafts at the Casa del Obispo (p123), off the plaza's north side.

6 Ex Convento de San Jacinto Cross the plaza and enter the serene, manicured gardens that once formed the atrium of the San Jacinto monastery (p100). The small baroque church on the west end features an eye-catching gilt altar.

7 Plaza de los Licenciados Beyond Plaza Tenanitla, you enter the idyllic cobblestoned end of the quarter. Proceed westward down Calle Juárez to Árbol, where you'll find the Plaza de Los Licenciados, a tranquil enclave which seems a universe away from hectic Av Revolución.

8 Calle Reina Turn right on Reina. You'll pass more stately private homes with massive wooden doors, pots of geraniums behind window grills and bougainvillea spilling over stone walls. Reaching the spooky cylindrical cross at the corner (in front of the former chapel of El Zacatito), jog left and continue up Reina.

9 Casa de los Delfines Turn left onto Lazcano, where some homes boast carved stone shields over their doorways. A short detour left on La Cita will take you to the Casa de los Delfines, a two-centuries-old house with fanciful dolphin decorations on its facade.

10 San Ángel Inn Return to Lazcano, retrace your steps 30m, and turn left (north) up jacaranda-lined Calzada de Santa Catarina. Follow this around a bend and keep going west. You emerge onto a plaza, opposite the San Ángel Inn (p153). Cross Av Altavista (with extreme caution) and stop in for one of its excellent margaritas.

11 Museo Casa Estudio Diego Rivera y Frida Kahlo Just above the San Ángel Inn, where Av Altavista bends east, is the Museo Casa Estudio Diego Rivera y Frida Kahlo (p100). The Diego–Frida complex should be immediately recognizable to anyone who's seen the movie *Frida*. Across from the museum, 'Metro Viveros' buses head down Altavista for Insurgentes and Coyoacán.

CIUDAD UNIVERSITARIA

Eating p155; Sleeping p212

The University City (Map p105; www.unam.mx/en; Ⓜ Universidad), 2km south of San Ángel, is the main campus of the Universidad Nacional Autónoma de México (UNAM). With over 280,000 students and 31,000 teachers, it is Latin America's largest university. Five former Mexican presidents are among its alumni, as is Carlos Slim Helú, ranked the world's richest man in 2007.

Founded in 1551 as the Royal and Papal University of Mexico, UNAM is the second-oldest university in the Americas. It occupied various buildings in the center of town until the campus was transferred to its current location in the 1950s. Standing upon part of a vast dried-up lava field called El Pedregal, it was constructed by a team of 150 young architects, sculptors and technicians headed by José García Villagrán, Mario Pani and Enrique del Moral. With its buildings covered in optimistic murals linking Mexican and global themes, the university is a monument to national pride. An architectural showpiece, it was placed on Unesco's list of World Heritage Sites in 2007.

Although it is a public university open to all, UNAM remains 'autonomous,' meaning the government may not interfere in its academic policy. It has often been a center of political dissent, most notably prior to the 1968 Olympics, held in Mexico City, when protests culminated in the tragic massacre at Tlatelolco (see p21).

In normal times during the school semesters, the campus is busy with student life; out of term, when its libraries, faculties and cafés are closed, it's very quiet but still open to visitors.

The campus is divided into two main parts. Most of the faculty buildings are scattered over an area about 1km square at the north end. The second section, about 2km further south, includes the Centro Cultural Universitario. Student cafés, open to everyone during academic sessions, are in both the architecture and philosophy buildings at the Jardín Central's west end, and in the Centro Cultural Universitario.

NORTHERN SECTION Map p105

As you enter the northern part of the campus from Insurgentes, it's easy to spot the Biblioteca Central (Central Library) – 10 floors high, almost windowless and covered on every side with colorful, complicatedly symbolic mosaics by Juan O'Gorman. The south wall, with two prominent zodiac wheels, covers colonial times, while the north wall deals with Aztec culture.

La Rectoría, the administration building at the west end of the vast central lawn, has a vivid, three-dimensional Siqueiros mosaic on its south wall, showing students urged on by the people.

The building south of La Rectoría contains the campus's Librería Central (Central Bookstore). Adjacent to it, the Museo Universitario de Ciencias y Artes (☎ 5622-0305; www.muca.unam.mx; admission free; ID required; ☉ 10am-6pm Tue-Sun) hosts eclectic, often polemical, exhibitions from the university collection.

The Auditorio Alfonso Caso, at the bottom (east) end of the Jardín Central, has on its north end a mural by José Chávez Morado showing the conquest of energy. Humanity progresses from the shadow of a primitive Jaguar god to the use of fire and then the atom, before emerging into an ethereal, apparently female, future. The east side of the same building depicts a similarly didactic mural about progress in mining.

A little further east, on the west wall of the Facultad de Medicina, a mosaic in Italian stone by Francisco Eppens interprets the themes of life and death in Mexican terms. The central mask has a Spanish profile on the left and an indigenous one on the right, together making up a mestizo face in the middle. An ear of maize and symbols of Aztec and Mayan gods represent the forces of life and death.

ESTADIO OLÍMPICO Map p105

☎ 5522-0491; Insurgentes Sur 3000

The Olympic Stadium stands on the west side of Av Insurgentes opposite the northern part of the campus. Built of volcanic stone for the 1968 Olympics, it is designed to resemble an elliptical volcano cone. With seating for over 72,000, it is now home to UNAM's Pumas soccer club, which competes in the national Primera División league (p190). Over the main entrance is Diego Rivera's

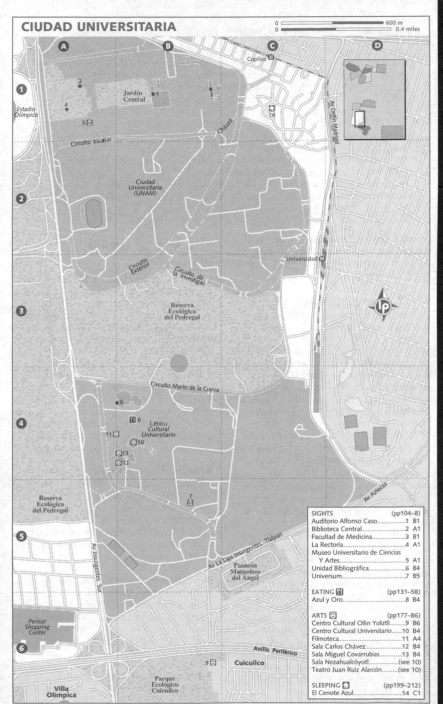

CIUDAD UNIVERSITARIA

0 — 600 m
0 — 0.4 miles

SIGHTS	(pp104–8)
Auditorio Alfonso Caso	1 B1
Biblioteca Central	2 A1
Facultad de Medicina	3 B1
La Rectoría	4 A1
Museo Universitario de Ciencias Y Artes	5 A1
Unidad Bibliográfica	6 B4
Universum	7 B5

EATING 🍴	(pp131–58)
Azul y Oro	8 B4

ARTS 🎭	(pp177–86)
Centro Cultural Ollin Yoliztli	9 B6
Centro Cultural Universitario	10 B4
Filmoteca	11 A4
Sala Carlos Chávez	12 B4
Sala Miguel Covarrubias	13 B4
Sala Nezahualcóyotl	(see 10)
Teatro Juan Ruiz Alarcón	(see 10)

SLEEPING 🛏	(pp199–212)
El Cenote Azul	14 C1

TRANSPORTATION: CIUDAD UNIVERSITARIA

- Metro – from Metro Universidad (the last stop on Línea 3), the university runs three bus routes (free) between 6:30am and 10:30pm Monday to Friday. Ruta 1 goes west to the main part of the campus; Ruta 2 traverses the Circuito Exterior, flanking the main campus' southern edge; Ruta 3 heads southwest to the Centro Cultural Universitario. Copilco metro station is near the northeast edge of the campus, 1km east of the Biblioteca Central. Take the 'Cerro de los Tres Zapotes' exit and follow the students down Filosofía y Letras to the university entrance.
- Metrobus – take the metrobus to its southern terminus, Dr Gálvez, then catch a pesero (minibus) to the west side of the university (see below). Plans are afoot to extend the metrobus line further down Insurgentes as far as Tlalpan, so it won't be necessary to make the transfer.
- Bus – from the metrobus terminus, cross Av Altamirano and catch a southbound 'Villa Coapa' pesero. For the northern part of the campus, get off at the first yellow footbridge crossing on Av Insurgentes, just before the Estadio Olímpico. For the southern section, get off at the second yellow footbridge after the Estadio Olímpico. Returning, catch any pesero marked 'San Ángel-Revolución'; to catch the metrobus, get off just after it turns left.

dramatic sculpted mural on the theme of sports in Mexican history. You can peep inside when it's closed by going to Gate 38, at the south end.

SOUTHERN SECTION Map p105

The Centro Cultural Universitario (University Cultural Center) is the focus of the southern part of the campus, about 2km south of the Estadio Olímpico. Entering off Av Insurgentes, go down the steps behind Rufino Tamayo's tall black sculpture, *La Universidad Germen de Humanismo y Sabiduría* (The University, Seed of Humanism and Wisdom). You'll find the Sala Nezahualcóyotl (p179), a major concert hall, down here on the left, and a collection of theaters, cinemas and smaller concert halls to the right. Nearby is the Universum (Museo Universitario de Ciencias; ☎ 5622-7287; www .universum.unam.mx, in Spanish; adult/child M$40/35; ☒ 9am-6pm Mon-Fri, 10am-6pm Sat & Sun), a science museum with kids' activities and workshops.

The large Unidad Bibliográfica (Bibliographic Unit), which houses part of Mexico's National Library, is about 200m north of the Centro Cultural. A short distance east of the library is the university's Espacio Escultórico (Sculpture Garden), with a trail leading through volcanic fields past a dozen or so innovative pieces. The most formidable work, by sculptor Mathias Goeritz, is found just north of the cultural complex. *Corona del Pedregal* comprises an enormous ring of concrete blocks, which surround an exposed section of the lava bed upon which the university was built.

THE ART OF UNAM
Walking Tour

1 Metro Copilco Take metro línea 3 (Dirección Universidad) to the next-to-the-last stop, Copilco. Before leaving the station, have a look at the megamural above the platform, El Perfil del Tiempo (p26), a survey of world painting by Durango artist Guillermo Ceniceros. Take the 'Cerro de los Tres Zapotes' exit.

2 UNAM Leaving the station, turn around and follow the students (down Calle Filosofía y Letras) to the university entrance. You'll cross a corridor lined with stalls serving a variety of snacks. Enter the campus through the ground floor passageway of the Facultad de la Medicina, emerging on the medical mall.

3 Facultad de la Medicina To your right is the medical school's north wing, dominated by a mosaic mural on its curved west wall which is packed with indigenous imagery. Concerts are performed beneath the mural every Friday. The zone buzzes with white-coated students engaged in between-class snacking and socializing.

4 Facultad de Odontología Looking north, you'll see an even trippier mosaic on the wall of the Facultad de Odontología (School of Dentistry), featuring a treelike figure whose head appears to be vaporizing. Head straight west, past a soccer court, to the next group of buildings.

5 Antigua Facultad de Ciencias Continue straight ahead, traversing a corridor between two buildings. The comic-bookish mural at your left, adorning the top part of the old sciences building, shows mankind's conquest of energy.

6 Biblioteca Central To the west spreads the university's main esplanade. Take a ramble across this grassy expanse to the campus' main section. The imposing Biblioteca Central (p104), with its four walls of murals by Juan O'Gorman, stands on the north side.

7 Rectoría Directly in front of you, across the west lawn, is the Torre de la Rectoría, the administrative tower, with an abstract Siqueiros mural on the lower portion. Circle around this building to the left to see a politically inspired three-dimensional mosaic, also by Siqueiros.

8 Estadio Olímpico Universitario Exiting the campus underneath Av Insurgentes, you arrive at the Estadio Olímpico Universitario (p104), the former Olympic stadium and now home of UNAM's Pumas team. Peer through the fence to admire Diego Rivera's dramatic sculpted mural over the stadium entryway on the theme of sports in Mexican history.

WALK FACTS

Start Metro Copilco
End Espacio Escultórico
Distance 3.2km
Duration 2 hours
Fuel stops Student cafeterias in the Architecture and Philosophy buildings

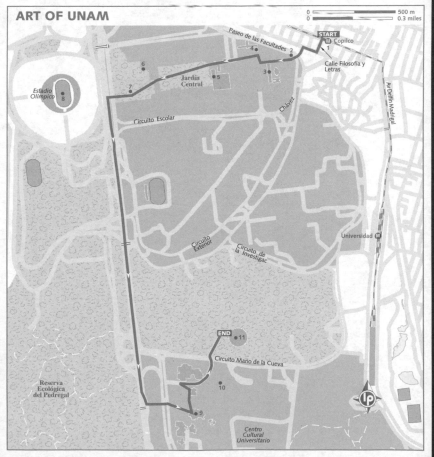

ART OF UNAM

NEIGHBORHOODS CIUDAD UNIVERSITARIA

9 Centro Cultural Universitario To continue the tour, catch any pesero down Av Insurgentes and get off at the second yellow footbridge. Take the bridge over Insurgentes, then follow the signs to the 'CUC.' You'll arrive in the middle of a plaza surrounded by five theaters and two cinemas.

10 Sculpture Garden Skirt the left side of the Sala Nezahualcóyotl (the pyramidal concrete structure to the north); a path leads to another complex with the Hemeroteca Nacional (the periodicals library). To your right, enter the university sculpture garden, where a trail leads through volcanic fields past a dozen or so innovative pieces.

11 Espacio Escultórico Leaving the garden, continue north and cross the road to find a major sculptural work by Mathias Goeritz, an enormous ring of concrete blocks around a lava bed. To return downtown, it's a 400m walk to Av Insurgentes; any 'San Ángel' bus will arrive at the metrobus terminus.

Eating, p155; Drinking p165

Tlalpan is 'what Coyoacán used to be' – an outlying village with a bohemian atmosphere, a grid of idyllic cobblestoned streets and some impressive colonial architecture. Municipal seat of the city's largest *delegación* (borough), Tlalpan sits at the foot of the southern Ajusco range and enjoys a cooler, moister climate. There are some fine restaurants along the arcades of the cute little plaza and an atmospheric cantina nearby, La Jalisciense (p165).

'Terra firma' in the indigenous tongue of Náhuatl, Tlalpan was inhabited as early as 800 BC, when a civilization arose at nearby Cuicuilco and thrived until a volcanic eruption obliterated the settlement. The formidable remains of Cuicuilco's ceremonial center are still on view on a hilltop park north of the village center. In 1645, the community was dubbed San Agustín de las Cuevas, a reference to the network of caves that were formed when subterranean gases perforated the volcanic ash. The name still belongs to Tlalpan's main temple, which stands alongside the square, and San Agustín is paid homage the last weekend of August during the Fiestas de San Agustín, a boisterous blend of processions, performances of traditional dance, gambling, cockfights and *charreadas* (rodeo displays).

MUSEO DE HISTORIA DE TLALPAN
Map p109
☎ 5485-9048; Plaza de la Constitución 10; admission free; ☺ 10am-7pm Tue-Sun
Half a block from the plaza, the Tlalpan history museum hosts compelling historical and art exhibits in naturally lit galleries off the courtyard.

CAPILLA DE LAS CAPUCHINAS SACRAMENTARIAS Map p109
☎ 5573-2395; Hidalgo 43; admission M$50; ☺ 10am-noon & 4-6pm Mon-Thu
There's a sublime simplicity about this chapel of a convent for Capuchine nuns, designed by modernist architect Luis Barragán in 1952. The austere altar, free of the usual iconography, consists only of a trio of gold panels. Visit in the morning to appreciate how light streams through the stained-glass window by Mathias Goeritz.

TLALPAN PRANCE
Walking Tour
1 Antigua Hacienda de Tlalpan Arriving on the bus from San Ángel (labeled 'Villa Coapa'), get off at the corner of San Fernando and Calzada de Tlalpan. A block south, past a large fountain, is the entrance to the Antigua Hacienda de Tlalpan (p155). Follow the white peacocks around the broad lawn that fronts the elegant restaurant and reception hall.

2 Casa Chata At the next corner south (Hidalgo), go right. A magnificently carved

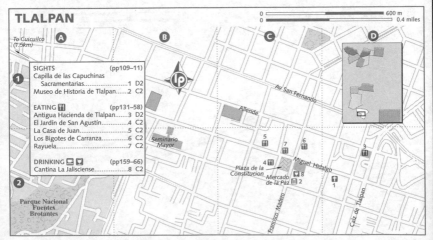

TLALPAN

0 — 600 m
0 — 0.4 miles

To Cuicuilco
(1.5km)

SIGHTS (pp109–11)
Capilla de las Capuchinas
  Sacramentarias..............1 D2
Museo de Historia de Tlalpan......2 C2

EATING (pp131–58)
Antigua Hacienda de Tlalpan......3 D2
El Jardín de San Agustín.............4 C2
La Casa de Juan...........................5 C2
Los Bigotes de Carranza.............6 C2
Rayuela.......................................7 C2

DRINKING (pp159–66)
Cantina La Jalisciense.................8 C2

Av San Fernando
Allende
Seminario Mayor
Miguel Hidalgo
Plaza de la Constitución
Mercado de la Paz
Parque Nacional
Fuentes Brotantes
Francisco Madero
Calz de Tlalpan

doorway at the next street gives access to the Casa Chata (☎ 5655-0158; admission free; ☼ 10am-6pm Mon-Fri). The 18th-century building houses a social-anthropology research center, with a library and bookstore off the patio.

3 Barragán Chapel About midway down the next block west is the convent of the Capuchin sisters of the Sacred Heart (p109), with a chapel designed by renowned Mexican architect Luis Barragán. Ring the bell to get a tour of the beautifully austere interior.

4 San Agustín de las Cuevas Proceeding west on Hidalgo, toward the end of the next block enter the grounds of the Parroquia de San Agustín de las Cuevas (☎ 5573-2373; ☼ 6am-6pm) on your left. Dating from the 1600s, the church features an oddly modernist contemporary altar, no doubt owing to Barragán's influence. Exit through the woodsy atrium which fronts the church.

5 Jardín Principal You exit onto Tlalpan's delightfully compact main plaza, centered on the sort of cute little gazebo that graces so many Mexican towns. Stop for coffee at Café

WALK FACTS

Start Av San Fernando at Calzada de Tlalpan
End Parque Nacional Fuentes Brotantes
Distance 2km
Duration 3 hours
Fuel stops Various restaurants and cafés on Jardín Principal

TRANSPORTATION: TLALPAN

- Metrobus – take the Insurgentes metrobus to the end of the line, and catch a pesero to Tlalpan (see below). By the time your read this, the metrobus line may be extended all the way to Tlalpan, making the transfer unnecessary.
- Bus – from the metrobus terminus, cross Altamirano and catch a southbound 'Villa Coapa' pesero. Get off at Calle Juárez, and walk three blocks south to Tlalpan's main square.

de La Selva or lunch at any of the restaurants behind the arched *portales* on the plaza's north side.

6 Casa Frissac On the far (west) side of the plaza, go through a formidable arched brick gateway to the Casa Frissac. Built by prerevolutionary oligarch Jesús Pliego, the handsome mansion today hosts concerts and art exhibits. A pathway weaves through the hilly grounds; note the tiled minaret on the other side of the far wall.

7 Government buildings At the bottom of the main square, you'll see the Edificio Delegacional, the administrative seat of Mexico City's largest borough. Take a moment to study the murals on the building's facade, which illustrate Tlalpan's history. Glyphs around the entryway refer to the indigenous tribes that populated the region.

8 Cocktails and History Across the street (to your left as you're facing the town hall),

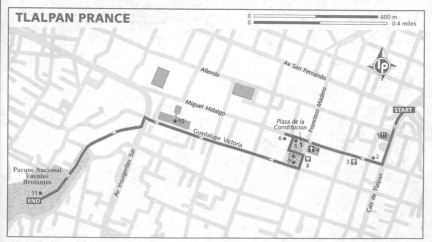

TLALPAN PRANCE

pop into the Cantina La Jalisciense (p165), a favorite local watering hole, and order a 'bull,' a refreshing vodka cocktail. Next door you'll find the Museo de Historia de Tlalpan (p109), with excellent historical exhibits.

9 Market Across the street from the history museum and directly behind the town hall is the Mercado de la Paz, the central market building. Take a wander amid the busy stalls, perhaps stopping to quaff a fresh-squeezed juice or to admire the hills of *moles* being sold.

10 Seminary Exit the market on the south side, then proceed west along Guadalupe Victoria, flanked by attractive buildings. Two blocks down, past Calle Abasolo, you'll see the imposing Seminario Mayor on your right, faced with maroon *tezontle* stone. Swarming with kids in red-and-white uniforms, this parochial school is definitely 'old school.'

11 Spring Time Reaching Av Insurgentes, take the footbridge over the busy thoroughfare. At the bottom, proceed to the next corner and turn right. The street winds uphill, past several food stalls, eventually entering the Parque Nacional Fuentes Brotantes (☎ 5424-5981; ☾ 6am-6pm), a national park built around natural springs. At the top of the trail, about 1km southwest of Av Insurgentes, is a large reservoir inhabited by ducks.

XOCHIMILCO & AROUND

Shopping p130; **Drinking** p166

Almost at the southern edge of the Distrito Federal, this network of canals flanked by gardens is a vivid reminder of the city's pre-Hispanic legacy. Xochimilco is famous for its *chinampas*, where the indigenous inhabitants grew their food. Remnants of these 'floating gardens' are still in use today, as are the waterways, even if the focus has shifted from agriculture to tourism. Gliding along the canals in a fancifully decorated *trajinera* (gondola) is an alternately tranquil and festive experience that may seduce even the most jaded traveler.

As if that weren't reason enough for an excursion, Xochimilco boasts one of the city's best art museums, the Museo Delores Olmedo Patiño. There's also a bustling public market and a handful of visitor-friendly *pulquerías* (drinking venues serving *pulque*).

A range of other attractions, including an ecological park, can be found in the surrounding area. To reach the Nativitas and Zacapa *embarcaderos* (boat landings), some 2km southeast of central Xochimilco, board a 'Galeana' pesero southbound on Ramírez del Castillo, a block west of the plaza. This or a 'Tulyehualco' pesero from the same place will take you to the Museo Arqueológico.

See the Directory chapter for locations of information modules in Xochimilco (p260).

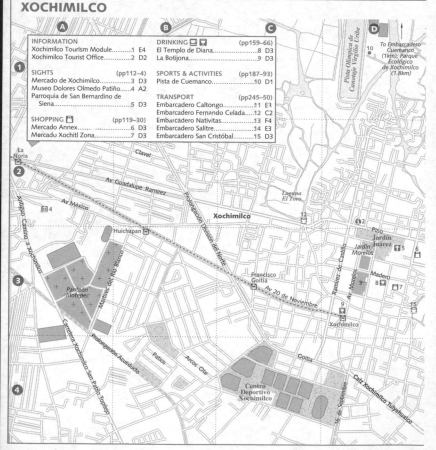

XOCHIMILCO

INFORMATION	
Xochimilco Tourism Module	1 E4
Xochimilco Tourist Office	2 D2

SIGHTS	(pp112–4)
Mercado de Xochimilco	3 D3
Museo Dolores Olmedo Patiño	4 A2
Parroquia de San Bernardino de Siena	5 D3

SHOPPING	(pp119–30)
Mercado Annex	6 D3
Mercado Xochitl Zona	7 D3

DRINKING	(pp159–66)
El Templo de Diana	8 D3
La Botijona	9 D3

SPORTS & ACTIVITIES	(pp187–93)
Pista de Cuemanco	10 D1

TRANSPORT	(pp245–50)
Embarcadero Caltongo	11 E3
Embarcadero Fernando Celada	12 C2
Embarcadero Nativitas	13 F4
Embarcadero Salitre	14 E3
Embarcadero San Cristóbal	15 D3

To Embarcadero Cuemanco (1km); Parque Ecológico de Xochimilco (1.8km)

MUSEO DOLORES OLMEDO PATIÑO
Map pp112–13

☎ 5555-1221; Av México 5843; admission M$40, Tue free; ⏰ 10am-6pm Tue-Sun

Possibly the most important Diego Rivera collection of all belongs to the Olmedo Patiño museum, ensconced in a peaceful 17th-century hacienda 2km west of central Xochimilco.

Dolores Olmedo Patiño, who resided here until her death in 2002, was a socialite and a patron of Rivera. The museum's 144 Rivera works – including oils, watercolors and lithographs from various periods – are displayed alongside pre-Hispanic figurines and folk art. Another room is reserved for Frida Kahlo's paintings, including an especially anguished self-portrait depicting her spine as a stone column broken in several places. Outside

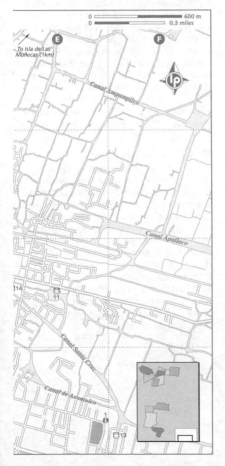

the exhibit halls, you'll see xoloitzcuintles, a pre-Hispanic hairless canine breed, roaming the estate's extensive gardens.

To get here take the Tren Ligero (light rail) from metro Tasqueña and get off at La Noria. Leaving the station, turn left at the top of the steps, walk down to the street and continue to the intersection with the footbridge. Here turn a sharp left, almost doubling back on your path, onto Antiguo Camino a Xochimilco. The museum is 300m down this street.

CANALS Map pp112–13
Xochimilco (Náhuatl for 'Place where Flowers Grow') was an early target of Aztec hegemony, probably due to its inhabitants' farming skills. The Xochimilcas piled up vegetation and mud in the shallow waters of Lake Xochimilco, a southern offshoot of Lago de Texcoco, to make fertile gardens called chinampas, which later became an economic base of the Aztec empire. As the chinampas proliferated, much of the lake was transformed into a series of canals. Approximately 180km of these waterways remain today and provide a favorite weekend destination for defeños. The chinampas are still under cultivation, mainly for garden plants and flowers such as poinsettias and marigolds. Owing to its cultural and historical significance, Xochimilco was designated a Unesco World Heritage Site in 1987.

On weekends a fiesta atmosphere takes over as the waterways become jammed with boats carrying large groups of families and friends. Local vendors and musicians hover alongside the partygoers serving food and drink, playing marimbas and taking photos with old box cameras. (Midweek, the mood is far more mellow.)

Hundreds of trajineras await passengers at the village's nine embarcaderos. Nearest to the center are Salitre and San Cristóbal, both 400m east of the plaza, and Fernando Celada, 400m west on Guadalupe Ramírez. Boats seat 14 to 20 persons; official cruise prices (M$140 to M$160 per hour) are posted at the *embarcaderos*. On Saturdays, Sundays and holidays, 60-person *lanchas colectivos* (collective boat taxis) run between the Salitre, Caltongo and Nativitas *embarcaderos*, charging M$20 per passenger round-trip.

Fixed prices for food, drink and even music on the waterways are also posted at the *embarcaderos* – one tune costs M$25 on marimbas, M$50 *norteño* (northern) style, and M$70 by mariachis! You can arrange for your *trajinera* to stop at Nativitas *embarcadero* for some shopping at its large *artesanías* (handicrafts) market.

While it is possible to get a taste of Xochimilco in an hour, it's worth going for longer; you'll see more and get a proper chance to relax.

XOCHIMILCO CENTER Map pp112–13

Though the canals are definitely the main attraction, Xochimilco village should not be overlooked. East of Jardín Juárez stands the 16th-century Parroquia de San Bernardino de Siena (7am-1pm & 4:30-8pm), with an elaborate gold-painted *retablo* (altarpiece) and a large tree-studded atrium. South of the plaza, the bustling Mercado de Xochimilco covers two vast buildings: the one nearer the Jardín Juárez has colorful flower displays and an eating annex for tamales and other prepared foods, while the one nearer the train station sells mostly produce and household goods, with a few pottery stalls.

PARQUE ECOLÓGICO DE XOCHIMILCO off Map pp112–13

☎ 5673-8061; Periférico Oriente 1; adult/senior & child M$20/5; 9am-6pm

Despite Xochimilco's Unesco World Heritage status, encroaching urbanization and illegal settlement along the canals continue to strain this unique habitat. At least one endemic species of the zone, the *axolotl* (a fishlike salamander) is in danger of extinction. Thus in 1991 the Ecological Park of Xochimilco was established, about 3km northeast of downtown Xochimilco, both to recover the fragile ecosystem and to provide a retreat for stressed-out urbanites.

Covering some 2 sq km, the protected area comprises a botanical garden and artificial lakes, home to a variety of waterbirds. Stroll the pleasant pathways, or rent a bicycle or a pedal boat for more extensive exploration. In the park's southeast corner, *chinampas* have been set aside to demonstrate traditional indigenous cultivation techniques. A visitors center has displays on plants and birds.

Trajineras departing from Embarcadero Cuemanco, 2km west of the park entrance, ply this lower-key section of the canals.

To reach Parque Ecológico de Xochimilco, take the Tren Ligero to the Periférico station. Exit on the Xochimilco-bound side, then go through the tunnel that underpasses the Periférico freeway. Emerging from the tunnel, turn right and walk to where you catch a 'Cuemanco' pesero; the park entrance is a 10-minute ride.

ISLA DE LAS MUÑECAS

For a truly surreal experience, hire a *trajinera* to the Island of the Dolls. Whatever festive mood you may have set out with will turn to dread approaching this remote spot, where thousands of dolls, many partially decomposed or missing limbs, hang from trees and rafters. The installation was created by recently deceased island resident Don Julián, who fished the playthings from the canals to mollify the spirit of a girl who had drowned nearby. The best departure point for the four-hour round-trip is the Cuemanco landing, near the Parque Ecológico de Xochimilco.

CUICUILCO

One of the oldest significant remnants of pre-Hispanic settlement within the DF, Cuicuilco (Map pp42–3; ☎ 5606-9758; Insurgentes Sur; admission free; ☷ 9am-5pm) echoes a civilization that stood on the shores of Lago de Xochimilco as far back as 800 BC. In its heyday in the 2nd century BC, the 'place of singing and dancing' counted as many as 40,000 inhabitants and rivaled Teotihuacán in stature. The site was abandoned a couple of centuries later, however, after an eruption of the nearby Xitle volcano covered most of the community in lava.

The principal structure is a four-tiered circular platform, 118m wide and 23m high, faced with volcanic-stone blocks. Atop the building are the remains of an altar, evidence that Cuicuilco was some kind of ceremonial center for an organized, priest-dominated society. (Earlier temples in the Valle de México were thatch-roofed affairs on low earth mounds.)

Set amid a park studded with cacti and shade trees, the platform can be easily scaled for sweeping views of the southern districts, including the formidable Xitle. The site hosts a small museum.

The archaeological site is set just back from the east side of Av Insurgentes, just over 1km south of the southern section of the Ciudad Universitaria.

To get to Cuicuilco, take the Insurgentes metrobus to the end of the line, then cross Altamirano to catch a southbound 'Villa Coapa' pesero. You'll see the entrance to the Cuicuilco archaeological park just south of the Periférico freeway.

TLATELOLCO

The northern district of Tlatelolco seems like a nondescript residential area whose most prominent feature is a series of low-income housing blocks. But beneath the surface is evidence of a stormy history.

The excavated remains of a major ceremonial complex attest to the zone's prominence in pre-Hispanic times, when it occupied an island in the lake. Tlatelolco was the site of the iconic clash between Cortés and Cuauhtémoc that forged modern Mexico.

Four and a half centuries later, more blood was spilled as government forces cracked down on protesters in 1968. This incident is extensively documented in a brand-new museum and cultural center, which also houses a cache of canvasses by some of Mexico's most important artists.

PLAZA DE LAS TRES CULTURAS
Map pp42–3

☎ 5583-0295; cnr Eje Central Lázaro Cárdenas & Flores Magón; admission free; ☷ 8am-5:30pm; ☷ Trolleybus 'Central Autobuses del Norte'
So named because it symbolizes the fusion of pre-Hispanic and Spanish roots into the Mexican mestizo identity, the Plaza of the Three Cultures displays the architectural legacy of three cultural facets: the Aztec pyramids of Tlatelolco, the 17th-century Spanish Templo de Santiago and, on the south side, the modern tower that now houses the Centro Cultural Universitario. A calm oasis north of the city center, the plaza is nonetheless haunted by echoes of its turbulent history.

Recent archaeological finds have altered long-held views about Tlatelolco's history. According to the conventional version, Tlatelolco was founded by an Aztec faction in the 14th century on a separate island in Lago de Texcoco and later conquered by the Aztecs of Tenochtitlán. But a pyramid excavated on the site in late 2007 actually predates the establishment of Tenochtitlán by as much as 200 years. All agree, however, that Tlatelolco was the scene of the largest public market in the Valle de México, connected by causeway to Tenochtitlán's ceremonial center.

During the siege of the Aztec capital by the Spaniards, Cortés defeated Tlatelolco's defenders, led by Cuauhtémoc. An inscription about that battle in the plaza translates: 'This was neither victory nor defeat. It was the sad birth of the mestizo people that is Mexico today.'

Tlatelolco is also a symbol of modern troubles. On October 2, 1968, 300 to 400 student protesters were massacred by government troops on the eve of the Mexico City Olympic Games (see the boxed text, p21). The area subsequently suffered some of the worst damage of the 1985 earthquake when apartment blocks collapsed, killing hundreds.

You can view the remains of Tlatelolco's main pyramid-temple and other Aztec buildings from a walkway around them. Like the Templo Mayor of Tenochtitlán, Tlatelolco's main temple was constructed in stages, with each of the seven temples superimposed atop its predecessors. The double pyramid on view, one of the earliest stages, has twin staircases which supposedly ascended to temples dedicated to Tláloc and Huizilopochtli. Numerous calendric glyphs are carved into the outer walls. Recognizing the significance of the site, the Spanish erected the Templo de Santiago here in 1609, using stones from the Aztec structures as building materials. Just inside the main (west) doors of this church is the baptismal font of Juan Diego, the man to whom Nuestra Señora de Guadalupe appeared in 1531 (see right).

CENTRO CULTURAL UNIVERSITARIO TLATELOLCO Map pp42–3

☎ 5597-4061; www.tlatelolco.unam.mx; Flores Magón 1; admission M$20; ☼ 10am-6pm Tue-Sun

Inaugurated in 2007, the Centro Cultural Universitario Tlatelolco occupies the former Foreign Relations Secretariat building (the agency has since moved to the Plaza Juárez complex on the Alameda Central). A component of the UNAM, the cultural center contains two interesting permanent exhibits. The Colección Andrés Blaisten, on the first floor, comprises the largest privately owned collection of Mexican 20th-century art, with over 650 paintings, prints and sculptures by both obscure and famed artists such as Rufino Tamayo, María Izquierdo and Juan Soriano. Downstairs, the Memorial del 68 both chronicles and memorializes the 1968 student massacre at Tlatelolco (p21). Through film clips, newspaper articles, photos, posters and numerous taped interviews with leading intellectuals (in Spanish), the exhibit evokes the mood of the times and follows the sequence of events leading up to the government-sponsored slaughter of hundreds of student protesters on October 2.

LA VILLA DE GUADALUPE

La Villa de Guadalupe encompasses Mexico's most important shrine, the Basilica de Guadalupe. According to legend, it was here that Mexico's beloved saint, the Virgin of Guadalupe, appeared to the indigenous peasant Juan Diego. It is an annual pilgrimage site for millions of Mexicans, necessitating an elaborate infrastructure to accommodate them. In addition to the modern big-top basilica, the pilgrimage complex is a veritable theme park of religious architecture, gardens and shrines, surrounded by a warren of vendor stalls with all manner of Guadalupe iconography and snacking options. Easily accessible from the center of town by bus or metro, 'La Villa' should be visited by anyone wanting to tune in to Mexico's spiritual wavelength.

BASÍLICA DE NUESTRA SEÑORA DE GUADALUPE Map pp42–3

☎ 5577 6022; www.virgendeguadalupe.org.mx; Plaza de las Américas 1; ☼ 6am-9pm; Ⓜ La Villa-Basilica

In December 1531, as the story goes, an indigenous Christian convert named Juan Diego stood on Cerro del Tepeyac (Tepeyac Hill), site of an old Aztec shrine, and beheld a beautiful lady dressed in a blue mantle trimmed with gold. She sent him to tell the bishop, Juan de Zumárraga, that he had seen the Virgin Mary, and that she wanted a shrine built in her honor. But the bishop didn't believe him. Returning to the hill, Juan Diego had the vision several more times. After the lady's fourth appearance, her image was miraculously emblazoned on his cloak, causing the church to finally accept his story, and a cult developed around the site.

Over the centuries Nuestra Señora de Guadalupe came to receive credit for all manner of miracles, hugely aiding the acceptance of Catholicism by Mexicans. Despite the protests of some clergy, who saw the cult as a form of idolatry with the Virgin as a Christianized version of the Aztec goddess Tonantzin, in 1737 the Virgin was officially declared the patron of Mexico. Two centuries later she was named celestial patron of Latin America and empress of the Americas, and in 2002 Juan Diego was canonized by Pope John Paul II. Today the Virgin's image is seen throughout the country, and her shrines around the Cerro del Tepeyac are the most revered in Mexico, attracting thousands of pilgrims daily and hundreds of thousands on the days leading up to her feast day, December 12 (see p13). Some pilgrims travel the last meters to the shrine on their knees.

By the 1970s the old yellow-domed basilica, built around 1700, was swamped by worshipers, so the new Basílica de Nuestra Señora de Guadalupe was built next door. Designed by Pedro Ramírez Vázquez, it's a vast, round, open-plan structure with a capacity for over 40,000 people. The image of the Virgin hangs above and behind the main altar, with moving walkways to bring visitors as close as possible.

Stairs behind the Antigua Basílica (Old Basilica) climb about 100m to the hilltop Capilla del Cerrito (Hill Chapel), where Juan Diego had his vision, then lead down the east side of the hill to the Parque de la Ofrenda, with gardens and waterfalls around a sculpted scene of the apparition. Continue on down to the baroque Templo del Pocito, a circular structure with a trio of tiled cupolas, built in 1787 to commemorate the miraculous appearance of a spring where the Virgin of Guadalupe had stood. From there the route leads back to the main plaza, re-entering it beside the 17th-century Capilla de Indios (Chapel of Indians).

MUSEO DE LA BASÍLICA DE GUADALUPE

☎ 5577-6022; admission M$5; ⏰ 10am-6pm Tue-Sun; Ⓜ La Villa-Basilica

The rear of the Antigua Basílica is now the basilica museum, with a fine collection of colonial art interpreting the miraculous vision. Various galleries on two floors display mostly large-scale works, including one of a procession along a causeway on Lago de Texcoco, one of the rare depictions of the lake before it was drained. The walls in the entry hall are covered with ex-votos – naive paintings on squares of metal that are done as an act of thanks for some miracle.

top picks

- Centro de Artesanías La Ciudadela (p123)
- Plaza del Ángel Shopping Arcade(p124)
- Condesa (p126)
- Bazar Sábado (p123)
- Perfumería de Tacuba (p122)

SHOPPING

Shopping in Mexico City has real treasure-hunt appeal, with a tantalizing combination of *artesanía* markets, street-side hawkers selling indigenous crafts, kitsch and quirky shops, and those old-fashioned stores with faded-cream paintwork and piled-high dusty shelves that appear to have been in the same family for generations. There is a flip side, of course: a sophisticated strut of designer shops (with a rare lack of pedestrians) which would seem happily at home in the center of Beverly Hills. Shopping malls do exist here as well, although they tend to be on more of a human scale than the anonymous concrete jungles you may be used to back home.

This city is also a good place to get things like shoe soles and cameras repaired – Mexicans prefer to mend things if they are mendable, rather than throw them away – and plenty of small street-corner workshops supply this need.

In the Centro Histórico, in particular, shops tend to be grouped together according to what they are selling. This drives prices down, saving you both time and money, and is very convenient if you are seeking something specific.

Given the diversity and surprise appeal of the shopping experience here, aim to approach your consumer experience unhurried and with an open mind and prepare to be rewarded by a truly rich experience.

SHOPPING AREAS

Mexico City's shopping map is fairly well-defined between swish and expensive, cutting edge and trendy, ordinary and everyday, and cheap, cheerful essentials.

If you're after top-designer threads, have an amble around Polanco where you can flash your gold card at Armani, and similar.

Condesa has mid-priced interesting and quirky shops, galleries, boutiques and craft outlets, particularly near the Parque Mexico and northwest around Roma.

The Zona Rosa is a shopping hotchpotch of gay accessory stores, quality shoes, Spanish chain-stores, great antique and craft markets and the occasional brash or dated boutique (where polyester reigns supreme and prices are rock-bottom).

Another shop-happy district is the Centro Histórico, especially the streets around the Zócalo and the Alameda Central, where you'll find clusters of shops all offering one particular type of merchandise, sometimes filling whole blocks, or more. In Plaza Santo Domingo, for instance, scribes peddle decorative custom-made invitations and announcements.

If you can take the clamor and the crowds, Mexico City's craft markets and bazaars may be the most memorable shopping experience of all (see the boxed text, p123)

top picks

SHOPPING STRIPS

- Av Presidente Masaryk (Map p84) in Polanco is designer-shop heaven for the cash-flush customer.
- Av Francisco Sosa (Map p95) in Coyoacán is best known for its stunning colonial architecture, but is also home to an increasing number of fascinating shops.
- Londres (Map pp74–5) in the Zona Rosa has the best selection of *tiendas*.
- Pasaje Polanco (Map p84) in Polanco is flanked by intriguing small boutiques.
- Plaza San Jacinto (Map p101) in San Ángel is surrounded by one-offs shops and galleries.

OPENING HOURS

Most stores are open from 9am to 7pm, Monday to Saturday, although some more traditional shops close at 2pm Saturday. Stores in malls are often open on Sunday.

CENTRO HISTÓRICO

Shopping in the historic center can be fascinating or daunting, depending on your viewpoint and map-reading ability. One moment you can be on a wide shopping street next to looming department stores, the next amid a *medina*-style street-life frenzy of food vendors, market stalls, manic traffic and no discernable way to cross the road. Approach it all with an open mind and zipped-up money belt and you should have fun. Don't miss the scribes who set up under the arches in Plaza Domingo, reflecting an ancient tradition that the computer age has yet to steamroller into oblivion.

ARTE MEXICANO PARA EL MUNDO
Map pp48–9   Artesanía
☎ 5521-3424; Monte de Piedad 11; ⏱ 9am-7pm Mon & Tue, to 8pm Wed-Sun; Ⓜ Zócalo
Explore three floors of quality arts and crafts from all over Mexico, including rugs, jewelry, pottery and delightful shocking-pink papier-mâché dolls with plenty of glitter and attitude. The first floor has an excellent bookshop with coffee-table-style tomes on Mexican design, cookery and architecture. There's a cafeteria on the sixth floor with sweeping Zócalo views.

NACIONAL MONTE DE PIEDAD
Map pp48–9   Artesanía
☎ 5278-1700; Monte de Piedad 7; Ⓜ Zócalo
Sells traditional black pottery from Oaxaca, including intricately-carved pots and masks. The shop is located to the right of this lofty historical arcade, where several of the galleries double as pawnshops, with silverware and jewelry at excellent prices. Seek out Salon Esmeralda halfway down on your left; the items with a color tag are secondhand.

PALACIO DE LAS MÁSCARAS
Map pp48–9   Artesanía
☎ 5529-2849; Allende 84; Ⓜ Garibaldi
The use of masks in Mexico dates from 3000 BC, when they were used by priests to summon the power of deities in pre-Hispanic Mexico. If you are interested in summoning a couple into your suitcase, there are an astonishing 5000-plus to choose from, most of which are produced in Guerrero state.

AMERICAN BOOKSTORE Map pp48–9 Books
☎ 5512-0306; Bolívar 23; Ⓜ Allende
Don't expect a Dalton's, but this place does have a small and classy selection of novels and books on Mexico in English, plus a solid range of Lonely Planet guides and some maps.

LIBRERÍA MADERO Map pp48–9   Books
☎ 5510-2068; Madero 12; Ⓜ Allende
If you read Spanish and are interested in boning up on Mexican history, art and architecture, you will find plenty of exquisitely bound and illustrated books to peruse here, including secondhand editions.

LA BODEGUITA DEL HABANO
Map pp48–9   Cigars
☎ 5510-1750; Bolívar 43; Ⓜ San Juan de Letrán
An old-fashioned cigar shop run by an old-fashioned lady. One Cuban cigar will cost you M$70, a handsome box of 25, more like M$500. All the big puffers are here, including Montecristo and Quintero.

EL PALACIO DE HIERRO
Map pp48–9   Department Store
☎ 5278-9905; Av 20 de Noviembre 3; Ⓜ Zócalo
This is the city's smartest chain with all the standard departments, including cosmetics and perfumes, men's and women's fashion, shoes, accessories and homewares at prices that shouldn't blow your budget. Across the street is Liverpool (☎ 5133-2800; Venustiano Carranza 92), a similar breed of department store, only slightly cheaper; the building also charmingly dates from the '30s. Both stores have other branches in the city, but these two are the biggest and the best.

DULCERÍA DE CELAYA Map pp48–9   Food
☎ 5521-1787; Av 5 de Mayo 39; ⏱ 10:30am-7pm; Ⓜ Allende
This traditional candy store has been serving its sweet treats since 1874. Indulge in a few candied fruits or coconut-stuffed lemons or, at the very minimum, check out the ornate building which creates the perfect frame for the colorful confectionery display.

SUPER SOYA Map pp48–9   Food
☎ 5521-5073; República de Brasil 11; Ⓜ Zócalo
A whole-foods shop where you can find all the normal healthy fare, including various nutty breads and biscuits, soy products, natural vitamins and minerals, sugarless sweets and invigorating power snacks for keeping up your pavement-pounding momentum.

TARDAN Map pp48–9   Hats
☎ 5512-3902; Plaza de la Constitución; Ⓜ Zócolo
A wonderfully old-fashioned hat shop with 1950s-style custard colored walls and shelves displaying every kind of hat imaginable, including the ubiquitous sombrero (to greet the folks back home), safari hats, panamas, trilbies, tweed caps, straw and cowboy hats.

top picks

BOOKSTORES

- Gandhi (right)
- Palacio de Bellas Artes (opposite)
- Centro Cultural Bella Época (p126)
- Cafebrería el Péndulo (p124)

LA PALESTINA Map pp48–9   Leather Goods

☎ 5512-8129; Av 5 de Mayo 20; Ⓜ Allende

You can pick up a magnificent saddle here, plus the leather Stetson to complete the yee-ha look. Altogether tamer, but of superb quality, are the classic leather briefcases which are so much classier for your laptop than the black vinyl norm.

LE PARFUM Map pp48–9   Perfume

☎ 5512-6005; Motolinia 15; Ⓜ Allende

Essential aromatherapy oils, natural flower essences, various soaps (including one for insomnia), and chemical-free cosmetics are sold here, along with imitations of big-name perfumes from Givenchy, Dior and Lancôme.

PERFUMERÍA DE TACUBA
Map pp48–9   Perfume

☎ 5521-5912; Tacuba 13; Ⓜ Allende

This place has remained firmly in '50s mold, with its shelves of old-fashioned bottles containing perfume essences. You can pick up a 10g vial of perfume – a sniff at just M\$3.50. At that price it may be worth trying out a few more, with tantalizing names like 'honey', 'vogue', 'cappuccino' and, er, 'Christmas'.

FLORICENTRO Map pp48–9   Souvenirs

☎ 5542-6074; Venustiano Carranza 116; Ⓜ Zócalo

Mexicans love their vibrantly-colored artificial flowers. You may not be of the same persuasion but this place is superbly kitsch, with a display that includes fake fruit that you would never be tempted to bite into.

LAS FÁBRICAS DE MEXICO
Map pp48–9   Textiles

☎ 5542-7129; Pino Suárez 17; Ⓜ Zócalo

The name says it all, except what is so great about these fabrics is that they are 100% cotton. Tablecloths, blankets and, yes, all-cotton underwear can be purchased here, as well as a range of super soft babygros.

ALAMEDA CENTRAL & AROUND

This area flows seamlessly from the Centro Histórico with a similar combination of small (and grander) shops, teeming markets and squeeze-through narrow sidewalks. Get your bearings by standing in the massive forefront of the Palacio de Bellas Artes. Avenida Juárez across the way is a good place to start exploring, with its large, easily accessible bookshops and Sears department store; useful if you need to pick up any last-minute essentials (like some comfortable walking shoes).

FONART Map p64   Artesanía

☎ 5563-0171; Juárez 89; ☺ 10am-7pm Mon-Sat; Ⓜ Bellas Artes

The well-known government-run handicrafts shop displays beautiful wares from around the country, ranging from Olinalá lacquered boxes to Oaxacan *alebrijes* and blankets from Teotitlán del Valle. Prices are fixed and higher than you pay in the Ciudadela market around the corner, but the quality is undeniably up there as well. The larger, original branch (Map pp42–3) is out at Patriotismo 691, Colonia Mixcoac, between the Bosque de Chapultepec and San Ángel.

MUSEO DE ARTE POPULAR
Map p64   Artesanía

☎ 5510-2201; www.map.org.mx; Revillagigedo 11; Ⓜ Zócalo

Opened in 2006, this museum showcases the country's finest folk art and handicrafts, so expect high quality and matching prices at the gift shop, which sells handmade Mexican crafts from all over the country, including delicate silver filigree earrings and embroidered shirts and dresses from Chiapas.

GANDHI Map p64   Books

☎ 5510-4231; www.gandhi.com.mx; Juárez 4; Ⓜ Bellas Artes

This is your best overall bet for both English language and Spanish books. It has a well laid-out selection, including magazines, journals, greeting cards and a fairly extensive array of DVDs. There are several other smaller branches around town; check the website for the exact location.

BAZAARS & MARKETS

Tianguis Cultural del Chopo (Map pp42–3; Nepomuceno; 10am-4pm Sat; M Buenavista) A gathering place for the city's various youth subcultures. Punks, goths, metalheads and all the other urban tribes gravitate here each Saturday to buy and trade CDs, hear live bands and exchange ideas.

Casa del Obispo (Map p101; 11am-6pm Wed-Sat; M Miguel Ángel de Quevedo) Has a divine setting with its hacienda-style courtyard and central fountain. There are mainly jewelry and *artesanía* stores and prices tend to be comparable or slightly higher than the nearby Bazaar Sábado.

Bazar Sábado (Map p101; 11am-6pm Sat; M Miguel Ángel de Quevedo) If you are ready to shift your credit card into overdrive on classy crafts, jewelry, art work, sculpture and similar, then make a trip here your Saturday date. Don't miss the jewelry stall by the main entrance, where Rosalba Poulat makes her baubles in the same style as her father, who created jewelry for Frida Kahlo.

Mercado Insurgentes (Map pp74–5; 9.30am-7.30pm Mon-Sat, 10am-4pm Sun; M Insurgentes) Between Florencia and Amberes, and packed with crafts – silver, textiles, pottery, leather and carved wooden figures – but you'll need to bargain to get sensible prices.

Centro de Artesanías La Ciudadela (Map p64; 10am-6pm; M Balderas) A favorite destination for various good stuff from all over Mexico. Worth seeking out are Oaxaca *alebrijes* (whimsical representations of animals in wood) and the Huichol beadwork ranging from masks to bowls and jewelry. Prices are generally fair even before you bargain.

Bazar de la Roma (Map pp92–3; Sat & Sun; M Cuauhtémoc) This market has used and antique items, large and small: books, beer trays, posters and furniture. There is also a similar antiques and art market along Álvaro Obregón on the same days.

Bazar del Oro (Map pp74–5; Calle de Oro; Sat & Sun; Durango) This upscale street market between Insurgentes and Plaza Cibeles has clothing, gifts and an excellent eating section.

LA TORRE DE PAPEL Map p64 — Books

☎ 5512-9703; Filomeno Mata 6a; M Allende

There are a handful of souvenir books here, plus maps. Perhaps of more interest to news-hungry folk will be the English-language newspapers, including the *Financial Times*, the *Wall Street Journal* and the *Daily Telegraph* (the latter photocopied). You can also buy stamps, another bonus.

PALACIO DE BELLAS ARTES

Map p64 — Books

☎ 5512-2593; cnr Av Juárez & Eje Central; M Bellas Artes

Located on the mezzanine floor of this magnificent palace, this bookshop has a superb selection of art books in English and Spanish, as well as posters, cards and various nifty gift items.

BENE PASTA Map p64 — Food

☎ 5512-8012; Ayuntamiento 12; M San Juan de Letrán

Somehow you don't associate Mexico with homemade pasta, although this company has been going for some 100 years.

As you would expect, the pasta is wonderfully colorful: fusilli coils of red, purple, green and orange. If this sounds too much of an indigestible dazzle, they also sell traditional white, plus jars of homemade sauce.

LA EUROPEA Map p64 — Food

☎ 5512-6005; Ayuntamiento 21; M San Juan de Letrán

Stocks imported goodies from Spain including all variety of tinned seafood, like *mejillones* (mussels) and sardines, plus olives and sweet treats. There is also an excellent wine and spirits selection, including the ubiquitous tequila.

LA VINA DEL SOL Map p64 — Wine & Liquor

☎ 5512-3355; Ayuntamiento 14; M San Juan de Letrán

There are 100-plus tequilas to select from here, including grand reserves, gift packs with glasses and the more pedestrian plonk. Take a tequila maestro along, if you can, to help you make your selection, or ask the assistant nicely in your best Spanish.

ZONA ROSA, CUAUHTÉMOC & JUÁREZ

The Zona Rosa and surrounding neighborhoods are home to a potpourri of tacky, expensive and quality shops. You can update your hip weekend wardrobe, replenish your English lit library, stock up on cut-price underwear and peruse some seriously classy antique and art shops. The tree-lined streets west of Génova in the heart of the Pink Zone are a good place to start your shopoholic strolling.

ARTESANOS DE MEXICO

Map pp74–5   Artesanía

☎ 5514-7455; Londres 117; ✆ 10am-7pm Mon-Fri; Ⓜ Insurgentes

Elderly owner Antonio Frausto is a real charmer and will explain the origins of the intriguing items for sale here, which include furniture, masks, lacquered and painted trays, paintings and ceramic pottery. The prices are as good as the markets. Ask Antonio to show you the photo of him with Reagan in the '70s; it will make his day.

PLAZA DEL ÁNGEL SHOPPING ARCADE Map pp74–5   Antiques

Londres; ✆ 10am-8pm Mon-Fri, to 4pm Sat & Sun; Ⓜ Insurgentes

There are more than 40 stores here, between Calles Amberes and Florencia, selling high-end antique silver jewelry, paintings, ornaments and furniture mainly dating from the mid-to-late 19th century. On Saturdays the number of stallholders typically triples, as an antiques flea market expands onto the sidewalk with all the associated banter, barter and bargains; the best time to visit is around 11am; a smaller flea market takes place here on Sunday.

CAFEBRERÍA EL PÉNDULO Map pp74–5 Books

☎ 5208-2327; Hamburgo 126; Ⓜ Insurgentes

A branch of this classy local chain with the usual quietly bookish and elegant atmosphere. There are two levels with all the categories of books you could think of, including some English-language classics and novels. Arty greeting cards are also on sale, plus there's a small restaurant (p140).

ZINIK Map pp74–5   Boutique

☎ 5208-3747; Londres 101; Ⓜ Insurgentes

There are plenty of one-offs here if you are pencil thin and looking for urban chic fashion to dazzle them on the dance floor, including tit-tight tops, skimpy skirts, jeans and sequined (or similar) dresses. Top off the outfit with some killer multicolored boots.

MIXUP Map pp74–5   Music

☎ 0180-0006-4987; www.mixup.com.mx; Génova 76; Ⓜ Insurgentes

This music junkie chain-store has one of the biggest ranges of recorded music (both Mexican and international) in the city. Just south of here, if you are heading for the Insurgentes metro station, the sidewalk stalls that crowd the entrance include many vendors of pirated DVDs (average M$15) but there's always the risk of a dud.

DIONE Map pp74–5   Shoes

☎ 5514-5907; Hamburgo 124; Ⓜ Insurgentes

This Mexican shoe designer from Guadalajara creates classic shoes for women in the softest of leather. There are Spanish Pons Quintana boots here, as well as fellow Spaniard Baltarini's stylish line. Bags and wallets are also top notch; for the best deals head for the '50% off' rack at the back of the shop.

VIA SPIGA Map pp74–5   Shoes

☎ 5207-9224; Hamburgo 136; Ⓜ Insurgentes

One of four Via Spiga stores in the city all specializing in classic and high-fashion men's and women's shoes and boots, with imports from Brazil and Italy. Coordinate your look with a snazzy leather bag and belt.

PLAZA LA ROSA SHOPPING ARCADE

Map pp74–5   Shopping Center

Londres; Ⓜ Insurgentes

A manageable-sized shopping mall between Génova and Ambero, with stores including Men's Factory, Campanita children's wear, Diesel for the streetwise look, Nutrisa health food store and Sorrento for shoes. There's a Starbucks too for those homesick for their daily slug of latté.

PLAZA REFORMA MALL

Map pp74–5   Shopping Center

www.reforma222.com; Paseo de la Reforma 222; Ⓔ Metrobus Hamburgo

Opened in November 2007, this dramatic great slab of a building is home to all the usual international and local high street chains like C&A, Zara, Women's Secret, Bershka, Pull & Bear and, surprise surprise, yet another branch of the ubiquitous Sanborns.

SOMOS PLATA Map pp74–5 — Silverwork
☎ 5511-8281; Amberes 24; Ⓜ Insurgentes

All the silver jewelry on display here is by Mexican designers. There is a good choice of earring and necklace sets, mainly simple fine designs (rather than the chunky modern look). The same owner runs the adjacent shop of ornate silver ornaments for gathering dust on the mantelpiece.

MINIATURAS FELGUÉREZ
Map pp74–5 — Souvenirs
☎ 5525-0145; Hamburgo 85; Ⓜ Insurgentes

This is one souvenir you can fit in your luggage. These tiny figurines are well made and amusing and emulate the Italian *presepe* (nativity) style with scenes ranging from a group of mariachis to a cheerful family of naturists! There are thousands of individual pieces to choose from as well.

RIO BRAVO Map pp74–5 — Tailors
☎ 5514-0095; Hamburgo 175; Ⓜ Insurgentes

A classic tailor's which, with its wood-paneled interior and dapper service, is straight out of London's Jermyn Street. Choose from pure cashmere or slum it with a wool-and-cashmere mix. Expect to pay in the region of M$3500 for the privilege, with an approximate time span of 10 days from tape-measure day.

POLANCO

Polanco's Av Presidente Masaryk, lined with designer shops, has a global anonymity, especially when compared to the street market bustle of the center. All the big players are here, including Cartier, Louis Vuitton, Hermés, Mont Blanc, Hugo Boss and Dior, located on a stretch of a few blocks between Aristóteles and Moliere. There *are* options for less cash-flush customers, mainly heading the other direction on Masaryk between Aristóteles and Hegel and around the Parque Lincoln to the south.

The futuristic-looking Plaza Molière mall at Moliere and Horacio contains a branch of the classy El Palacio de Hierro department store dealing mainly in clothes, toys and cosmetics.

AMERICAN VINTAGE Map p84 — Boutique
☎ 5250-1348; Presidente Masaryk 169; Ⓜ Polanco

Vintage clothing surely never looked this good back then. Tucked into a corner inside the American Apparel boutique, there is a great selection of threads here, including '60s frocks, floral-print sweaters, Capri pants and Art Deco scarves.

MARINGO Map p84 — Boutique
☎ 800-627-4646;www.maringo.com; Presidente Masaryk 274; Ⓜ Polanco

At last. Somewhere on the presidential street that sells great fashion at a price that won't force you to take out an extra mortgage. The range is extensive and, although top designers like Carolina Herrera are represented, there are less costly fashions, as well as shoes and accessories.

SICARIO Map p84 — Boutique
Séneca 41; Ⓜ Polanco

Refurbish your indie weekend wardrobe here; this boutique specializes in fun, non-conformist garments, so you can expect lots of hippy-style flowing skirts and dresses, plus hats and fun accessories, most of which are real one-offs.

VILEBREQUIN Map p84 — Boutique
☎ 5282-0741; Plaza Zentro; Ⓜ Polanco

Top up your swimming trunks collection here, a French company with a sense of humor. They come with every imaginable design, including flowers, stripes, birds and flocks of sheep (handy for counting if you can't sleep). You can even buy an oh-so-cute matching towel.

CATIMINI Map p84 — Children
☎ 5281-0741; Presidente Mazaryk 350; Ⓜ Polanco

Stylish kiddies wear with top international names like Lili Gaufrette, Ikks, Kenzo and Osh Kosh and a range of cuddly to cool threads from 0 to 16 years, plus accessories.

LA VILLA DE MADRID
Map p84 — Food, Wine & Liquor
☎ 5281-3588; Alejandro Dumas 78; Ⓜ Auditorio

An institution in these parts, this is where homesick Spaniards come to stock up on

CLOTHING SIZES

Women's Clothing

Aus/UK	8	10	12	14	16	18
Europe	36	38	40	42	44	46
Japan	5	7	9	11	13	15
USA	6	8	10	12	14	16

Women's Shoes

Aus/USA	5	6	7	8	9	10
Europe	35	36	37	38	39	40
France only	35	36	38	39	40	42
Japan	22	23	24	25	26	27
UK	3½	4½	5½	6½	7½	8½

Men's Clothing

Aus	92	96	100	104	108	112
Europe	46	48	50	52	54	56
Japan	S		M	M		L
UK/USA	35	36	37	38	39	40

Men's Shirts (Collar Sizes)

Aus/Japan	38	39	40	41	42	43
Europe	38	39	40	41	42	43
UK/USA	15	15½	16	16½	17	17½

Men's Shoes

Aus/UK	7	8	9	10	11	12
Europe	41	42	43	44½	46	47
Japan	26	27	27½	28	29	30
USA	7½	8½	9½	10½	11½	12½

Measurements approximate only, try before you buy

their Manchego cheese and Marques de Cáceres vintages. You can also buy imported *fino* (sherry) here, plus a wide range of tequilas and liquors.

PASAJE POLANCO Map p84   Shopping Center
Pasaje Polanco; Ⓜ Polanco
This classy pedestrian walkway between Musset and Anatole France is flanked by equally sophisticated boutiques. One of the more unusual is Casa Toroda (☎ 5281-6097; local 105), which has beautiful engraved glass plates from Senegal, Kenyan masks, and Brazilian jewelry embellished with turquoise and coral. Shoe addicts can drool over the exquisite soft-leather shoes and boots at Macarena Gutiérrez (☎ 5282-3209; local 21B) by the designer of the same name. Las Artesanías (☎ 5280-9515; local 360) has a large showroom of local crafts, including lacquer ware, woven textiles, leather items and silver jewelry at only marginally higher prices than elsewhere (given the location).

LA DIVINA Map p84   Wine & Liquor
☎ 5250-1546; Newton 136; Ⓜ Polanco
Enter the revolving door to be confronted by shelf upon shelf of more than 200 different brands of tequila, plus everything else guaranteed to put hair on your chest. There are fancy gift packs available and, if the garish signs are to be believed, everything is permanently cut price.

CONDESA

Condesa has a hip Greenwich Village feel about it, with its leafy streets, sidewalk cafés and enticing combo of trendy boutiques and quirky shops. The dilemma is trying to actually *locate* anything, as there is nothing as predictable as a Condesa High Street. Instead, shopping is a constant adventure, or frustration, with the shops arbitrarily located throughout the neighborhood. Don't forget your map and be prepared to ask for directions or walk in ever-despairing circles, particularly around the *parques*.

CENTRO CULTURAL BELLA ÉPOCA
Map p88   Books

☎ 5276-7110; Tamaulipas 202; Ⓜ Patriotismo
A sprawling, but well laid-out, bookstore with all the categories you could possibly hope for, including an extensive Mexican and Spanish cookery section. Most of the books are in Spanish, but there are a few worthy classics (and similar) in English.

HEADQUARTERS Map p88   Boutique
☎ 5211-7389; Atlixco 118; Ⓜ Patriotismo
An artful store with a black ceiling and warehouse look selling the retro-chic fashion look, with Mexican brands like Reme Ritas and Sweet & Dandy cashing in on NaCo's success with their slogan-style T-shirts. The back of the store is a surprising flip into baby pink Japanese-style accessories by Guadalajara company Tatéi (www.tatei.com).

KUSS KUSS Map p88   Boutique
☎ 3547-3448; www.kusskussshop.com; Alfonso Reyes 123; Ⓜ Patriotismo
A funky small space selling NaCo T-shirts and sweatshirts, and shiny lacquered floral bags and flat pumps made by Mexican designers like Mauricio Eduardo and García Gutierrez, plus the classic Jelly shoes from Brazil.

ARE YOU A NACO?

It roughly translates as 'cracker,' meaning 'bad mannered, uneducated and lower class' (although it has been used to describe tacky nouveau riche types). Though traditionally a derogatory term, *naco* has lately been adopted by streetwise city folk who claim to admire the direct, uncomplicated iconography of everything from *lucha libre* characters to soft drink bottles. In urban chic terms, it means the hottest look in casual wear to hit the streets since the days of grunge. Founded by a couple of college pals and now counting Diego Luna (of *Y Tu Mamá También* and *Frida* fame) among investors, the NaCo clothing line concentrates on T-shirts emblazoned with an edgy or graphic message. These often relate to Mexican pop culture and have clever multiple meanings, like *Brown is the New White*, which actually refers to rice, not people. The line also includes sweaters and tracksuit jackets and is fast obtaining a global profile, with sales to the US booming and a possible partnership with fashionable Brazilian shoemaker Havana on the books. Check out the NaCo Miscelánea shop in Condesa and stock up on these oh-so-trendy T-shirts (below).

MILAGRO Map p88   Boutique
☎ 5286-5764; www.collection-milagro.com; Atlixco 38; Ⓜ Patriotismo
Designer Sandra Gutiérrez works with local artisans to create a natty line of tightly woven raffia and embroidered bags in brilliant colors and designs and all shapes and sizes, including one for your lap top. Also stocks original jewelry and belts.

NACO MISCELÁNEA Map p88   Boutique
☎ 5255-5286; Yautepec 126B; Ⓜ Patriotismo
This cheeky streetwear store is in the heart of Condesa. The first surprise is the size of the place: tiny, the walls papered with lurid photos of strung-up chickens. The logos vary from 1950s Mexican truck companies to Superman. There are also tweed caps and sweatshirts for sale.

BRIGUETTE Map p88   Chocolates
☎ 5286-3939; Fernando Montes de Oca 81; Ⓜ Patriotismo
Fabulous locally produced chocolates, featuring flavors such as tea, kiwi, lavender, marzipan and pistachio, mixed spices and creamy truffle. You can buy one or two or float away on a chocoholic cloud and pick up a couple of hundred grams of your favorites.

BODEGA DE QUESOS Map p88   Food
Fernando Montes de Oca 147; Ⓜ Chapultepec
Join the line of cheese-lovers at this corner shop, with its vast choice of national and international cheeses, including *requesón* from Chiapas, creamy Brie, Camembert, feta, gorgonzola, fresh mozzarella, parmesan and the costly cured Spanish Manchego (at M$436 per kilo).

GREEN CORNER Map p88   Food
☎ 5211-0276; Mazatlán 81; ⏲ 7:30am-10pm; Ⓜ Chapultepec
This natural food store stocks everything you could possibly shake a carrot stick at, including organic juices, tofu, nuts and dried fruits, whole-wheat pasta (a rarity here), organic spreads, jams and herbal teas. There's a restaurant, too.

ESRAWE Map p88   Interior Design
☎ 5255-9611; www.esrawe.com; Alfonso Reyes 58; Ⓜ Patriotismo
This local Mexican designer goes for the minimalist look, with his futon-style modular furniture in lime green and chocolate brown. The retro-style cabinets have hidden drawers, while the imported Naninarquina rugs from Spain give a whole new meaning to 'shag' rugs, with their incredible texture finishes in the shape of leaves and flowers.

ENTENAYA PLATA Map p88   Jewelry
☎ 5286-1535; Montes de Oca 47; ⏲ 11am-8pm Mon-Sat; Ⓜ Chapultepec
Seven talented local jewelry designers have their work on display here. Silver is combined with coral, turquoise, seeds and semiprecious stones and each piece has a detailed explanation. Credit cards are accepted, so come prepared to spend.

ZEMBU Map p88   Souvenirs
☎ 5211-7504; Michoacán s/n; Ⓜ Patriotismo
You can buy your hubble-bubble pipe direct from Cairo here (M$675), plus the flower and fruit tobaccos, including rose, kiwi, melon, lemon and grape (M$50). Alternatively, purchase a puff (or three) for around M$20.

top picks

ARTESANÍA & CRAFTS

- Arte Mexicano Para el Mundo (p121)
- Nacional Monte de Piedad (p121)
- Fonart (p122)
- Casa del Coleccionista (opposite)
- Rinconcito Maya (opposite)

ROMA

In comparison to Condesa, Roma is grid-system straightforward, with plenty of restaurant- and retail-therapy appeal spread along attractive leafy streets. Like its neighbor, Roma is interspersed with some stunning Art Deco architecture and is becoming increasingly well known for its dynamic art scene (p184).

CHÍC BY ACCIDENT Map pp92–3 Antiques
☎ 5514-5723; Colima 180; ☼ 10am-8pm Mon-Fri, to 5pm Sat; Ⓜ Insurgentes

Featured in stylish *wallpaper** magazine, French owner Emmanuel Picault has a fascinating collection of 20th-century furniture and objects here, ranging from a quirky giant walrus to a sumptuous abstractly designed quilt. Picault has published a book on contemporary furniture with Philippe Starck *(Book by Accident)*. The adjacent showroom, Sex By Accident, concentrates on the erotica in art and sculpture.

ARTE PREHISPÁNICO Map pp92–3 Artesanía
☎ 5574-7202; Córdoba 148; ☼ 11am-7pm Tue-Sat, Ⓜ Insurgentes

This is the place to pick up your Aztec mask or sculpture; the copies here are excellent, as good as those at any museum. Other *artesanías irresistibles* include the woven wraps from Chiapas and the reasonably-priced *Día de Muertos* figures from Michoacán.

LIBRERÍA TEOREMA Map pp92–3 Books
☎ 5525-2188; Álvaro Obregón 153; Ⓜ Insurgentes

One of several secondhand bookstores on this stretch, with shelves stretching as far as the eye can see, packed with dusty titles. Dig around (or ask the appropriately

elderly owner) where the English books are; there are a few, particularly cookbooks.

LEMUR Map pp92–3 Boutique
☎ 3547-2182; Jalapa 85; Ⓜ Insurgentes

This funky store sells original toys, clothes and accessories by brands like Insight and Modern Amusement, plus a streetwise range of slogan T-shirts, shiny bags, and made to stand out (and on) shoes and boots.

EL CIGARRITO Map pp92–3 Cigars
☎ 5511-8392; Oaxaca 116; Ⓜ Insurgentes

According to convivial owner Carlos, this is the only cigar store in Mexico City – indeed Mexico! – that carries such a wide range of *puros*, imported from the Dominican Republic, Honduras, Nicaragua and Cuba, plus local Mexican stock.

LA TRUFFE Map pp92–3 Food
☎ 5511-3949; Orizaba 101; Ⓜ Insurgentes

Lots of imported and local gourmet goodies, including cheese, wine, pasta, mustards, pickles, jams, dried chilies, organic marmalades and jams. La Truffe also organizes wine tasting events.

ELFOS Map pp92–3 Souvenirs
☎ 2454-3118; Guanajuato 202; Ⓜ Insurgentes

If you believe in fairies (it happens!), this shop will delight. There are shelves and shelves of models crafted in Alicante, Spain. They are fabulously made and up to 41cm high, choose from Dagowill (protector of children), Gaer (good for your love life), Dagda (for wealth and health) and many more for those seeking total ethereal coverage.

COYOACÁN

As one of the most charming neighborhoods in the city, Coyoacán is increasingly catering to its admiring visitors with intriguing small shops, which fit in well with the aesthetic appeal of the place. Some of the best are located around the central Jardín del Centenario.

ALEGRA Map p95 Artesanía
☎ 5658-4482; Malitzin 6; ☼ 11am-9pm; Ⓜ Viveros

A small space crammed with textiles, crafts and jewelry, including beaded bags, leather belts with colorful ceramic-painted buckles and unusual earrings and brooches decorated with tiny pressed flowers.

ARTESANÍAS SOLER ARUMI
Map p95   Artesanía
Francisco Sosa 349; Ⓜ Viveros
This hole-in-the wall sells classic and modern designed frames, bowls, plates, teapots, candlesticks – you name it – made out of pewter so shiny you can see your reflection.

CASA DEL COLECCIONISTA
Map p95   Artesanía & Antiques
☎ 5658-7099; Fransisco Sosa 1; Ⓜ Viveros
A treasure-trove of local crafts, including miniatures, silver jewelry and beaded bags. There are also antiques and collectables here, like gaudily-painted tin trays from '50s cantinas and brightly decorated gourds.

GANDHI Map p95   Books
☎ 2625-0606; www.gandhi.com.mx; Felipe Carrillo Puerto 6; Ⓜ Viveros
Yet another branch of this excellent bookshop with a solid selection of fiction and nonfiction with both English and Spanish titles. Gandhi also sells DVDs and magazines. Note that there are two more Gandhi branches in nearby San Ángel.

NALANDA LIBROS Map p95   Books
☎ 5554-7522; Centenario 16; ◷ 10am-7pm Mon-Fri Ⓜ Viveros
This well-established bookstore specializes in esoteric and religious books, with a healthy selection in English. There are DVDs of sacred music to put you in the mellow mood.

AYLLU Map p95   Boutique
☎ 5538-8564; Francisco Sosa 9; ◷ 11am-8pm; Ⓜ Viveros
This local designer has come up with a cool and comfortable line of women's fashion, using all-cotton fabrics in colors like salmon, Mediterranean blue and cream. Embroidered shawls complete the flowing summery look with the prices more off-the-peg than off-the-wall.

MINERALIA COYOACÁN Map p95   Jewelry
☎ 5659-5157; Ortega 32; ◷ 11am-9pm; Ⓜ Viveros
The name says it all; this shop has two showrooms lined by shelves of wonderful stones, painted seeds and semiprecious

top picks
FOOD & WINE

- Briguette (p127)
- Bodega de Quesos (p127)
- La Europea (p123)
- La Villa de Madrid (p125)

gems. Choose several different colored strings and buy the clasp separately to create a show-stopping original piece.

PASAJE COYOACÁN Map p95   Souvenirs
☎ 5659-2432; Cuauhtémoc; Ⓜ Viveros
A great browsing space if you have no idea what you are looking for but the peso purse is heavy. Peruse local pottery, woven and embroidered bags, straw and knitted hats, funky lights, rugs, candles, dried flowers and colorful reeds and furniture.

SAN ÁNGEL
Follow the shopping baskets here on Saturdays when the classy Bazar Sábado attracts the crowds, including arty types, for the original canvases displayed in the Plaza del Carmen and Plaza San Jacinto. The streets are also lined with vendors, selling everything from brightly colored woven baskets to intricately beaded bowls and decorative pieces.

CASA AZUL Map p101   Artesanía & Antiques
☎ 5550-3223; Plaza del Carmen 25; Ⓜ Miguel Ángel de Quevedo
Walk up the wide steps to the terrace and grand entrance of this colonial-style grand house, which today creates a fitting showcase for antiques and crafts. There is a beguiling combination of kitsch, historic and current day *artesanía* items spread over three large creaking rooms.

RINCONCITO MAYA Map p95   Artesanía
☎ 5424-5925; Plaza San Jacinto 3; ◷ 10am-6pm Sat; Ⓜ Miguel Ángel de Quevedo
These stunning quilts from Chiapas, brightly colored and hand stitched, all tell a folksy (or frightening) story. Plus there are blankets, shawls and other textiles from Yucatán, Guatemala and Honduras. The prices are up there, but so is the quality.

EL TALLER DEL MUEBLE

Map p95   Artesanía & Furniture

☎ 5616-6121; Madero 8a; ✆ 9.30am-8pm
Ⓜ Miguel Ángel de Quevedo

Despite the name, this shop sells far more than just furniture – which may not fit in your hand luggage. There are some unusual pottery and ceramic pieces, including folksy painted plates and cups, Aztec sculpture copies, wall hangings and unusual masks. Prices are fair.

GLOBAL BOOK Map p95   Books

☎ 5550 2383; www.globalbook.com.mx; Centro Comercial Plaza del Carmen; Ⓜ Miguel Ángel de Quevedo

A rare all-English-language bookshop with a solid collection of literature, bonkbusters, bestsellers, coffee-table tomes on art and design, children's books and travel guides, including Lonely Planet; includes a cafeteria.

PLAZA LORETO Map p95   Shopping Center

Altamirano 46; 🚍 Metrobus Doctor Gálvez

Plaza Loreto, a 600m walk south of Plaza San Jacinto, is an unusually attractive shopping mall converted from an old paper factory. Several patios and courtyards are set between the brick buildings and it's a lot more than just a place to shop. You'll find a miniamphitheater for free concerts and puppet shows; two multiscreen cinemas (one of them, Cinemanía, devoted to classic and art-house movies and endowed with a nice little lobby bar); a cabaret club, La Planta de Luz (p174); an excellent art museum (p102), and one of the city's best restaurants, Taberna de León p154). There are plenty of up-market shops as well, including boutiques and jewelers, plus a branch of Sanborns and the Mixup music store.

XOCHIMILCO Map pp112–13

The central market here is spread between two buildings: the older Xochitl Zona (Map pp112–13), which mainly sells food, plus several stalls selling pottery, piñatas, bags and backpacks and cheaper off the peg clothing, plus an annex (Map pp112–13), famed for its colorful flower market. There is a reasonable *artesanía* market which runs most of the length of the *embarcaderos* (boat landings).

top picks

- **El Cardenal** (p135)
- **El Bajío** (p147)
- **María del Alma** (p148)
- **Contramar** (p151)
- **Tierra de Vinos** (p151)
- **Águila y Sol** (p144)
- **Fonda El Refugio** (p140)
- **Taberna de León** (p154)
- **Lampuga** (p148)
- **Los Girasoles** (p136)

What's your recommendation? www.lonelyplanet.com/mexico-city

EATING

These days, Mexico City is a whole lot more than tacos and enchiladas. As internationally acclaimed chefs continually refine the art of fusing European and Asian styles with Mexican ingredients, the capital has become a significant port of call on the food and travel trail. Visitors can now choose from any number of fusion-fare restaurants, where auteur chefs forge exciting new recipes. Add to this a growing appreciation on the part of *defeños* (people native to DF) for foreign cuisines, and you've got a truly impressive panorama. In the Condesa neighborhood in particular, there's been a remarkable proliferation of exciting eateries of all styles, and on any given evening intrepid eaters can choose from fine French bistros, Argentine steakhouses, Mediterranean seafood purveyors, sushi houses and British pub grub. Not to mention those tacos and enchiladas.

Fusion and global cuisines aside, it's the traditional favorites that keep many coming back. What's prepared in the humblest *taquerías* (taco stalls), markets and lunch halls is often just as thrilling, minus the price tag or pretensions. *Taquerías,* both upscale (El Califa, p150) and down (El Borrego Viudo, p157), season their meaty morsels with the zestiest salsas imaginable. Tamales, the best of which are found inside markets or on the street (Tamales Chiapanecos María Geraldine, p153), are a unique delicacy – slowly simmered packages of cornmeal blended with savory sauces, pork or chicken, nuts and fruit and so on, invariably accompanied by a piping hot cup of the corn-based beverage called *atole*. Other traditional places specialize in *pozole,* a wonderful pork-and-hominy broth served with a table full of garnishes (La Casa de Toño, p157).

In addition, thousands of holes-in-the-wall put together traditional multicourse lunches (*comida corrida*) just like *abuelita* used to (Restaurant Dzib, p138). Market buildings are good places to look for these while *tianguis* (weekly street markets) customarily have an eating section offering tacos, *barbacoa* (Mexican-style barbecue) and quesadillas (cheese folded between tortillas and fried or grilled).

Good opportunities also exist for authentic international cuisine, with restaurants catering to the capital's sizeable Lebanese, Jewish, Japanese and Cuban communities. Restaurants in the Zona Rosa's growing Korean community are only just beginning to attract a wider audience, so the food remains avowedly Korean (U Rae Ok, p142).

Despite this extraordinary culinary bounty, many Chilangos prefer to spend their time in modern chain restaurants, where predictable menus make a sound, if unexciting, fallback. Branches of VIPS, Sanborns, Wings and California restaurants serve US-style coffee-shop fare and Mexican standards. International chains, from KFC to Starbucks are also well represented.

HISTORY & CULTURE

The first Spaniards to enter Moctezuma's grand city of Tenochtitlán found markets overflowing with many previously unseen foodstuffs, such as beans, squash, peanuts, vanilla, sweet potato, and of course, the maize that we call corn – the staple of the indigenous diet.

Half a millennium later, it's in the corn-based dishes that we see the vestiges of the pre-Hispanic diet and cooking methods. Corn was – and is – ground and made into tortillas, then cooked on a fired-clay platter known as a *comal* (these days, it's more likely to be made of metal). These edible utensils delivered bits of cooked foods into Mexican mouths. Corn was also made into tamales and filled with beans, fish, flowers, fruits and vegetables then wrapped in corn husks or banana leaves. It was even used to make drinks, such as the *atole* found on Mexico City street corners early each morning.

While Mexican ingredients certainly changed the way the rest of the world ate, in return the new settlers brought along their own fare. Before their arrival, the primary sources of protein in Mexico had been insects and small animals such as rabbits, the indigenous dogs, armadillos, possums, and a wide variety of fowl. The Spanish contributed cows, pigs, goats and sheep, adding both the animal's meat and their lard, milk and cheese. The result was an early fusion cuisine that resulted in the Mexican food we typically think of today.

HOW DEFEÑOS EAT

Following the centuries-old fascination with European culture, many Mexico City inhabitants wake up with a pastry and coffee or just dash off to work. For the millions who ride public transit, breakfast awaits outside the metro entrances and on nearly every street corner. Especially in the office zones of Colonia Cuauhtémoc and the Zona Rosa, it's hard to walk more than a block without some irresistible item popping up en route. Tamales filled with chicken or pork and red, green or *mole* sauce, then wrapped in corn husks or banana leaves, are hearty enough to keep you going for a few hours; stuffed into a large *bolillo* (bread roll), it's a super carb charge. Fresh-squeezed orange or carrot juices are never far away.

Although the lunch break isn't until much later, by mid-morning cafeterias like the ubiquitous Los Bisquets Obregón (p152), VIPs and Sanborns teem with people noisily chatting over *huevos a la mexicana* (eggs scrambled with finely minced tomato, onion and chili) and glasses of *café con leche* (coffee with milk).

Around 3pm, throngs of office workers step out for a cheap *comida corrida* – the modern substitute for the multicourse meals traditionally served at home when businesses shut down in the afternoon. At neighborhood *fondas* (small, often family-run eateries) an inexpensive *comida corrida* includes a choice of soups, followed by rice or pasta, then a selection of three or four mains (sometimes one of them is vegetarian). Finally, there's a small dessert that could be as ordinary as a lone marshmallow or a simple piece of cake. The cheapest meals frequently include a pitcher of *agua de fruta,* a blend of watered-down seasonal fruit juice and sugar. For executives who linger over their midday meal, traditional places like Café de Tacuba (p136) or El Cardenal (p135) in the Centro Histórico are popular. A tequila or two might even accompany these meals.

Back home in the evening, average Josés and Josefinas relax with a cup of coffee or chocolate and some rolls or pastries (often delivered by bicycle) before bed. Meanwhile, a more energetic, well-heeled bunch fill the trendy cafés and bistros of Colonia Roma or Condesa, or enjoy fine dining in Polanco.

After an evening on the town, rich and poor alike belly up to late-night taco stands like El Tizoncito (p150) or El Borrego Viudo (p157) for a half-dozen *taquitos al pastor* (tiny tacos topped with shavings of grilled roasted pork from a big skewered cone) before finally crawling home.

ALTA COCINA MEXICANA

Highly innovative and deeply pleasing to the eye and palate, Mexico's haute cuisine is causing a stir in international gastronomic circles. A new generation of chefs are boldly blending the world's great cuisines with the flavors and textures of both indigenous and post-conquest Mexico. Their philosophy of food, cooking and eating yields a plethora of dishes old and new.

Affluent Polanco is perhaps the foremost destination for the best of these exciting hybrids. At places like Pujol (p145), Izote (p146) and Águila y Sol (p144), fresh local ingredients such as avocado, cilantro, cactus paddle, squash blossom and *huitlacoche* (a mushroom that grows on corn) find their way into inventive versions of pastas, pesto, tempura and desserts. Another breed of chef prefers to refine the classics of the masses, much as modern composers borrow folk melodies for their symphonies. Classically updated versions of such common fare as *barbacoa, carnitas, mole* and enchiladas are best enjoyed at El Bajío (p147) or El Cardenal. Another innovation adds flair to the seminal dishes of a particular region, as at La Sabia Virtud (p149), whose Puebla-inspired dishes reflect centuries-old Spanish and indigenous blends, and María del Alma (p148), where uniquely Tabascan seafood and tamale recipes are perfected for the contemporary diner.

Mexico has recently come into its own in wine production as well, and most of these places maintain an extensive cellar of the best Mexican and international vintages to highlight their signature dishes.

STREET EATS

In Mexico City, the term 'eating out' can often be taken literally. Instead of going to restaurants, many Chilangos prefer to dine on the street, often standing up – and not just because it's invariably quicker and cheaper than eating in a restaurant. Some of the city's thousands of street stalls offer superior fare, and the most popular ones go on to become restaurants (though faithful fans might complain they lose something in translation!).

Besides the stationary vendors reviewed here, certain items can be found all over

CULINARY COURSES

There is no more excuse for producing blimp-sized burritos stuffed with anything that happens to be in the fridge. Just as Mexico City is fast gaining a reputation as an exciting culinary capital, so several reputable cooking schools and courses have been established where you can hone your tortilla and tamale-making skills and learn how to make traditional and more sophisticated Mexican dishes. Check the respective websites for current schedule and prices.

Centro Culinario Ambrosia (Map pp42–3; ☎ 5550-7843; www.ambrosia.com.mx; Av San Jerónimo 243) Cooking courses are held in a grand historic building, both for professional and amateur chefs and cooks. Courses in English were introduced in April 2008. There is also a restaurant on site where you can sample the service and dishes first-hand.

Cocinar Mexicano (off Map pp42–3; ☎ 739-395-0433; www.cocinarmexicano.com; Tepoztlán) One-week master classes in traditional and contemporary Mexican cuisine, with hands-on classes taught by Mexico's top chefs and village women. Run by a native New Yorker, Magda Bogin, who also incorporates cultural trips into the week and runs separate writing workshops.

Mexico Soul & Essence (Map p88; ☎ 5564-8457; www.mexicosoul&essence.com; Amsterdam 269) Can organize your culinary tour, including restaurant bookings and cooking courses.

Pujol (Map p84; ☎ 5545-4111; www.pujol.com.mx; Petrarca 254) This top restaurant offers regular cooking courses, usually covering five once-weekly sessions, with a total of 15 hours.

town. In the evening, tamales are delivered by bicycle, their arrival heralded by an eerie moan through a cheap speaker. You'll know the *camote* (sweet potato) man is coming by the ear-splitting steam whistle emitting from his cart, heard for blocks around. The same vendor offers delicious baked plantains, laced with cream on request.

VEGETARIANS & VEGANS

Mexico City is probably the best place in Mexico for vegetarians, and even serious vegans need not dismay. The capital's *mercados* (markets), *tianguis* (weekly street markets) and even supermarkets abound with some of the freshest and widest choices of fruits and vegetables anywhere. Aside from a few good vegetarian and organic restaurants (p155), the popular fusion places prepare some interesting salads and pastas. Vegetarians might also browse the appetizer lists for items like braised eggplant and mushrooms or steamed artichokes.

PRACTICALITIES
Opening Hours

There's always something to eat somewhere in Mexico City. In the Centro and Zona Rosa, a few cafeteria-type places stay open 24 hours. The most popular taco stands are open until 2am or 3am, closing barely long enough to wash everything down and start again by 10am or 11am the next morning. Even some

of the more upscale taco places in Condesa and Coyoacán feed the after-bar crowd.

Breakfast is served from 7am or 8am until 11am or noon. In Mexico City, the afternoon lunch, known as *comida,* is still one of the most important events in the day, and extends over a two- to three-hour period in the late afternoon. Anyone looking for a lunch menu before 2pm may have a hard time.

Business at the restaurants along the shady streets and plazas of Coyoacán, Condesa, Roma or Polanco ebbs and flows throughout the day. Some open for breakfast around 8am. Otherwise, service begins around 1pm. There's a slowdown about 5pm, but by 8pm or 9pm a reservation or an extended wait is necessary.

How Much?

It's easy to spend a fortune on eating in Mexico City, and sometimes it's worth it, but even Mexico's wealthiest residents realize that some of the best stuff can be consumed at inexpensive taco stands or at quesadilla grills in the street markets.

Two people savoring the latest Alta Cocina Mexicana or the better international dishes with wine and a couple of margaritas to start will easily spend M$500 or more per person.

At the better hotels and restaurants, expect to spend M$70 to M$120 for breakfast. Lunch with a set menu will run M$90 to M$200. In the small restaurants at the lower end, you can get by for M$30 for a plate of eggs, beans and tortillas, or M$35 to M$40 for a budget three-course *comida corrida.*

PRICE GUIDE

$$$	mains over M$130
$$	mains M$70-130
$	mains under M$70

Among the popular places of Condesa, pastas and salads go for M$70 to M$100, and a decent steak runs from M$180 to M$200. Late-night tacos will set you back M$15 to M$40 each, depending on the setting.

Drinks always take a bite out of the budget. A glass of wine will cost M$45 to M$80. By the bottle might be a better deal, with some starting at M$180 to M$200, but the better quality wines, both Mexican and imported, will rival the prices at any fine restaurant in the US or Europe.

CENTRO HISTÓRICO

The historic center is a great place to enjoy traditional Mexican dishes in elegant surroundings. In general, though, it's more of a daytime than evening destination, with many places only open for breakfast and lunch. Restaurant options tend to be sparse after dark, though a few places stay open till midnight and one, Café El Popular, around the clock.

Contrary to expectations, the recent restoration of the zone west of the Zócalo has not been accompanied by a wave of trendy restaurants, though many of the older establishments continue to flourish. You'll find some Mexican chains here as well, serving up reliable (if bland) variations on traditional fare. Working Chilangos tend to head for the set lunch and *torta* (Mexican-style sandwich in a bread roll tostada) places on Calle 5 de Mayo and República de Uruguay, as well as along pedestrian thoroughfares Motolinia and Gante.

Perhaps the quintessential Mexico City experience is dining or sipping cocktails overlooking the vast Zócalo with the Mexican *tricolor* waving proudly over the scene. The three upscale hotels overlooking the plaza offer abundant buffet breakfasts most days, and two new Zócalo restaurants – Puro Corazón and La Terraza – serve classic Mexican cuisine with the views.

EL CARDENAL Map pp48–9 Traditional Mexican $$$
☎ 5521-8815; Palma 23; dishes M$90-280;
ⓨ 8am-7pm Mon-Sat, to 7pm Sun; Ⓜ Zócalo

Possibly the finest place in town for traditional Mexican fare, El Cardenal is a family-run institution frequented by politicians and businessfolk – former Mayor López Obrador used to hold breakfast meetings here. The restaurant occupies three floors of a Parisian-style mansion with a pianist playing sweetly in the background. Breakfast is a must: a tray of just-baked sweet rolls and a pitcher of frothy, semi-sweet chocolate are a prelude to eggs, scrambled with *chilorio* (Sinaloa-spiced minced pork) or Puebla Hacienda style (garnished with *poblano* chili strips). For lunch, go for the oven-roasted veal breast, Oaxaca-style *chiles rellenos,* or in summer, *escamoles* (ant larvae, a much coveted specialty). Another branch is inside the Sheraton Centro Histórico.

RESTAURANTE CHON
Map pp48–9 Traditional Mexican $$$
☎ 5542-0873; Regina 160; dishes M$180; ⓨ lunch Mon-Sat; Ⓜ Pino Suárez

Pre-Hispanic fare is the specialty of this cantina-style restaurant. Sample maguey worms (in season), grasshoppers, wild boar, and other items that have gone from being customary fare on Mexican tables to gourmet delicacies. Fortino Rojas, Chon's adventurous chef, incorporates these primordial ingredients into dishes Moctezuma could never have imagined. How about deer meatballs in *huitlacoche* sauce, chrysanthemums filled with ant larvae, crocodile steaks laced with pumpkin seed sauce? (Note: armadillo, in danger of extinction, has been taken off the menu.)

LA CASA DE LAS SIRENAS
Map pp48–9 Contemporary Mexican $$$
☎ 5704-3345; República de Guatemala 32; mains M$160; ⓨ 8am-11pm Mon-Thu, to 2am Fri & Sat, to 7pm Sun; Ⓜ Zócalo

Housed in a 17th-century relic, this restaurant has a series of atmospheric salons on three floors connected by creaky staircases. However, the only real place to dine is the top-floor terrace overlooking the Plaza del Templo Mayor. It's an ideal perch to nibble on mushrooms simmered with chipotle chilies, stuffed chilies laced with walnut sauce, or other Oaxaca-influenced fare – along with a shot of tequila from the downstairs cantina's extensive selection. Service is spotty.

HOSTERÍA DE SANTO DOMINGO

Map pp48–9   Traditional Mexican $$$

☎ 5526-5276; Belisario Domínguez 72; mains M$70-180; ⏰ 9am-10pm; Ⓜ Allende

Whipping up classic Mexican fare since 1860, this hugely popular (though not touristy) restaurant has a festive atmosphere enhanced by chamber music. It's famous for its enormous *chiles en nogada* (M$180; large green chilies stuffed with meat and fruit, covered with a creamy white walnut sauce and sprinkled with red pomegranate seeds – representing the colors of the Mexican flag), an Independence Day favorite, served here year-round. Other recipes handed down through the generations include the *pechuga ranchera con nata* (chicken breast in cream laced with *chile pasilla*) and *frijoladas* (bean puree served over lightly fried tortillas). Formerly part of the Santo Domingo monastery, the ancient building features two floors of dining rooms, seasonally festooned with *papel picada* (doilies).

LOS GIRASOLES

Map pp48–9   Traditional Mexican $$$

☎ 5510-0630; Plaza Manuel Tolsá; dishes M$120-150; ⏰ 1pm-midnight Tue-Sat, to 9pm Sun & Mon; Ⓜ Allende

Beside the Museo Nacional de Arte, this fine restaurant specializes in *alta cocina mexicana*, with recipes contributed by some of the stars of the genre. The menu boasts an encyclopedic range of Mexican fare, from pre-Hispanic (grasshoppers), to colonial (turkey in tamarind *mole*), to contemporary (snapper fillet in rosehip salsa). Cozy salons, done up colonial style, tend to fill up with foreign tourists in the evening, while at lunchtime they may be occupied by legislators from the nearby Senate building. Try to get a table overlooking the Plaza Tolsá, or on the terrace adjacent to it.

CAFÉ DE TACUBA

Map pp48–9   Traditional Mexican $$

☎ 5518-4950; Tacuba 28; mains M$70-150; ⏰ 8am-11:30pm; Ⓜ Allende

Before the band there was the restaurant. A fantasy of colored tiles, brass lamps and oil paintings, this mainstay has served *antojitos* (traditional Mexican snacks or light dishes – literally 'little whims') since 1912. The food is overrated, but the atmosphere is just right for *pambazos* (filled rolls fried in chili sauce) or tamales with hot chocolate.

CASINO ESPAÑOL

Map pp48–9   Spanish & Traditional Mexican $$

☎ 5510-2967; Isabel La Católica 29; 4-course lunch M$93; ⏰ lunch Mon-Fri; Ⓜ Allende

The old Spanish social center, housed in a fabulous Porfiriato-era building, has a popular cantina-style eatery downstairs and an elegant restaurant upstairs. Stolid execs loosen their ties in the former for a long leisurely lunch, and the courses keep coming. Spanish fare, naturally, highlights the menu (Thursday there's *cocido madrileño*, a stew of chick peas and sausage), though *tacos dorados* (chicken tacos, rolled and deep fried) and *chiles en nogada* are equally well-prepared.

PURO CORAZÓN

Map pp48–9   Contemporary Mexican $$

☎ 5518-0300; Monte de Piedad 11; breakfasts M$65-95; ⏰ 8am-9pm; Ⓜ Zócalo

This new Zócalo option has heart-thumping views of the cathedral from its 6th-floor perch, as well as a less stodgy vibe than its hotel counterparts. There's a novel spin on home-grown ingredients like *pulque* (fermented maguey beverage) and *flor de calabaza* (squash blossoms). Watch the flag being raised as you dig into a *huitlacoche* omelet, or lowered while savoring a shrimp cocktail laced with tequila.

AL-ANDALUS

Map pp48–9   Middle Eastern $$

☎ 5522-2528; Mesones 171; dishes M$90-125; ⏰ 8am-6pm; Ⓜ Pino Suárez

Al-Andalus caters to the capital's substantial Lebanese community, serving shawarma, kebabs, kibbe (spiced lamb fritters), felafel and so on in a superb colonial mansion in the Merced market district. Dine in one of the wood-beamed halls or on a terrace overlooking the courtyard. After lunch, choose from a tempting array of baklavas and other syrupy pastries, then kick back with a hookah.

LA TERRAZA DEL ZÓCALO

Map pp48–9   Regional Mexican $$

☎ 5521-7934; Plaza de la Constitución 13, 6th fl; mains M$110-150; ⏰ 1-8pm Sun-Thu, to midnight Fri & Sat; Ⓜ Zócalo

With dining on a broad balcony overlooking the Zócalo toward the national palace, La Terraza makes a promising new alternative to the ho-hum hotel restaurants on

DRINKS (& GREAT FOOD!) IN THE CANTINA   Mauricio Velázquez de León

When it comes to food, our city has no match. It is said that *capitalinos* (as we are called) can eat breakfast, lunch and dinner in a different place in Mexico City for a year without ever repeating the venue. Urban myth? Maybe. But think about it. There are more than 20 million hungry souls in this city, so we munch day and night, enjoying our vibrant street-food culture, our endless collection of eateries *(loncherías, taquerías, torterías)* and our restaurants. But even this is hardly enough! We also eat in bars, especially our cantinas. And we eat very well, if I may say.

Cantinas have a long history in Mexico. They were once at the centre of every Mexican man's social life, a monument of machismo with a more than shady reputation. Legendary signs at the door of cantinas read 'No minors, no women, and no military staff.' Patrons drank on bare-wood tables with glass holders attached to its legs, in order to leave the surfaces clean to play dominoes. Tequila, *mezcal* and whiskey flowed freely, and food, when available, was terrible.

Today, these century-old cantinas retain their long wooden bars, bare-wood tables and extended stained mirrors. Most of their patrons are still male, but if there were a sign at the door it would read 'No Smoking.' Best of all, while a reputation for rough edges is maintained, cantinas are completely women friendly and have given tequila and beer an ideal companion: great food.

Most cantinas will offer free meals in return for drinks purchased. Food is served in small portions, called *botanas*, but it will keep coming as long as you keep ordering drinks. You can also order from the menu and eat as though you're in a traditional restaurant.

Here is a totally subjective list of cantinas worth a visit, thanks to their food, sense of history, or both.

- La Ópera (☎ 5512-8959; Av 5 de Mayo 10; ☯ 1pm-midnight Mon-Sat, to 6pm Sun; Ⓜ Allende) Many *capitalinos* will tell you to visit this elegant cantina (founded in 1870) to see the hole in the ceiling shot by Pancho Villa. But you may want to go to check out the delicious escargots in *chipotle*. The setting is atypically stylish for a cantina; gazing at the elegant chandeliers and velvet drapes you can travel back to a time when Mexico was in love with all things French.
- El Mirador de Chapultepec (☎ 5286-2165; Chapultepec 606, San Miguel Chapultepec; ☯ 1:30-10pm Mon-Fri, to 7pm Sat) Another cantina with a great legend. It is said that Mexican dictator, Porfirio Díaz, used a tunnel that connected the cantina to Chapultepec Castle. If true, he may have journeyed frequently to try *huachinango a la veracruzana* (red snapper Veracruz-style) or even the *criadillas* (mountain oysters).
- Covadonga (☎ 5533-2922; Puebla 121, Colonia Roma; ☯ 1pm-3am Mon-Fri; Ⓜ Insurgentes) Nicknamed 'Covita,' and *the* place to see journalists, celebrities and government officials, this is the trendiest cantina in the city. A better reason to visit is the *tortilla española*.
- Bar Montejo (☎ 5516-5851; Benjamín Franklin 261, Colonia Condesa; ☯ 1pm-1am Mon-Sat; Ⓜ Chilpancingo) A paradise for office workers, Bar Montejo is always jam-packed. Come early and leave late. The constant stream of *botanas* is one of the best in the city, starting with shrimp soup, continuing with tacos fritos and peaking with paella. But the real treat is *cochinita pibil* (pork marinated in chilies, wrapped in banana leaves, and pit-cooked or baked). It also has two floors that serve food in a traditional restaurant setting. If you are in the city when el Tri (Mexico's national football team) is playing a game, get a table next to one of the large plasma screens and be ready to cheer and scream. Bar Montejo also has two floors that serve food in a traditional restaurant setting.
- La Guadalupana (☎ 5554-6253; Higuera 2, Coyoacán; ☯ noon-12:30am Mon-Sat; Ⓜ Viveros) In the heart of Coyoacán, next to what once was Hernán Cortés' home, this cantina is a meeting place for writers, revolutionaries and other intellectuals. It serves a fantastic *lengua a la veracruzana* (tongue Veracruz-style). For some reason the kitchen closes at 6pm, but don't worry: you can order quesadillas and *tortas* from the mercado down the block.
- La Puerta del Sol (☎ 5512 7244, Av 5 de Mayo 54; ☯ 11am-11pm Mon-Wed, to midnight Fri-Sat; Ⓜ Zócalo) This quintessential cantina, founded in 1887, still has the double-leaf doors that machos like to push with brio when entering the watering hole. It serves an array of *botanas* and is famous for its *chamorros* (marinated pork shank).

the same side of the plaza. Oaxaca-style enchiladas and *cecina de Yecapixtla* (thinly sliced salted meat from a town in the state of Morelos) highlight a menu of regional classics. Enter at ground level through the jewelry arcade (there are various foreign flags above the entryway) and look for the elevator.

SANBORNS CASA DE AZULEJOS
Map pp48–9   Café $$
☎ 5512-9820; Madero 4; dishes M$60-80; ☯ 7am-1am; Ⓜ Allende

The original branch of the citywide chain of coffee shops is worth visiting mainly to admire its main dining hall within a magnificently preserved baroque courtyard.

It's a perennially popular meeting place for Chilangos and tourists alike, with rows of tables between octagonal pillars, roof beams alternating with strips of French tile, and a lovely Moorish fountain behind an ornately carved archway. The former marquis' palace was converted to a soda fountain in 1925 by Ohioan Frank Sanborn, who added the peacock murals. Despite the fabulous setting, the food is unremarkable coffee shop fare, with bland versions of Mexican standards.

CAFÉ LA BLANCA Map pp48–9 Café $$
☎ 5510-9260; Av 5 de Mayo 40; antojitos M$40-65, set lunch M$76; ☟ 8am-midnight; Ⓜ Allende
White-coated waiters and orange upholstery set the tone for this 1960s relic offering hearty breakfasts and daily lunch specials. Sit at the U-shaped counter or grab a table by the window for people-watching over a cappuccino.

CAFÉ EL POPULAR Map pp48–9 Café $
☎ 5518-6081; Av 5 de Mayo 52; dishes M$40-60; ☟ 24hr; Ⓜ Allende
So popular was this tiny round-the-clock café that they opened another more amply proportioned branch next door to catch the considerable overflow. Fresh pastries and good combination breakfasts (fruit, eggs, frijoles – beans – and coffee) are the main attractions. Café con leche (M$1) is served chino style (ie you specify the strength).

VEGETARIANO MADERO
Map pp48–9 Vegetarian $
☎ 5521-6880; Madero 56, 1st fl; set lunch from M$63; ☟ 8am-7pm; Ⓜ Allende; Ⓥ
Despite the austere entrance, there's a lively restaurant upstairs where a pianist plinks out old favorites. The meatless menu includes tasty variations on Mexican standards. Balcony seating lets you observe the street activity. A nearby street-level branch, Restaurante Vegetariano (☎ 5510-0113; Filomena Mata 13), displays the day's offerings out front.

COOX HANAL Map pp48–9 Regional Mexican $
☎ 5709-3613; Isabel La Católica 83, 2nd fl; dishes M$40-60; ☟ 10:30am-7pm; Ⓜ Isabel La Católica
Founded in 1953 by boxer Raúl Salazar from Mérida, this establishment, situated over a billiard hall, prepares Yucatecan fare just as it's done in Don Raúl's hometown. The poc chuc (grilled pork marinated in sour orange juice), papadzules (tacos stuffed with chopped hard-boiled egg and laced with pumpkin seed sauce) and cochinita pibil (pork marinated in chilies, wrapped in banana leaves, and pit-cooked or baked) are of a high standard, and tables are set with the obligatory marinated red onions and four-alarm habanero (a fiery chili) salsa. Yucatecan troubadours perform on the central stage come lunchtime.

EL CHARCO DE LAS RANAS
Map pp48–9 Taquería $
☎ 1054-4567; República de Uruguay 43; tacos M$35-45; ☟ 8am-6pm; Ⓜ San Juan de Letrán
Men in white bonnets work the big, gleaming grill at 'the frog pond,' a modern branch of the renowned taquería located in the southern DF. Aside from the well-crammed tacos al pastor and huge alambres (kebabs of beef, peppers, onions and bacon) – best washed down with an ice-cold horchata – you might try the chicharrón de queso (rolled sheets of crispy fried cheese).

CHURRERÍA EL MORO Map pp48–9 Café $
☎ 5512-0896; Eje Central Lázaro Cardenas 42; hot chocolate with 4 churros M$25; ☟ 24hr; Ⓜ San Juan de Letrán
A fine respite from the shopping hordes of the Eje Central, El Moro manufactures long, slender deep-fried churros (doughnut-like fritters), just made to be dipped in thick hot chocolate. It's a popular late-night spot as well, perfect for winding down after hours.

RESTAURANTE DZIB
Map pp48–9 Comida Corrida $
☎ 5709-9402; Regina 54; set lunch M$23; ☟ lunch; Ⓜ Isabel La Católica
This deceptively large dining hall must be the ultimate comida corrida joint, serving toothsome three-course lunches. Start with a hearty caldo de habas (bean soup), followed by a plate of rice or spaghetti, then choose from an extensive selection of mains, which change daily (Friday is seafood day). TVs showing the afternoon soap opera are conveniently placed at the front of each room.

TAQUERÍA LOS PAISÁS

Map pp48–9   Taquería $

☎ 5542-8139; Jesús María 131; tacos M$10;
⊙ 8am-midnight; Ⓜ Pino Suárez

There's always a crowd spilling out of this corner taco stand amidst the wholesale paper district east of the Zócalo, and that's reason enough to join them. Run by three goateed brothers, the place offers overstuffed steak, sausage and *pastor* tacos – or *campechano*, all mixed up. Help yourself from the heaving trays of garnishes: mashed potatoes, *pico de gallo*, cactus paddles and *habanero*-spiked onions, among others. As there's just one narrow steel table, most patrons have a stand-up chomp.

TACOS DE CANASTA CHUCHO

Map pp48–9   Taquería $

☎ 5521-0280; Av 5 de Mayo 17A; tacos M$5;
⊙ 9am-6pm Mon-Fri, 8am-5pm Sat; Ⓜ Allende

These bite-sized tacos are stuffed with fillings such as refried beans, *chicharrón* (fried pork skin) and *mole* (just the sauce), and arranged in a big basket. A couple of pails contain the garnishes: spicy guacamole and marinated carrot chunks and chilies.

PASTELERÍA IDEAL Map pp48–9   Bakery $

Calle 16 de Septiembre 18; pastries M$8-15;
⊙ 6:30am-9:45pm; Ⓜ San Juan de Letrán

Mexico's most glorious array of wedding cakes is on offer at this old-fashioned bakery: this is the place if you need a 70kg, multistory gâteau for your nuptials. Otherwise, there's a huge variety of breads and pastries with odd names like 'railroads' and 'dark rocks', whose allusions can only be guessed at. Grab a pair of tongs and stack up your steel tray, then get rung up by one of the scores of girls in blue aprons.

JUGOS CANADÁ Map pp48–9   Juice Bar $

Av 5 de Mayo 47; dishes M$1.75-$3.25; ⊙ 8am-
10pm Mon-Sat, 9am-9pm Sun; Ⓜ Allende

A veritable juice-squeezing factory, with oranges, pineapples, watermelons and so on temptingly displayed on shelves. Choose from juices and *licuados* (milkshakes). Check the board for a menu of fantastic permutations. Ever tried a guava-mamey cocktail? Fruit salads and big fat *tortas* are also prepared.

ALAMEDA CENTRAL & AROUND

Owing to the recent renovations performed around this iconic city park, eating options reflect the schizophrenic nature of the zone. Places on the immediate perimeter of the Alameda cater to an upscale clientele, and the Plaza Alameda mall, next door to the Sheraton, has plenty of global franchises. But head down Luis Moya or along Ayuntamiento, south of the Alameda, for pockets of the neighborhood's rustic heritage in the form of *torta* stands and chicken-soup vendors. Mexico City's modest Chinatown covers a single paper-lantern-strung block of Dolores, a couple blocks south of the park.

EL REGIOMONTANO

Map p64   Regional Mexican $$$

☎ 5518-0196; Luis Moya 115; grilled goat M$187;
⊙ 11am-10pm; Ⓜ Balderas

Lettered on the window is the message 'BABY GOATS VERY YOUNG KIDS,' and there they are, splayed on stakes and grilling over a circle of coals, just as they're done in Monterrey or Saltillo. A single platter serves two.

CUATRO MARES Map p64   Chinese $$

☎ 5510-4675; Dolores 27; chow mein M$85, mains
M$120; ⊙ 11am-10pm; Ⓜ San Juan de Letrán

If you're looking for authentically prepared Chinese food, you won't find it in the capital's diminutive Chinatown, which serves up a generally bland Chinese-Mexican hybrid that's heavy on the sweet-and-sour sauce. Of the half-dozen restaurants along Dolores, this one has the best Peking duck and shrimps in lobster sauce. Dine outdoors on the plaza or inside with the Chinese dragons.

CAFETERÍA DEL CLAUSTRO

Map p64   Café $

☎ 5518-2266; Hidalgo 45; salads & baguettes
M$35-45; ⊙ 10am-5pm Tue-Sun; Ⓜ Bellas Artes

If you're touring the Alameda museums, put this self-service café, inside the tranquil courtyard of the Museo Franz Mayer (p65), on your itinerary. The light fare includes Italian cold cuts on *chapata* rolls, ample green salads, quiches and excellent cakes, with seating at marble tables and baroque music to set the mood.

top picks

LATE NIGHT EATS

- Café El Popular (p138)
- El Tizoncito (p150)
- Mercado San Camilito (p156)
- Barracuda Diner (p152)
- Churrería El Moro (p138)

EL CUADRILÁTERO Map p64   Tortería $
☎ 5521-3060; Luis Moya 73; tortas M$35-70;
☼ 7am-8pm Mon-Sat; Ⓜ Juárez
Owned by *luchador* (wrestler) Super Astro,
this shrine to *lucha libre* features a wall of
wrestlers' masks, many donated by his ring
pals and enemies. Not just wrestlers, but also
ordinary denizens of the Centro frequent the
joint for its gigantic tortas, versions of which
are displayed at the entrance. If you man-
age to consume a 1.3kg cholesterol-packed
Torta Gladiador in 15 minutes, it's free.

CAFÉ COLÓN Map p64   Café $
☎ 5521-6343; Colón 1; breakfasts M$30-49,
4-course lunch M$40; Ⓜ Hidalgo
Dishing out traditional fare from this location for almost half a century, Café Colón
remains popular with local office workers
who pour in mid-morning for coffee or
mid-afternoon for the filling *comida*. The
café's two neatly renovated rooms retain
old maps of the Alameda and vintage light
fixtures.

TACOS XOTEPINGO Map p64   Taquería $
☎ 5709-4548; Marquez Sterling 42; tacos M$13-35;
☼ 11am-11pm; Ⓜ Balderas
With seating inside the big dining hall, on
the sun-dappled patio or alongside the
formidable grill, this taco temple makes a
great pit-stop after shopping at the Ciudadela crafts market, opposite.

MI FONDA Map p64   Café $
☎ 5521-0002; López 101; paella M$37; ☼ noon-
5pm; Ⓜ San Juan de Letrán
Working-class Chilangos line up here for
their share of *paella valenciana,* made fresh
daily and patiently ladled out by women in
white bonnets. Jesús from Cantabria over-
sees the proceedings. Space is limited but
you can share a table.

PLAZA DE LA REPÚBLICA & SAN RAFAEL

Though not considered a culinary destination
by any means, this mixed hotel and residential
zone has several small, homey, neighborhood
restaurants and *taquerías*.

BOCA DEL RÍO Map p71   Seafood $$
☎ 5535-0128; Ribera de San Cosme 42; fish from
M$95; ☼ 9am-11pm; Ⓜ San Cosme
This large, old-fashioned dining hall has its
fish delivered daily from the coast. Take a
seat at the long stainless-steel counter and
enjoy shrimp, oyster or octopus cocktails
(from M$50, or eat all three in one serve,
campechano-style), served with a lemon
squeezer, a bottle of *habanero* salsa and a
package of Saltines.

LA LONA VERDE Map p71   Seafood $$
☎ 5546-5781; Pedro Baranda 4; fish fillets M$60,
comida corrida M$85; ☼ noon-7pm Mon-Sat;
Ⓜ Revolución
This humble and friendly establishment
does some very tasty seafood dishes. Start
off with fried shrimp quesadillas or *mixiote
de mariscos* (a flavorful shellfish broth), then
have a fish fillet *al ajillo* (laced with a garlic
and chlli sauce). Being an Oaxacan-run
establishment, they also make *tlayudas,*
those great big crispy tortillas with a variety
of toppings.

EL CALIFA DE LEÓN Map p71   Taquería $
Ribera San Cosme 56B; tacos from M$22; ☼ 11am-
2am; Ⓜ San Cosme
Practically hidden amid the surrounding *am-
bulante* activity, this standing-room-only joint
is sought out by taco mavens from all over.
Unlike at thousands of similar places, the
twist here is that the beef is not chopped up
but grilled in thin slices. The salsas – chipotle
and *salsa verde* – are exceptional.

ZONA ROSA, CUAUHTÉMOC & JUÁREZ

The Zona Rosa's main pedestrian thoroughfare, Génova, can seem an edgy chaos of food
vendors, bemused tourists, gay couples, pan-
handlers and people on the move – mainly
towards the Insurgentes metro station, which
lies four blocks south of Paseo de la Reforma.

Watch this street theater from one of Génova's terrace cafés or sidestep off to a quieter restaurant in Cuauhtémoc or Juárez.

TEZKA Map pp74–5 — Spanish $$$
☎ 5228-9918; Amberes 78; dishes M$195-275; Ⓜ Insurgentes
This restaurant showcases contemporary Basque cuisine created by Master Chef Juan Mari Arzak, a native of San Sebastián. Seafood is the specialty, with dishes like sea bass and red snapper in a green chili sauce or codfish in a garlic and red pepper marinade. Desserts include a truly decadent warm chocolate torte with fresh berries. The dining room is one of the most stylish in town, accentuated by dramatic copper metalwork.

LES MOUSTACHES Map pp74–5 — French $$$
☎ 5533-3390; Río Sena 88; dishes M$160-200; ⏱ 1-11:30pm Mon-Sat, to 6pm Sun; Ⓜ Insurgentes; Ⓟ
An old-school traditional French restaurant, with tables in an elegant patio surrounded by ivy-clad walls. Start off with pâté de foie gras, then choose from duck in Grand Marnier sauce, beef Wellington or lobster Thermidor. For dessert, there are tempting crepes and soufflés.

ANGUS Map pp74–5 — Argentine $$$
☎ 5511-8633; Copenhague 31; steaks M$80-150; Ⓜ Insurgentes
This steak place attracts a slick business crowd, here for the excellent prime cuts and, possibly, the scantily-dressed waitresses in cowgirl gear. The vast closed-in terrace is the place to be; the interior dining room has stuffy burgundy upholstery and a private men's-club look. The meaty choices include rib-eye and T-bone steaks, plus surf-and-turf steak or lobster and shrimp. Seriously homesick Yanks can kick-start their appetite with a bowl of clam chowder.

RAFFAELLO Map pp74–5 — Italian $$$
☎ 5525-6585; Londres 165; pizzas M$95, pasta M$125-145; Ⓜ Insurgentes
Elderly bow-tied waiters provide attentive service at this charming Italian restaurant with its cosmopolitan-style enclosed sidewalk terrace and elegant dining room. There's an upper-crust pizza choice, plus all the pasta favorites and a few rogue dishes, such as shrimp curry and goulash.

top picks
ETHNIC EATING

- French: Les Moustaches (left)
- Italian: Il Postino (p151)
- Japanese: Sushi Shalala (p149)
- Korean: U Rae Ok (opposite)
- Lebanese: Al-Andalus (p136)
- Russian: Kolobok (p157)
- Spanish: Tierra de Vinos (p151)

FONDA EL REFUGIO
Map pp74–5 — Traditional Mexican $$
☎ 5525-8128; Liverpool 166; dishes M$110; Ⓜ Insurgentes
The Fonda was founded 50 years ago by the late Judith Martínez Ortega, whose folkloric collection of copper pots, colorful paintings and whimsical ceramic ornaments still decorate the dining rooms. Fortunately, she also collected recipes, which her family continues to create flawlessly today. Favorites include mole poblano (breast of chicken drenched in a rich chocolate-based sauce) and albondigas chipotle (meatballs laced with spicy chili).

BLAH BLAH Map pp74–5 — Argentine $$
☎ 5514-6753; Florencia 44; mixed grill for two M$230; Ⓜ Insurgentes
Mysteriously described as a progressive bar in their advertising, this Argentinean parrilla (grill) is, indeed, run by an enthusiastic young team and the decor is modern(ish), with stone-clad walls and earth colors, but the food is meaty and traditional, with gut-busting grills like sausage, gizzard, beef and ribs. There are dishes that don't require finger bowls, such as chicken breast with orange sauce and apple and, for the truly faint-hearted, Greek salad.

KONDITORI Map pp74–5 — Scandinavian $$
☎ 5511-0722; Génova 61; salads, sandwiches & dishes M$65-110; Ⓜ Insurgentes
This Scandinavian café attracts well-heeled regulars to see and be seen on this, the Pink Zone's main pedestrian thoroughfare. The salads, Danish sandwiches and cakes are good bets; some people make a special trip here for the weekend brunch (M$120) accompanied by live jazz.

CHALET SUIZO Map pp74–5 Swiss $$
☎ 5511-7529; Niza 37; fondues M$65-75, meat & fish dishes M$80-95; Ⓜ Insurgentes
Dating from 1950, this Alpine-feel restaurant is gingerbread cute, with beamed ceilings and Swiss ornaments and photos spread throughout five small dining rooms. Fondues include chocolate and Chinese, aside from the more conventional cheese or meat *bourguignon*. Other menu choices include veal goulash, trout in a white wine sauce and a creamy broccoli soup starter.

SANBORNS Map pp74–5 Traditional Mexican $$
☎ 5525-4039; Londres 130; breakfast M$65-90; ☺ 7am-1am; Ⓜ Insurgentes
Although not as splendid as the Sanborns original in the historic district, the interior here is still magnificent with ivy-twined columns, looming stained glass windows and a lofty vaulted ceiling. The food is, sadly, only average – aside from the breakfast, order *chilaquiles* (crushed soft corn tortillas covered in green chili sauce and topped with cheese).

CAFEBRERÍA EL PÉNDULO
Map pp74–5 Contemporary Mexican $$
☎ 5208-2327; Hamburgo 126; omelets M$59, dishes M$85-120; Ⓜ Insurgentes
An elegant café within a classy bookshop. Come here for a breakfast *omelette Juliette* with spinach, tomato and goat cheese, surrounded by books and cosseted by classical music, (live on Sunday mornings). More substantial fare includes pasta and fish dishes, plus there's a cut-price children's menu.

LA TERRAZA DEL QUETZAL
Map pp74–5 Contemporary Mexican $$
☎ 5511-1464; Río Tiber 104; dishes M$80-90; ☺ 8am-10pm Mon-Fri, to 1pm Sat; Ⓜ Sevilla
La Terraza opened in late 2007. Sit on the upstairs terrace or in one of the cute dining rooms with primary-color tablecloths and giant prints of fruit and veg. Dishes include a recommended tortilla soup topped with cheese and avocado, tacos with various fillings and a specialty pasta *quetzal* with cheese, broccoli, mushrooms and chicken.

RESTAURANTE VEGETARIANO YUG
Map pp74–5 Vegetarian $$
☎ 5553-3872; Varsovia 3; buffet M$75, dishes M$60-75; ☺ 7am-9pm Mon-Fri, 8:30am-8pm Sat & Sun; Ⓜ Insurgentes; Ⓥ

The menu is gastro-heaven for vegetarians and vast enough for most carnivore folk to find something they fancy – even if it is a soy-substitute burger. Go the buffet route for ample choice or choose from specialties like squash flower crepes and chop suey with brown rice. The wine is nonalcoholic but the desserts are un-piously sweet and delicious; think cheese cake with fresh berries. The green-painted furnishings are rustically appropriate.

LA POLAR Map pp74–5 Regional Mexican $$
☎ 5546-5066; Guillermo Prieto 129, San Rafael; birria M$85; ☺ 8am-1am; Ⓜ San Cosme; Ⓟ
Run by a family from Ocotlán, Jalisco, this boisterous beer hall has essentially one menu item: *birria*, a soulfully spiced goat stew. Their version of this Guadalajara favorite is considered the best in town. Spirits are also raised further by mariachis and *norteño* combos, who work the salons here.

BLU Map pp74–5 Seafood $$
☎ 5525-7598; Río Lerma 156; 6 oysters M$60, dishes M$75-80; Ⓜ Sevilla
A rare oyster bar among this energetic stretch of restaurants on Río Lerma between Río Tiber and Río Guadalquivir. There are just a handful of tables, plus the adjacent bar, which is bathed with dated '60s blue neon light. Dishes include an oyster starter, salmon grill, grilled meats and salads.

U RAE OK Map pp74–5 Korean $$
☎ 5511-1233; Hamburgo 232; dishes M$60-85; ☺ Mon-Sat; Ⓜ Insurgentes
The core of the Korean community, the Zona Rosa has several authentic restaurants catering to this discerning and traditional local crowd. This simple upstairs locale has the finest *bul-go-gi* (grilled marinated beef) and *chigae* (hearty soup), at the best prices.

CAFÉ MANGIA Map pp74–5 International $
☎ 5533-4503; Río Sena 85; paninis M$65, salads M$65, breakfast M$40; ☺ 8am-8pm Mon-Fri; Ⓜ Insurgentes
Enjoy an uncomplicated menu of panini with fillings such as pesto and smoked cheese, roast beef, cheese and herbs and smoked salmon with cream cheese. There's a healthy salad and breakfast choice, plus fresh juices and seriously good coffee. The atmosphere is boho-arty with white-painted brick walls, challenging artwork

MEXICAN COOKBOOKS

The high priestess of Mexican cookbooks, in English, is Diana Kennedy. British by birth, she moved to Mexico in 1957 after marrying the foreign correspondent for the *New York Times*. Diana began teaching Mexican cooking classes and in 1972 published her first of numerous cookbooks. She has been decorated with the Order of the Aztec Eagle, the highest honor bestowed on foreigners by the Mexican government and lives much of the year in her ecological adobe house in Michoacán, Mexico. Her latest book, *The Art of Mexican Cooking,* published by Random House in April 2008, includes more than 200 recipes, ranging from the ultra sophisticated to traditional, pure and simple.

Other books for inclusion on your Mexican-food-to-impress bookshelf include *Larousse de la Cocina Mexicana* by Alicia Gironella and Giorgio de'Ángeli (republished in 2006), which has more than 500 recipes for starters, soups, mains, sauces, breads and sweets, as well as traditional methods of preparation of fruits, vegetables, meat and fish. Each recipe explains the origin of the plate, preparation time, grade of difficulty and even the approximate cost of the ingredients.

For vegetarians, Kippy Nigh's *A Taste of Mexico* (1996; Book Publishing Company) features meatless recipes from all over Mexico and includes the background to each dish as well as a breakdown of calories, protein, fat and carbohydrates. Kippy has lived in Mexico since the early 1980s and opened her first bakery (La Casa del Pan) in Mexico City in 1989, followed in 1993 by a second bakery, plus a vegetarian restaurant in her subsequent home, San Cristóbal de Las Casas in Chiapas.

and an outside terrace. All the vegetables are organically grown.

LA CASA DE LAS ENCHILADAS

Map pp74–5   Traditional Mexican $
☎ 5211-2247; Tokio 110; dishes M$60;
Ⓜ Chapultepec

Indecisive Librans should avoid this place; five choices of tortilla, 11 of filling, 10 of sauces, and seven of topping, including cilantro, cheese and sour cream. You can't go far wrong (or leave hungry), whatever three-enchilada *plato* you choose. The look is scrubbed pine, bright lights and pastel walls. There is a second restaurant at Liverpool 169 in Zona Rosa, complete with a children's play area; a definite family favorite.

V ZONA ROSA Map pp74–5 Traditional Mexican $
☎ 5514-8079; Varsovia 14; tacos M$8, 3-course menu M$42; ◷ 8am-8pm Mon-Fri; Ⓜ Insurgentes

This justifiably popular restaurant is fronted by a taco stand with freshly prepared fillings. Inside, the decor is of the Formica-style school with three TVs, efficient (elderly) service, a congenial English-speaking manager and a great-value three-course lunch menu. Enchiladas, *tortas*, soups, chicken *chilaquiles* and fresh fruit salads are a taster of what's on offer.

KING FELAFEL Map pp74–5   Middle Eastern $
☎ 5514-9030; Londres 178; sandwiches M$22, salads M$35 ◷ 9am-8pm Mon-Fri, to 6pm Sat; Ⓜ Insurgentes

This Middle-Eastern fast-food place serves traditional dishes like falafel, hummus and tabouleh, and is run by a Syrian Jew who knows all the family recipes and is suitably spirited with the spices.

BOSQUE DE CHAPULTEPEC

The *primera* (1a) *sección* of the park has a convenient strip of snack and drink stalls overlooking the southern tip of the Lago de Chapultepec. To get here cross the underpass from Paseo de la Reforma and turn right just past the Monumento a los Niños Héroes. Look for the colorful menus and signs off the main drag to the right; there will probably be a few punters handing out leaflets, as well.

There are around 10 cafés here, with not much to choose between them. Most have outside seating overlooking the lake, complete with fountain. The approximate price for a taco or *torta* is M$10 – this is probably your best bet. There is also a fairly ordinary cafeteria inside the Museo Nacional de Antropología. For better quality head for the more formal and pricier restaurants in the *segunda* (2ª) *sección* of Chapultepec and the Lago Menor and Lago Mayor lakes, or double back to Reforma via the underpass, where several good restaurants cater to the discerning office workers in Torre Mayor, across from the entrance.

DEL BOSQUE Map p78   Traditional Mexican $$$
☎ 5273-2918; Margen Oriente 2a; buffet breakfast & lunch M$189-249; ◷ 7am-1am; Ⓜ Constituyentes; Ⓟ

Part of a lakeside trio, Del Bosque overlooks the smaller, more tranquil (ie no *pedalos*) Lago Menor. Brilliant blue wine-and-water glasses on the tables catch any sun rays, brightening up an otherwise somewhat stuffy dining room. The weekend buffets are your best value, with an expansive breakfast and lunch spread available. Afterwards you can waddle round the lake for exercise.

JARDÍN DEL CORREGIDOR

Map p78   Spanish $$$

☎ 5271-1956; General Cano 22; dishes M$200-235; Ⓜ Constituyentes

Just across from one of the southern exits of the park, this Spanish-owned restaurant (part of the Park Villa hotel) has a magnificent lion and lioness in a large back garden pen; apparently bought on the street and brought home by the owner's son when they were cubs (a step up from the usual abandoned kitten!). The food is traditionally Spanish; try the garlic mushrooms, followed by *pulpo a la gallega* (octopus Galician style) and chocolate fondue with fruit.

MERIDIEM Map p78   Traditional Mexican $$$

☎ 5273-3599; Lago Mayor, 2a sección; dishes M$89-170, buffet M$170; Ⓜ Constituyentes; Ⓟ

At the northern end of the lake, the Meridiem has soothing lake and fountain views and a bumper daily buffet (1:30pm to 5pm) with plenty of hot and cold choices; the latter generally including dishes like *pescado de ajillo* (fish with garlic). Lesser appetites can eat relatively inexpensively here by ordering the tacos, which are well prepared and filling.

EL LAGO Map p78   Traditional Mexican $$$

☎ 5515-9586; Lago Mayor, 2a sección; dishes M$150-170; Ⓜ Constituyentes; Ⓟ

This restaurant is more famous for its fabulous views and who's who clientele than (of late) for its food, which is good, rather than exceptional. Push the boat out with a seafood dish like grilled sardines with a arugula salad and grab a pew next to the picture window overlooking the lake. The dining room is seriously grand and the service predictably efficient.

LA LANTERNA Map p78   Italian $$$

☎ 5207-9969; Paseo de la Reforma 458; pasta & pizza M$115, steak M$160; ☙ 1pm-10:30pm Mon-Sat; Ⓜ Chalpultepec

This smart Italian restaurant has an intimate feel with its low ceilings, dark wood-and-tile decor and shelves lined with fine wines. Businessmen from the nearby Four Seasons Hotel can forge deals over a fiery dish of *penne all'arrabbiata* (spicy chili and tomato sauce) or get heavy with a fillet of steak with all the trimmings.

BOLUDO Map p78   Argentine $$

☎ 5286-0179; Río Lerma 303; steaks M$130, dishes M$75; Ⓜ Chalpultepec

A slick modern interior combined with hearty cuts of imported Argentinean steak makes this a favorite with the briefcase brigade. Those with a lighter appetite can opt for enchiladas, sandwiches or a vegetable grill.

POLANCO

Polanco is the Beverly Hills of Mexico City so, together with designer shops and miniature poodles, you can expect to find some fine dining among the inevitable rip-off establishments. Note that it is wise to reserve ahead at all the top-end restaurants located here.

ÁGUILA Y SOL

Map p84   Contemporary Mexican $$$

☎ 5281-8354; Emilio Castelar 127; dishes M$250-375; ☙ 1-11pm Mon-Sat; Ⓜ Polanco; Ⓟ

A modern temple of somewhat stark decor coupled with exciting updated Mexican flavors, Martha Ortiz is something of a culinary goddess in these parts. Start in style by sipping a *bandera mexicana,* so named because it features the colors in the

top picks

REGIONAL EATING

- Chiapas: Tamales Chiapanecos María Geraldine (p133)
- Guerrero: Pozolería Tixtla (p157)
- Jalisco: La Polar (p142)
- Norteño: El Regiomontano (p139)
- Oaxaca: La Lona Verde (p140)
- Puebla: La Sbia Virtud (p149)
- Tabasco: María del Alma (p148)
- Veracruz: El Bajío (p147)
- Yucatán: Coox Hanal (p138)

CELEBRITY CHEFS

Mexico City is fast becoming Central America's gourmet capital, with a wave of *nueva cocina* restaurants that challenge and express traditional Mexican ingredients, recipes and culinary conventions in new and exciting ways.

Martha Ortiz Chapa is the chef behind the highly acclaimed Águila y Sol (opposite) and one of several female chefs to attract international recognition for her visionary take on Mexican food. 'My recipes reflect the pre-Columbian and European roots of Mexican cuisine, as well as being very sensual and feminine.

'I am continuing a tradition here; women have always done the cooking in Mexico and consider their mealtime to be something sacred; we leave the men to be the politicians! Mexican women have inherent strength and passion, which are motivating forces behind culinary creativity.

'I think great cooks are like artists. I read a lot, love music, poetry and painting; my food is all about texture and colors, as well as taste.'

Martha's menu changes regularly and is typically based on a central theme: for example, the color black was unsurprisingly chosen in early November for the *Día de los Muertos*; the meal kicking off in style with black margaritas.

Mónica Patiño has four children, three restaurants, two TV cooking shows, part-owns a gourmet delicatessen and has written three cookbooks. Like Martha Ortiz, she is passionate about Mexican cuisine. 'When I traveled to India I saw that the top hotels served Indian cuisine, they were proud of their culinary heritage whereas, for years, the hotel restaurants here would be Italian or French. Fortunately this is gradually changing.'

Mónica has grown her own organic vegetables for 30 years and also believes in offering diners the option of a lighter cuisine. In her MP Bistro (☎ 5280-2506; Andrés Bello 10; dishes M$150-250; ⏱ 1.30-11.30pm Mon-Wed, to 12.30am Thu-Sat; Ⓜ Polanco), for example, she blends Eastern and Western flavors with remarkable success: 'I think the combination of a little acid and chili works very well.' In her flagship La Taberna de León (p154), the focus is a similar combo of local and international, like salmon with soy sauce and teppanyaki vegetables. Again, like Martha, she believes that women's sensitivity is an advantage over men in the kitchen. 'My food is infused with emotions. I knead corn dough like a caress.'

Sonia Arias who, with her American partner, executive chef (and a *man*!) Jared Reardon runs Jaso (p146), learnt to cook from her grandmother. 'Mexican women have always played an important culinary role here.' However, Sonia describes her menu as American contemporary 'with touches of Mexican'.

'Essentially our cuisine is dictated by the availability of what is fresh in the market. We change our menu constantly, printing it ourselves for that reason. For example, if Jared finds excellent red snapper in the fish market, he will prepare a dish around it for that evening.

'Presentation is also very important, we are extremely picky with the little details: the fresh flowers, welcome canapé and even the music, which is provided for us by the DJ from New York's Buddha Bar.'

Looks good, tastes good, sounds good: these restaurants all have something special to offer; exercise your taste-buds (ok, and your wallet) and check them out.

Mexican flag (green, white and red): three shot glasses filled with oak-barrel aged tequila *reposada, sangrita* — a tomato citrus drink — and lime juice. The menu includes traditional dishes given the dynamic taste sensation treatment, like the succulent pork loin in yellow mole with gingered mango.

HACIENDA DE LOS MORALES
Map p84   Traditional Mexican $$$
☎ 5096-3054; Vázquez de Mella 525; dishes M$270-350; Ⓜ Polanco; Ⓟ
Often the setting for banquets and receptions, the 400-year-old former silk-producing hacienda serves sumptuous variations on Mexican and Spanish classics in its regally luxurious dining room, surrounded by lush gardens. Recommended

dishes include *chiles en nogada* and the mango flambé. Reservations are essential and the dress is bib-and-tucker formal.

PUJOL Map p84   Contemporary Mexican $$$
☎ 5545-4111; Petrarca 254; dishes M$250-350; ⏱ 1-11pm Mon-Sat; Ⓜ Polanco; Ⓟ
This smartly minimalist dining room with black-and-white decor is punctuated by the brilliant crimson of red carnations on the tables. The menu reflects a creative approach to classic Mexican and Spanish recipes with a *soupcon* of French influence – and a sense of humor, as evident in the starter of what looks like a quail egg (topped with caviar) in a Chinese soup spoon, actually created from mango and cauliflower. Signature dishes include zucchini-blossom cappuccino

(more of a soup served in a highball glass) and duck carpaccio with *pipian* (pumpkin seed) vinaigrette and *mezcal* foam. If you fancy gleaning a little Pujol culinary flair, consider enrolling in one of the cooking courses (see *p134*).

BIKO Map p84   Contemporary Mexican & Spanish $$$

☎ 5282-2064; Presidente Mazaryk 407; dishes M$220-350; ⏱ 1:30-11pm Tue-Sat, to 6pm Sun; Ⓜ Polanco

Co-owned by San Sebastián chef Bruno Oteiza, the menu is based on traditional Basque recipes that have been given the *nouvelle* treatment, such as tuna steaks served with ham and dried fruits. The dining room is unostentatiously chic and less bleakly minimalist than some top-end restaurants in these parts. There is an adjacent bar with bucket seats, intimate lighting and rooftops views.

IZOTE Map p84   Contemporary Mexican $$$

☎ 5280-1671; Presidente Mazaryk 513; dishes M$230-300; ⏱ 1-11pm Mon-Sat; Ⓜ Polanco; Ⓟ

Patricia Quintana is the celebrated owner of this fashionable upbeat restaurant with its innovative menu and uncluttered dining room highlighted by a traditional-style mural. The presentation is superb, minus the tendency to overdose on towering stacks decorated with drizzle, and the relatively simple dishes include chopped cactus and tomato salad, lamb barbecued in a banana leaf and red mullet with crushed pistachios in a *mole* sauce. The restaurant is named after the exquisite white flower that adorns the yucca plant.

JASO Map p84   Contemporary American $$$

☎ 5545-7476; Newton 88; dishes M$200-250; Ⓜ Polanco

Smoothly run by husband-and-wife team, Jared Reardon and Sonia Arias, who met at the New York-based Culinary Institute of America, progressive palates can dine on dishes such as red snapper with giant asparagus or roast pepper porcini with citrus sauce, all relying on impeccably sourced ingredients. The homemade ice cream choice includes irresistible flavors like blueberry with triple cream cheese and raspberry with hazelnuts and chocolate. There's plenty of swagger on the interior front, with seductive small spaces and stylish decor touches.

PAMPANO Map p84   Contemporary Mexican $$$

☎ 5281-2010; www.modernmexican.com; Moliere 42; dishes M$195-225; ⏱ 1.30-11pm Mon-Sat, to 6pm Sun; Ⓜ Polanco)

Opened in November 2008 by opera legend (and part owner) Plácido Domingo, Pampano is one of the latest gourmet restaurants in Polanco (the original is in New York). High ceilings, a magnificent central candelabra and icy white walls with a sculpted, rippled effect create a minimalist dining space. The dishes include black bean soup with fresh cheese, plantains, avocado and strips of tortilla; and seafood specialties like tacos de *langosta* (lobster) and the exemplary *pescado de azteca* with *huitlacoche* in a chili sauce.

CAMBALACHE

Map p84   Contemporary Argentine $$$

☎ 5280-2080; Arquímedes 86; steak M$310, fondues M$85; ⏱ 1pm-1am; Ⓜ Polanco

You can expect a good grilling at this, one of the better steak houses in town. The front window provides a taste of what's to come, with steaks roasting on the spit. During the week, the low-ceiling dark wood dining room gets packed with local businessmen dining on a menu that, aside from the steaks, includes suckling pig, mixed grill, veal sweetbreads, fondues and (would you believe) a blessedly digestible watercress salad with a choice of Roquefort or bacon dressing.

SAINT HONORÉ Map p84   French $$$

☎ 5281-1065; Presidente Mazaryk 341; dishes M$150-220; Ⓜ Polanco

This restaurant is especially famous for its vast choice of excellent local and imported wines, having won a place on the *Wine Spectator*'s 'Outstanding Wines' list for four consecutive years. The romantic dining room has dreamy Mediterranean seascape murals and a menu that includes innovative French dishes like *escalopes de foie gras de canard chaud aux framboises* (slices of warm duck foie gras pâté with raspberries).

ENTREVINOS

Map p84   Contemporary European $$$

☎ 5582-1066; Oscar Wilde 9; dishes M$160-180; Ⓜ Polanco

Unostentatiously chic restaurant where Spanish and French dishes are made with salutary (and salivatory) attention to detail.

There are just a few tables, where diners can enjoy French classics such as coq au vin or Spanish paella; the latter is good value if you are a gaggle, at M$320 for six.

VILLA MARÍA Map p84   Traditional Mexican $$$
☎ 5203-0306; Homero 704; dishes M$95-$180; ⏱ 1:30pm-midnight Mon-Sat, to 7pm Sun; Ⓜ Polanco; Ⓟ
A large spread with an invariably celebratory atmosphere, the Villa María makes a good choice for that special meal *a la mexicana*. Original recipes like *infladitas* (mini quesadillas) and *sopa capilla* (with local cheese, squash flowers and corn) incorporate regional styles from around the Republic. Megamargaritas come in 10 flavors.

EL BAJÍO Map p84   Traditional Mexican $$
☎ 5281-8246; Alejandro Dumas 7; dishes M$70-120; Ⓜ Auditorio
Owner Carmen Titita Hernandez Oropeza (better known as Titita) is one of the best-known and best-loved culinary figures in the city. She has written several cookbooks and built a reputation on producing down-home Veracruz-style food. One of five restaurants in the city, this branch has striking folkloric-inspired decor, with one entire wall decorated with colorful woven baskets, another with framed hand-woven fabrics. For starters try the *sopa de fideo seco* (pasta soup with tomato, avocado, cilantro and cream) followed by sea bass in banana leaves or chicken with *mole*.

CREPERIE DE LA PAIX Map p84   French $$
☎ 5280-5859; France 79; crepes M$70-90, salads M$75; Ⓜ Polanco
There's a Parisian feel to this *crepería*, with its Toulouse Lautrec posters, bustling corner location and attractive outside terrace. The menu includes savory and sweet crepes, a few pasta choices and small or large salads, including goat cheese with walnuts.

OTTO Map p84   Contemporary European $$
☎ 5282-3861; www.otto-bistro.com; Julio Verne 89; dishes M$50-80; ⏱ 8am-11pm Mon-Wed, to 12:30pm Thu-Sat; Ⓜ Polanco
The duck-egg blue and burgundy two-tone paintwork equals a fashionable look at this bistro-style restaurant where white-smocked waiters serve up dishes like risotto

top picks
TAQUERÍAS
- El Califa (p150)
- El Borrego Viudo (p157)
- Supertacos Chupacabras (p153)
- Taquería Hola (p150)
- Taquería Los Paisás (p139)
- Tacos de Canasta Chucho (p139)
- El Farolito (below)
- El Tizoncito (p150 & p153)

with fish and mushrooms, salmon with couscous and pineapple, and *crema de flor de calabaza con coco* (soup of squash flowers with coconut). Breakfast goodies include bagels with salmon and cream cheese.

BREADHAUS Map p84   International $
☎ 5281-0173; Presidente Mazaryk 350; sandwiches & salads M$59; Ⓜ Polanco
Everything costs M$59 on this menu, including baguettes, *paninis*, *ciabatta* and fat *focaccias* stuffed with a nine-filling choice like serrano ham, roast beef and salmon. If you want to lay off the dough, go for one of their mixed-leaf salads. The space is inside-outside and attracts local business types with limited lunch breaks and expansive appetites.

EL FAROLITO Map p84   Traditional Mexican $
☎ 5250-2322; Newton 130; tacos M$28-34, salads M$48-70; Ⓜ Polanco
An old-fashioned place with smiley service, a vast outside terrace and a menu including tacos, quesadillas and salads (such as Cesar and Greek) plus, astutely reflecting current cholesterol-obesity concerns, a list of taco 'light' choices, such as chicken breast.

KLEIN'S Map p84   Traditional Mexican $
☎ 5281-0862; Presidente Mazaryk 360; dishes M$59; Ⓜ Polanco
More New York diner than the swanky Polanco norm, Klein's is a popular hang-out for the local Jewish community, although most of the fare is typically Mexican – enchiladas, *pollo y frijoles* (chicken with beans), *sopa de fideos* (soup with noodle-style pasta). You can also get bagels or a plate of kosher salami and eggs.

CONDESA

Condesa (or more cheekily, Condechi) has become the hub of the eating-out scene, and dozens of informal bistros and cafés, many with sidewalk tables, compete for space along key streets. Most of the restaurants are clustered near the convergence of Calles Michoacán, Vicente Suárez and Tamaulipas, while other pockets are found along Montes de Oca, Nuevo León and Mazatlán. Another area to investigate is along the streets that ring the Parque México, with some particularly inviting options opening on that oval of greenery.

It must be added, however, that style often triumphs over substance here, and popularity does not necessarily correlate with quality. Condesa's culinary renaissance is a recent phenomenon, and some places make it on the neighborhood's trendy image rather than their kitchen skills. We've listed some of the more reliable options below.

Most higher-end Condesa restaurants offer valet parking for around M$25 (though you may wonder how they manage it!).

HIP KITCHEN Map p88   Café $$$
☎ 5212-2110; México 188; mains M$165-270; ☽ 1pm-midnight Mon-Sat; 🚍 Metrobus Sonora; 🅿
At the stylish bistro of Roma's new Hippodrome Hotel (see p210), star chefs fuse Mexican and Asian ingredients in exciting ways: miso-glazed salmon gets brushed with *chipotle*, and *pico de gallo* is served alongside your saku tuna. Dining is in a narrow, romantic space with a wall-length sofa and Art Deco fixtures. Reservations are highly recommended.

LAMPUGA Map p88   Seafood $$$
☎ 5286-1525; Ometusco 1; mains M$135-160; ☽ 2pm-midnight Mon-Sat, to 6pm Sun; 🅜 Chilpancingo
Fresh seafood is the focus of this French-bistro-style restaurant, where a blackboard over the bar announces the daily specials and brown paper tablecloths enable sloppy eaters. Tuna tostadas make great starters, as does the Greek-style octopus; for a main course, have the catch of the day grilled over coals. It may be hard to find a table at lunchtime.

EL ZORZAL Map p88   Argentine $$$
☎ 5273-6023; Alfonso Reyes 139; steaks M$130-250; ☽ 1-11pm; 🅜 Patriotismo; 🅿

Run by Buenos Aires expats, this is the best of many options for Argentine fare, with imported cuts, as well as fresh pasta and generous salads. The *parrillada* (M$460), a mixed grill served on a chopping board, feeds at least two. The small, unpretentious dining room is adorned with photos of Argentine songbird Carlos 'El Zorzal' Gardel.

FONDA GARUFA Map p88   Argentine $$$
☎ 5286-8295; Michoacán 93; pasta M$85, steaks M$140-200; ☽ 2pm-midnight Mon, 8am-midnight Tue & Wed, 8am-1am Thu-Sat, 8am-11pm Sun; 🅜 Patriotismo; 🅿
One of the first in the zone to put tables on the sidewalk and fire up a grill, La Garufa is amidst Condesa's liveliest corridor – expect to be serenaded by street musicians and asked for change. The place owes its longevity to the quality of its Argentine cuts and better-than-average pastas, as well as a romantic candlelit ambience.

CAFÉ LA GLORIA Map p88   French $$
☎ 5211-4180; Vicente Suárez 41; dishes M$85-100; ☽ 1pm-midnight Mon-Sat, to 11pm Sun; 🅜 Patriotismo; 🅿
A hip bistro in the heart of the zone, La Gloria remains a popular meeting place for both Chilangos and foreigners, thanks to their generous salads, zesty pastas and surprising blackboard specials, not to mention the quirky art on display.

BISTROT MOSAICO Map p88   French $$$
☎ 5584-2932; Michoacán 10; mains M$80-170; ☽ 1-11:30pm Mon-Sat, to 5:30pm Sun; 🅜 Chilpancingo; 🅿
A slice of Paris just west of Av Insurgentes, this unpretentious bistro is the successful creation of French restaurateur François Avernin. It's trendy for a reason: the service is stellar, the salads fresh and varied, and the wines well chosen. Picnickers can stock up on pâté and escargots at the deli counter.

MARÍA DEL ALMA
Map p88   Regional Mexican $$$
☎ 5553-0403; Cuernavaca 68; mains $100-165; ☽ 1:30-11pm Mon-Fri, to 1:30am Sat, to 6pm Sun; 🅜 Patriotismo; 🅿
A culinary escape to the Mexican state of Tabasco, María del Alma is a bit removed from the Condesa hubbub. Dining is in a leafy patio among singing birds and

a romantically inclined pianist. Enjoy a *guanabana* margarita as *tabasqueño* owners Jorge and Fernando describe such regional items as tamales *de chipilín*. For a main dish, try sea bass steamed in aromatic herbs. The mind-blowing desserts, say, *dulce de coco con almendra* (a scoop of sweet, shredded coconut spiked with chocolate) are excellent.

PHOTO BISTRO Map p88 French $$$

☎ 5286-5945; Citlaltépetl 23; mains M$100-170; 🚌 Metrobus Campeche

A French bistro cum photo gallery – how could it miss in Condesa? Indeed on any given evening, a smart set fills the intimate Photo Bistro, one of several fine eateries facing the fountain of tiny Plaza Citlaltépetl. Mexican ingredients enliven some of the artistically presented French fare here: slices of jicama add crunch to the spinach salad, and the salmon carpaccio rests on a bed of honeyed amaranth.

ROJO BISTROT Map p88 French $$$

☎ 5211-3705; Ámsterdam 71; mains M$90-150; 🕑 2pm-midnight Mon-Sat, to 6pm Sun; 🚌 Metrobus Sonora

On a leafy corner near Parque México, this eatery is popular as much for its vibrant social scene as the French-inspired cuisine. The ambience is pure Condesa: loud chatter competing with thumping music, sexy waitstaff, and sidewalk seating behind a plastic curtain. Regulars recommend the duck in passion fruit sauce, or the octopus risotto.

LA SÁBIA VIRTUD

Map p88 Regional Mexican $$

☎ 5286-6480; Tamaulipas 134B; mains M$100; Ⓜ Patriotismo; Ⓟ

Nouvelle cuisine from Puebla is lovingly presented at this cozy spot. *Mole* is the main thing, prepared in the classic Santa Clara convent style or the restaurant's own *verde* version. It laces enchiladas, various kinds of stuffed chilies, and *champandongo*, a sort of tortilla lasagna, which readers of the novel *Like Water for Chocolate* may recall as a dish the protagonist, Tita, prepares for one of her suitors.

EL DIEZ Map p88 Argentine $$

☎ 5276-2616; Benjamín Hill 187; steaks M$88; 🕑 1pm-midnight Sun-Thu, to 1am Fri & Sat; Ⓜ Patriotismo; Ⓟ

The overwhelming popularity of this unpretentious steak place might be attributed to its prices. Quality Argentine cuts, served on a cutting board with zestily dressed salad alongside, average under M$100, and Malbec wines are similarly reasonable. Those with less carnivorous appetites can order pizza by the square meter.

SUSHI SHALALA Map p88 Japanese $$

☎ 5286-5406; Tamaulipas 9; sushi from M$20, noodle & rice dishes M$90; 🕑 1-11pm Mon-Sat, to 8pm Sun; Ⓜ Patriotismo; Ⓟ Ⓥ

This long-standing Japanese deli is noted for its authenticity (owner Hiroshi is from Tokyo) and casual atmosphere. Standouts include the tempura and *negitoro don* (fresh tuna with sesame oil served on a bed of rice).

LA RAUXA Map p88 Comida Corrida $

☎ 5211-2927; Parras 15; 4-course lunch M$70; 🕑 1-6pm Mon-Sat; 🚌 Metrobus Sonora; Ⓥ

Here's an interesting twist on the *comida corrida* concept, featuring uniquely created Catalan-influenced fare by chef/owner Quim Jardí. Instead of a printed menu, Quim describes what's being served, with at least one vegetarian main course option daily. Pleasant terrace seating under a big tree is usually filled by 2:30pm.

ORÍGENES ORGÁNICOS Map p88 Café $$

☎ 5208-6678; Plaza Popocatépetl 41A; salads M$40-85, 3-course lunch M$120; 🕑 8am-10pm Mon-Fri, 9am-7pm Sat, 10am-6pm Sun; 🚌 Metrobus Sonora; Ⓥ

More than just a place to buy soy milk, granola bars and certified-organic produce, this store-café facing one of Condesa's cutest plazas prepares tasty meals with an emphasis on fresh, seasonal, organic ingredients. Besides the veggie crepes, tofu fajitas and so on, there are a dozen salads to choose from.

FRUTOS PROHIBIDOS Map p88 Café $

☎ 5264-5808; Ámsterdam 244; sandwiches & wraps M$45-60; 🕑 8am-10pm Mon-Fri, 10am-6pm Sat & Sun; 🚌 Metrobus Campeche; Ⓥ

When you need a break from *bistek,* Forbidden Fruits puts together healthy salads, wraps and fruit-juice combos. Consider taking out for a picnic in nearby Parque México.

DON KESO Map p88 Tortería $

☎ 5211-3806; Amsterdam 73; baguettes & salads M$40-50; ☻ 10am-midnight Mon-Wed, to 2am Thu-Sat, 1-10pm Sun; 🚇 Metrobus Sonora
This casual, reasonably priced hangout near Parque México has great baguettes and salads, plus an exciting cocktail selection. Crowds rush in for the good-value *comida corrida* (M$65).

EL CALIFA Map p88 Taquería $

☎ 5271-7666; Altata 22; tacos M$30; ☻ 1:30pm-3:30am; Ⓜ Chilpancingo; Ⓟ
This very popular *taquería* on Condesa's southern edge puts its own spin on the classic Mexican snack, grilling thin slices of beef and tossing them on handmade tortillas. Tables are set with a palette of savory salsas in sturdy clay bowls. Often jammed well past midnight, the place attracts after-hours prowlers in the mood for comfort food.

EL TIZONCITO Map p88 Taquería $

☎ 5286-7321; Tamaulipas 122; tacos from M$8.50; ☻ noon-3:30am Sun-Thu, to 4:30pm Fri & Sat; Ⓜ Patriotismo
The original branch of the city-wide chain has been going for nearly 40 years. It claims to have invented tacos *al pastor* (ie cooked on a spit, shepherd style), and half the fun is watching the grillmen deftly put them together. If there are no seats, try the bigger location two blocks east on Campeche.

NEVERÍA ROXY Map p88 Ice Cream Parlor $

☎ 5286-1258; Mazatlán 81; scoop M$12, banana split M$45; ☻ 11am-8:30pm; Ⓜ Chapultepec
A throwback to a less-franchised era, the old-fashioned Roxy makes its own ice cream and sherbet onsite, including such tropical flavors as *zapote* (sapodilla) and guava. Another branch is at Tamaulipas 161, close to metro Patriotismo.

EL FIGONERO Map p88 Comida Corrida $

☎ 5211-9951; www.elfigonero.com; Campeche 429-C; set lunch M$40; ☻ 8:30am-4pm Mon-Sat; Ⓜ Patriotismo
In the midst of all the trendiness is this little neighborhood place, offering a three-course *comida corrida* that's a bit more creative than usual. Show up before 3pm to avoid the lunchtime rush. There's sidewalk seating or you can squeeze into the crowded little *comedor*.

TAQUERÍA HOLA Map p88 Taquería $

☎ 5286-4495; Ámsterdam 135; tacos M$11; ☻ 9am-5:30pm Mon-Fri, to 2pm Sat; 🚇 Campeche
Midmorning, locals crowd this friendly hole-in-the-wall for a stand-up snack. Choose from a remarkable array of fillings, including sardines, green sausage, stuffed chilies and *quelites* (a seasonal green), all temptingly displayed in clay dishes. Tacos are served on two tortillas, the second to catch the overflow, and garnished on request with guacamole or crumbly white cheese.

ROMA

Bohemian Colonia Roma has traditionally been known for its café society rather than its restaurants. Several longstanding coffee shops along Avenida Álvaro Obregón reinforce that image. But Roma has increasingly become the place to go for an evening glass of wine and quiet conversation accompanied by pasta or salad, particularly at some of the sidewalk bistros along Calle Orizaba and around the delightful Parque Luis Cabrera. Another area to investigate is the Plaza Villa de Madrid (aka Plaza de Cibeles) which has recently flourished as a culinary point of reference with some of the neighborhood's finest eateries.

Roma is also a great destination for fans of street food. Besides the numerous street corner vendors of tamales, quesadillas and hamburgers, several weekly *tianguis* (markets) contain popular food sections, with a bewildering array of cheap and tasty snacks.

IXCHEL Map pp92–3 Contemporary Mexican $$$

☎ 3096-5010; Medellín 65; mains M$120-280; ☻ 8pm-3:30am Mon-Sat; 🚇 Metrobus Durango; Ⓟ
'Fusion' is an overused term among Condesa and Roma bistros, but this late-night supper club takes it seriously. Ixchel's innovative chef deftly fuses Mexican elements (grasshoppers, squash blossoms) with Mediterranean and Asian fare (risotto and tempura). The upstairs club, Love (p170), adds another dimension (Wednesday to Saturday nights), with DJs supplying the appropriately chilled ambience.

LAMM Map pp92–3 Contemporary Mexican $$$

☎ 5514-8501; www.lamm.com.mx; Álvaro Obregón 99; mains M$150-180; ☻ 8am-2am Mon-Fri, 9am-2am Sat, 9am-6pm Sun; Ⓜ Insurgentes
The restaurant of Colonia Roma's Casa Lamm cultural complex occupies a multi-

LITTLE WHIMS

Antojitos – literally, 'little whims', are traditional Mexican snacks or light dishes. On some menus they're listed as *especialidades mexicanas* or *platillos mexicanos*. Some *antojitos* are actually small meals in themselves. They can be eaten any time, and either on their own or as part of a larger meal. There are many, many varieties, but here are some of the more common ones:

burrita – flour tortilla folded over a filling of ham and cheese, heated a little to make the cheese melt

burrito – any combination of beans, cheese, meat, chicken or seafood seasoned with salsa or chili and wrapped in a flour tortilla

chilaquiles – fried tortilla strips cooked with a red or green chili sauce, and sometimes meat and eggs

chiles rellenos – chilies stuffed with cheese, meat or other foods, deep fried and baked in sauce

empanada – small pastry with savory or sweet filling

enchilada – ingredients similar to those used in burritos and tacos, rolled up in a tortilla, dipped in sauce and then baked or partly fried; enchiladas Suizas (Swiss enchiladas) come smothered in a blanket of creamy sauce

enfrijolada – soft tortilla in a frijole sauce with cheese and onion on top

entomatada – soft tortilla in a tomato sauce with cheese and onion on top

gordita – fried maize dough filled with refried beans and topped with cream, cheese and lettuce

guacamole – mashed avocados mixed with onion, chili, lemon, tomato and other ingredients

quesadilla – flour tortilla topped or filled with cheese and occasionally other ingredients, then heated

queso fundido – melted cheese served with tortillas

sincronizada – a lightly grilled or fried flour-tortilla 'sandwich,' usually with a ham and cheese filling

sope – thick patty of corn dough lightly grilled then served with *salsa verde* or *salsa roja* and frijoles, onion and cheese

taco – the número uno Mexican snack: soft corn tortilla wrapped or folded around the same fillings as a burrito

tamal – corn dough stuffed with meat, beans, chilies or nothing at all, wrapped in corn husks or banana leaves and then steamed

torta – Mexican-style sandwich in a bread roll

tostada – thin tortilla fried until crisp that may be eaten as a nibble while you're waiting for the rest of a meal, or can be topped with meat or cheese, tomatoes, beans and lettuce

---

level glass-walled pavilion opening on the center's enclosed gardens. It's an appealingly serene setting for fusion fare *a la mexicana*, such as tamarind tuna and *esmedregal* (cobia, a prized game fish) in tequila cream sauce. After hours, the restaurant morphs into the city's toniest *antro* (p170).

TIERRA DE VINOS Map pp92–3 Spanish $$$
☎ 5208-5133; Durango 197; dishes M$120-240; 1-8pm Mon & Tue, to midnight Wed-Sat; Metrobus Durango; P

The focus is on the wine, with hundreds of vintages lining the cellar-like walls, but there's fine Spanish cuisine to complement your chosen tipple. The mood is smart but not snooty: waiters gladly suggest what to have with, say, a plate of paprika-laced *patatas bravas* (shiraz), or sea bream over black rice (a barrel-aged tempranillo).

IL POSTINO Map pp92–3 Italian $$$
☎ 5208-3644; Plaza Villa de Madrid 6; dishes M$100-165; Metrobus Durango

Run by a pair of chefs from Rome and Milan, this superior restaurant features sidewalk terrace dining on an arc of the Plaza Cibeles (aka Villa de Madrid). You might start off with an octopus carpaccio, followed by sea bass wrapped in calzone on a bed of capellini pasta. Otherwise, ask chef Claudio for his inspiration of the day. Don't pass on dessert – the profiteroles with homemade ice cream merit applause.

CONTRAMAR Map pp92–3 Seafood $$
☎ 5514-9217; Durango 200; mains M$130-150; 1:30-6:30pm; Metrobus Durango; P

Fresh seafood, artfully prepared, is the star attraction at this stylish dining hall with a seaside ambience. The specialty is tuna fillet Contramar style – split, swabbed with red chili and parsley sauces, and grilled to perfection.

BARRACUDA DINER Map p88   Café $$

☎ 5211-9480; Av Nuevo León 4A; burgers M$70-90; ⏱ 1pm-2am Sun-Wed, to 3am Thu-Sat; Ⓜ Sevilla

This retro-style diner does a fine facsimile of gringo comfort food, including cheeseburgers, onion rings, and macaroni and cheese. The late-night hangout also sets up some pretty far-out milkshakes (mmm, mamey).

NON SOLO PANINO Map pp92–3   Italian $

☎ 3096-5128; Plaza Luis Cabrera 10; sandwiches M$50-70; Ⓜ Insurgentes; Ⓟ

The plaza's dancing fountains make a lovely backdrop for Italian sandwiches, with things like mozzarella, pesto and smoked salmon stuffed into fresh baked *chapatas* – Mexico's version of baguettes. More than just a snack center, 'Non Solo' is a cozy haunt for Roma's artistic set.

EL 91 Map pp92–3   Comida Corrida $

☎ 5208-1666; Valladolid 91; mains M$50-60; ⏱ 1-7pm Sun-Fri; Ⓜ Sevilla

Lunch is served to piano accompaniment at this triple-decker restaurant-bar – dumbwaiters deliver the food to the top terrace. It offers a different menu daily, with a long list of homemade soups and mains.

LOS BISQUETS OBREGÓN Map pp92–3 Café $

☎ 5584-2802; Álvaro Obregón 60; breakfast M$45, antojitos M$50; Ⓜ Insurgentes; Ⓟ ✕

The flagship branch of this nationwide chain overflows most mornings; fortunately there are a couple more nearby. Chilangos flock here for the *pan chino* (Chinese pastries) and *café con leche,* dispensed from two pitchers, Veracruz style.

TAQUITOS FRONTERA Map pp92–3 Taquería $

☎ 5207-4546; Frontera 120; tacos M$19; ⏱ 1:30pm-4am Mon-Thu, to 6am Fri & Sat; Ⓜ Insurgentes

One of a few late-night *taquerías* along Roma's main drag, this is a humble alternative with cheerful staff, a smoky open grill and leather tables and chairs. In addition to the main attraction, there are great sides like

frijoles charros (cowboy beans) and *cebollitas* (grilled green onions).

COYOACÁN

More like a small town than part of the city, the center colorfully fills up with local families at weekends, which means a shortage of chairs on the square at the terrace restaurants. In the unlikely event you are in a rush (or just feel like a mid-morning snack) head for the Mercado de Antojitos just round the corner on Higuera, where a huddle of stalls sell tacos, *gorditas* (thick, fried tortillas, split apart and stuffed with a variety of fillings), tostadas and *pozole*. Brave souls can seek out Don Fello, in the far corner, who stuffs his tacos with pork or beef *lengua* (tongue), *sesos* (brains) or *ojo* (eyes) – a snip (ouch!) at just M$12 apiece.

LOS DANZANTES

Map p95   Contemporary Mexican $$$

☎ 5658-6054; Jardín del Centenario 12; breakfast M$80, dishes M$75-M$150; Ⓜ Viveros

Located on the plaza, the restaurant is an indoor-outdoor space with a slick modern bar backed with cobalt-blue glass in the main dining room and an elegant outdoor terrace. The Swiss-trained chef prepares innovative dishes like squid in beet sauce on creamy rice, surrounded by *cabuches* (the fruit of the *viznaga* cactus). Relax your belt a notch further with the chocolate truffle pie. You'll also find *mezcal* (an alcoholic drink similar to tequila) cocktails available upstairs in the bar; Danzantes now has its own tequila label.

ENTRE VERO Map p95   Uruguayan $$$

☎ 5659-0066; Jardín del Centenario 14C; pizza M$80, dishes M$80-150; Ⓜ Viveros

Enjoying a fabulous location overlooking the park, this restaurant has maintained a high reputation. Palate-pleasing touches include starter strips of warm pita bread with a tangy chili-based sauce and the excellent Mexican and international wines available by the glass. Try dishes like the tuna steaks, grilled vegetable platter or Neapolitan style thin-crust pizzas.

LA PAUSE Map p95   Contemporary Mexican $$

☎ 5658-6780; Francisco Sosa 287; salads & pasta M$80; 8am-8pm Sun-Thu, to 1am Fri & Sat; Ⓜ Viveros

An effortlessly cool bookshop, art gallery and restaurant, with plenty of vegetarian options; the salads are excellent, especially the La Pause special with spinach, lettuce, serrano ham and goat cheese. Kick back and peruse the art books over a cup of chai, or join the squirrels and birds in the courtyard garden.

EL CARACOL DE ORO
Map p95   International $$
☎ 5658-9489; Higuera B16; dishes M$65-80; Ⓜ Viveros

Oozes cosmo kitsch with jazzily designed painted tables (chessboards, faces, flowers – get the picture?) and equally flamboyant paintings on the walls. Pretend-to-be-arty types can tuck into interesting flavors like apple curry with chicken and goat cheese, or chiles rellenos stuffed with mango.

EL JARDÍN DEL PULPO Map p95   Seafood $$
Mercado Coyoacán; fish dishes M$75; ⊗ 11am-5pm; Ⓜ Viveros

At weekends this timeless classic gets packed out as locals descend on the long shared tables to devour shrimp tacos, fried whole fish, shrimp and oyster cocktails, caldos (broths) and the namesake pulpo en su tinta (octopus cooked in its own ink).

CAFÉ PARNASO Map p95   Traditional Mexican $
☎ 5554-2225; Carrillo Puerto 2, Plaza Jardín del Centenario; dishes M$65; ⊗ 9am-10pm Mon-Fri, to 11pm Sat & Sun; Ⓜ Viveros

The place to linger, not only over countless cappuccinos, but also a groaning plato combinado with Spanish tortilla, cheeses, ham, empanadas (small pastry with savory or sweet filling) and sweet pastries. Tip the scales with a chocolatine, gooey layers of chocolate cream between sticky filo pastry.

MÉSON DE LOS LÉONES
Map p95   Traditional Mexican $
☎ 5554-5916; Allende 161; dishes M$55-65; ⊗ 11am-6pm Sun-Fri; Ⓜ Viveros

This family-run restaurant has been attracting punters for decades with its unwaveringly authentic menu and genial atmosphere. The half-tiled dining room has a photo display of happy diners enjoying specialty dishes like carne asada estilode Léon con mole, rajas poblana, guacamole y frijoles (roasted meat with mole sauce, roasted peppers, guacamole and beans).

EL TIZONCITO Map p95   Traditional Mexican $
☎ 5554-7712; Aguayo 3; tacos & quesadillas M$25; Ⓜ Viveros

This is a branch of the popular chain that originated in Condesa. The atmosphere is, well, nil – unless you like bright lights and modern diner-style decor, but the place is spotless, the quesadillas and tacos are particularly good (try the taco al pastor filled with spiced slivered pork) and the creamy horchata is heaven in a glass.

TAMALES CHIAPANECOS MARÍA GERALDINE Map p95   Regional Mexican $
☎ 5608-8993; Plaza Hidalgo; tamales M$24; ⊗ noon-9pm Sat, 8am-9pm Sun

At the passageway next to the arched wing of San Juan Bautista church, look for these incredible tamales by native chiapaneca doña María Geraldine. Wrapped in banana leaves, stuffed with ingredients like olives, prunes and almonds, and laced with sublime salsas, they're a meal in themselves.

SUPERTACOS CHUPACABRAS
Map p95   Taquería $
cnr Avs Río Churubusco & México; tacos M$8; ⊗ 7am-3am; Ⓜ Coyoacán

Named after the mythical 'goat sucker' (something like the Loch Ness monster), this mega taco stall has a new home beneath a freeway overpass, but true mavens should not be deterred. The beef and sausage tacos (with 'a secret ingredient of 127 spices') can be enhanced by availing yourself of the fried onions, nopales (prickly pear) and other tasty toppings that fill half a dozen huge clay casseroles in front.

SAN ÁNGEL
This attractive pueblo-style neighborhood is a favorite haunt for tourists on Saturdays, here for the shopping at the art markets in the squares and sophisticated Bazaar Sabado (see p129). During the week, San Ángel slumbers in preparation for the weekly onslaught and is a far quieter place, so pick your restaurant day carefully, depending on whether you fancy an atmosphere of calm or of clamor and crowds.

SAN ÁNGEL INN
Map p101   Traditional Mexican $$$
☎ 5616-1402; Diego Rivera 50; dishes M$200-350; ⊗ 1pm-1am Mon-Sat, to 10pm Sun; Ⓟ

This famous inn is located in a magnificent former Carmelite monastery so opulent that the Emperor Maximilian lived here for a while, as well as several Spanish Viceroys. Dine in one of a series of elegant dining rooms filled with antiques and evocative old oil paintings. The food is fittingly classical, start with *crepas de huitlacoche,* followed by the classic *pollo en mole poblano* or *chiles en nogada.* Even if you don't splurge for dinner, have one of its renowned margaritas in the garden. Walk or take a taxi 1km northwest from San Ángel's Plaza San Jacinto.

TABERNA DE LEÓN
Map p101   Contemporary Mexican $$$
☎ 5616-2110; Plaza Loreto 173; dishes M$155-270;
Ⓜ Miguel Ángel de Quevedo

Chef Monica Patiño is one of the new breed of female Mexican chefs who are stirring up traditional cuisine in the most delightful and innovative ways (p145). This is her original restaurant and it remains the most popular, especially at weekends when it is packed out with elegant local families with their well-behaved (and fashionably dressed) children. Seafood is the specialty, with highlights including Baja California stone crab and corn blinis with Norwegian salmon and caviar. Those nostalgic for Venice should choose the carpaccio Harry's Bar-style. The desserts are a work of art and taste pretty good as well.

PAXIA
Map p101   Contemporary Mexican $$$
☎ 5550-8355; Av de la Paz 47; dishes M$130-285; Ⓨ 1pm-midnight Mon-Thur, to 1am Fri-Sat;
Ⓜ Miguel Ángel de Quevedo

The achingly cool reception area here has a giant plasma screen where you can watch the food being prepared. The *menú de degustación verde* costs M$430 but is a real banquet if you are a serious (very hungry) gourmet, with seven courses, including *sopa de alcachofa y pistache pulverizado* (creamed artichoke and pistachio soup) and *raviolis rellenos de huitlacoche en salsa de tres quesos* (ravioli stuffed with truffle-like corn fungus in a three-cheese sauce).

FONDA SAN ÁNGEL
Map p101   Traditional Mexican $$
☎ 5550-1641; Plaza San Jacinto 3; dishes M$90;
Ⓜ Miguel Ángel de Quevedo; Ⓟ

On weekends you can sit under the sun brollies on the vast terrace and multitrip to the ample brunch, with all kinds of egg dishes, pastries and fresh-squeezed juices, plus great quesadillas. The menu includes some unusual dishes like chicken filled with goat cheese. There's a fine Mexican wine list varying from M$175 to M$630 a bottle.

BISTROT LA BOURGOGNE
Map p101   French $$
☎ 5616-8685; Av de la Paz 32; dishes M$90;
Ⓜ Miguel Ángel de Quevedo

There's a real inside-outside feel to the dining room here, with its glass ceiling and ivy-draped rafters. Wicker furniture and red geraniums complete the sunny Mediterranean look, while the menu is of the bistro rather than blue-ribbon variety, with classic dishes like snails, terrines, moist tuna steaks and creamy foie gras. Chef Fernand Gutiérrez is used to the discerning bourgeoisie, having worked in the Ritz Carlton and Four Seasons hotels.

SAKS
Map p101   Contemporary Mexican $$
☎ 5616-1601; Plaza San Jacinto 9; dishes M$75-120;
Ⓨ 7:30am-6pm Sun-Thu, to midnight Fri & Sat;
Ⓜ Miguel Ángel de Quevedo; Ⓥ

Sitting here on the terrace, bathed in sunshine with live music, a cosmopolitan clientele and a view through the leaves to the art stalls, you could be in Montmartre – except the food and weather here are arguably better. Choose from meatless specialties like *poblano* chilies stuffed with *huitlacoche,* Camembert soufflé, huge salads and squash-blossom crepes. The dining room is reminiscent of a monastery cellar, with its arched windows and vaulted ceilings but, thankfully, more cheerful given the good-humored staff and bright artwork on the walls.

CLUNY
Map p101   French $$
☎ 5550-7350; Av de la Paz 57; dishes M$75;
Ⓜ Miguel Ángel de Quevedo

This place has history, dating back to 1974 when it was one of a rare breed of French restaurants in the city. Cluny continues to hit the spot for unpretentious French cuisine, but don't expect much that is nouvelle. Quiche, salad, crepes, decadently delicious desserts and happily generous portions are the order of the day.

SUMO
Map p101   Japanese $$
☎ 5550-8355; Av de la Paz 47; dishes M$65-75;
Ⓜ Miguel Ángel de Quevedo

An elegant Japanese restaurant with a feng shui minimalist look and lots of white, beige and tubular steel furniture. The food is Asian-authentic, with a vast menu that includes deep-fried noodles, sashimi, sushi, noodles, tempura and various imaginative tofu dishes. Wind up with a shot of cold sake.

CRÊPERIE DU SOLEIL Map p101 · Crepes $

☎ 5550-2585; Madero 4; crepes M$65;
Ⓜ Miguel Ángel de Quevedo
A long-time classic on the Plaza del Carmen, this tiny crêperie has a handful of tables and a steady stream of regulars, here for the reliably-good sweet and savory crepes, *chapatas* and coffee.

EL SECRET GOURMET

Map p101 · International $

☎ 5616-4511; Av de la Paz 58; dishes M$45;
Ⓜ Miguel Ángel de Quevedo
A rare combination of gourmet restaurant and TV dinners; if you are renting an apartment, the frozen or refrigerated selection of dishes available here may appeal. They include various mousses, like salmon, Roquefort and olive, Middle Eastern choices, such as hummus and tabouleh, plus pastas, stuffed tacos, chicken and vegetarian dishes. There is also a deli section selling organic produce, including jams, chutneys and sauces.

CAPICUA Map p101 · Spanish $

☎ 5616-5211; Av de la Paz 14B; tapas & raciones M$40-65; Ⓜ Miguel Ángel de Quevedo
One of several restaurants in a little mall off Av de la Paz, Capicua is a lot smarter than your average Spanish tapas bar, but offers familiar favorites like *pulpos a la gallega*, *tortilla de patatas* (potato omelet), *boquerones alinadas* (anchovies in a vinaigrette dressing), and slices of crumbly Manchego cheese. There's an excellent wine list with riojas.

CIUDAD UNIVERSITARIA & TLALPAN

The university city mainly caters to students living on a shoestring so, if your budget is similarly restricted, you can find plenty of inexpensive, fairly standard, places to eat, with the exception of the excellent Azul y Oro. Cuicuilco is famed for its circular temple, rather than its culinary appeal, while

top picks
VEGETARIAN EATS

Tlalpan is fast competing with San Angel as a favorite for leisurely weekend brunches. The best restaurants here overlook a bustling central plaza, surrounded by the faded grandeur of colorful colonial-era buildings. There is also a daily market behind the town hall with food for sale (and to eat), which is inexpensive and, judging by the turnover, reliably fresh and good.

ANTIGUA HACIENDA DE TLALPAN

Map p109 · Traditional Mexican $$$

☎ 5655-7315; Calz de Tlalpan 4610, Tlalpan; dishes M$200-220; ⏰ 1pm-1am Mon-Sat, to 7pm Sun; 🚍 Metrobus Dr Gálvez, pesero 'Villa Coapa'
The setting is sublime; an 18th-century hacienda tastefully resurrected into one of the city's quintessential colonial-style restaurants. The dining rooms are set around lovely gardens, complete with showy peacocks and a small pond with swans. The menu reads like a novel, with a vast choice including some delectable soups: pumpkin flower, cold avocado, lobster bisque and black bean. Follow this with a fish or spicy meat dish like roast pork loin in a chili sauce.

EL JARDÍN DE SAN AGUSTÍN

Map p109 · Traditional Mexican $$

☎ 5485-3409; www.eljardindesanagustin.com; Plaza de la Constitución 9, Tlalpan; dishes M$75; Ⓜ Tasqueña
The cuisine here is authentic Yucatecan, with dishes like *sopa de lima* (chicken soup with limes, coriander, onions and garlic), *arroz con platano* (rice with plantains), and *la milanesa con papas* (steak baked or fried in egg and breadcrumbs with roasted potatoes) on the menu. The dining room is large and cheerful with brightly painted tables and chairs overlooking the plaza. There is live music at weekends.

MARKET FARE

Some of the best eating in Mexico City is not found in any restaurant but in the big covered *mercados* and *tianguis*. Fortunately, these long-standing favorites remain impervious to trends.

- **Mercado San Camilito** (Map pp48–9; Plaza Garibaldi; pozole M$44; ⏰ 24hr; Ⓜ Garibaldi) The block-long building contains over 70 kitchens serving Jalisco-style *pozole* (specify *maciza* if pig noses and ears fail to excite you). Also served are *birria* and *tepache*.
- **Mercado Medellín** (Map pp92–3; Coahuila; ⬛ Metrobus Campeche) Features an extensive eating area with cheap and filling *comidas corridas*, as well as several excellent seafood restaurants.
- **Parrillada Bariloche** (Map pp92–3; Bazar de Oro, Calle de Oro; ⏰ Wed, Sat & Sun; ⬛ Metrobus Durango) This stall along the southern aisle of an upscale street market grills some of the least-expensive Uruguayan-style steaks and sausages in town, along with excellent side salads.
- **Tianguis de Pachuca** (Map p88; Melgar; ⏰ 10am-4pm Tue; Ⓜ Chapultepec) The food section at the north end of the weekly Condesa street market offers many tempting options, but none so mouthwatering as the *mixiotes*, steamed packets of seasoned mutton, whose contents may be rolled into thick tortillas and garnished with fiery *chiles de manzana* (very hot, yellow chili peppers).
- **Mercado de Antojitos** (Map p95; Higuera; Ⓜ Coyoacán) Near Coyoacán's Plaza Hidalgo, this busy spot has all kinds of snacks, including deep-fried quesadillas, *pozole, esquites* (boiled corn kernels served with a dollop of mayo), tamales and *flautas* (chicken tacos, rolled long and thin then deep-fried; garnished with lettuce and cream).
- **Tostadas Coyoacán** (Map p95; ☎ 5659-8774; Allende; tostadas M$20-30; ⏰ noon-6pm Ⓜ Viveros) Inside Coyoacán's main market (between Malitzin and Xicoténcatl) an attractive array of platters here will stop hungry visitors in their tracks. Tostadas are piled high with things like seviche, marinated octopus and pig's trotters, mushrooms and shredded chicken.

AZUL Y ORO Map p105 Contemporary Mexican $
☎ 5623-3500; Centro Cultural Universitario; set menu M$50, dishes M$65; ⏰ 10am-6pm Sun-Tue, to 8pm Wed-Sat

Ricardo Muñoz Zurita famously travels throughout the country searching out traditional Mexican dishes which he then re-creates in the kitchen here with delicious results. There are four seasonal menus, special dishes that change monthly, and a daily three-course menu, made affordable for students on a budget, at just M$50. The antithesis of the fast-food campus norm, dishes on the Autumn menu include *crema de cilantro con almendras* (cream of coriander soup with almonds) and *tamalitos de acelga* (starter-size tacos stuffed with chard). A second restaurant opened in 2007 in the Faculty of Engineering building in the north end of the campus and yet another is planned for the Centro Histórico. No alcohol.

RAYUELA Map p109 Contemporary European $
☎ 5655-8456; Plaza de la Constitución s/n, Tlalpan; breakfast & dishes M$65; ⏰ 9am-12:30pm Tue & Wed, to 11:30pm Thu-Sat, to 8pm Sun; Ⓜ Tasqueña

Join the line for breakfast on Sunday mornings. Chef Raul's fluffy herb, cheese or mushroom omelets with a fresh tomato sauce are legendary. His mother, charming Socorro, runs the show, and her interest in art is reflected in the decor and paintings (for sale). Eat inside or under the archways on simple tasty dishes like spaghetti with pesto, fondue, crepes and *chilaquiles rojos* (fried strips of tortilla in a tomato and chili-based sauce, sprinkled with cheese).

LA CASA DE JUAN
Map p109 Traditional Mexican $
☎ 5655-9444; Plaza de la Constitución 5, Talpan; dishes M$50; ⏰ 10am-9pm; Ⓜ Tasqueña

This is a place where you want to hang around a while; it has a more European café than restaurant feel, with its small beamed rooms, challenging artwork, board games and wrought-iron balconies overlooking the square. Aside from breakfast, the daily menu changes and will usually include enchiladas, or similar, at a very reasonable price.

LOS BIGOTES DE CARRANZA
Map p109 Traditional Mexican $
☎ 5134-4241; Francisco Madero 16, Tlalpan; dishes M$40-48; ⏰ 8am-8pm; Ⓜ Tasqueña

There are just a few tables here upstairs and down, plus a spotless, open-plan kitchen and a reassuringly brief menu of traditional favorites like *chiles rellenos,* tacos, chicken dishes and steak. Proudly unpretentious, the decor is as dated as the menu, but has plenty of charm.

OTHER NEIGHBORHOODS

KOLOBOK Map pp42–3 Russian $

☎ 5541-7085; Díaz Mirón 87, Santa María La Ribera; salads M$30, mains M$35; ⊙ 10am-8pm Tue-Sun; Ⓜ Buenavista

Run by a family from Kazan, Russia, this humble place facing the charming Alameda of the Santa María La Ribera neighborhood has excellent layered salads, tasty 'Russian empanadas' and borscht, of course.

LA CASA DE TOÑO

Map p71 Regional Mexican $

☎ 2630-1084; Sabino 166; pozole M$34; ⊙ 9am-11pm; Ⓜ Buenavista

A major destination for families in Santa María la Ribera, this classic dining hall occupies one of the neighborhood's typical old houses, with tables in a series of salons connected by arched passageways and colorful murals of historic figures chowing down. The main attraction is Toño's hearty *pozole,* served with big sides of crispy *chicharrón* (pork rinds) and limes, but most patrons order a platter of fried quesadillas or tostadas to start. For dessert, Grandma's special flan is the utmost indulgence.

FONDA MARGARITA

Map pp42–3 Traditional Mexican $

Adolfo Prieto 1364; mains half/full portion M$21/32; ⊙ 5:30-11:30am Mon-Sat; ⊜ Metrobus Parque Hundido

Possibly the capital's premier hangover-recovery spot – witness the line down the street on Saturday mornings – the humble eatery under a tin roof whips up big batches of comfort food for the day ahead. Soulful fare like pork back in *chile guajillo* sauce is doled out of giant clay dishes. Don't miss the *huevos refritos* (eggs scrambled with refried black beans). The *fonda* is beside Plaza Tlacoquemécatl, six blocks east of Av Insurgentes.

EL BORREGO VIUDO Map pp42–3 Taquería $

Revolución 241, Tacubaya; tacos M$5-8; ⊙ noon-3am; ⊜ San Ángel-M Barranca del Muerto

More than a dozen white-capped men labor over a steaming grill at this busy neighborhood *taquería* just below the Viaducto freeway. The menu announces the taco variations in sparkly type: *suadero* (beef), *longaniza* (sausage), tender tongue, and their specialty, *pastor,* sliced off a huge cone by the entrance. The tacos are small but substantial, bathed in a potent *salsa verde,* and are best washed down with a mug of *tepache,* a pineapple drink fermented in a wood barrel.

POZOLERÍA TIXTLA

Map pp42–3 Regional Mexican $

☎ 5538-8120; Hernández y Dávalos 35; pozole M$50; ⊙ 11am-9pm; Ⓜ Lázaro Cárdenas

East of Roma, in working-class Colonia Algarín, this old-fashioned dining hall attracts plenty of families with hefty appetites. The specialty (they've been perfecting it for almost 40 years) is Guerrero-style green *pozole,* a soulful variation on the classic pork and hominy broth, garnished with crackling chicharrón and creamy avocado slices.

top picks

Cafés, bars, cantinas and *pulquerías* are all key social venues on the capital's landscape. The traditional watering holes are, of course, cantinas – no-nonsense places with simple tables, long polished bars and serious waiters in formal white jackets. Traditionally male domains reserved for domino playing, tequila sipping and sports viewing, in recent years these establishments have opened their swinging doors to women.

A humbler kind of drinking venue rooted in ancient Mexican tradition, *pulquerías* serve *pulque*, a slightly slimy pre-Hispanic beverage. These relics are worth seeking out for a glimpse of the past. They are lately experiencing a resurgence, with young Chilangos rediscovering the joys of sharing a pitcher of the milky quaff. Another drink being reclaimed by Mexican youth is *mezcal*, the rustic mother of tequila, with *mezcalerías* popping up for hip aficionados to sample crafted batches from Oaxaca, Zacatecas and elsewhere.

Starbucks is a latecomer to a long-standing café tradition fueled by beans from Veracruz, Oaxaca and Chiapas. Coyoacán in particular is jammed with java joints.

Opening Hours

Bars generally open their doors around 7pm, though people don't start pouring in till around 10pm or 11pm, especially toward the weekend. Last drinks are served around 1:30am or 2am, later on Friday and Saturday. Cantinas, many of which double as eating establishments, open earlier, from around 1pm and tend to close as early as 10pm, though there are a few late-night cantinas, such as El Tenampa on Plaza Garibaldi. *Pulquerías* are daytime drinking places; they may open as early as 10am and usually shut down by sundown.

How Much?

Prices of beer and liquor are very much a result of the neighborhood and type of establishment. Expect to pay significantly more in the bars of Condesa or Polanco than you would in your average cantina.

Beer is generally cheap, with bottles of Corona or Victoria going for around M$20 (M$30 in Condesa or Polanco), with more refined brews like Bohemia or Negra Modelo costing slightly more. If you're with friends, you can save by springing for a *cubeta* (ice-filled steel bucket) of six beers. Expect to pay M$70 or M$80 for a shot of top-shelf whiskey or tequila. A bottle of fine tequila, like Her-radura Reposado, could set you back M$950, Bacardi rum (complete with mixer, ice and hovering waiter) M$550. You'll pay around M$40 for a Cuba Libre in an ordinary cantina, M$70 to M$100 for cocktails in Condesa.

Wine may be more expensive than back home. It's not uncommon to spend M$60 to M$80 on a glass of wine, while bottles of anything decent may go for anywhere from M$200 to M$800.

Tipping

Waiters in bars and cantinas will fully expect a tip of 10% to 15%, with the higher rate anticipated in the upscale dens of Condesa and Polanco. In dance clubs, a service charge of 10% may be added to your bill, but they'll still expect you to shell out an additional 5%.

CENTRO HISTÓRICO

Alcohol runs like a river through the ancestral memory of these streets. Everyone should enjoy a *trago* (drink) or two inside an elegant wood-carved booth at La Ópera Bar, or drown their sorrows with the mariachis at El Tenampa (p176) on Plaza Garibaldi. More adventurous aficionados can survey Calle Bolívar's cantina row, west of the Zócalo.

BAR MANCERA Map pp48–9   Bar
☎ 5521-9755; Venustiano Carranza 49; cover Fri & Sat night M$50; ⏱ noon-10pm Mon-Thu, to 2am Fri & Sat; Ⓜ San Juan de Letrán
This atmospheric gentlemen's salon seems preserved in amber, with ornate carved paneling, flowery upholstered armchairs and well-used domino tables. Lately it's been adopted by young clubbers who set up turntables Friday nights from around 9pm.

HOSTERÍA LA BOTA Map pp48–9   Bar
☎ 5709-1117; 1er Callejón de Mesones 7; ⏱ 11am-8pm Tue, to 1:30am Wed-Sat; Ⓜ Isabel la Católica

This fun and funky bar is one component of the Casa Vecina community arts center, a cultural beachhead in the rough-and-tumble southern fringe of the Centro. Tapas and tequilas are served amidst a profusion of warped bullfighting bric-a-brac and mismatched furniture.

LA GIOCONDA Map pp48–9 Bar
☎ 5518-7823; Filomena Mata 18; ☽ 4-11pm Mon-Thu, to 2am Fri & Sat; Ⓜ Allende
Dark and light draft beer are poured by the pint in this happening little pub, located off a pedestrian thoroughfare. By around 7pm, the stone-walled space is usually buzzing with a varied crowd in the mood for relaxed conversation and a bit of rock 'n' roll.

LA ÓPERA BAR Map pp48–9 Cantina
☎ 5512-8959; Av 5 de Mayo 10; ☽ 1pm-midnight Mon-Sat, to 6pm Sun; Ⓜ Allende
With booths of dark walnut and an ornate tin ceiling (said to have been punctured by Pancho Villa's bullet on an otherwise slow night), this late-19th-century watering hole remains a bastion of tradition. Enjoy a watercress salad or dish of snails in *chipotle* sauce alongside your tequila and *sangrita*.

SALÓN CORONA Map pp48–9 Cantina
☎ 5512-5725; Bolívar 24; ☽ 8am-midnight Sun-Wed, to 2am Thu-Sat; Ⓜ Allende
Punks and suits help make up the crowd in this boisterous, no-nonsense beer hall, which has been running since 1928. The amiable staff serve up *tarros* (mugs) of light or dark *cerveza de barril* (draft beer) and bottles of almost every known Mexican beer, along with tasty *bacalao* (salt cod) and turkey sandwiches. The photo mural behind the counter, by the way, captures the patrons' stunned reaction when soccer star Hugo Sánchez missed a penalty kick back in the '86 World Cup against Paraguay.

LA HERMOSA HORTENSIA
Map pp48–9 Pulquería
Plaza Garibaldi 4; ☽ 10am-midnight; Ⓜ Garibaldi
Opening onto Plaza Garibaldi, this is a good *pulquería* for beginners: its hygiene is above the norm, they're used to seeing foreigners, and the atmosphere is 100% *'familiar.'*

top picks
CANTINA CRAWL

- La Ópera Bar (left)
- Cantina Covadonga (p164)
- Cantina La Jalisciense (p165)
- Salón Corona (left)
- La Guadalupana (p165)

CAFÉ JAKEMIR Map pp48–9 Café
☎ 5709-7038; Isabel la Católica 88; ☽ 9am-8pm Mon-Sat; Ⓜ Isabel la Católica
Run by a family of Lebanese coffee traders from Orizaba, this old distribution outlet was transformed into a popular café and has excellent and inexpensive cappuccinos, as well as baklava and other pastries. Bulk buyers will find bins of beans from Veracruz, Oaxaca and Chiapas below the counter.

LA SELVA CAFÉ Map pp48–9 Café
☎ 5521-4111; Bolívar 31; Ⓜ Allende
When the crowds and street noise begin to rattle you, duck into this branch of the Chiapas coffee trader, ensconced in the stunning patio of a colonial building.

ALAMEDA CENTRAL & AROUND
In contrast to the tony cafés that occupy the museums and malls in the immediate vicinity of the Alameda Central, plenty of workaday coffee houses and drinking establishments are scattered around the chaotic shopping district south of the park, though these options tend to diminish after dark.

LAS DUELISTAS Map p64 Pulquería
Aranda 30; ☽ 9am-9pm; Ⓜ Salto del Agua
Now graffitied with pre-Hispanic psychedelia behind the swinging doors, this large *pulquería* alongside the Mercado San Juan has become the domain of young Chilangos who've rediscovered the virtues of their ancestral beverage. Despite the interior's new look, the *pulque* is still dispensed straight out of the barrel in a variety of flavors, including mango and coconut.

PULQUERÍAS

Before discotheques, even before cantinas, Mexico had *pulquerías*. Named after the drink they served, these seedy hovels were *the* working-class watering hole for the better part of 400 years, before refrigeration and more conventional beverages starting pushing them to the side.

When the Aztecs ruled Mexico, *pulque,* extracted from the maguey plant, was used only in rituals and by the elite. Its production was strictly controlled and drunkenness was severely punished. When the Spanish arrived, *pulque* hit the streets. The milky, low-alcohol brew was sold from open-air stands and the method of service was just as primitive: purveyors would ladle the drink from large basins into earthenware cups. As the day wore on, these cups would be smashed by rowdy patrons once the contents were drained – *¡epa!*

The ancient beverage was widely consumed in Mexico City throughout the colonial period, chiefly among the city's underclasses – statistics of the era show an annual per capita consumption among adults of 187 gallons. In the mid-17th century there were some 200 *pulquerías* operating in the Centro. The government restricted their locations to outlying neighborhoods, a factor that may have contributed to the wicked brew's eventual demise. In the meantime, other potent potables, such as beer brought by German immigrants, as well as *mezcal* and tequila, began to gain greater popularity and supplant *pulque* as the intoxicant of choice. True *pulque* is homemade, not bottled, and therefore not viable for large-scale commercial production.

Nowadays just a handful of *pulquerías* still function. They tend to be extremely rustic places, and some remain male-only enclaves. However, they are highly social venues with patrons in a conversant mood. Food is served (often for free) and jukeboxes are normally set just below blast volume. The viscous white liquid may be served straight up or in the somewhat more palatable *curado* (flavored form). Coconut, pineapple and mango are popular, along with some odd variations like beet, oat (sprinkled with cinnamon) and celery.

ZONA ROSA, CUAUHTÉMOC & JUÁREZ

The Pink Zone, the capital's international party center, boasts the highest concentration of bars and clubs in town, and prices at the numerous venues along Londres and Florencia reflect its tourist orientation. Male pedestrians in this area should be prepared for aggressive invitations from numerous street-corner hustlers to 'ladies' bars' and 'table dance clubs.' Calle Amberes has become the hub of the gay and lesbian-oriented bar scene (p196).

CAFÉ LA HABANA Map pp74–5   Café
☎ 5546-2555; Morelos 62; Ⓜ Juárez
This grand coffeehouse is a traditional haunt for writers and journalists, who linger for hours over a *café americano*. Legend has it that Fidel and Che plotted strategy here prior to the Cuban revolution.

CAFETERÍA GABI'S Map pp74–5   Café
☎ 5511-7637; Nápoles 55; ☾ Mon-Sat;
Ⓜ Insurgentes
Cluttered with caffeine-related paraphernalia, this family-run coffeehouse perks with conversation midmornings and early evenings, when the occupants of neighboring offices pour in for a rich *café con leche*

(coffee with milk) and a crispy *banderilla* (stick-like glazed pastry).

PAPA BILL'S SALOON Map pp74–5   Bar
☎ 5207-6669; Río Guadalquivir 88; ☾ 1pm-midnight or 1am Mon-Sat, to 8pm Sun;
Ⓜ Insurgentes
For those in need of their sports fix, this sprawling gringo-style parlor has plenty of flat-screen TVs showing the big game. Happy hours are from 2pm to 9pm.

HOSTAL TEQUILERÍA CIELO ROJO
Map pp74–5   Cantina
☎ 5525-1196; Génova 70; ☾ noon-1am Sun-Thu, to 3am Fri & Sat; Ⓜ Insurgentes
Besides offering the most extensive selection of tequilas this side of Jalisco, this boisterous salon on the Zona Rosa's main pedestrian thoroughfare also stocks some fine handmade *mezcals* from the La Venencia distillery in Oaxaca, including a 15-year-old *arroqueño*. Mariachis perform nightly, greatly enhancing the whole sampling process.

POLANCO

The bars of upscale Polanco can be more democratic than you might expect. Everyone seems to want to bask in the exclusive, electronica-fueled aura exuded by the hotel bars in the Zona Hotelera and along Presidente Masaryk,

top picks

CAFÉS

- Caffé Toscano (right)
- Cafetería Gabi's (opposite)
- Café La Habana (opposite)
- Café El Jarocho (p165)
- Los Enanos del Tapanco (p165)

and they're willing to pay the price for the sexy cocktails dispensed therein.

BIG RED Map p84 — Bar
☎ 5255-5277; Presidente Masaryk 101; 8:30am-2am Mon-Sat; Ⓜ Polanco
Big Red is a volume dealer. Drinks are priced by the ounce (M$14 for Bacardi, M$16 for Centenario tequila), plus your choice of mixer. Thus the place attracts a broader cross-section of the populace than the usual Polanco *antro* (bar). Rather than the icy electronica favored by such places, Big Red dares to blare *banda* (brass band music from northern Mexico) and pop.

SEGAFREDO Map p84 — Café
☎ 5281-1203; Dumas 71C; 8am-midnight Sun-Wed, to 2:30am Thu-Sat; Ⓜ Polanco
The Bologna-based chain expertly prepares all the espresso variations, from *caffé latte fredo* to *macchiato con panna*. Try a Caffé Maya, spiked with the Yucatecan anise liqueur Xtabentún. Attracted by wireless access, laptop-users often occupy the upper level, which has an open-air terrace attached.

CONDESA

Well-known as a culinary and nightlife destination, Colonia Condesa also abounds in casual sidewalk cafés serving espressos and lattes, particularly along Calle Tamaulipas (not to mention a couple of Starbucks branches). More recently, several *mezcal* tasting salons have popped up in the neighborhood (p164), to wildly positive response.

BLACK HORSE Map p88 — Pub
☎ 5211-8740; Mexicali 85, cnr Tamaulipas; 6pm-2am Mon-Sat; Ⓜ Patriotismo
It isn't just because they prepare bangers and mash and screen the soccer match

that this authentic British pub has earned a spot on the Condesa map. The place also boasts an international social scene and has excellent bands playing in the back room midweek.

CAFÉ BOLA DE ORO Map p88 — Café
☎ 5286-5659; Nuevo León 192B; 7am-10pm Mon-Fri, 9am-7pm Sat; Ⓜ Chilpancingo
An outlying branch of the Xalapa coffee purveyor, this is a good place to score a bag of Coatepec beans or simply enjoy a cup of Veracruz' fine, full-bodied blends.

CAFFÉ TOSCANO Map p88 — Café
☎ 5584-3681; Michoacán 30; Ⓜ Metrobus Sonora
This sidewalk café opens onto a delightful corner of Parque México, making a fine setting for a latte and the morning paper – grab one off the rack.

CANTINA EL CENTENARIO
Map p88 — Cantina
☎ 5553-5451; Vicente Suárez 42; noon-midnight Mon-Sat; Ⓜ Patriotismo
Behind the swinging doors is an enclave of tradition in the heart of modish Condesa, brimming with bullfighting memorabilia and adorned with Spanish *azulejo* tiles. Sure, hipsters fill the place every evening, but the domino bouts, roving musical trios and tasty drinking snacks are the same as ever.

LA BOTICA Map p88 — Mezcalería
☎ 5212-1167; Alfonso Reyes 120; 5pm-midnight Mon-Tue, to 1:30am Wed-Sat; Ⓜ Patriotismo
Like an old apothecary's, La Botica dispenses its elixirs from squat little bottles lined up on the shelf (these make nifty souvenirs). Available varieties are suitably scribbled on pieces of cardboard – try the *cuesh*, distilled from a wild maguey in Oaxaca. La Botica has been such a roaring success, they've opened other branches with similar hours at Campeche 396 in Condesa and Orizaba 161 in Colonia Roma.

PASTELERÍA MAQUE Map p88 — Café
☎ 2454-4662; Ozulama 4; Ⓜ Metrobus Campeche
Condesa sophisticates gather mornings and evenings at this Parisian-style café-bakery near the south end of Parque México. Waiters bring around trays of fresh-baked croissants and *conchas* (round pastries sprinkled with sugar) – point to your preference.

MEZCAL RENAISSANCE

Mezcal, known erroneously as 'that drink with the worm in it,' is finally getting the respect it deserves. (The worm was a marketing gimmick for gullible American consumers.) A spirit whose origins date back to pre-Hispanic times, *mezcal* has languished in Mexico, overshadowed by other liquors, like rum and brandy. Many think of it as a rustic relative to the more refined tequila, when in fact tequila is just one form of *mezcal* derived from a particular plant that grows in the state of Jalisco – the blue agave. But *mezcals* are produced from many varieties of agave (or maguey) throughout Mexico, including the states of Durango, Zacatecas, Michoacán, Guerrero and, most famously, Oaxaca.

It is estimated there are some 136 varieties of the succulent plant, and each one produces a different version. New laws now require *mezcals* from the various regions to be labeled with an appellation of origin, as wines from regions in Europe are denominated. Due to worldwide demand, the production of tequila has become industrialized, while many small-scale *mezcal* makers still produce the drink in limited, hand-crafted batches.

Another difference is that *mezcals* are customarily produced by roasting the *piña* – the pineapple-shaped heart of the agave – over a fire in an underground pit, which lends the drink its characteristic smoky flavor, while in the tequila process the *piña* is steamed.

Straight up, *mezcal* is typically served with slices of orange and an orangey salt blended with chili and – old myths die hard – a powder made from maguey worms, and chased by a Victorita mini bottle of beer. And, like a fine single-malt scotch, it's meant to be savored slowly rather than knocked back.

Places like the Mestizo Lounge (below) and Los Danzantes (p152), which has its own distillery in Santiago Matalán, Oaxaca, serve *mezcal* to a new breed of discerning aficionados. Another, the Taberna Red Fly (below) in Colonia Roma, organizes monthly tastings. La Botica (p163), with branches in Condesa and Roma, dispenses *mezcal* from old-fashioned pharmacy bottles and serves it in fruity cocktails.

ROMA

Colonia Roma remains a bohemian enclave where artists and intellectuals engage in animated conversation at Parisian-style cafés. Like Condesa, it's a center of the *mezcal* revival (see above), with various tasting venues found along Calle Orizaba.

CANTINA COVADONGA Map pp92–3 Cantina
☎ 5533-2922; Puebla 121; ⏱ 1pm-3am Mon-Fri; Ⓜ Insurgentes

Echoing with the sounds of clacking dominoes, the old Asturian social hall is a traditionally male enclave, though hipsters of both sexes have increasingly moved in on this hallowed ground.

MESTIZO LOUNGE Map pp92–3 Mezcalería
☎ 2454-1662; Chihuahua 121; ⏱ 6pm-2am Tue-Sat; Ⓜ Insurgentes

This highly social hole-in-the-wall run by gregarious hosts Gina and Manuel is very much at the heart of the *mezcal* renaissance. Taste a smoky *cenizo* (a Zacatecas variety) or have a *mezcal* martini. They make excellent sandwiches, too.

TABERNA RED FLY Map pp92–3 Lounge
☎ 1054-3616; Orizaba 143; ⏱ 6pm-midnight Mon-Wed, to 2am Thu-Sat; Ⓜ Álvaro Obregón

An elegantly furnished space in a typical Porfiriato-era residence, the Red Fly organizes monthly *mezcal* tastings, where aficionados can appreciate the subtle gradations in flavor, based on where the beverage is distilled.

TIERRA DE VINOS Map pp92–3 Wine-tasting salon
☎ 5208-5133; Durango 197; ⏱ 1-8pm Mon & Tue, to 1pm-midnight Wed-Sat; Ⓜ Metrobus Durango

Mexico is not a nation of oenophiles, so this salon is a pleasant surprise. The wine list changes monthly, with most of the world's vineyards represented. Sit at the front bar and nosh on tapas while sampling the month's featured vintage or take a table in the lively rear dining room (see p151).

TRAVAZARES TABERNA Map pp92–3 Pub
☎ 5264-1142; Orizaba 127; ⏱ 1pm-2am; Ⓜ Metrobus Álvaro Obregón

The downstairs adjunct of a cultural center, this popular Roma hangout strikes a suitably bohemian tone. Recycled objects furnish a series of cozy, candlelit salons where artistically inclined youth sip wine or Cerveza Cosaco (a Mexican mircrobrew). The fusion menu is hit-or-miss, depending on who's in the kitchen.

CAFÉ DE CARLO Map p92–3 Café
☎ 5574-5647; Orizaba 115; ⏱ 8am-10pm Mon-Sat, to 5pm Sun; Ⓜ Insurgentes

Coffee connoisseurs head for this unassuming sidewalk café, with an aromatic roaster and a vintage espresso machine. Across the street is a relic of 1950s Roma, La Bella Italia. It's an old-fashioned ice cream parlor that sees few customers these days.

CAFÉ VILLA DE MADRID Map pp92–3 Café
☎ 5208-8549; Plaza Villa de Madrid; ☽ 8:15-6:30pm Mon-Sat; ⓜ Metrobus Durango

With just a few sidewalk tables at the top of the Plaza Villa de Madrid (aka Plaza Cibeles), this longtime storefront operation roasts beans from the family *finca* in Chiapas (they also roll their own cigars). Espressos are just M$8.50 a shot (about half what Starbucks charges).

LOS ENANOS DEL TAPANCO
Map pp92–3 Café
☎ 5564-2274; Orizaba 161; ☽ 8am-11:30pm Mon-Fri, 9am-11:30pm Sat, 3:30-10:30pm Sun; ⓜ Centro Médico

Possibly Mexico City's coolest café, the 'Dwarves of the Loft' doubles as an art gallery. Cappuccinos and quiches are served along with an eclectic music selection. There's live music Friday and storytelling Tuesday evening.

MESÓN DE THÉ CARAVANSERAI
Map pp92–3 Tea room
☎ 5511-2877; Orizaba 101; ☽ 10am-9:30pm Mon-Fri, 12:30pm-9:30pm Sat, 3:30-9:30pm Sun; ⓜ Insurgentes

This French-managed tea room has over 100 blends, carefully categorized by their intended effects (Tokyo Springtime is 'a subtle tea for the afternoon'). Guests lounge on sofas and pillows to enjoy a pot of their chosen brew, which is ceremoniously served on silver trays.

COYOACÁN

Weekend hangout that it is, this southern district probably has more cafés per square inch than anywhere else in town. The cafés are mainly on the streets radiating off the two central plazas and along tranquil Francisco Sosa. One of them, Café El Jarocho, is a genuine Coyoacán institution. Nearby is the recently opened La Bipolar, an odd new hybrid of working class dive and hipster hotspot.

LA GUADALUPANA Map p95 Cantina
☎ 5554-6253; Higuera 2; ☽ noon-12:30am Mon-Sat; ⓜ Viveros

Serving spirits for over seven decades, this venerable tavern breathes tradition, from the bulls' heads on the walls to the blasé waiters in white coats. The setting is just right for a tequila, served with homemade *sangrita* and/or a few Bohemias. There are *botanas* and tortas as well as heartier fare like *cabrito* (goat).

LA BIPOLAR Map p95 Cantina
☎ 5484-8230; Mallntzln 155; ☽ 1pm-2am; ⓜ Viveros

Owned by Mexican heartthrob Diego Luna of *Y Tu Mamá También* fame, this popular new cantina displays a *naco* aesthetic (see p127), playing up the kitschier elements of Mexican popular culture. Inside, the walls are fashioned from plastic crates and the light shades are sliced tin buckets while the 50s-era jukebox spins a remarkably eclectic music selection. Besides the Coronas and *mezcal* shots, they've got updated versions of classic Mexican snacks.

CAFÉ EL JAROCHO Map p95 Café
☎ 5658-5029; Cuauhtémoc 134; ☽ 6am-1am; ⓜ Coyoacán

This immensely popular joint churns out M$7 cappuccinos for long lines of java hounds. As there's no seating inside, people have their coffee standing in the street or sitting on curbside benches. The branch just around the corner makes great tortas, and both branches have terrific doughnuts. Another branch at El Jarocho (Map p95; ☎ 5659-9107; Av México 25-C) is convenient to Viveros park.

OTHER NEIGHBORHOODS
TLALPAN
CANTINA LA JALISCIENSE
Map p109 Cantina
☎ 5573-5586; Plaza de la Constitución 6; ☽ noon-12:30am Mon-Sat

One of the best reasons to make the trip down to Tlalpan, this always lively neighborhood cantina is frequented by the arty characters who populate the southern

BLOODY MARÍA

A good shot of tequila should be sipped and appreciated. In Mexico, it is often accompanied by an equal cup of *sangrita* (literally, little blood). This nonalcoholic chaser can range from sweet to spicy. The sweeter varieties contain mostly grenadine and orange juice, while the spicier ones have a tomato base with chili added. The best bars and restaurants make their own *sangrita*, and the spicier version predominates.

This recipe is the creation of owner and chef Fernando Ramírez at María del Alma (p148). Any combination of non-chunky or strained hot sauce can be substituted for the local brands mentioned here. (In a pinch, *sangrita* can be made by spicing up some Bloody Mary mix.)

Sangrita María del Alma

Blend and strain tomatoes to make 1L undiluted tomato juice. Add the following:

- 2 oz grenadine
- 6 oz orange juice
- 1 oz Clamato juice
- 2 oz lemon juice
- 1 oz Valentina hot sauce
- 1 oz Bufalo hot sauce
- 1 oz Tabasco sauce
- salt & pepper to taste

Optional:
- Puree and add 50g of celery and 50g of cucumber

Serve in a hollowed out Roma tomato; garnish with a small green chili.

district, though it has a distinctly down-to-earth atmosphere. In operation since 1870, in the revolutionary era it was a parting stop for gun-toting bandidos bound for the hills. Gregarious owner Miguel Ángel Fernández carries forward the legacy with his homemade sangría and toothsome *bacalao* sandwiches. But take heed: swearing is strictly prohibited. For transport information, see p110.

XOCHIMILCO

EL TEMPLO DE DIANA Map pp112–13 Pulquería
☎ 5653-4657; Madero 17; ⌚ 9am-9:30pm; Ⓜ Xochimilco

This classic *pulquería,* a block east of the main market, has a cheerful sawdust-on-the-floor vibe, with patrons from a broad age range enjoying giant mugs of the maguey-based beverage behind the swinging doors. Even a few females may pop in. *Pulque* is delivered fresh daily from Hidalgo state, and expertly blended with flavorings like mango, tomato and pine nut.

LA BOTIJONA Map pp112–13 Pulquería
Morelos 109; ⌚ 9am-9:30pm; Ⓜ Xochimilco

Possibly the cleanest *pulque* dispenser in town, this institutional-green hall near the train station is a friendly family-run establishment with big plastic pails of the traditional quaff lining the shelves. Coconut and celery are among the more intriguing *curados* (flavored *pulques*) on offer.

top picks

- **Auditorio Nacional** (p171)
- **El Bataclán** (p173)
- **Salon Tenampa** (p176)
- **El Hijo del Cuervo** (p169)
- **La Casa de Paquita La del Barrio** (p173)
- **Mamá Rumba** (p172)
- **Pasagüero** (p173)
- **Pata Negra** (p170)
- **Salón Los Ángeles** (p171)
- **T-Gallery** (p170)

What's your recommendation? www.lonelyplanet.com/mexico-city

After-hours, the capital's attractions are just as lively and varied as they are by day. Chilangos take their nighttime pursuits seriously. Whether bouncing around on a dance floor, taking in a concert or gathering with friends at a nightclub, they devote considerable energy to the activity.

Nighttime entertainment tends to follow class lines. The DF's working classes may strut their stuff in large, elegant dancehalls like the Salón Los Angeles, crowd the Zócalo for free concerts by *norteño* bands, or sing along with Paquita La del Barrio, the popular recording star, at her own cabaret (p173). Better-off *capitalinos* may prefer to squeeze into postmodern clubs and groove to DJ-driven beats and consume exotic cocktails at Polanco nightspots, or catch the jazz and pop stars who regularly perform at clubs and concert halls. But as an outsider, you can drop in anywhere and enjoy the scene.

Certain parts of town light up after dark. In the Zona Rosa and Condesa, revelers may hoof it from one venue to the next, while in Polanco or along Av Insurgentes Sur, it's customary to leave the car with the valet. The action is somewhat sparser if no less lively in the Centro Histórico, where the action unfolds in various colonial palaces and mansions.

To find out what's going on, check the 'Noche' or 'Conciertos' sections of the Spanish-language *Tiempo Libre* magazine, or scour the listings in *Chilango* and *Dondé Ir*, monthly magazines with extensive nightlife coverage. For more information on these and other entertainment publications, or about where to purchase tickets for events, see the information section in The Arts (p178).

ANTROS

Halfway between a bar and a dance club, the *antro* is the unit of nightlife currency for with-it young *defeños* (DF natives). The concept varies, but *antros* usually have loud recorded music, maybe video screens, and enough space to dance if the mood takes you. Some *antros* lean more toward the bar end of the spectrum, while others are closer to a *discoteca*; some host live music a few nights of the week. Most *antros* will have a restaurant component, with snacks such as pizza or spring rolls to nibble on, and there will certainly be a range of colorful cocktails on offer. Polanco and Condesa offer the trendiest scenes, and there's more upscale action down in San Ángel.

top picks

GLITTERATI SPOTTING

- Condesa DF (opposite)
- Área (right)
- Momma (p170)
- Bengala (opposite)
- Tiki Bar (p170)

ÁREA Map p84

☎ 5282-3100; Presidente Masaryk 201, Polanco; ✆ 7pm-midnight Mon-Wed, to 2am Thu-Sat; Ⓜ Polanco

Atop the Hábita Hotel, this open-air roof lounge does a brisk trade in exotic martinis, with sweeping city views as a backdrop and videos projected on the wall of a nearby building for entertainment. On chilly evenings beautiful scenesters gravitate toward the wall-length fireplace; in warmer weather they cool their toes in the pool on the deck below.

GO GO LOUNGE Map p84

☎ 5281-8974; Dumas 105, Polanco; cover M$100; ✆ 10pm-5am Thu-Sat; Ⓜ Polanco

The honeycombed decor in this *antro* over a sushi bar seems lifted from *Kill Bill*, and features what is supposedly the largest mirror ball in Latin America. Merengue, reggaeton and pop keep a post-pubescent crowd bouncing in a series of packed salons. When it gets too sweaty, make your way to the terrace bar and order a Takeshi (sake and mango ice cream cocktail).

BAR MILÁN Map pp74–5

☎ 5592-0031; Milán 18, Juárez; ✆ 9pm-3:30am Wed-Sat; Ⓜ Cuauhtémoc

Tucked away on a quiet backstreet east of the Zona Rosa, this cave-like hangout gets as crowded as the metro, with a boisterous blend of college students and expats. Purchase drink tickets ('milagros'), then make your way over to the cactus-trimmed bar. The soundtrack ranges from classic rock to Café Tacuba; don't be surprised when the crowd spontaneously bursts into chorus.

BENGALA Map pp92–3
☎ 5211-4690; Sonora 34A, Roma Norte; ☽ 9pm-4am Thu-Sat; Ⓜ Chapultepec
This low-lit concept bar evokes a desert trek, with decor influenced by *Casablanca* and *The Sheltering Sky*, though disco-friendly DJs may put you on an entirely different plane. Its slightly out-of-the-way location only adds to the conspiratorial air. Have a 'Module' (a green cocktail of cucumber, Pernod and mescal) and mingle with the film and TV figures who customarily pop up here.

CELTICS Map p88
☎ 5211-9081; Tamaulipas 36, Condesa; ☽ 1:30pm-3am Mon-Sat, 6pm-1am Sun; Ⓜ Patriotismo
An Argentinian-run facsimile of an Irish pub, Celtics remains hugely popular with young *defeños*. A Guinness will set you back M$70 here, a draft Sol M$35. The soundtrack is more U2 than Chieftains; bands play Sunday to Tuesday evenings.

CIBELES Map pp92–3
☎ 5208-2029; Plaza Villa de Madrid 17, Roma; ☽ 7pm-2am Tue-Sat; Ⓜ Metrobus Durango
This fashionable new *antro* is a low-ceilinged, L-shaped living room with a perversely eclectic array of mismatched sofas, armchairs and coffee tables. The mood swings throughout the week from quiet and conversational (Tuesday) to loud and raucous (Friday, when DJs mix '80s hits with lounge-y beats). Reservations are a must on weekends.

CINNA BAR Map p88
☎ 5287-8456; Nuevo León 67; ☽ 7pm-2am Tue-Sat, to 1am Sun; Ⓜ Patriotismo
Looking at Parque España through red-tinted windows, this lounge-cum-dining room sports a self-consciously minimal aesthetic. Smartly outfitted professionals stop in after work to nosh on Vietnamese spring rolls, sip raspberry martinis and groove on sounds concocted by DJs with iBooks.

CONDESA DF Map p88
☎ 5241-2600; Veracruz 102, Condesa; ☽ 1pm-midnight Mon-Wed, to 1:30am Thu-Sat, to 11pm Sun; Ⓜ Chapultepec
The bar of the fashionable boutique hotel has become an essential stop on the Condesa nightlife circuit. Action focuses on the triangular atrium and wackily decorated alcoves around it, where businessfolk, artists and the occasional film star gather before moving on to still-hotter spots. Up on the roof terrace, guests lounge on wicker sofas, nibble on sushi and enjoy views of verdant Parque España across the way.

EL HIJO DEL CUERVO Map p95
☎ 5658-7824; www.elhijodelcuervo.com.mx; Jardín Centenario 17, Coyoacán; ☽ 4pm-midnight Mon-Wed, 1pm-1:30am Thu, 1pm-2:30am Fri & Sat, 1-11:30pm Sun; Ⓜ Viveros
A Coyoacán institution, this enormous stone-walled hall on the Jardín del Centenario is a sort of thinking man's-drinking man's habitat. Groups of friends pack into its various salons to share pitchers of beer, snack on boards of Spanish cheeses and engage in animated conversation. Assorted musical ensembles perform Wednesday and Thursday nights in a small theater toward the back.

HOOKAH LOUNGE Map p88
☎ 5264-6275; Campeche 284, Condesa; ☽ 1pm-12:30am Mon-Wed, to 2am Thu-Sat; Ⓜ Chilpancingo
Moroccan tapestries and scimitars set the tone for this North African fantasy. The fun revolves around the water pipes (from M$100), available in a bewildering array of flavors. Wednesday to Saturday nights, DJs produce an eclectic mix of chill-out and Arab rhythms, with no fewer than four turntables. There are also Middle-Eastern snacks.

LA BODEGUITA DEL MEDIO Map pp92–3
☎ 5553-0246; Cozumel 37, Roma; ☽ 1:30pm-1am Sun-Wed, to 2am Thu-Sat; Ⓜ Sevilla
The walls are scribbled with verses and messages at this animated branch of the famous Havana joint where the *mojito* was reportedly invented. (Here the cocktail is prepared in classic style with white rum, mint leaves and brown sugar.) Excellent *son cubano* combos perform in the various interconnected salons above the bar. For

top picks

HIPPEST DF NIGHTSPOTS

- T-Gallery (right)
- Cibeles (p169)
- Malafama (below)
- Pata Negra (right)
- La Bodeguita del Medio (p169)

snacks, try the *masitas de cerdo* (fried pork chunks) or stuffed plantains.

LAMM Map pp92–3

☎ 5514-8501; Álvaro Obregón 99, Roma; ☾ to 2am Mon-Sat; Ⓜ Insurgentes

In the evening the open-air restaurant of the Lamm (p150) turns into a hip lounge where luminaries from the academic, artistic and political spheres converge until the wee hours. There's live *música cubana* and jazz Tuesday and Wednesday respectively.

LOVE Map pp92–3

☎ 5564-7823; Medellín 65, Roma; admission M$70; ☾ 11pm-3:30am Tue-Sat; 🚍 Metrobus Sonora

Socialites line up for Love, upstairs from the fusion restaurant Ixchel (p150), in a typically ornate Colonia Roma mansion. You're unlikely to get in without reservations, and even then it'll depend on your looks. Once inside the velvet-draped lounge, order an apple martini and party like it's 1983 – the DJ will help you remember what that was like.

MALAFAMA Map p88

☎ 5553-5138; Av Michoacán 78, Condesa; tables per hr M$80; Ⓜ Patriotismo

As trendy as its bars and cafés, Condesa's sleek billiard hall doubles as a gallery of photo art. The well-maintained tables are frequented by both pool sharks and novices.

MOMMA Map p84

☎ 5281-1537; Tennyson 102, Polanco; cover varies; ☾ 10pm-2am Mon-Sat; Ⓜ Polanco

Currently Polanco's hottest *antro*, Momma attracts hordes of party people. Beyond a chic, minimalist restaurant, the brightly lit hall of mirrors resounds with pop *en español* and hits from past decades. As elsewhere in Polanco, expect a discretionary admission policy.

PATA NEGRA Map p88

☎ 5211-5563; Tamaulipas 30, Condesa; ☾ 1:30pm-2am; Ⓜ Patriotismo

Nominally a tapas bar, this oblong salon draws a friendly, clean-cut crowd of 20-something Chilangos and expats. There's live music on both levels, with the upper Salón Pata Negra striking a more bohemian tone.

REXO Map p88

☎ 5553-5337; Saltillo 1, Condesa; ☾ 1:30pm-1am Sun-Tue, to 2am Wed-Sat; Ⓜ Patriotismo

A minimalist, triple-decker supper club, the perennially popular Rexo really packs them in toward the weekend. There's dining on the upper levels, though the focus is on the lit-from-below bar at the bottom, which fuels the revelry with mezcaltinis and other unusual cocktails.

T-GALLERY Map p88

☎ 5211-1222; www.tgallerydesign.com; Saltillo 39, Condesa; ☾ 5pm-2am Mon-Sat; Ⓜ Patriotismo

A low-key crowd kick back with cocktails in the various salons of this lovely old Condesa home, each appointed with a splendid array of kitschy sofas, coffee tables and mirrors. It's like going to a party at your hippest friend's house, with a difference – you can purchase any of the furniture that appeals to you. Jazz, blues and bossa nova combos jam downstairs nightly.

TIKI BAR Map pp92–3

☎ 5584-2668; Querétaro 227, Roma; ☾ 6pm-3am Wed-Sat; 🚍 Metrobus Sonora

Amidst the salsa dance clubs, this South Pacific spree spreads on the kitsch with bamboo-fringed walls and teak floors. The wacky cocktails are the real draw: not just mai-tais but chocotikis, mojotikis and various other rum creations that thrill a celebrity-studded crowd.

LIVE MUSIC

However the evening is enjoyed, it will probably involve some kind of musical performance. Cuban dance ensembles stir up the salsa at the various tropical dance halls, blues and rock groups entertain aficionados at smoky clubs, singer-songwriters deliver sensitive balladry at cozy cafés, mariachis belt out heartfelt ballads at Plaza Garibaldi, and globally known pop groups play concert halls and sports arenas.

CONCERTS

Mexico City has emerged as a prime stop on the international touring circuit, and you're as likely to catch such foreign visitors as Bob Dylan, Kenny G or Korn as homegrown artists like Maná, Alejandro Fernández or Banda El Recodo. As elsewhere, the size of the venue will depend on the artist's fame. Big acts will likely perform at the Auditorio Nacional or Palacio de Deportes sports arena, while lesser-known figures may play medium-sized halls like the Teatro Metropolitán or Vive Cuervo Salón. Check www.ticketmaster.com.mx to see what's coming up, and purchase tickets at Ticketmaster outlets (p178).

AUDITORIO NACIONAL Map p78

☎ 5280-9250; www.auditorio.com.mx in Spanish; Paseo de la Reforma 50; Ⓜ Auditorio

Major rock and pop artists take the stage at the 10,000-seat Auditorio Nacional (National Auditorium). Mexican stars like Luis Miguel, Maná and Gloria Trevi invariably pack the surprisingly intimate space, as do occasional foreign visitors like John Fogerty, Caetano Veloso and Joaquín Sabina.

TEATRO METROPOLITÁN Map p64

☎ 5510-1035; Independencia 90; Ⓜ Juárez

Artists as diverse as Café Tacuba, Buddy Guy and the Russian National Ballet have played this medium-sized hall near the Alameda Central. An old movie palace dating from the 1940s, the lavishly decorated theater holds around 3000, with an upper deck high above the stage.

VIVE CUERVO SALÓN Map p84

☎ 5255-1496; Lago Andrómaco 17; admission M$250-550

A warehouse-sized venue for touring salsa stars as well as rock, world and other performers. With excellent sound, wall-length bar and dance floor for thousands, this is one of Mexico's most attractive clubs.

TROPICAL

A dozen or more clubs and large *salones de baile* (dance halls) are devoted to salsa, merengue, cumbia, danzón and other Cuban and Caribbean dances. The city's many aficionados can go to a different hall each night of the week, some capable of holding thousands of people. Even if you can't dance a step, you might enjoy listening to the great *salseros* on

top picks

TROPICAL MUSIC/ DANCING VENUES

- Salón Los Ángeles (left)
- Mamá Rumba (p172)
- El Gran León (below)
- California Dancing Club (below)
- Barfly (below)

stage, including many Cuban imports, and watching the smartly dressed couples hit the dance floor.

You might learn a few steps beforehand at the Plaza de Danzón (Map p64), northwest of La Ciudadela near metro Balderas. Couples crowd the plaza every Saturday afternoon to do the *danzón*, an elegant and complicated Cuban step that infiltrated Mexico in the 19th century. Lessons in *danzón* and other steps are given from around 3:30pm to 5:30pm.

BARFLY Map p84

☎ 5282-2514; www.bar-fly.com.mx; Presidente Masaryk 393, 1st fl; cover M$140; ⌚ 9pm-3am Tue-Sat; Ⓜ Polanco

Upstairs at the Plaza Masaryk shopping mall, this small supper club jumps to live Cuban sounds most nights. This being Polanco, it's a well-coiffed crowd that fills the tiny dance floor, situated just below the stage.

CALIFORNIA DANCING CLUB Map pp42–3

☎ 5539-3564; Calz de Tlalpan 1189; admission men/women M$45/40 Fri, Sat & Mon, M$75 Sun; ⌚ 6-11pm Fri, Sat & Mon, to 5am Sun; Ⓜ Portales

More *popular* (low-brow) than the Colonia Roma clubs, this old-fashioned hall has marathon dance sessions, with half a dozen bands on the bill. Hundreds of couples bounce around a vast tiled floor flanked by stout mirrored columns as groups like Los Escorpiones de Durango keep the *cumbias* (Colombian dance music) coming. Beer and soft drinks are dispensed from two humble bars.

EL GRAN LEÓN Map pp92–3

☎ 5564-7110; Querétaro 225, Roma; cover M$60; ⌚ 9pm-3:30am Thu-Sat; 🚌 Metrobus Sonora

Two or three top-notch Cuban *son* ensembles take the tropical stage nightly at this old-school club. Unescorted (and escorted)

HAVANA, DF

Ever since Hernán Cortés set sail from La Habana for the coast of Veracruz, the fates of Cuba and Mexico have been closely linked. In contrast to its northern neighbor, Mexico has long displayed a benevolent attitude toward Cuba, and the island is frequented by vacationing Mexicans. Fidel Castro was a regular at Mexico City's Café La Habana (p162) before the revolution. Now Cubans are establishing a beachhead in Mexico City, and their presence has injected a healthy energy into the city.

With easy connections between the two countries, Mexico makes a convenient way station for Cubans en route to the US, and many use it for that purpose. But others come as tourists, students on scholarships or on cultural exchange programs and choose to stick around. Unlike their counterparts in the US, Cubans who settle in Mexico tend not to rail against the island's regime; their motivation for staying is often more economic than political. It's also much easier to maintain contact with the island from Mexico than from the US, as they're free to travel back and forth.

Though Cubans tend to integrate freely within Mexican society and many marry Mexicans, they fiercely maintain their Cuban identity, most visibly through their music and dance. Fortunately, Mexicans tend to be fans of Cuban culture and envy Cubans' capacity to party, not to mention their much-vaunted sex appeal. As demonstrated by the perennial popularity of the Cuban-influenced *danzón* in Mexican ballrooms, there's been a long tradition of musical borrowing. Cuban musicians are in great demand in the capital and many migrate here to cash in on that appreciation.

If there is a Little Havana, it's in Colonia Roma, particularly along Calle Querétaro, where many Cubans reside and the flames are fanned nightly at the various dance clubs clustered along the street. The spirit of Celia Cruz is regularly invoked at Mamá Rumba (see below), while Cuban salseros keep the floors filled at the nearby clubs El Gran León (p171) and El Rincón Cubano (☎ 5264-0549; Av Insurgentes, cnr Querétaro, Roma; ☼ 8pm Thu-Sun; admission M$50-70; ⧉ Metrobus Sonora). Other Cuban ensembles jam in the relaxed setting of La Bodega (below), in Condesa. The *mojitos* flow freely at La Bodeguita del Medio (p169), a franchise of the legendary Havana club with a full menu of Cuban specialties. For island fare like *moros y cristianos* (black beans and rice), Cubans head for La Fonda Cubana (☎ 5584-2825; Insurgentes 200, Roma; ☼ noon-7pm Thu-Tue; ⧉ Metrobus Sonora); to stock their pantries they shop at the Mercado Medellín (p156) for items like green bananas and *malanga*, a root vegetable used in soups and stews.

women should expect to be invited up onto the tightly packed dance floor.

LA BODEGA Map p88

☎ 5511-7390; www.labodega.com.mx; Popocatépetl 25, Roma; ☼ 1pm-1am Mon-Sat; ⧉ Metrobus Álvaro Obregón

Fans of the Buena Vista Social Club will appreciate the Cuban combos who perform throughout the day in this rambling, tropically decorated Condesa home. *Rumbas, boleros* and *sones* accompany Mexican food, cocktails and dominoes in airy, high-ceilinged salons on both floors. Upstairs is the cabaret club El Bataclán (opposite).

MAMÁ RUMBA Map pp92–3

☎ 5564-6920; Querétaro 230, Roma; cover M$70-80; ☼ 9pm-3:30am Wed-Sat; ⧉ Metrobus Sonora

Managed by a Havana native, Mamá Rumba features contemporary salsa, with music by the house big band. Instructors will get you started Wednesday and Thursday evenings. On alternate Saturdays the invariably packed club hosts reggaeton DJs and cabaret acts.

SALÓN LOS ÁNGELES Map pp42–3

☎ 5597-5181; Lerdo 206, Colonia Guerrero; admission M$40; ☼ 6-11pm Tue & Sun; Ⓜ Tlatelolco

'Those who don't know Los Ángeles don't know Mexico' reads the marquee, and for once the hyperbole is well deserved. Cuban-music fans won't want to miss the outstanding orchestras here nor the incredibly graceful dancers who fill the vast floor. Particularly on Tuesday evening, when an older crowd comes for *danzones*, it's like the set of a period film. Salón Los Ángeles is in a rough area, so take a taxi.

ROCK

Mexico has come a long way since the dark ages (prior to 1990) when appearances by foreign rock groups were officially suppressed. (After the disastrous 1971 rock festival at Avándaro, Mexico's version of Woodstock, bands were not granted visas until 1989, when Rod Stewart played in Querétaro.) Nowadays, groups like Yo La Tengo, The Hives, King Crimson and The Cure regularly quench the rock-thirsty masses, while the *rock en español* scene thrives at downtown clubs, concert halls and festivals. A good place to catch free performances is the Tianguis del Chopo (p123), an alternative street market, where young-and-hungry bands take the stage every Saturday afternoon.

DADA X Map pp48–9

☎ 2454-4310; www.recia.org/dadax, in Spanish; Bolívar 31; cover free-M$200; ⌚ from 9pm Thu-Sat; Ⓜ San Juan de Letrán

Black-clad youth gravitate toward this space on the upper floor of a magnificent colonial building. The varied program includes cult films, poetry readings and live music, which might be anything from ska to electronica.

HARD ROCK LIVE Map p84

☎ 5327-7101; cover from M$220; Campos Elíseos 290; Ⓜ Auditorio

Occupying a superb old Polanco mansion near the Auditorio Nacional, this branch of the international club hosts the cream of *rock en español,* with groups like La Cuca, the Nortec Collective, La Gusana Ciega, Zoe and Molotov on stage.

MULTIFORO ALICIA Map pp92–3

☎ 5511-2100; www.myspace.com/foroalicia; Av Cuauhtémoc 91; cover M$70; ⌚ 9pm-2am Fri & Sat; Ⓜ Cuauhtémoc

Behind the graffiti-scrawled facade is Mexico City's premier rock club. A suitably smoky, seatless venue, the Alicia stages up-and-coming punk, surf and ska bands, who hawk their music at the store downstairs. As many as half a dozen groups crowd the bill at the unapologetically *naco* space, with images of wrestling combatants as a backdrop to the performances.

PASAGÜERO Map pp48–9

☎ 5512-6624; www.pasaguero.com; Motolinía 33; cover M$100; ⌚ 10pm-2:30am Thu-Sat; Ⓜ Allende

Some visionary developers took a historic building and transformed its ground level into a space for various cultural happenings, particularly rock and electronica gigs. When buzzworthy bands visit Mexico, they'll likely be playing here. Located off a pedestrian esplanade, El Pasagüero features a front café-bar (from 11am to 11pm) with cheap *chelas* (cold beers), making for a fine pre-show hangout.

CABARET

The musical revues now in vogue at the following venues update the old tradition of the *carpas,* impromptu tent shows that were performed in neighborhoods outside the Centro (where the more established theaters drew higher-class audiences). The *carpa* shows included comic sketches that dealt with the political and social concerns of the day, and unlike their Centro counterparts were delivered in the spoken and visual language of the working classes. Actors like Tin Tan and Cantínflas cut their teeth in these venues before moving on to the Mexican silver screen. The most successful of today's cabaret performers, like Jesusa Rodríguez and Astrid Haddad, update the *carpa* tradition to a German cabaret-type forum, still cleverly skewering the hypocrisies of the country's political classes whilst retaining the kitschy costumes and nutty slapstick of the old tent shows.

BAR EL VICIO Map p95

☎ 5659-1139; www.lasreinaschulas.com, in Spanish; Madrid 13; cover M$100-200; Ⓜ Coyoacán

With liberal doses of politically and sexually irreverent comedy and a genre-bending musical program, this offbeat cabaret is appropriately located in Frida Kahlo's old neighborhood. It's also the showcase for Las Reinas Chulas, an all-girl troupe who put a feminist spin on the normally macho-intensive *grupera* genre.

EL BATACLÁN Map p88

☎ 5511-7390; www.labodega.com.mx; Popocatépetl 25; cover M$100-200; ⌚ 9pm Tue-Sat; 🚌 Metrobus Álvaro Obregón

A theater within a club (La Bodega, see above), this intimate cabaret showcases some of Mexico's most vivid performers, with frequent appearances by the wonderfully surreal Astrid Haddad. Cocktails and *antojitos* are served, with tables on stepped levels leading up from the stage. Afterwards, catch top-notch Cuban *son* combos in La Bodega's various salons.

LA CASA DE PAQUITA LA DEL BARRIO Map pp42–3

☎ 5583-8131; Zarco 202; ⌚ 8:30pm Fri & Sat; cover M$150; Ⓜ Guerrero

Located in the rough-and-tumble Guerrero district, this bastion of popular culture is the frequent venue for TV and recording star Paquita La del Barrio. The corpulent chanteuse customarily performs a sublime set of plaintive ballads, almost all of which express disdain for her suitors – her asides are deliciously bitter. Phone ahead to see if Paquita herself is performing.

LA PLANTA DE LA LUZ Map p101

☎ 5616-5238; Plaza Loreto; www.laplantadeluz
.com.mx; admission M$150-250; ☻ 9pm-3am
Wed-Sat; ⊞ Metrobus Dr Gálvez

The 'power plant,' inside the Plaza Loreto shopping mall, is the creation of raconteur and *Reforma* columnist Germán Dehesa (sometimes called the Mexican Woody Allen). The large supper club alternates between Dehesa's own comedic revues and music performances by well-regarded folk, rock and pop artists.

JAZZ, BLUES & WORLD

The term 'Latin jazz' may most often be associated with Cuban and Caribbean artists, but Mexico City's jazz scene has been blossoming, thanks to a recent crop of clubs. Besides these venues, concerts by jazz and world artists are sometimes staged at the Centro Cultural Universitario, the Teatro de la Ciudad and the Centro Nacional de las Artes (p178), the last of which stages the annual Euro Jazz festival in March.

CULTURAL ROOTS Map pp48–9

☎ 5521-6622; Tacuba 81; cover M$25; ☻ 4-11pm
Fri & Sun, 9pm-2am Sat; Ⓜ Allende

Portraits of Marcus Garvey, Haile Selassie and Emiliano Zapata glare down over the throngs of skanking youth who fill this warehouse-sized room, where DJs pump out a heady blend of contemporary reggae. Despite the pervasive aroma, signs remind you that ganja use is prohibited.

LUNARIO DEL AUDITORIO NACIONAL Map p78

☎ 5280-9250; www.lunario.com.mx; admission
M$350-700; Ⓜ Auditorio

Major jazz artists from throughout the hemisphere perform at this large, classy nightclub adjacent to the national auditorium. Seating is at tables that ascend back from the stage, and cocktails and snacks are served. Enter off the right side of the Auditorio.

NEW ORLEANS Map p101

☎ 5550-1908; Av Revolución 1655, San Ángel;
admission M$50-150; ☻ 9pm-3am Tue-Sun;
⊞ Metrobus La Bombilla

Littered with bric-a-brac, the DF's longest-running jazz club has a relaxed, homey ambience, and the kitchen prepares home-made pastas and salads. Gregarious owner Ángel keeps things eclectic, staging everything from Dixieland jazz to scat singing to funk and fusion.

PAPA BETO Map pp74–5

☎ 5592-1638; www.papabeto.com, in Spanish;
Villalongín 196, Cuauhtémoc; cover M$80-120;
☻ 1st/2nd set 9:30pm/11pm Tue-Sat

Run by a Japanese expatriate to highlight the impressive wealth of local talent, this excellent salon remains the city's top jazz venue. Tuesday night is reserved for jam sessions with surprise guests. It's a bit out of the way, though – six blocks north of Paseo de la Reforma via Río Sena. From Metro Chapultepec, take a pesero marked 'La Raza'.

RUTA 61 Map p88

☎ 5511-7602; Baja California 281; cover M$60-200;
☻ music from 10pm Thu-Sat; ☎ Chilpancingo

Catering to Mexico City's denim-clad blues cult, this split-level venue stages electric blues artists in the Buddy Guy-Howlin' Wolf mold. About once a month there's a direct-from-Chicago act, though you're more likely to see one of the many local cover bands.

ZINCO JAZZ CLUB Map pp48–9

☎ 5512-3369; www.zincojazz.com; Motolinía 20;
cover M$100-200; ☻ 9pm-2am Wed-Sat;
☎ Allende

A vital component in the Centro renaissance, Zinco is a subterranean supper club featuring local jazz and funk outfits and occasional big-name touring artists. Located downstairs from the Art Deco Banco Mexicano building, the intimate room fills up fast, so reserve ahead.

TROVA & TRADITIONAL

Situated well outside the commercial mainstream, Mexico's *trovadores* – more singer-songwriters than troubadours – perform in a number of casual cafés around town. Taking their cue from such Cuban artists as Pablo Milanés and Silvio Rodríguez, they write songs that are deeper and more poetic than the usual pop fare, with lyrics that touch on political and personal themes. The website www.trovamex.com does a good job of compiling events, venues and artists.

If you're looking for traditional Mexican songsters, you're as likely to find them in the local cantina or on a nearby street corner as in clubs or concert halls. Too often undervalued by their own compatriots, itinerant musicians are forced to scrounge for tips from bar patrons or passersby. One venue that gives regional styles their due is the Museo Nacional de Culturas Populares (p94) in Coyoacán, which regularly stages indigenous artists.

CAFÉ CORAZÓN Map p101
☎ 5550-8854; Frontera 4; cover M$60-80; ⊙ 9:30pm Fri & Sat; ⓔ Metrobus La Bombilla

Folk singers in the Silvio Rodríguez mold take the small stage at this temple of *trova* near San Ángel's Plaza San Jacinto.

CAFEBRERÍA EL PÉNDULO Map p88
☎ 5286-9493; www.pendulo.com, in Spanish; cover varies; Av Nuevo León 115; Ⓜ Chilpancingo

Leading Mexican *trovadores* play this café-bookstore-CD shop toward the weekend. 'The Pendulum' is frequented by a well-read, mature crowd who actually prefer to listen to the lyrical content of such singer-songwriters as Fernando Delgadillo and Hernaldo Zuñiga. There's another branch in the Zona Rosa (☎ 5208-2327; Hamburgo 126; Ⓜ Insurgentes).

EL BALCÓN HUASTECO Map pp42–3
☎ 5341-6762; www.elbalconhuasteco.com; Sor Juana Inés de la Cruz 248, Colonia Agricultura; cover M$40; ⊙ from 6pm Thu-Sat; Ⓜ Normal

This center for the preservation of the Huastec culture of Hidalgo and Veracruz stages performances by the region's fiery trios. There are wooden platforms for traditional *zapateando* dancing and snacks from the area.

CLUBBING

The capital's thriving club scene has become an obligatory stop on the international DJ circuit, and on any given weekend young Chilangos turn out in droves to dance the night away to *punchis-punchis* (Mexican slang for electronic music). The venues in this category are especially ephemeral and news is generally communicated by word of mouth or on Myspace pages. To find out what's going on, pick up flyers at Condesa's Malafama billiard hall (p170). Some of the hottest clubs are gay-oriented venues that are open to adventurous scenesters of all stripes – check the Gay & Lesbian chapter for listings (p197).

ALTAVISTA 154 Map p101
☎ 5616-7504; Av Altavista 154, San Ángel; ⓔ Metrobus Altavista

This San Ángel club has three rooms: red, yellow and blue. Superior DJs rule the red room, laying down such dense grooves that even certified nondancers must get up and move their butts. A lounge and bar occupy the other rooms. Admission is free though cocktails are typically pricey for the zone.

CENTRO CULTURAL DE ESPAÑA
Map pp48–9
☎ 5521-1925; www.ccemx.org; Guatemala 18; admission free; ⊙ 10pm-2am Thu-Sat; Ⓜ Zócalo

Young hipsters pack the roof terrace of the Spanish cultural center each weekend for its excellent DJ sessions. Located directly behind the cathedral, the rebuilt colonial structure is usually quaking by midnight.

CREAM Map pp74–5
☎ 5292-6114; Versalles 52; cover M$120; ⊙ from 10pm Thu-Sat; Ⓜ Cuauhtémoc

The longstanding El Colmillo club has been spruced up and reborn as one of the city's premier electronica venues. Beyond the ghoulishly red narrow front room, steps lead down to a hallucinatory party lounge, where internationally renowned DJs work from a catwalk above a laser-lashed dance floor.

PATIO DE MI CASA Map pp74–5
Versalles 68, Juárez; admission M$50; ⊙ 10pm-6am Thu-Sat; Ⓜ Cuauhtémoc

This low-key venue is a new addition to the clandestine club zone on the east edge of Colonia Juárez. Minus the exclusive attitude of some venues, it's simply a gathering place for fans of electronic music that has managed to attract such globally prominent figures as Alan McGee and Jeremy Scott. After a few Mezcal Sunrises, the warped decor begins to make sense.

PERVERT LOUNGE Map pp48–9
☎ 5510-4457; República de Uruguay 70, Centro Histórico; cover M$100; ⊙ 10:30pm-5am Thu-Sat; Ⓜ Isabel la Católica

A pioneering electronica venue in the heart of the Historic Center, the Pervert routinely hosts DJs the stature of Luca Ricci and Satoshi Tomiie. Tribal house, deep house and progressive house are among the featured styles heard within the narrow, stone-walled room.

RIOMA Map p88

☎ 5366-6593; Insurgentes Sur 377, Condesa; admission M$100; ⓨ 11pm-3am Thu-Sat; ⓔ Metrobus Campeche

Once a restaurant owned by Mexican screen star Cantínflas (the name is a jumbled version of the actor's first name), Rioma is now an exclusive lounge attracting a sexy 20-something crowd. The below-street-level space retains the restaurant's original mahogany paneling, with the red polka dots contributed by Japanese designer Yayoi Kuzama. Star DJs fire up the turntables.

MARIACHIS

Plaza Garibaldi (Map pp48–9; take the metro to Bellas Artes or Garibaldi), five blocks north of the Palacio de Bellas Artes, is where the city's mariachi bands gather in the evenings. Mexico's most characteristic music, mariachi originated in the state of Jalisco, but Plaza Garibaldi remains a landmark for the tradition, featuring bronze statues of such musical icons as Pedro Infante and Juan Gabriel.

Outfitted in silver-studded *charro* suits and broad brimmed sombreros, the musicians stand around with drinks until approached by someone who's ready to pay for a song (M$70) or whisk them away to entertain at a party. The typical mariachi ensemble consists of seven to 12 members, playing trumpets, violins and guitars of various sizes, including the bass-toned *guitarrón* and the five-stringed

vihuela. Rather than one particular type of song, the mariachi repertoire actually consists of a variety of styles, including *boleros, ranchera* songs, and *huapangos*. The players are usually men but they don't have to be – the all-female group Mariachi Sonidos de América Feminil also work the plaza, offering a refreshing spin on the macho tradition.

The plaza gets going by about 8pm and stays busy until midnight or so. Besides the mariachis, other small combos perform *sones jarochos* – the sweet harp-driven music of Veracruz – and *norteño* polkas. You can wander and listen to the mariachis in the plaza for free, but if you're celebrating something and feel like being serenaded, request a classic tune like *El Rey, Amorcito Corazón* or *Ay Jalisco No te Rajes*. For food, try the Mercado San Camilito (p156) north of the plaza.

The biggest mariachi gathering of the year coincides with the Fiesta de Santa Cecilia (November 22), when a stage is set up on the plaza for performances by stars of the style.

SALÓN TENAMPA Map pp48–9

☎ 5526-6176; www.salontenampa.com; Plaza Garibaldi 12; ⓨ 1pm-3am; Ⓜ Garibaldi

Graced with murals of the giants of Mexican song and enlivened by its own songsters, this historic cantina on the north side of the plaza is an obligatory visit. Founded in 1925 by a Jalisco native, the cavernous hall is always in a festive mood, with carved wood booths around the perimeter and roving mariachi bands performing for groups of revelers. It's the ultimate setting for *el último trago,* the evening's final shot of tequila.

top picks

- Ballet Folclórico de México (p100)
- Sala Carlos Chávez (p179)
- Foro Shakespeare (p182)
- Sala Nezahualcóyotl (p179)
- Palacio de Bellas Artes (p179)

One Sunday morning in May 2007 approximately 18,000 people stripped down for US photographer Spencer Tunick in the Zócalo, setting a new record for his famed mass nude photo shoots. Tunick told the local press that attention had turned to Mexico City to appreciate how a country can be free and treat the naked body as art.

Take this wonderful sense of inhibition, combine it with the exuberance and inherent creativity of the people, and it is no wonder that Mexico City has one of the most flourishing contemporary art scenes in Latin America – as witnessed by the sheer number of galleries opening up all the time, particularly in the boho-chic area of Roma.

The city also prides itself on its music, and well it might: its palatial Palacio de Bellas Artes is one of the most important concert halls in this part of the world and emotional and highly theatrical opera has always been close to the Mexican heart. The Palacio is also the official home of the Mexico City Philharmonic Orchestra, which occupies a very important place in Mexico's rich musical life. The orchestra has made more than 50 recordings, as well as playing with such legendary soloists and conductors as Plácido Domingo and Leonard Bernstein.

Theater too is increasingly seeking to forge its own voice, with the trend in new writing moving toward the more idiomatic and away from the influence of European and US theatrical models. And, if you are a movie buff, then the sheer number of cinemas here will guarantee that you don't have to suffer one night's deprivation of popcorn-fueled big-screen entertainment.

Information

One of the best sources of 'what's on' information is the Spanish language *Tiempo Libre*, which is published weekly on Thursday and includes events and gallery listings for the week ahead, plus concerts, film and theater events. Other useful guides include the comprehensive monthlies *Donde Ir* and *Chilango*, the latter with a *Time Out*-style supplement. *Primera Fila*, a Friday section of the *Reforma* newspaper, also includes entertainment listings. The Palacio del Bellas Artes publishes *Agenda Arte*, a small comprehensive monthly guide to concerts, theater and dance productions, which you can pick up free at tourist kiosks and performing arts venues.

Tickets & Reservations

TICKETMASTER

☎ 5325-9000; www.ticketmaster.com.mx
Tickets for major venues are available via internet, phone or at any of these outlets.

Auditorio Nacional (Map p78; Paseo de la Reforma 50, Bosque de Chapultepec; ⏰ 11am-6pm; Ⓜ Auditorio)

Liverpool Centro (Map pp48–9; Venustiano Carranza 92, Centro; ⏰ 11am-7pm; Ⓜ Zócalo); Polanco (Map p84; Mariano Escobedo 425, Polanco; ⏰ 11am-8pm; Ⓜ Polanco)

Mixup Centro Histórico (Map pp48–9; Madero 51, Centro; ⏰ 10am-9pm Mon-Sat, 11am-8pm Sun; Ⓜ Zócalo); Calle 16 de Septiembre (Map pp48–9; Calle 16 de Septiembre 14, Centro; Ⓜ San Juan de Letrán); Zona Rosa (Map pp74–5; Génova 76, Zona Rosa; ⏰ 9am-9pm; Ⓜ Insurgentes)

CLASSICAL MUSIC

Mexico City is arguably the best place to enjoy classical music in Mexico, for both the high caliber of the musicians and also the exceptional acoustics and theater spaces of the top venues. Together with the philharmonic and symphony orchestras, there are several smaller ensembles, including the Carlos Chávez Youth Symphony, the New World Orchestra (Orquesta del Nuevo Mundo), the National Polytechnical Symphony and the Bellas Artes Chamber Orchestra (Orquesta de Camara de Bellas Artes). In addition to the following listings, several museums also hold occasional classical concerts, and some of the swankier five-star hotels have a string quartet to accompany cocktail hour.

AUDITORIO BLAS GALINDO Map p95

☎ 1253-9400, ext 1607; Centro Nacional de las Artes, cnr Río Churubusco & Thalpan; tickets M$40-100; www.ticketmaster.com.mx; Ⓜ General Anaya
This good-size auditorium in the south of the city has a regular program of classical music concerts performed by the Carlos Chávez Symphony Orchestra, and visiting international youth orchestras; check

listings in the local press. The auditorium is also one of the main venues for performances by musicians participating in the *Foro Internacional de Musica Nueva* (International Competition for New Music), an annual event since 1977.

CENTRO CULTURAL OLLIN YOLIZTLI
Map p105
☎ 5606-6089; Periférico Sur 5141, Ciudad Universitaria
Regular year-round free concerts of chamber ensembles and string recitals are held at this Cultural Center's Sala Herminio Novelo, with music students and professionals consistently delivering polished performances. Admission is free and, at the time of writing, the concerts took place weekly at 8pm on Thursday (although confirm, if possible, before setting out). This Cultural Center is one of the most active on the classical music scene, however several other similar centers, as well as museums, in the city present occasional classical music performances; check *Tiempo Libre* or Friday's *La Jornada* for listings. For transport information, see p106.

NATIONAL MUSIC CONSERVATORY
Map p84
☎ 5280-6347; Auditorio Silvestre Revueltas, Av Presidente Masaryk 52, Polanco; Ⓜ Polanco
The country's most important music conservatory was founded at the beginning of the 20th century and still produces some of the country's top classical musicians, like current golden boy José Antonio Espinal, recognized as one of the most talented young conductors, pianists and musicians in Mexico today. The Conservatory holds regular free concerts, but is not famed for its publicity or advance notice. Keep a close eye on the local press, stop by or telephone the information office.

PALACIO DE BELLAS ARTES Map p64
☎ 5512-2593; www.bellasartes.gob.mx; Av Hidalgo 1, Centro; tickets M$100-300; box office Ⓧ 11am-7pm; Ⓜ Bellas Artes
The fabulous Art Nouveau extravaganza which is the Palacio de Bellas Artes creates a glittering showcase for classical music concerts. And, encouragingly, if you are a classical music buff, you are not alone; according to Palacio program manager, Claudia González Romero, although clas-

sical music has taken an overall dip in the global hit parade, there is still an enthusiastic audience for the big orchestras here.

The resident orchestra, since 1975, is the Orquesta Filarmónica de la Ciudad de México (Mexico City Philharmonic Orchestra) under the artistic direction of Jorge Mester (described by the *Los Angeles Times*' art critic as 'a master … who finds the depth, complexity and power in the music'). Leading international musicians and conductors also make frequent guest appearances, while chamber groups appear at the Palacio's recital halls. Tickets are usually available on the previous or actual day of the concert at the ticket windows in the lobby, open 11am to 7pm Monday to Saturday, 9am to 7pm Sunday. You can also get them from Ticketmaster.

SALA CARLOS CHÁVEZ Map p105
☎ 5622-6958; www.musicaunam.net in Spanish; Centro Cultural Universitario, Av Insurgentes Sur 3000, Ciudad Universitaria; tickets M$50-75; box office Ⓧ 10am-2pm Tue, to 2pm & 4:30-8:30pm Wed-Sat, to 1:30pm Sun, concert days 4:30-7.45pm Sat, to 6.45pm Sun
Named after the famous 20th-century Mexican composer, this small *sala* with seating for just 165 (and designed so no big hairdos can obstruct the view of the stage), is the ideal intimate space for enjoying chamber music (for which Chávez was particularly famed) and soloists (including classical guitarists). For transport information, see p106.

SALA NEZAHUALCÓYOTL Map p105
☎ 5622-7125; www.musicaunam.net, in Spanish; Centro Cultural Universitario, Av Insurgentes Sur 3000, Ciudad Universitaria; tickets M$50-100; box office Ⓧ 10am-2pm Tue, to 2pm & 4:30-8:30pm Wed-Sat, to 1:30pm Sun
This impressive concert hall with the impossible-to-pronounce name is located at the heart of the University's Cultural Center. The design emulates Amsterdam's late-19th-century Concertgebouw theater, with the seats extending to the sides and rear of the orchestra platform, creating the ultimate surround-sound experience. This is further accentuated by the 'canopy' over the stage. The university has its own UNAM Philharmonic Orchestra, which regularly stages concerts here. The Nezahualcóyotl is also a respected venue for world-renowned

musicians, along with the Palacio. The concert season runs from September to June. For transport information, see p106.

TEATRO DE LA CIUDAD Map pp48–9

☎ 5510-2942; Donceles 36, Centro; tickets M$50-100; ☎ 9am-5pm Tue-Sun; Ⓜ Allende

Dating back to 1918, this was the first theater to be built in Mexico City and, after being closed for several years, has been exquisitely restored to its former glory. The elaborate neoclassical facade is a suitable taster of what's to come: a sumptuous Art Nouveau interior reflecting the belle époque style of the period. The 1300-seat theater is the venue for a healthy selection of musical genres, including classical orchestras, recitals and blues (John Lee Hooker Jnr was a recent sold-out star).

DANCE

Mexico City is home to one of the oldest dance companies in the country. Founded in 1952 by Amalia Hernández, now managed by her daughter, the *Ballet Folclórico de México* has developed the choreography for 40 so-called 'ballets' that are based on folk dances from all over the country. Other companies of a similarly high caliber to look out for are the *Compañía Nacional de Danza Folclórica* (formed in 1984 under the direction of Nieves Paniagua) and the *Ballet Folklórico Mexicano Fuego* (established in 2005 with members from the former *Ballet Nacional de Aztlan*).

A free and always entertaining spectacle is provided by the Conchero dancers who gather informally every day in the Zócalo to carry out sweaty pre-Hispanic dances – or their interpretation; no one can really verify the authenticity. They are very photogenic though, in their feathered headdresses and *concha* (shell) anklets and bracelets, dancing to the rhythm of big booming drums. The classical flipside has to be the national dance company's performance of Swan Lake, generally performed on islands in the Lago Chapultepec, in the first section of the Bosque de Chapultepec, at 8pm Wednesday to Sunday from late February to early April.

Although contemporary dance and ballet both have sizable followings here, one of the longest established ballet companies, the Ballet Teatro del Espacio, was forced to close in 2007 for lack of funding – for which they vociferously blamed the government in the local press.

As well as the following venues, several of the theaters listed under Classical Music also stage occasional dance productions.

PALACIO DE BELLAS ARTES Map pp48–9

☎ 5512-2593; www.bellasartes.gob.mx; Av Hidalgo 1, Centro; tickets M$360-600; box office ◐ 11am-7pm; Ⓜ Bellas Artes

Performances of the dramatic *Ballet Folklórico de México* are normally at 8:30pm Wednesday and 9:30am and 8:30pm Sunday. Despite the show's popularity, tickets are usually still available on the day at the ticket windows in the lobby, open 11am to 7pm Monday to Saturday, 9am to 7pm Sunday. You can also get them from Ticketmaster (see p178) or in advance from the theater.

SALA MIGUEL COVARRUBIAS Map p105

☎ 5622-6958; www.musicaunam.net, in Spanish; Centro Cultural Universitario, Av Insurgentes Sur 3000, Ciudad Universitaria; tickets M$50-75; box office ◐ 10am-2pm Tue, to 2pm & 4:30-8:30pm Wed-Sat, to 1:30pm Sun, concert days 4:30-7.45pm Sat, to 6.45pm Sun

This contemporary dance venue programs exceptional and diverse performances. Recent shows include performances by La Rossignol, an Italian company that

top picks

FESTIVALS & FAIRS

- Festival de Cine Franco-Mexicano (French-Mexican Film Festival; ◐ Nov; see p183)
- Festival Cinematografico de Verano (Summer Film Festival; www.unam.mx, in Spanish; ◐ Jun-Aug; see p184)
- Feria de México Arte Contemporáneo (Contemporary Mexican Art Fair; www.macomexico.com; ◐ Apr; see p185)
- Festival Internacional de Musica y Escena (International Festival of Music & Scenery; www.musicaunam.net, in Spanish; ◐ Aug; see above)
- Foro Internacional de Musica Nueva (International Competition for New Music; www.cnca.gob.mx; ◐ May; see p178)
- Muestra Internacional de Cine (International Film Festival; www.mexicofilmfestival.com; ◐ Jun; see p183)

delivers an evocative show of Renaissance music and dance. The auditorium also serves as the venue for the *Festival Internaciónal de Musica y Escena* (International Festival of Music and Scenery), an annual event since 1998. For transport information, see p106.

TEATRO DE LA DANZA Map p78
☎ 5280-6228; Centro Cultural del Bosque cnr Paseo de la Reforma & Campo Marte, Bosque de Chapultepec; box office ⌚ noon-3pm & 5-7pm Mon-Fri & prior to events; Ⓜ Auditorio
The Centro Cultural del Bosque complex behind the Auditorio Nacional features six theaters, including the Teatro de la Danza, established in 1969 and dedicated to modern dance. There are just 340 seats in this elegant auditorium, so advance reservations are recommended for the higher-profile performances. As with classical music, Mexico City's cultural centers frequently stage classical and contemporary dance performances. Watch out for announcements in *Tiempo Libre* and Friday's *La Jornada*.

OPERA
The Palacio de Bellas Artes, home of the esteemed Opera Nacional de México is *the* place to see opera in the city. Maria Callas famously sang in several productions at the Palacio early in her career, and recordings exist of several of her performances here. Plácido Domingo, who lived in Mexico City for much of his early life and apparently considers himself equally Mexican and Spanish, also launched his career here at the premiere of *My Fair Lady* (1961), as well as a subsequent production of *The Merry Widow*, singing either the role of Camille or Danilo. Unfortunately for opera fans, his commitment to the city seems to be more culinary than operatic of late (see p146). Other venues that stage opera include the Teatro de la Ciudad and the Auditorio Blas Galinda (see p178).

THEATER
Although there's no distinct West End-style theater district here, the world of theater is alive and well, with plenty of stages located around the city. The more contemporary avant-garde productions often take place in cultural centers, or on a makeshift stage in a Condesa café (or similar), while the larger

top picks
FOR KIDS

- Teatro de la Danza (left) On Saturday and Sunday afternoons, children's plays and puppet shows are staged at the Centro Cultural del Bosque.
- Cineteca Nacional (p183) Cartoons are a staple at cinemas around town, including weekend matinees here.
- Ballet Folclórico de México (opposite) The costumes, color and spirited music and dance can't fail to delight the kiddies.
- Teatro Polyforum Siqueiros (p183) Has a regular program of musicals and shows specifically geared for children.

theaters will pull in the crowds with the more commercial productions and musicals.

Although the theater scene here can be vastly entertaining, a command of Spanish is essential for the more contemporary productions, which often play on subtle nuances relating to the current political and socio-economic climate.

The websites www.mejorteatro.com.mx, www.cenart.gob.mx and www.conaculta.gob.mx (all in Spanish) cover the major theaters. Performances are generally Thursday to Sunday evenings, with weekend matinees.

CASA DE CULTURA JESÚS REYES HEROLES Map p95
☎ 5659-3937; Francisco Sosa 202, Coyoacán; Ⓜ Miguel Ángel de Quevedo
This cultural center is set in a gorgeous colonial-style building, with arches, patios and bubbling fountains. The modest theater stages plays (free), as well as small concerts featuring local musicians. There's also an exhibition space; pick up a copy of the monthly *Cartelera Cultural Coyoacanense*, which includes a theater program. The center is located in Santa Catarina's pretty main square, also home to the larger Teatro Santa Catarina (☎ 5658-0560; www.teatrounam.mx), a UNAM theater which primarily stages serious drama productions (in Spanish).

CAFÉ 22 Map p88
☎ 5212-1533; Montes de Oca 22, Condesa; tickets M$100-180; performances ⌚ 9pm Mon-Sat; Ⓜ Chapultepec

STARS IN YOUR EYES

'The Mexican audience is becoming increasingly sophisticated,' comments Orly Beigel, founder of Orly Beigel Productions, a leading Mexico City music promotion company, which she founded in 1980. 'As well as huge names like Academy Award-winning composer Philip Glass, we have also had seats sell out with famous, but more experimental performance artists, like Laurie Anderson.

'However, in a city of some 24 million, it's hardly surprising that there is a public for everything. I think one reason for our success is that we carefully target our publicity.'

Other big names in the classical music world who Orly exclusively represents in Mexico include American opera singer Jessye Norman, 'who has a majestic stage presence!', Portuguese *fado* and folk group Madredeus, the classical Kronos String Quartet, Israeli clarinetist Giora Feidman and Zubin Mehta and the Israel Philharmonic Orchestra.

In January 2006 several of these musicians, plus others of similar international renown, took part in one of the most poignant concerts ever to take place at the Palacio de Bellas Artes. Titled *Never Again, A Concert to Life,* musicians paid tribute to the six million people murdered by the Nazis. As Orly explains: 'My mother was a Holocaust survivor, the purpose of this concert was to raise awareness of violence and intolerance via this thought-provoking and poignant concert.'

Unsurprisingly, the audience's standing ovation was one of the longest and most emotional ever to be witnessed at the Palacio de Bellas Artes.

This chilled-out theater-club in the informal environment of a café stages experimental contemporary productions like *Ni Princesas Ni Eslavas* with a three-woman cast, described as being more daring than *Desperate Housewives,* and more revealing than *Sex & the City.* The cover price includes a beer, or similar.

CENTRO CULTURAL HELÉNICO Map p101

☎ 3640-3139; www.helenico.gob.mx, in Spanish; Av Revolución 1500, Guadalupe Inn; tickets M$250; box office noon-2pm & 4-8:30pm Mon-Fri, 11am-2pm & 4-8:30pm Sat & Sun; Metrobus Altavista
One of the city's most prominent of the larger theaters, established in the late '80s, with a vigorous program, including the occasional English-language production. The comfortable Helénico performs everything from comic farce to monologues and drama. Productions take place from Fridays to Sundays and tickets can be purchased at the box office, by phone, Internet or Ticketmaster.

FORO SHAKESPEARE Map p78

☎ 5553-4642; www.foroshakespeare.com; Zamora 7, Roma; tickets M$120-250; box office 10am-3pm Mon-Fri; Chapultepec
Originally a bookshop specializing in theatrical tomes, the Foro opened in 1982 as one of the first venues to stage alternative theater productions. Located in the cosmopolitan surroundings of Condesa, this barrio theater continues to produce an eclectic, often edgy, program, including ex-

perimental theater and stand-up comedian shows. The venue includes an exhibition space for local artists and photographers.

TEATRO BLANQUITA Map pp48-9

☎ 5512-8264; Eje Central Lázaro Cardenas, Centro; tickets M$100-175; Chapultepec
There is something very traditional about this theater, located a sombrero-spin from the mariachi musicians in Plaza Garibaldi. One of the city's older theaters, it has long been regarded as the best place in town to enjoy musicals and comedy, as well as popular plays, generally geared toward a family night out. The seats are comfortably cushioned and priced.

TEATRO EL GALEÓN Map p78

☎ 5280-6228; Centro Cultural del Bosque, cnr Paseo de la Reforma & Campo Marte, Bosque de Chapultepec; box office noon-3pm & 5-7pm Mon-Fri & prior to performance; Auditorio
One of several theaters within this vibrant cultural center, the Galeón stages evocative thought-provoking plays by primarily Mexican writers. Most recently, these have included the acclaimed *Rashid 9/11,* written by Jaime Magnus, which obtained first prize in the *Premio Nacional de Dramaturgia Victor Hugo* (a national playwrights' competition) in 2006.

TEATRO JUAN RUIZ ALARCÓN Map p105

☎ 5665-0709; www.teatrounam.mx, in Spanish; Centro Cultural Universitario, Av Insurgentes Sur

3000, Ciudad Universitaria; tickets M$50-100; box office ☺ 10am-2pm Tue, to 2pm & 5-8pm Wed-Fri, to 1:30pm & 4:30-7.45pm Sat, 10:30am-1:30pm & 4:30-6:30pm Sun

This plush 466-seat theater, within the university's Cultural Centre, has a large stage and excellent lighting and acoustics, so is the frequent venue for large-cast musicals and similar, as well as Shakespearean and other classic drama. For transport information, see p106.

TEATRO POLYFORUM SIQUEIROS
Map pp42-3

☎ 5606-8028; www.marioivanmartinez.com, in Spanish; Insurgentes y Filadelfia, Del Valle; tickets M$250-300; box office ☺ noon-2pm & 4-7:30pm Mon-Fri, 11am-2pm & 4-8:30pm Sat & Sun; ⊜ Metrobus Poliform

A friendly small theater auditorium with wrap-around seats surrounding a central stage. The productions regularly include programs designed for children which, even if Spanish does not trip easily off your tiny tot's tongue, can be colorful and entertaining. Classic comedies are also regularly staged.

FILM

Mexicans love going to the cinema and the city is a world-class banquet for filmgoers. Almost everything is screened here, from corny American blockbusters to obscure foreign-language films. Admission prices are around M$40, with many places offering discounts on Wednesday and showings before 6pm. Except for children's fare, movies are in original languages with Spanish subtitles. *Reforma* and *La Jornada* have daily listings.

The following multiplexes have mostly Hollywood mainstream films, with the odd Mexican hit.

CINEMARK Map pp74-5

☎ 5432-6789; www.cinemark.com.mx; Paseo de la Reforma 222, Zona Rosa; adult/child M$33/28; ☺ 12:30am-10:30pm; ⓜ Insurgentes

This Cinemark complex opened in November 2007, as part of the spanking new Plaza Reforma Mall (see p124); the company is massive throughout Mexico with a total of 29 complexes (nine in the city). This one has 11 modern auditoriums, equipped with Dolby sound and THX, comfortable seats and digital image. There is a car park and a kick-back lounge-cafeteria.

CINEMEX PALACIO Map p64

☎ 5512-0348; www.cinemex.com; Iturbide 25, Centro; adult/child M$44/36; ☺ 11am-11.05pm; ⓜ Juárez

One of over 30 multiplexes in the capital, Cinemex is the largest chain of movie theaters in Mexico City. It was founded back in 1993 by three astute Harvard college students (majoring, naturally, in Business Studies) after regulations were lifted with the new Cinematography Law. Known for their bigger screens, plush carpeting, well-lit interiors and US-style food and drink vendors, back in the mid-'90s this was also the only chain in the world with 100% digital sound. Cinemex is well-represented throughout all districts. To find the most convenient location, check the easy-to-navigate website (in Spanish), scrolling down on the *complejos* (venues) box.

CINÉPOLIS DIANA Map pp74-5

☎ 5511-3236; Paseo de la Reforma 423, Zona Rosa; adult/child M$38/28; ☺ 11:30am-11.15pm; ⓜ Sevilla

Yet another cinema chain, although Cinépolis has a modest half-dozen complexes. This one has a manageable, six-screen choice with air con, comfortable reclining seats, Dolby sound and a cafeteria. Matinees are shown at weekends. This cinema is also the venue of the *Festival de Cine Franco-Mexicano* held annually during the second week in November.

CINEMEX CASA DE ARTE Map p84

☎ 5280-9156; www.cinemex.com in Spanish; France 120, Polanco; admission M$40; ☺ 11:30-10:30pm; ⓜ Polanco

This Cinemex Casa de Arte (*House of Art*) screens independent first-run and foreign films in its four-screen complex, which also thoughtfully caters to the hearing-impaired. The venue is also the annual host to the *Muestra Internacional de Cine* (International Film Festival), when a selection of some of the most exceptional foreign films is screened.

CINETECA NACIONAL Map p95

☎ 1253-9390; www.cinetecanacional.net, in Spanish; Av México-Coyoacán 389, Coyoacán; admission M$35; ☺ 4:30-10pm; ⓜ Coyoacán

Thematically-focused film series are shown on six screens here, with at least one regularly devoted to Mexican cinema. You can eat, drink and read here as well, as the complex includes cafés and bookstores. Located 700m east of metro Coyoacán, *Tiempo Libre* devotes two weekly pages to the Cineteca's city-wide programs.

FILMOTECA Map p105

☎ 5665-0709; Centro Cultural Universitario, Insurgentes Sur 3000, Ciudad Universitaria; admission M$25; ⏰ 6:30-11:30pm

UNAM's two cinemas screen films from its collection of over 35,000 titles, selected from an archive (founded in 1960) that has played a pivotal role, not only in Mexican but in international film culture. Among its activities, the Filmoteca actively seeks long-lost films for preservation. It has also played a vanguard role in international film culture, organizing the first Mexican film festival in Paris back in 1963. You can catch the *Festival Cinematografico de Verano* (Summer Film Festival) between June and August. For transport information, see p106.

LUMIERE REFORMA Map pp74–5

☎ 5514-0000; Río Guadalquivir 104, Zona Rosa; admission M$45; ⏰ 11:30am-12.50pm; Ⓜ Sevilla

This theater has four screening rooms with just 50 seats apiece, as well as the technology to show the same film simultaneously in more than one *sala*. Screens quality art-house and foreign releases with a liberal dose of the quirky and unconventional.

EL LUNARIO Map p78

☎ 5280-9250; www.lunario.com.mx; Costado Poniente, Bosque de Chapultepec; admission M$50; ⏰ 6:30-11pm; Ⓜ Auditorio

Regular weekly cinema screenings take place every Thursday at this see-and-be-seen fashionable theater, film-house, cabaret and good-time bar (see also p174).

VISUAL ARTS

Contemporary and controversial Turner Prize (UK) winner, Damien Hirst, is just one of many leading international artists who has been enthralled and influenced by the Mexican culture. His US$100 million diamond-encrusted skull, unveiled in June 2007, was the result of time spent here, and the influence of the elaborately decorated skulls of the extraordinary annual celebration: Día de Muertos.

Mexicans are also justifiably proud of their artistic heritage, as witnessed when you visit any local gallery or museum and do a nationality head count. The virtual cult status of Frida Kahlo and Diego Rivera throughout the world has also obviously played its part in raising national awareness of today's Mexican art world.

Roma is gradually evolving as the hip new place for contemporary art galleries in DF, while adjacent Condesa also has a few good galleries. Polanco is predictably more upmarket and conservative, but it has some great exhibition spaces. Be prepared that many galleries have gone the unfriendly, locked-door route and don't even have window displays, which is mildly disquieting if you are a casual art appreciator and would rather look around relatively incognito. But persevere, doors will be opened and gallery owners are generally friendly and informative.

Likewise, art aficionados (especially hungry ones) should keep an eye on the local press for art openings. Members of the public are almost always welcome and, as well as enjoying the occasion, the company and the art, you will in all likelihood be offered some hearty snacks and drinks as well. Pick up the freebie monthly art map and guide (www.arte-mexico.com), available at galleries and museums, with its comprehensive list of exhibition inaugurations.

ART GALLERIES

ARRÓNIZ Map pp74–5

☎ 5311-7965; www.arroniz-arte.com; Plaza Río de Janeiro 53, Roma; Ⓜ Insurgentes

Despite its location on an elegant leafy square, this gallery has a raw urban energy, with its Soho-style space and basic concrete floors. This is the only gallery in the country specializing in limited-edition engravings and prints. Artists include the new and the emerging as well as the established. A modest number of paintings and photography is generally on show here, too. Exhibitions change every three months.

CENTRO CULTURA DE CASA LAMM Map pp74–5

☎ 5525-1322; www.galeriacasalamm.com.mx; Álvaro Obrego 99, Roma; Ⓜ Insurgentes

The beautiful art deco building creates a perfect ambience for this private art college, which offers lectures and courses, as well as a video club, café, bookshop, library and excellent art gallery exhibiting the work of talented contemporary artists such as Cuban Eduardo Roca Salazar (Choco).

CINCO CLÁSICOS Map pp74–5
☎ 5525-4079; Estocolmo 26, Zona Rosa; Ⓜ Insurgentes
This small gallery in an exquisitely restored 1930s dollhouse of a building deals with mainly contemporary Latin American and Mexican art. The painters include Francisco Toledo, Sergio Hernandez and Rafael Coronel. The congenial owner, Simón Alkón, speaks excellent English.

CÍRCULO AZUL Map p95
☎ 5659-1881; Fransisco Sosa 363, Coyoacán; Ⓜ Viveros
The picturesque courtyard, with its tiles and 16th-century fountain, is a fitting introduction to this fine gallery, with its classic and contemporary artwork and sculpture. There's an original painting signed by Diego Rivera, plus some stunning charcoal and ink drawings by contemporary Mexican artist, Raquel Chávez Lanz.

GALERÍA DE ARTE MEXICANO Map p78
☎ 5272-5529; www.artegam.com; Rebollar 43, Bosque de Chapultepec; Ⓜ Constituyentes
The first contemporary art gallery to open in Mexico City (way back in 1935). Since this time, the gallery has held close to 1000 shows, with exhibitions of smock-and-beret masters like Diego Rivera, Miguel Covarrubias, Rufino Tamayo and Frida Kahlo. The gallery continues to promote established and emerging Mexican artists and remains one of the most exciting and extensive in the city.

GALERÍA JUAN MARTÍN Map p84
☎ 5280-0277; Dickens 33, Polanco; Ⓜ Polanco
A welcoming two-story gallery with a light, airy feel and an exciting permanent collection of paintings, pottery and photography by Mexican and international artists, as well as regular temporary exhibitions. The variety and combination of styles and themes contributes towards the appeal of the place.

GALLERY 13 Map pp92–3
☎ 5525-6077; Orizaba 92, Roma; Ⓜ Insurgentes
This is a young dynamic gallery that typically displays up-and-coming artists and photographers under the age of 30. The exhibition spaces are spread over two floors with five well-lit galleries. Definitely one to watch.

GARASH Map pp92–3
☎ 5207-9858; Alvaro Obregón 49, Roma; Ⓜ Insurgentes
A gregarious toddler on the contemporary art scene, Garash was established in 2003 in this classic early 20th-century building, complete with original columns. Exhibitors are mainly Mexican and Japanese and tend to be in the innovative genre of Hisae Ikenaga, the Madrid-based sculptor famed for transforming mass produced modular furniture into startlingly contemporary sculpted forms (which is what many of us end up doing naturally when trying to assemble an Ikea flat pack!) and who has had a successful solo exhibition here. This is one of the galleries to participate in the annual MACO art fair, established in 2004 and held during the last week of April. This is considered the most important event of its kind in the Latin American contemporary art world. Check the website (www.macomexico.com, in Spanish) for a list of participating galleries in the city.

JARDÍN DEL ARTE Map pp74–5
Juaréz; ☾ Sun; ◻ Metrobus Reforma
A small art market, between Sullivan and Villalongín, and also known as the Sullivan Market, has a large selection of paintings and art supplies, plus some food.

LOURDES SOSA Map p84
☎ 5280-6857; www.lourdessosagaleria.com; Ibsen 32, Polanco; Ⓜ Polanco
A small one-room gallery with regular exhibitions of paintings, sculptures and graphic art by renowned national artists such as Manuel Felguérez, whose massive *Puerta 1808* sculpture (Map p64) graces the intersection between Paseo de la Reforma and Juaréz near the city center.

MUCA Map pp92–3
☎ 5511-0925; Tonalá 51, Roma; Ⓜ Insurgentes
This gallery is a branch of the national university's Museo Universitario de Ciencias y Artes (p104). The range of exhibits is impressive, covering both traditional and cutting-edge contemporary Mexican art, like the pop art style installations of Manolo Arriola

for which he projects images on to the wall via a dazzle of neon lights.

GALERÍA NINA MENOCAL Map pp74–5

☎ 5564-7209; www.ninamenocal.com; Zacatecas 93, Roma; Ⓜ Insurgentes

Established in 1990, this sophisticated Cuban-owned gallery became initially famous for representing legendary Cuban artists like Félix González and still represents several Cuban artists, as well as Mexican and European contemporary artists and sculptors. The gallery's setting is a classic colonial-style '40s building with galleries situated around a central ivy-flanked courtyard.

OMR Map pp92–3

☎ 5207-1080; www.galeriaomr.com; Plaza Río de Janeiro 54, Roma; Ⓜ Insurgentes

Housed in a grand Art Nouveau gem of a building with soaring ceilings, OMR adds its own slant to contemporary with a floor that tilts to one side, the result of settling soil (Roma is built on a dry lake bed). The gallery holds six to eight exhibitions per year and represents a broad spectrum of the most prominent painters, sculptors and photographers on both the Mexican and international art scene, like Mauricio Alejo, Rafael Lozano-Hemmer, José Leon Cerrillo and Spanish artist Félix Curto.

PROBERT Map p101

☎ 5616-4675; San Jacinto 20, San Angel; Ⓜ Miguel Angel de Quevedo

A quality gallery specializing in contemporary works by Mexican and Latin American artists, plus paintings by several European and American artists now resident in Mexico. The latter include respected Dublin-born artist Phil Kelly, who has lived here since 1989 and paints evocative landscapes. Also here to tempt you is a selection of exquisite and unusual glass and ceramic beaded jewelry.

SPORTS & ACTIVITIES

top picks

SPORTS & ACTIVITIES

The exuberance that Mexicans have for life reaches crescendo pitch when it comes to certain sports. It's no surprise that the so-called Mexican wave originated here; this loony arm-waving custom dates back to the 1986 World Cup finals held in Mexico City. Although originally intended to distract competitors, the wave's ripple effect and the good cheer and congeniality it suggests is the exact opposite to the football thuggery so typical of football matches in northern Europe.

Overall, spectator sports are the big noise here, Mexicans are not as keen on donning the Lycra and sweating their way through a body-pump class as in, say, the US. That said, although crowded central Mexico City is not overly endowed with sports halls, if you feel like working off all those refried beans and tortillas, you don't have to go far to find somewhere to work on your muscle tone.

No sport ignites Mexicans' passions as much as *fútbol*, while rodeos and bullfighting share a vigorous fan base. And, approached with an open mind and a sense of humor, watching a flamboyant and quirky *lucha libre* match could well be the highlight of your trip.

ACTIVITIES

If you are peso poor, but want to exercise those new Nikes, there are several leafy parks with jogging pathways which provide a great escape from the traffic fumes. Use your common sense and only jog during daylight hours. Other available sports include tennis and ice-skating, and adventure sports are on the increase. If you want to fire up your adrenalin on all cylinders, *Tiempo Libre* has a sports page with listings that generally include canoeing, mountain climbing and rafting organizations.

CYCLING

On Sunday mornings Paseo de la Reforma is closed to traffic from Bosque de Chapultepec down to the Alameda Central, and you can join the legions of Chilangos who happily skate or cycle down the avenue each week.

For a more ambitious trek, the urban cycling group Bicitekas (Map p88; www.bicitekas.org, in Spanish) organizes rides starting from the Monumento a la Independencia at 9pm every Wednesday. Groups of up to 100 cyclists ride to destinations like Coyoacán and Ciudad Satélite. Participants must be sufficiently robust to handle treks of up to 40km. Helmets and rear lights are required.

For information on renting bicycles and around-town routes, see p246.

ICE SKATING

As part of Mayor Marcelo Ebrard's campaign to bring fun recreational activities to the city's poorer inhabitants, a huge ice skating rink (reportedly the world's largest) is installed in the Zócalo during the Christmas holiday season, from early December through January. Loans of ice skates are provided free of charge – if you don't mind waiting as much as two hours to get them.

PISTA DE HIELO SAN JERÓNIMO
Map pp42–3
☎ 5683-1929; Av Contreras 300, Colonia San Jerónimo Lídice; admission per hr/day M$34/48; ⏰ 11am-8pm Tue-Sun
Located 2.5km west of the Ciudad Universitaria. To get here hop on a 'Contreras' pesero from Copilco metro station; get off at the Glorieta San Jerónimo intersection on the Periférico ring road. admission includes skate hire

JOGGING

BOSQUE DE TLALPAN Map p109
Camino a Santa Teresa, Tlalpan; Ⓜ Tasqueña
This beautiful forest contains several jogging and hiking trails, as well as numerous picnic areas where you can kick back with your water bottle and muesli bar. Springtime is stunning with a dazzle of wildflowers. From metro Tasqueña, take the Tren Ligero to the Estadio Azteca station, then catch a Tlalpan pesero, which will drop you at the park.

PISTA DE CUEMANCO Map pp112–13
Esquina de Periférico Sur y Canal Nacional, Xochimilco; Ⓜ Tasqueña

Following the trail around the Canal Nacional, one of the web of waterways in Xochimilco and a wonderful setting for jogging. From the metro continue on the Tren Ligero to the last stop, from where bicycle taxis will shuttle you to the canals.

VIVEROS DE COYOACÁN MAP p95
Av Universidad 2100, Coyoacán; M Coyoacán
This pretty wooded park has a 2.1km winding *circuito atlético* which is marked every 100m, so you can keep pace with your progress. For strollers, the *sendero didáctico* (educational trail) has Spanish-language signs identifying the surrounding trees.

TENNIS

SHERATON MARÍA ISABEL HOTEL
Map pp74–5
☎ 5242-5555, ext 3934; Paseo de la Reforma 325, Zona Rosa; per person per hr M$200; ⊗ 10am-5pm; M Insurgentes
One of the most central venues for tennis enthusiasts. With only two courts available, though, be sure to reserve in advance, via phone or in person, before you swagger on court accompanied by your killer serve.

HEALTH & FITNESS
If you are staying in one of the city's top-end hotels, you will probably have a gym available to indulge in a little weight-training before your double helping of *huevos rancheros*. Some

hotels, especially those with spas, also have day rates available for nonguests. Otherwise there are several city gyms where you can use the equipment and take classes inexpensively.

GYMS

EQUILIBRIUM Map pp74–5
☎ 5207-5045; Rio Papaloapan 3, Juaréz; classes M$45; ⊗ 7am-10pm; M Insurgentes
A modest gym with friendly staff and a small weight room with good equipment, this place offer lots of regular classes, including spinning, Pilates, yoga and Latin rhythm. It lacks a website so you will have to make a trip here to find out the current schedule.

CENTRO CABA Map pp92–3
☎ 5574-1976; Álvaro Obregón 160, Roma; per day M$45; ⊗ 7am-10pm Mon-Fri, 8am-10pm Sat, 9am-4pm Sun; M Insurgentes
This sweaty gym has been a hit with pumping bodies for a decade. Classes, including Pilates, rumba Cubana and kickboxing, are (amazingly) included in the day-pass price, as are use of the small (but efficient) weight room and sauna.

CENTRO QI Map p88
☎ 5584-4880; www.qi.com.mx, in Spanish; Amsterdam 317, Roma; per day M$185; ⊗ 6am-11pm Mon-Thu, 8am-6pm Sat, 9am-4pm Sun; M Insurgentes
Centro QI is an exclusive gym and spa located in Roma. It is considered one of

---

SPA TIME OUT
The antithesis of the chaos and noise of Mexico City street life, there are several spas here where you can luxuriate in self-pampering bliss.

- **aWay Mexico City** (Map p84; ☎ 5255-9138; www.whotels.com; W Mexico City Hotel, Campos Eliseos 252, Polanco; per day M$500; ⊗ 6:30am-10:30pm; M Auditorium) The only place in town where you can enjoy a renewing session in a *temascal* (traditional adobe sweat lodge). This classy marbled space includes a gym, jet pools, steam rooms, and sun beds on the rooftop terrace from where you can enjoy sweeping city views. There's also a small bar for invigorating fruit juices and Vogue magazine for inspiration.
- **Spa Gran Melia** (Map p64; ☎ 5128-1212; www.solmelia.com; Hotel Gran Melia Mexico Reforma, Paseo de la Reforma 1, Juaréz; per day M$250; ⊗ 6am-8pm; M Hidalgo) Well-priced for the facilities which include a superb gym with round-the-clock trainer, three Jacuzzi spas with skylights, a small indoor pool, a sauna and a steam room. Therapies and treatments on offer include shiatsu, volcanic mud, lip wrap, body scrub and the enticing-sounding body wine massage (Chardonnay apparently, such a waste...).
- **Spa Marquis** (Map pp74–5; ☎ 5229-1200; www.marquisreforma.com; Hotel Marquis Reforma, Paseo de la Reforma 465, Zona Rosa; per day M$310; ⊗ 7am-9pm; M Chalpultepec) The day fee covers use of the separate-sex Jacuzzi, sauna and steam room and mixed gym and pool. There are sitting areas with magazines, complimentary juices and coffee and domed skylights. Massages cost an average of M$90 for 50 minutes and additional treatments, including mud therapy and various facials, are available.

BUILDING SANDCASTLES IN THE CITY

The city's mayor, Marcelo Ebrard, apparently inspired by the artificial beaches in European capitals like Paris and Budapest, has created four urban beaches in the city, using 130 tons of sand brought from Boca del Río in Veracruz. To add to the holiday-by-the-sea feel, each beach has ice-cream vendors and live music at weekends.

There has been predictable controversy surrounding the urban beaches with the criticism almost exclusively coming from wealthier locals, who typically trip off to Acapulco for their hols and see the sand-in-the-city idea as an unnecessary waste of public funds and a bit of an eyesore.

Not so all the thousands too poor to vacation anywhere, many of whom have never seen a beach. Now they can have a quasi-family holiday every weekend: build sandcastles, play volleyball and enjoy a picnic with sand in between their tacos and toes.

The beaches are located in far-flung parts of the city: the park built for the 1968 Summer Olympics, the northeastern Gustavo A Madero district, the eastern district of Iztacalco and Azcapotzalco, in the far north.

'I don't know why this is annoying people so much,' Ebrard told the local press. 'It doesn't cost the government much work to adapt spaces so people can have a good time with their families. To those who don't want to use the beaches, it seems a bad idea. But to most people, it's great…'

the best health clubs in the city for both its stylish design and the diversity of its services. Facilities include a climbing wall, massage rooms, tanning beds and every class you could possibly think of like Pilates, spinning, body combat, body pump, belly dancing, yoga, chi kung and (if it all sounds too much) meditation.

SPECTATOR SPORTS

Events such as soccer games, bullfights and wrestling can be fascinating: even if the action doesn't especially interest you, the crowd probably will. Most of the daily newspapers will have a generous sports section, where you can find out who is kicking which ball where (and similar). True enthusiasts should look for *La Afición* (www.laaficion.com), a Spanish-language daily devoted to sports.

SOCCER (FOOTBALL)

Soccer (or *fútbol* as it is known here) is *the* national sport, followed fanatically by millions of Mexicans. Even if you are only mildly interested in the game, attending a *partido* can be very entertaining. In general, games are an appealingly relaxed affair, with rival fans sitting close to each other exchanging good-hearted competitive banter that rarely resorts to violence – aside from the occasional good-humored soft whack in the face by a toilet roll (or similar) on its missile route to the pitch. Face painting contributes to the good time atmosphere, together with the steady supply of drinks and food that are sold directly to spectators at their seats.

The capital stages two or three soccer matches almost every weekend in the national Primera División. Mexico City's four teams are: América nicknamed Las Águilas (the Eagles), and the most popular in the country; Las Pumas, of UNAM, which come second in popularity; followed by Cruz Azul (known as Los Cementeros); and lastly, Atlante (Los Potros).

The soccer calendar is divided into a *torneo de invierno* (winter season, August to December) and a *torneo de verano* (summer season, January to May), each ending in eight-team playoffs (*liguillas*) and eventually a two-leg final to decide the champion. Games follow a baffling system which involves a certain amount of unpredictability. For example, it is feasible that a team can come top in the league and be subsequently relegated to a lower position as the latter placement is decided by the overall previous season's results.

The biggest match of all is El Clásico, between América and Guadalajara, which typically fills the Estadio Azteca with 100,000 flag-waving fans. This is about the only game of the year when you should get tickets in advance. Crowds at other games range from a few thousand to around 70,000.

Tickets (M$80 to M$450 for regular season games) are usually available at the gate right up to game time, or can be purchased from Ticketmaster (see p178). There are several stadiums that host games. The newspapers *La Afición* and *Esto* have the best soccer coverage and there are plenty of websites related to Mexican soccer, including the comprehensive www.futmex.com and www.femexfut.org.mx.

ESTADIO AZTECA Map pp42–3

☎ 5617-8080; www.esmas.com/estadioazteca, in Spanish; Calz de Tlalpan 3665, Tlalpan

The country's largest stadium (capacity 114,000) is home to both the América and Atlante clubs. Presided over by an enormous sculpture by the late American artist, Alexander Calder, games are played on weekend afternoons; check the website for kickoff times. Take the Tren Ligero from metro Tasqueña to Estadio Azteca station.

ESTADIO AZUL Map pp42–3

☎ 5563-9040; www.cruz-azul.com.mx, in Spanish; Indiana 260, Colonia Nápoles; 🚌 Metrobus Ciudad de los Deportes

The stadium is next door to the Plaza México bullring. Cruz Azul home games kick off at 5pm on Saturday.

ESTADIO OLÍMPICO Map pp42–3

☎ 5522-0491; www.pumasunam.com.mx, in Spanish; Insurgentes Sur 3000, Ciudad Universitaria

This is the home of the UNAM Pumas. Games start at noon on Sunday and are always well attended and entertaining; the exuberant university fan clubs are well known for their raucous chants. See p106 for directions.

BULLFIGHTING

The most important bullring in the city is the aptly named Monumental Plaza, one of the world's largest bullrings, where the main season runs from October or November to March.

If you're not put off by its very concept, a *corrida de toros* (bullfight) is quite a spectacle, from the milling throngs and hawkers outside the arena to the pageantry and drama in the ring itself and the crowd response it provokes. Six bulls are usually fought in an afternoon, two each by three matadors.

From October or November to March or April, professional fights are held at the Monumental most Sundays, starting at 4pm. There are sometimes extra *corridas* – often with star Mexican and visiting Spanish matadors. The veteran Eloy Cavasos, from Monterrey, is often acclaimed as Mexico's best matador. Ignacio Garibay, José Luis Angelino and José María Luevano are younger stars. From June to October, junior matadors fight young bulls. Some are as young as 10 (the age minimum in Spain is 16). The youngest matador on record is Rafita Mirabal who, in 2005, at only eight years old was facing lethal young bulls in the ring. This fad for child *toreros* continues to be attacked by child protection groups, antibullfighting organizations and doctors. However

LA CORRIDA

This most machismo of spectator sports is one of the world's most controversial: to *aficionados* the pitting of man against bull is nothing less than an art form, while critics see it more as a one-sided ghoulish exhibition of torture and slaughter.

Although Spain is its true home, *la corrida de toros* is also quintessentially Mexican – it's said that this is the only event locals ever arrive on time for (aside from weddings and funerals).

The *corrida* starts promptly generally in the afternoon on a Sunday. To the sound of, typically, a Spanish *paso doble*, the matador, in his twinkling *traje de luces* (suit of lights), and his *toreros* (assistants) give the traditional *paseíllo* (salute) to the fight authorities and the crowd. Then the first of the day's six bulls is released from its pen for the first of the three *suertes* (acts).

The cape-waving toreros first attempt to wear out the bull by luring him around the ring. Next, two *picadores*, on heavily padded horses, enter and jab long lances into the bull's shoulders to weaken him. This is a time you may want to look away, as it can be pretty gruesome.

Next, the band pipes up again, the *picadores* leave the ring, and the *suerte de banderillas* begins, as the *toreros* attempt to stab three pairs of elongated darts into the bull's shoulders without getting impaled on his horns. After the band signals the end of this second *suerte*, the final *suerte de muleta* is the climax in which the matador has exactly 16 minutes to kill the bull. Starting with fancy cape work to tire the animal, the matador then exchanges his large cape for the smaller *muleta* and takes sword in hand, baiting the bull to charge before delivering the fatal lunge with his sword. If the matador succeeds, and he usually does – if not always on the first attempt – the bull collapses and an assistant dashes into the ring to sever its jugular. If the applause from the crowd warrants, he will also cut off an ear or two and sometimes the tail for the matador. The dead bull is dragged from the ring to be butchered for sale.

A 'good' bullfight depends not only on the skill and courage of the matador but also the spirit of the bulls. Animals lacking heart for the fight bring shame on the ranch that bred them. Very occasionally, a bull that has fought outstandingly is spared – an occasion for great celebration – and allowed to return to its stud farm to live out its life in peace.

the temptation is there, especially for poorer families seduced by the idea of obtaining fame and wealth, with little apparent thought of the inherent danger involved.

MONUMENTAL PLAZA MÉXICO
Map pp42–3

☎ 5563-3961; Rodin 241, Colonia Nápoles; 🚇 Ciudad de los Deportes

This deep concrete bowl can hold 48,000 spectators. The *taquillas* (ticket windows) by the bullring's main entrance have printed lists of ticket prices. As a rule, the more expensive seats are in the *sombra* (shade), the cheaper are in the *sol* (sun). The cheapest seats of all are in the Sol General section – the top tiers of seating on the sunny side of the arena. Seats in the Sombra General – the top tiers on the shady side – cost slightly more. The best seats are in the Barreras, the seven rows nearest the arena which normally cost around M$175 to M$300.

Except for the biggest *corridas*, tickets are available right up to the time the third bull is killed, though the best seats may sell out early. You can buy advance tickets Thursday to Saturday from 9:30am to 1pm and 3:30pm to 7pm, and Sunday from 9:30am onward. Most major hotels and many travel agencies sell tickets at a markup.

BASEBALL
Mexico City has one team in the Liga Mexicana de Béisbol, the Diablos Rojos (www .diablos.com.mx), since their former second team, the Tigres, moved to nearby Puebla due to poor attendance. During the regular season (March to July), the Diablos play every other week with Sunday games played at noon. The playoffs take place in August. The league's website is www.lmb.com.mx.

FORO SOL Map pp42–3

☎ 5639-8722; cnr Av Río Churubusco & Viaducto Río de la Piedad; tickets M$25-90

This stadium seats 26,000 spectators and is located to the east of the city. Games usually start at 6:30pm. Ticketmaster sells tickets and the Afición sports paper details

---

LUCHA LIBRE

Violence, torture and extreme cruelty are on display in Mexico's capital three nights a week. *Lucha libre,* the Mexican version of pro wrestling, serves up this antisocial behavior as popular entertainment. Laden with myth, charged with aggression and chock-full of hilarious theatrics, it can be an amusing spectacle.

Mexico City's two wrestling venues, the 17,000-seat Arena de México (Map p64; ☎ 5588-0266; www .arenamexico.com.mx, in Spanish; Dr Lavista 197, Colonia Doctores; ⏰ 8:30pm Fri; tickets M$45-200; Ⓜ Balderas or Cuauhtémoc) and the smaller Arena Coliseo (Map pp48–9; República de Perú 77; ⏰ 7:30pm Tue, 5pm Sun; Ⓜ Allende) are taken over by a circus atmosphere each week, with roving vendors selling beer, sandwiches and wrestlers' masks. There are three or four bouts, building up to the most formidable match-ups. Sporting day-glo tights, flaming masks and rippling biceps and taking names like Tarzan Boy, Violencia, Virus, Satánico and Super Crazy, the flamboyant *luchadores* play up their superhero and super villain personae. After being ushered in by bikini-clad babes, the stars go at each other in teams or one-on-one. Though more a display of acrobatics and theatrical histrionics than an actual competition, their antics can be pretty impressive and not without bodily risk. Wrestlers catapult off the rope and launch into somersaults en route to pouncing their opponent, and it's not unusual to see a pair of combatants, locked in mortal embrace, go hurtling into the crowd. The predominantly working-class fans are happy to suspend their disbelief and enter the fray, with grandma shaking her fist and shouting, 'Kill him!'

Perhaps the sense of catharsis comes from witnessing an acting out of the unresolved struggle Mexicans observe on a daily basis in the political and social arenas – with the good guys winning for a change. *Lucha libre* (literally, 'free fight') means anything goes, and referees seem more like props than arbiters. The scenario invariably pits *técnicos* ('craftsmen') against *rudos* ('rulebreakers') in a mythic face-off between good and evil. The *rudos* usually wear black and engage in dirty tactics, not hesitating to grab a nearby piece of furniture to pummel an opponent. They usually get the upper hand early on, only to be pounded mercilessly by the *técnicos* in a stunning reversal toward the end of the match.

For seven decades, the Consejo Mundial de Lucha Libre has provided a forum for *lucha libre*'s popular heroes, who generally come from the city's rougher barrios. As with any sport, certain figures have loomed large. Undoubtedly the most charismatic figure was Santo, who hid his real identity behind a silver mask until his death in 1984. Santo consolidated his presence in popular culture by crossing over into cinema during Mexico's golden age of B movies, battling zombies and martians on the screen. Another *lucha libre* star, Super Barrio, went into politics, becoming a standard bearer for the leftist PRD (Party of the Democratic Revolution).

upcoming games. From the Ciudad Deportiva station, on metro Línea 9, it's a five-minute walk to the ballpark.

CHARREADAS

Much like their American counterpart *charreadas* (rodeos) are thrilling to watch and demonstrate superb ranching and equestrian skills. Check the website of the Asociación Nacional de la Charrería (www.nacionaldecharros.com in Spanish) for an up-to-date schedule. The main difference between a *charreada* and a US rodeo is that the Mexican riders compete in teams of up to eight people who ride in unison, as well as separately. Live mariachi music adds to the good-time atmosphere.

RANCHO DEL CHARRO Map pp42–3
☎ 5277-8706; Av Constituyentes 500, Bosque de Chapultepec; tickets M$25-90; Ⓜ Constituyentes
This permanent covered arena is located between the Panteón Civil de Dolores and the 3ª Sección of the Bosque de Chapultepec. The main charreada season is from mid-May to early June.

BOXING

Mexico has produced many world boxing champs and a big fight here is a major event, widely televised. The venues are the same as those used for *lucha Libre* (see opposite). For a schedule of matches, check the *La Afición* daily sports' newspaper.

GAY & LESBIAN MEXICO CITY

top picks

- Black Out (p198)
- Living (p198)
- La Perla (p198)
- Tom's Leather Bar (p198)
- Buttergold (p197)

In a land where macho attitudes rule and traditional family values remain strong, it should come as no surprise that little tolerance is shown for alternative orientations. Notwithstanding the prominence of such openly gay luminaries as singer/composer Juan Gabriel, artist Juan Soriano and essayist Carlos Monsiváis, until recently gay life was safely closeted and officially unmentionable in the media. The ascendance of the Partido de Acción Nacional (PAN), a right-of-center political party with close ties to the Catholic church, suggests a continuation of these long-prevailing attitudes.

But as in many other areas, the capital diverges from the mainstream. Dominated by the socially progressive PRD, which is nothing short of antagonistic toward the PAN presidency, the city assembly recently passed an initiative sanctioning same-sex partnerships by granting such unions the same legal advantages enjoyed by traditional married couples. While falling short of an actual legalization of gay marriage, the move seemed like a bold assertion of the capital's well-known tolerance for gays and lesbians.

Mexico City is a magnet for the first generation of Mexicans able to openly express their sexuality. This new openness has created a special energy in the capital. Gays and lesbians can now choose from a wide variety of venues appealing to different age groups and social classes.

The growing sense of tolerance means public displays of affection are no big deal anymore, at least in the capital's more cosmopolitan zones. To be sure, it's OK to hold hands in the Zona Rosa, but it won't raise any eyebrows in Colonia Condesa, Roma, Polanco or Del Valle either.

EATING

While gourmands of all persuasions gather in Condesa and Polanco for their dining experiences, the following places also function as gay social venues.

12:30 Map pp74 5
☎ 5514-5971; Amberes 13; Ⓜ Insurgentes
Located at the heart of the gay nightlife district, 12:30 is good for sandwiches, salads and other 'munchis'. In fact, the relaxed, social atmosphere may appeal to exhausted clubbers – the electronica soundtrack is usually low enough for actual conversation. Go upstairs to dine on a terrace overlooking Amberes. Service can be a challenge.

EL GENERALITO Map pp48–9
☎ 5518-3711; Filomena Mata 18G; comida corrida M$50; Ⓜ Allende
A longtime queer hangout in the Centro, this cozy restaurant opens on pedestrian lane Filomena Mata. Paintings by owner Juan Carlos cover the walls. There's a reasonably priced comida corrida and draft beer.

DRINKING

BGAY BPROUD CAFÉ MÉXICO Map pp74–5
☎ 5208-2547; Amberes 12B; ☽ 11am-11pm; Ⓜ Insurgentes

A good place to start your explorations, this casual café functions as a sort of nerve center for DF gay life, particularly amongst the younger crowd.

BLACK OUT Map pp74–5
☎ 5511-9973; www.black-out.com; Amberes 11; ☽ 5pm-2am; Ⓜ Insurgentes
The new kid on the Zona Rosa's hottest block is mostly male but frequented by buff clubbers of every persuasion. Designed by Frida art director Felipe Fernández del Paso to evoke the cosmopolitan New York theater world, the high narrow space is draped in black velvet, with a sky-high bar of status liquors.

EL VIENA Map pp48–9
☎ 5512-0929; República de Cuba 2E; Ⓜ Bellas Artes
The city's only gay cantina is a friendly if nondescript place, attracting a varied crowd (from truck drivers to journalists) and the jukebox is terrific. Most patrons move over to the next-door Oasis disco at some point in the evening.

PRIDE
☎ 5516-2368; Alfonso Reyes 281; ☽ 6pm-2am Tue-Sat; Ⓜ Chilpancingo
On the southeast corner of Condesa, Pride is a relaxed gathering place for a youthful,

CINEMA GAY

If movies hold up a mirror to society and serve as a gauge to what's considered appropriate behavior, the portrayal of gays and lesbians in Mexican film demonstrates a sea change in attitudes. In the past, if gay characters appeared at all, they were objects of scorn and ridicule, but recent films from Mexico feature frank portrayals of gay sexuality.

Prior to the 1970s, the *'marica'* was a stock character in Mexican comedies, a limp-wristed, rouged figure who was invariably disparaged by the other cast members. Such an exaggeratedly effeminate role appeared as far back as 1938 in the Mexican film *La Casa del Ogro* (The Ogre's House) and continued to pop up in any number of B-movies for cheap comic relief. The first sympathetic portrayal of a gay character awaited *El Lugar Sin Límites* (The Place Without Limits), a 1978 drama directed by Arturo Ripstein. Played by Roberto Cobo, who had made an indelible impression on audiences as a street derelict in Luis Buñuel's *Los Olvidados* (1950), the character of 'La Manuela' emerges as a tragic figure who is at once desired and victimized by the typically macho characters in a Mexican village. Less than a decade later, *Doña Herlinda y Su Hijo* (Doña Herlinda and Her Son;1984) was probably the first portrayal in Mexican cinema of a same-sex couple in love and struggling with familial pressures to conform to an image of normalcy. By the 1990s, gay issues were being dealt with more openly and two internationally successful films, *El Callejón de los Milagros* (Midaq Alley;1995) and *Y Tu Mamá También* (And Your Mother Too; 2001), explored the power of societal taboos and the psychological impact they have on Mexicans. A somewhat lighter look at the theme turned up in the 2004 film *Temporada de Patos* (Duck Season), in which an adolescent boy discovers his budding homosexuality.

The more recent emergence of a genuinely gay cinema in Mexico perhaps reflects a growing tolerance for non-heterosexual life, at least in the capital. The films *Mil Nubes de Paz Cercan el Cielo, Jamás Acabarás de Ser Amor* (A Thousand Clouds of Peace, 2003) and *El Cielo Dividido* (Broken Sky, 2006), both critically acclaimed works by the director Julián Hernández, allow viewers to observe relationships through the lens of gay desire.

To see current Latin American and international films dealing with gay themes, check what's playing at Contempo Cinema (Map pp74–5; ☎ 5208-4044; www.contempocinema.com; Londres 161, Zona Rosa; admission M$40; ⏰ 6:30-11:30pm; Ⓜ Insurgentes). Located inside the Zona Rosa's Plaza del Ángel shopping center, the Contempo screens contemporary Mexican and international films, with an emphasis on gay and erotic themes, as well as staging occasional theater and cabaret productions.

---

upscale LGBT crowd. Friends gather round the bar or head upstairs to lounge on sofas. It's conveniently nearby the popular taco joint, El Califa.

SANBORNS CAFÉ Map pp74–5

☎ 5207-9760; Londres 149; ⏰ 24 hr; Ⓜ Insurgentes

During the day, Chilangos customarily meet at Sanborns Café for a business breakfast or lunch (see p142). After hours, this round-the-clock coffee shop makes a convenient port-of-call between clubs. It's also considered a prime cruising locale, particularly the book-browsing section at the front.

NIGHTLIFE

The long-time core of gay nightlife is the Zona Rosa, with Calle Amberes rivaling San Francisco's Castro Street for bars, discos, nightclubs, restaurants and cafés. Other pockets of *de ambiente* activity exist in Colonia Roma and the Centro Histórico.

DANCE CLUBS

BOY BAR Map pp74–5

☎ 5511-3915; www.boybarclub.com; Amberes 14, admission incl one drink M$130; ⏰ from 10pm Thu Sat; Ⓜ Insurgentes

Steamiest of the clubs on the Amberes strip, this multi-level disco has won notoriety for its chiseled go-go dancers, not to mention a 'hot room' for advanced groping. If it gets too hot, catch a breeze up on the sandy terrace overlooking the street action.

BAR OASIS Map pp48–9

☎ 5521-9740; República de Cuba 2G, Centro; ⏰ 3pm-1am Sun-Thu, to 3am Fri & Sat; Ⓜ Bellas Artes

Next door to El Viena, this packed *antro* cuts across class lines, with both cowboys and businessmen dancing before a day-glo cityscape. Stick around past midnight for shows featuring lip-synching trannies.

BUTTERGOLD Map pp48–9

☎ 5761-1861; Izazaga 9; cover incl 2 drinks M$100; ⏰ 9pm-4am Tue-Sun; Ⓜ Salto del Agua

Buttergold (aka Butterflies, aka El Butter), across the street from metro Salto del Agua, is an airplane-hangar-sized space that still manages to get densely packed. The funhouse features five bars, a snack bar and a big stage for elaborately choreographed drag shows. It's fun for straights, too, as long as you don't mind crowds, thick smoke and loud, loud music.

EL ALMACÉN/EL TALLER Map pp74–5

www.eltaller-elalmacen.com.mx; Florencia 37; ⏰ 6pm-2am Tue-Sun; admission M$50; Ⓜ Insurgentes

Among the first in the Pink Zone to fly the rainbow flag, this perennially popular nightspot has two distinct levels. Upstairs, El Almacén (the warehouse) is a narrow low-lit bar featuring weekly cabaret programs. Downstairs, the men-only El Taller (the workshop) is a dark, industrially themed space with a crowded dance floor and continuous heavy breathing videos.

LA PERLA Map pp48–9

☎ 1997-7695; República de Cuba 44; cover M$120; ⏰ shows 11:30pm & 1:30am Fri & Sat; Ⓜ Bellas Artes

Once a red-light venue, this small cabaret has been reborn in the age of irony as a cradle of kitsch, with hilarious drag shows featuring traditional Mexican songstresses. It attracts a mixed crowd, perhaps more straight than gay, in the mood to slum it. Be sure to arrive by 10:30pm to get in.

LIPSTICK Map pp74–5

☎ 5514-4920; www.lipstickbar.com; Amberes 1; cover Wed & Thu M$100, Fri & Sat M$140; ⏰ Wed-Sat; Ⓜ Insurgentes

At this large (capacity 950) club for an upscale 18-to-35 set, the fun goes on in three different settings: a subdued lower lounge for chilling out with friends; a video bar with adjacent dark room for close encounters; and an excellent upper terrace for all-out revelry. Thursday is girls' night.

LIVING Map pp74–5

☎ 5286-0671; www.living.com.mx; Paseo de la Reforma 483; cover $150-170; ⏰ 10pm-4am Fri & Sat; Ⓜ Sevilla

Housed in a magnificent Italianate mansion near the Torre Mayor, Living is a temple of ecstatic nightlife for the 20-something set, both gay and straight. On the enormous

main dance floor, world-class DJs cook up high-volume house sessions as sculpted performance artists/exotic dancers gyrate. Other scenes unfold in other lounges.

TOM'S LEATHER BAR Map p88

☎ 5564-0728; Insurgentes Sur 357; www.toms mexico.com; cover M$120; ⏰ 9pm-4am Tue-Sun; 🚌 Metrobus Sonora

For those who would dare to get medieval, Tom's provides the props, with heraldic shields, crossed swords and candelabras highlighting a decidedly decadent decor. When you hear the fat lady sing, the show's about to begin.

SLEEPING

6M9 GUEST HOUSE Map pp74–5

☎ 5208-8347; www.purpleroofs.com/6m9-mx .html; Marsella 69, Colonia Juárez; s/d M$640/950; Ⓜ Insurgentes; 🏊

Oriented toward a gay male clientele, the 6M9 occupies a pretty Porfiriano-era building within walking distance of Pink Zone bars. The fun-filled facilities include a small pool, sun deck and tiled steam room, and guests can help themselves to complimentary beverages at the bar. There are nine spacious, well-maintained rooms (reservations by internet only).

HOTEL MARCO POLO Map pp74–5

☎ 5080-1445; www.marcopolo.com.mx; Amberes 27, Zona Rosa; s/d US$168/188; Ⓜ Insurgentes; Ⓟ ✕ 🐾 🖥

Not a gay hotel per se, this small, modern hotel near Paseo de la Reforma is in the heart of the gay nightlife district and is often identified as the best option nearby. The 59 bright rooms are done up in earthy tones, with plush beds and windows overlooking tree-lined Amberes. Rates are about 50% lower if booked online.

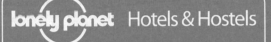

lonely planet Hotels & Hostels

Want more Sleeping recommendations than we could ever pack into this little ol' book? Craving more detail – including extended reviews and photographs? Want to read reviews by other travellers and be able to post your own? Just make your way over to **lonelyplanet.com/hotels** and check out our thorough list of independent reviews, then reserve your room simply and securely.

SLEEPING

top picks

- Gran Hotel Ciudad de México (p200)
- Casa González (p208)
- Red Tree House (p210)
- Mexico City Hostel (p202)
- Hábita Hotel (p209)
- Hippodrome Hotel (p210)
- La Casona (p211)
- Hotel Isabel (p203)
- Hostel Mundo Joven Catedral (p201)
- Hostal Frida (p212)

SLEEPING

As a frequent destination for both Mexican and foreign visitors, the DF (Federal District) overflows with lodging options, from no-frills guesthouses to top-flight hotels. Some of the most affordable places are clustered in the Centro Histórico, the vibrant center of the city, while more luxurious accommodations are concentrated in the Zona Rosa and Polanco neighborhoods, with branches of some major international chains represented. Midrange lodgings, most featuring restaurants and bars, abound in the Alameda and Plaza de la República areas; they tend to trade character for neutral modern comfort. (Note that places with the word 'garage' on the sign generally cater to short-term trysting guests.) Those on a tight budget will find an increasing number of low-cost hostels, particularly in the center of town.

Accommodations listings in this chapter are ordered by neighborhood, then by price from most to least expensive based on the price of a standard double. Unlike in Mexico's coastal resorts, rates do not vary by season in the capital. Generally we've quoted rack rates, though business hotels customarily offer substantial discounts, especially during slow periods.

CENTRO HISTÓRICO

For most nonbusiness travelers, the historic center is the obvious place to stay, brimming with shops, museums, government palaces and historic buildings, some of which house hotels. Ongoing renovations of its infrastructure and preservation of its many historic edifices have boosted the zone's appeal, attracting more visitors and encouraging installation of more lodgings, restaurants and clubs. But despite the center's renaissance and consequent gentrification, it remains one of the more affordable areas, and superior deals can still be found.

Three upmarket hotels stand right on the Zócalo (the city's vast central plaza) while an equal number of budget hostels are within a block of the square. At least a dozen midrange options line Av 5 de Mayo and other streets west of the Zócalo.

GRAN HOTEL CIUDAD DE MÉXICO
Map pp48–9   Historic Hotel $$$
☎ 1083-7700; www.granhotelciudaddemexico .com.mx; Av 16 de Septiembre 82; s/d M$1636/2691; Ⓜ Zócalo; Ⓟ ⊠ 🖵
The Gran Hotel flaunts the French art nouveau style of the prerevolutionary era. Crowned high overhead by a stained-glass canopy crafted by Tiffany in 1908, the vast atrium is a fin-de-siècle fantasy of curved

balconies, original wrought-iron elevators and chirping birds in zoo-sized cages. Rooms do not disappoint by comparison: fringed curtains, plush armchairs and canopied king-size beds boast a belle époque opulence. The rooftop terrace takes full advantage of the Zócalo setting. Observing the huge Mexican flag flapping in the wind from this perch, you may well be moved to shout 'Viva México!'

HOLIDAY INN ZÓCALO
Map pp48–9 Hotel $$$
☎ 5130-5130, 800-5521-2122; www.hotelescortes .com; Av 5 de Mayo 61; r from M$1264; Ⓜ Zócalo; Ⓟ ⊠ ⊠ 🖵
Northernmost of the three upper-echelon hotels facing the Zócalo, the Holiday Inn seems the least pretentious, eschewing colonial trimmings for contemporary comfort. And its rooftop-terrace restaurant, looking straight at the Metropolitan Cathedral, ranks with those of its neighbors.

HOTEL MAJESTIC
Map pp48–9   Hotel $$$
☎ 5521-8600; www.hotelmajestic.com.mx; Madero 73; r US$135, ste from US$172; Ⓜ Zócalo; Ⓟ ⊠ 🖵 ♿
This Best Western franchise has a lot going for it, including an attractive colonial interior, an unbeatable location and perhaps the most panoramic terrace restaurant on the Zócalo. Rooms, however, are less fabulous than you'd expect for these prices.

NH CENTRO HISTÓRICO
Map pp48–9 Hotel $$$
☎ 5130-1850; www.nh-hotels.com; Palma 42; r/suite incl breakfast M$1551/1693; Ⓜ Zócalo; Ⓟ ⊠ 🖵

PRICE GUIDE
$$$	over M$1000 double
$$	M$400-M$1000 double
$	under M$400 double

Riding the downtown development wave, Spanish chain NH placed one of its DF branches smack in the center. Lounges and rooms get a Euro-minimalist treatment normally associated with pricier digs. Spacious suites occupy the curved corners of the aerodynamically designed 1940s structure. Online rates are a terrific deal.

TULIP INN RITZ Map pp48–9   Hotel $$

☎ 5130-0160; www.tulipinnritzmexico.com; Madero 30; r/ste M$870/924; Ⓜ Allende
Popular with touring European groups, who appreciate its prime location, simpatico staff and secure installations, the 78-year-old Ritz was recently spruced up by new overseers from the Netherlands. About half of the 120 large rooms overlook Madero or Bolívar, while the rest face a tranquil patio.

HOTEL CATEDRAL Map pp48–9   Hotel $$

☎ 5518-5232; www.hotelcatedral.com.mx; Donceles 95; s/d M$475/660; Ⓜ Zócalo; Ⓟ ▭
Though short on colonial charm, this comfortable lodging has clearly considered its location, directly behind the Metropolitan Cathedral. South-facing rooms above the 4th floor offer reach-out-and-touch views of the colonial masterpiece, while units north take in stately Calle Donceles. Even if you get an interior room, you can lounge on the rooftop terraces, with cityscapes in all directions.

HOTEL GILLOW Map pp48–9   Hotel $$

☎ 5518-1440; www.hotelgillow.com; Isabel la Católica 17; s/d M$468/600; Ⓜ Zócalo; Ⓟ ▭
A historic building with standard midrange facilities, the Gillow boasts old-fashioned service and spacious carpeted rooms around a sunlit central courtyard. For views, request an Av 5 de Mayo or Isabel la Católica unit. With its marble floors, chandeliers and statuary, the lobby is a study in 1960s luxury.

HOTEL CANADÁ Map pp48–9   Hotel $$

☎ 5518-2106; www.hotelcanada.com.mx; Calle 5 de Mayo 47; s/d M$420/500; Ⓜ Allende; Ⓟ
This longstanding locale has performed a serious face-lift to boost its profile on hotel-packed Calle 5 de Mayo. Its smallish rooms have been done over tastefully, with fresh new carpets, peach-toned headboards and sepia photos of old Mexico. Affable gray-uniformed staff cater to a primarily business clientele, who may unwind in the TV amphitheater downstairs or quaff fresh-squeezed juices next door.

HOTEL CAPITOL Map pp48–9   Historic Hotel $

☎ 5512-0460; www.hotelcapitol.com.mx; República de Uruguay 12; s/d M$320/400; Ⓜ San Juan Letrán
Opposite the computer shopping center, this friendly relic of a hotel first opened its door a century ago as the Gran Hotel. Though it's lost some of its grandness since then, it still offers plain rooms around a central hall with fountain. Romantically inclined guests often opt for the Jacuzzi-equipped suites.

HOSTEL MUNDO JOVEN CATEDRAL

Map p48–9   Hostel $
☎ 5518-1726; www.hostelcatedral.com; República de Guatemala 4; dm incl breakfast M$140, d with shared bathroom M$380; Ⓜ Zócalo; ▭
Backpacker central in Mexico City, the capital's only HI affiliate is abuzz with a global rainbow of young travelers. Every facility you might need is here, the location couldn't be more central and the place is cordially managed. Four- and six-person dorms have polished hardwood floors, sturdy bunk beds and corresponding lockers. Other useful features include a youth travel agency, a relaxed ground-level café, and an excellent rooftop sun deck with bar and lounge chairs.

HOSTAL VIRREYES Map pp48–9   Hotel $

☎ 5521-4180; www.hostalvirreyes.com.mx; Izazaga 8; dm M$120, s/d M$320/370; Ⓜ Salto del Agua; ▭
A prestige hotel in the past, the Virreyes has quite naturally morphed into a hostel-student residence. Decor is bare bones but dorms provide plenty of breathing room for a half-dozen occupants and have proportionately large bathrooms done up in Talavera tile. The lobby lounge, which retains

some of the old hotel's more attractive elements, serves as an occasional live music venue, while the retro-fitted restaurant has a decent *comida corrida* (set lunch).

HOTEL AZORES Map pp48–9 Hotel $
☎ 5521-5220; www.hotelazores.com; República de Brasil 25; s/d from M$300/360; Ⓜ Zócalo; Ⓟ
Just off the fascinating Plaza Santo Domingo, the uncharacteristically modern Azores boasts a cheerily designed and scrupulously maintained interior. The 65 rooms are neither large nor luxurious but are in excellent shape. Just eight overlook the street through picture windows. The rest give onto a pair of bright interior courtyards, the lower one containing the pleasant lobby bar.

HOSTAL MONEDA Map pp48–9 Hostel $
☎ 5522-5803; www.hostalmoneda.com.mx; Moneda 8; dm incl breakfast & dinner M$120-155, d M$355; Ⓜ Zócalo; Ⓛ
On one of the city's most exuberant and historic streets, the Moneda is an altogether more modest affair than the nearby Hostel Mundo Joven Catedral, though it remains a favored stop on the international backpackers' circuit. Chief among its assets are a well-informed, bilingual staff and a terrific multipurpose rooftop, suitable for sending emails or swinging in a hammock.

HOSTAL AMIGO Map pp48–9 Hostel $
☎ 5512-3464; www.hostelamigo.com; Isabel la Católica 61; dm incl breakfast & supper M$115, d with shared bathroom M$333; Ⓜ Isabel la Católica; Ⓛ
Occupying a 250-year-old former nuns' residence, this recently inaugurated hostel retains some of the original architectural features. The atmosphere is aggressively casual, and if you like to party, you'll find plenty of amigos and amigas who share your interest. All that partying has taken a toll on the facilities, though, and the dorms can get mighty crowded.

HOTEL PRINCIPAL Map pp48–9 Hotel $
☎ 5521-1333; www.hotelprincipal.com.mx; Bolívar 29; s/d/tr M$225/315/410; Ⓜ Allende
A longtime favorite with frugal travelers, the Principal has a helpful staff with plenty of experience. Typical of the old Centro lodgings, it boasts enormous rooms with high ceilings surrounding a plant-draped central hall. A newly installed skylight and fresh paint considerably brighten the environment. Cafés and clubs dot the street.

HOTEL ROBLE Map pp48–9 Hotel $
☎ 5522-7830; www.hotelroble.com; República de Uruguay 109; s/d/tr M$275/310/520; Ⓜ Zócalo; Ⓛ
Used mostly by Mexicans visiting the capital on a shopping spree, the Roble is terrifically convenient to the numerous stores just south of the Zócalo. Despite its modern, concrete-block facade, however, the rooms could use an upgrade, with chipped furniture and stale-smelling carpet. A downstairs restaurant remains busy throughout the day.

HOTEL WASHINGTON Map pp48–9 Hotel $
☎ 5512-3502; Av 5 de Mayo 54; s/d/tr M$240/300/340; Ⓜ Allende
If you're sticking to a budget but don't want to sacrifice comfort and prefer to be right in the middle of things, the Washington will do nicely – and you'll likely be amid similar-minded travelers. Be sure to get a balcony room facing Av 5 de Mayo or Calle Palma; airless interior units are best avoided.

MEXICO CITY HOSTEL Map pp48–9 Hostel $
☎ 5512-3666; www.mexicocityhostel.com; República de Brasil 8; dm incl breakfast from M$100, s/d M$200/300; Ⓜ Zócalo; Ⓛ
Steps from the Zócalo, this colonial structure has been artfully restored, with original wood beams and stone walls as a backdrop for modern energy-efficient facilities. In the spacious dorms, three or four sturdy bunk beds stand on terracotta floors. Immaculate bathrooms trimmed with *azulejos* (coloured tiles) amply serve around 100 occupants. Rates include a buffet breakfast.

HOTEL RIOJA Map pp48–9 Hotel $
☎ 5521-8333; Av 5 de Mayo 45; s/d from M$220/250; Ⓜ Allende
The Rioja is a well-maintained lodging in the middle of everything, and the quality of its facilities matches those of places at twice the price. Front rooms (slightly pricier) have balconies suitable for observing the activity on Av 5 de Mayo. Interior units, opening on an echoing central court, tend to be dark but guarantee a peaceful night's sleep.

HOTEL JUÁREZ Map pp48–9 — Hotel $

☎ 5512-6929; hoteljuarez@prodigy.net.mx; 1er Callejón de 5 de Mayo; s/d M$190/250; Ⓜ Allende

Nestled in an L-shaped alley, the Juárez is another incredibly cheap but perfectly good choice in the thick of things, though just out-of-the-way enough to ensure a *tranquilo* night's sleep. True, its feng shui may need an overhaul, but the shoestring travelers who regularly check in here don't seem to mind.

HOTEL SAN ANTONIO Map pp48–9 — Hotel $

☎ 5518-1625; fax 5512-9906; 2a Callejón 5 de Mayo 29; d with private/shared bathroom M$220/200, tr M$320; Ⓜ Allende

Located inside an L-shaped passage linking Av 5 de Mayo with Palma, the Hotel San Antonio gives easy access to downtown shopping and sights while remaining slightly aloof from the bustle. Rooms are on the small side and face either the little-used alley or the whitewashed interior court. Join the mayor and his pals for breakfast at El Cardenal (p135), just off the Palma entry.

HOTEL ISABEL Map pp48–9 — Hotel $

☎ 5518-1213; www.hotel-isabel.com.mx; Isabel la Católica 63; s/d/tr with private bathroom M$220/320/460, s/d with shared bathroom M$150/220; Ⓜ Isabel la Católica; 🖳

The Isabel is a long-time budget travelers' favorite, and it's easy to see why. A few blocks from the Zócalo, it offers large, well-scrubbed rooms with old but sturdy furniture, high ceilings and great balconies, plus a hostel-like social scene. The classic arrangement has three floors of rooms around a skylit patio festooned with lots of plants.

HOTEL ZAMORA Map pp48–9 — Hotel $

☎ 5512-0245; hotelzamora@prodigy.net.mx; Av 5 de Mayo 50; s/d with private bathroom M$175/275, s/d with shared bathroom M$130/220; Ⓜ Allende

Absolutely no frills here, but it's clean, friendly and cheap. Rooms, around a skylit hall, have high ceilings with painted wood beams, plus there are springy mattresses; bathrooms range from primitive to nicely tiled. Ask for a front room: the balconies over Av 5 de Mayo are worth the price alone.

HOTEL SEÑORIAL Map pp48–9 — Hotel $

☎ 5709-3340; www.residenciasenorial.com; Callejón de la Esperanza 8; s/d per month M$1800/2150; Ⓜ Salto del Agua; Ⓟ 🖳

An old 'by-the-hour' hotel converted into a student residence, the Señorial is a haven for art students, but is open to anyone with an ISIC card. Rooms are austere, but students with a month to spend in the capital might find it an interesting option. Adjacent is the Plaza de las Vizcaínas, a pleasant (though sometimes derelict) patch of green.

ALAMEDA CENTRAL & AROUND

The area south of the Alameda Central abounds with unremarkable but perfectly comfortable midrange hotels, especially along Revillagigedo and Luis Moya. Some of these places customarily fill up with package tour groups from Europe. Like the Centro Histórico, this section is undergoing major renovations, with the recently built Sheraton as a symbol of its new ascendance, though pockets of neglect are reminders of the 1985 earthquake that devastated the zone. Though by day the neighborhood bustles with shoppers, after dark it quiets down considerably and, apart from its small Chinatown district, offers little incentive to wander.

HOTEL SHERATON CENTRO HISTÓRICO Map p64 — Hotel $$$

☎ 5130-5300; www.sheraton.com.mx; Juárez 70; r from US$220; Ⓜ Hidalgo; Ⓟ ⊠ 🅧 🖳 🈂 🖳

A cornerstone of this downtown redevelopment project, the sleek Sheraton towers above quaint Alameda Central. Most travelers are here on business, but anyone desiring a dose of comfort and sublime cityscapes should be more than satisfied. The 27-floor hotel contains more than 450 rooms, all above the 9th floor to maximize views. Classic rooms come in a range of soothing colors, from cobalt blue to cappuccino. The busy complex also boasts a branch of El Cardenal restaurant (p135) serving up *alta cocina mexicana* (see p133), and a huge fitness center with saunas, a massage clinic and a terrace café.

HOTEL DE CORTÉS Map p64 — Hotel $$$

☎ 5518-2181; www.hoteldecortes.com.mx; Hidalgo 85; traditional r/ste M$1385/1962, Virreinal M$2398/2992; Ⓜ Hidalgo; ⊠ 🖳

Once a hospice for pilgrims of the Augustinian order, this World Hotels property has a long history of sheltering travelers. Rooms encircle a lovely late-18th-century patio, where a buffet breakfast is served each morning and mariachis perform nightly. If you don't mind the price tag, staying here will give you a genuine taste of colonial Mexico.

HOTEL SAN FRANCISCO Map p64   Hotel $$
☎ 5533-1032; sanfrancisco@hotelesdelangel.com; Luis Moya 11; s/d M$700/760; Ⓜ Juárez; Ⓟ

With buildings springing up all around it, this longstanding Alameda tower has changed little over the years, though its views are now obstructed. Popular with Australian and European groups, it boasts spacious rooms with old-fashioned furniture and seriously dated lobby decor. Your best bet for Alameda views are the north-facing units above the 11th floor.

HOTEL MONTE REAL Map p64   Hotel $$
☎ 5518-1150; www.hotelmontereal.com.mx; Revillagigedo 23; s/d/tr M$650/700/800; Ⓜ Juárez; Ⓟ ⊠ ▱

Handily located across the way from the new Museo de Artes Populares (p63) and down the street from the Teatro Metropolitán (p171), this nine-level block makes a fine place to lay your head. Mexican handicrafts spice up the busy lobby and otherwise bland though well-maintained rooms. A genuinely cheerful staff has ample experience attending to foreign guests, especially French and German groups.

HOTEL MARLOWE Map p64   Hotel $$
☎ 5521-9540; www.hotelmarlowe.com.mx, in Spanish; Independencia 17; s/d/tr M$480/600/740; Ⓜ San Juan de Letrán; Ⓟ ⊠ ▱

The best of many midrange options in the south-of-Alameda zone, the peach-concrete Marlowe stands just across from Chinatown's pagoda gate. Above a bright, airy lobby are spacious, rooms colored salmon and champagne, with good carpet, colorful bedspreads, soothing art and inset lighting. Fitness freaks will appreciate the top floor gym-with-a-view.

HOTEL FLEMING Map p64   Hotel $$
☎ 5510-4530; www.hotelfleming.com.mx; Revillagigedo 35; s/d/tr M$360/460/490; Ⓜ Juárez; Ⓟ ▱

Just a block from the metro, the Fleming is one of the better deals in the zone. Though typically uninspiring in design or decor, the spacious, peach-toned rooms have all the comforts of pricier places in this category, plus ceiling fans and attractive painted ceiling beams. For some reason it's popular with French groups, who congregate in the decent ground-level restaurant.

HOTEL SAN DIEGO Map p64   Hotel $
☎ 5510-3523; Luis Moya 98; s/d M$250/400; Ⓜ Balderas

Though a bit far from the action, this generic option two blocks east of La Ciudadela should appeal to peso-pinchers unwilling to rough it. Above the lobby's imitation leather sofas and plastic plants are bright, decent-sized rooms with furniture of recent vintage and newly tiled bathrooms. Some may be put off by the antiseptic cleaning odor.

PLAZA DE LA REPÚBLICA & SAN RAFAEL

Farther from the Zócalo, the area around the Monument to the Revolution is awash in hotels of every category, with a number of by-the-hour dives interspersed amid the business-class establishments. Unaffected by the wave of development sweeping the Centro and Reforma corridor, the semiresidential zone offers glimpses of Chilango neighborhood life. Schoolchildren and office workers share the streets with hookers, troubadours and visitors from the provinces – add the strains of an organ grinder and you have all the elements for a neorealist film.

HOTEL CASA BLANCA Map p71   Hotel $$$
☎ 5096-4500; www.hotel-casablanca.com.mx; Lafragua 7; s/d M$1080/1350, ste from M$1588; Ⓜ Metrobus Tabacalera; Ⓟ ⊠ ▤

Here's a five-star hotel with all the trimmings for much less than the chains. A sexy new lobby bar jazzes up the otherwise '60s ambience, with a lavender color scheme in the 270 rooms. Bonus: a rooftop pool with adjacent lounge.

HOTEL JENA Map p71   Hotel $$
☎ 5097-0277; www.hoteljena.com.mx; Terán 12; s/d M$667/761, ste M$1287; Ⓜ Hidalgo; Ⓟ ⊠ ▱ ▤

Not as tall as it looks (the imposing black tower is strictly for show), the Jena has huge rooms that are among the most luxurious in this range. Wood paneling is a key element in the decor, lending everything a boardroom burnish, including the snappy cocktail lounge. An indoor pool and gym are additional attractions. The hotel is just a block and a half from Reforma.

HOTEL ASTOR Map p71 — Hotel $$
☎ 5148-2644; hotel.astor@mexico.com; Caso 83; s/d M$440/580; 🚍 Metrobus Reforma; 🅿 🗷 🖵
Glass turrets and cascading fountains front this sleek and sterile block, which seems designed for anonymity – the desk clerk sits inside a glass booth and cars huddle discreetly in an interior patio. Nevertheless, the Astor offers large, modern rooms that are as comfortable as they're unremarkable. Perhaps their most useful feature is the soundproof windows that muffle the traffic streaming down Caso. A block east is the classic Gran Premio, a neighborhood café with a vintage Italian espresso maker and great pastries.

HOTEL MAYALAND Map p71 — Hotel $$
☎ 5566-6066; www.hotelmayaland.com.mx; Antonio Caso 23; s/d M$430/560; Ⓜ Juárez; 🅿 🖵
Standing on a rather sterile street two blocks south of the Monument to the Revolution, this business-oriented hotel has well-maintained facilities with a Maya motif. Typically neutral-modern rooms feature textured pink walls, floral canvasses and inset lighting.

HOTEL MÓNACO Map p71 — Hotel $$
☎ 5566-8333; www.hotel-monaco.com.mx; Guerrero 12; s/d M$485/520; Ⓜ Hidalgo; 🅿 🗷
Steps from the metro and opposite cute Plaza San Fernando, this refurbished older hotel stands at the lower edge of run-down Colonia Guerrero but is more attuned to the nearby Reforma business corridor. Bellboys in blue suits proudly escort you down marble-floored hallways with piped-in muzak to your neatly furnished, color-coordinated room.

HOTEL NEW YORK Map p71 — Hotel $$
☎ 5566-9700; Édison 45; s/d M$310/520; Ⓜ Revolución; 🅿 🖵
A few blocks northeast of Plaza de la República, this is an upscale option in a zone crammed with cut-rate hotels. Though rooms are on the small side, they're a cut above your average sterile business hotel, with bold primary colors and stylish furniture. Rates include breakfast and wi-fi.

PALACE HOTEL Map p71 — Hotel $$
☎ 5566-2400; fax 5535-7520; Ignacio Ramírez 7; s/d M$351/409; 🚍 Revolución; 🅿
Run by a bunch of gregarious Asturians, the Palace has large, neatly maintained rooms in an appealing range of blue tones. Broad balconies give terrific views down palm-lined Ramírez to the Plaza de la Revolución. Cash-paying guests get substantial discounts.

HOTEL ÉDISON Map p71 — Hotel $
☎ 5566-0933; Édison 106; s/d/tr M$219/299/359; Ⓜ Revolución; 🖵
Beyond the grim, bunkerlike exterior, accommodations face a rectangular garden surrounded by pre-Hispanic motifs. Despite faded wallpaper and dated fixtures, rooms are amply sized, with massive closets and marble washbasins. Should you need them, there's a bakery and a laundry across the street.

CASA DE LOS AMIGOS Map p71 — Hostel $
☎ 5705-0521; www.casadelosamigos.org; Mariscal 132; dm M$100, r with shared bathroom M$290; Ⓜ Revolución; 🗷 🖵
Not technically a hostel, the Quaker-run Casa is primarily a residence for NGOs, researchers and others involved in peace and human-rights efforts, but it welcomes walk-in travelers. It attracts a more serious individual than the average hostel and thus has a lower-key atmosphere. Meditation sessions, discussions with community members and Spanish conversation are available to guests, who may volunteer to help run the Casa for a reduced rate. A hearty breakfast (M$15) is served Monday to Friday in the ground-floor dining room. There's a two-night minimum stay.

HOTEL OXFORD Map p71 — Hotel $
☎ 5566-0500; Mariscal 67; s/d M$120/200; Ⓜ Revolución
Some find a special allure in this art deco remnant of 1940s Mexico City which sits on the tranquil Plaza Buenavista behind the Museo Nacional de San Carlos. Others just call it a dive. Rooms 210 and 310 are best,

with handsome rounded balconies facing the plaza and goings-on within. If it's seedy charm you're after, the Oxford's bar will do nicely, and they'll send up drinks until 4am.

ZONA ROSA, CUAUHTÉMOC & JUÁREZ

Foreign businesspeople and tourists check in at the numerous glitzy hotels in this international commerce and nightlife area that's also the center of the city's gay culture. Though it's hardly representative of DF life, some may find the Pink Zone a reassuringly global bubble, where foreigners can move about without eliciting undue interest. Most of the international hotel chains have branches within the zone proper and along Paseo de la Reforma, while an assortment of less-expensive Mexican-run establishments dot the quieter streets of Colonia Cuauhtémoc, north of Reforma, and Juárez, east of Insurgentes.

FOUR SEASONS HOTEL

Map pp74–5   Luxury Hotel $$$
☎ 5230-1818; www.fourseasons.com/mexico; Paseo de la Reforma 500; r US$370; Ⓜ Sevilla; Ⓟ ✕ ✂ ▯ ▱ ⚅ ☗

One of the city's most elegant lodgings, the Four Seasons was designed to resemble a French-Mexican late-19th-century structure, an anomaly amid Paseo de la Reforma's glass-and-steel monoliths. Rather than flirting with modernity, the hotel goes for a classic opulence, from the lobby salons, with their Louis XV armchairs and settees, to the aristocratically furnished guest rooms, with an average 56 sq meters of floor space. Most of these face a beautifully landscaped central courtyard, a mix of tropical foliage and French renaissance.

SHERATON MARÍA ISABEL HOTEL

Map pp74–5   Hotel $$$
☎ 5242-5555; www.sheraton.com/mariaisabel; Reforma 325; r from US$252; Ⓜ Insurgentes Ⓟ ✕ ✂ ▯ ▱ ⚅ ☗

Overlooking the Independence monument and next door to the US embassy, the Sheraton's two towers have accommodated businesspeople, diplomats and journalists for over three decades. Among its varied attractions are a rooftop pool, fitness center, two lighted tennis courts, nightly mariachis and a Starbucks branch.

SAN MARINO HOTEL-SUITES

Map pp74–5   Serviced Apartment $$$
☎ 5207-9060; www.sanmarino.com.mx; Río Tiber 107; r M$1795; Ⓜ Insurgentes; Ⓟ ✂ ▯

Just up from the Ángel monument along a major northbound artery, this locale has slickly styled rooms – rather than suites – with faux-wood floors and marshmallow mattresses. The effect is undercut by the chintzy kitchen, but execs here are more likely to seek nourishment in the grotto-like restaurant downstairs. The hotel routinely offers hefty discounts for walk-in customers.

HOTEL IMPERIAL Map pp74–5   Hotel $$$
☎ 5705-4911; www.hotelimperial.com.mx; Paseo de la Reforma 64; r/ste M$1521/2457; Ⓜ Hidalgo; ✂ ▯

The dictator Porfirio Díaz unwrapped this cake wedge of a building in 1904, and it remains a refreshingly stylish structure alongside the Columbus traffic circle. Spacious suites occupy the upper turret levels while 50 standard rooms line the Paseo de la Reforma and Av Morelos sides. Unfortunately, room decor fails to match the building's Porfiriato splendor.

SUITES DEL ÁNGEL

Map pp74–5   Serviced Apartment $$$
☎ 5242-9500; www.hotelesdelangel.mexico -hoteles.com; Río Lerma 162; ste M$1460; Ⓜ Insurgentes; Ⓟ ✂ ▯

Sister to the nearby Hotel Del Ángel, this is designed for execs on longer stays. It's a great deal considering its central location and ample accommodations. Tri-chamber suites include a few sofas, huge closets, three TVs (one's in the bathroom should you need it), Jacuzzi and full kitchen. Front rooms have balconies overlooking traffic-clogged Calle Río Lerma.

HOTEL SEVILLA PALACE Map pp74–5 Hotel $$$
☎ 5705-2800; www.sevillapalace.com.mx; Paseo de la Reforma 105; r M$1328, ste from M$1907; Ⓜ Allende; ✂ ▱

While it won't win any awards for originality, this monolithic structure is built for comfort, with over 400 air-conditioned rooms featuring queen-size beds and cheery abstract art. Soaring up through the central atrium in a transparent vertigo-inducing elevator, you reach the 23rd floor, with a swimming pool beneath a protective canopy and a thatched *palapa* (thatch-roofed, open-sided beach shelter) for cocktails. Both the monumental Plaza de la Revolución and pleasant Parque Sullivan with its Sunday art market are within walking distance.

HOTEL GENEVE Map pp74–5 Hotel $$$
☎ 5080-0800; www.hotelgeneve.com.mx; Londres 130; r from M$1355; Ⓜ Insurgentes; Ⓟ ✖ ✗ ▣
Celebrating its centennial, this Zona Rosa institution strives to maintain a belle époque ambience in contrast to the globalized mishmash around it. The lobby breathes class, with lily-of-the-valley chandeliers, oil canvasses and dark wood paneling, as well as access to a skylit Sanborns café flanked by corkscrew-shaped columns. Rooms feature handsome carved wood headboards and colonial dressers and nightstands.

HOTEL MISIÓN REFORMA
Map pp74–5 Hotel $$$
☎ 5141-0442; www.hotelesmision.com.mx; Morelos 110; r M$1300, ste M$2303; Ⓔ Metrobus Reforma; Ⓟ ✗ ▣
One of several large business hotels around the Columbus traffic circle, this terracotta monolith is a branch of a Mexican chain. Its spacious rooms get liberal doses of color and comfort and afford fine views of the grand boulevard below. When it's time to turn in, inner shutters block out noise and light.

HOTEL DEL ÁNGEL Map pp74–5 Hotel $$
☎ 5533-1032; www.hotelesdelangel.mexico-hoteles.com; Río Lerma 154; s/d/tr M$761/878/995; Ⓔ pesero Reforma-Metro Hidalgo; Ⓟ ✗ ▣
Like the area, this hotel is in transition. Construction of the HSBC building next door has robbed the once-formidable tower of views of the iconic monument it is named for. But rather than brood, the hotel is jazzing up its facilities from the top down, trading the ho-hum wicker motif (still in evidence on the lower floors) for pomo furniture and fixtures in the uppermost units.

HOTEL MISIÓN ZONA ROSA
Map pp74–5 Hotel $$
☎ 5533-0535; www.hotelesmision.com.mx; Napoles 62; r incl breakfast M$877; Ⓜ Insurgentes; Ⓟ ✗ ▣

Rising like a pink pylon above a nondescript section of Colonia Juárez, this business-class hotel offers small neatly appointed suites with classy ceiling moldings, Talavera pottery and a raised wireless work area. A small gym on the top level affords cityscape views. Skip the complimentary breakfast and make for Gabi's, a popular café and gallery of coffee paraphernalia just down the street.

HOTEL CITYEXPRESS Map pp74–5 Hotel $$
☎ 5208-1717; www.cityexpress.com.mx; Havre 21; r incl breakfast M$807; Ⓔ Metrobus Hamburgo; Ⓟ ✗ ✗
A no-nonsense business-class hotel in a green glass tower, the new Cityexpress emphasizes comfort and functionality – a place to crash between deals. But the decor is a cut above the neutral modern favored by most hotels in this price class, with designer bedspreads, well-chosen art and captivating views of the nearby office towers springing up in this transitional zone.

HOTEL MARÍA CRISTINA Map pp74–5 Hotel $$
☎ 5703-1212; www.hotelmariacristina.com.mx; Río Lerma 31; s/d from M$695/775; Ⓜ Insurgentes; Ⓟ ✗ ▣
Dating from the 1930s, this facsimile of an Andalusian estate, north of Reforma, makes an appealing retreat, particularly the adjacent bar with its own patio seating. Rooms lack the lobby's colonial splendor, but are generally bright and comfortable.

HOTEL PRIM Map pp74–5 Hotel $$
☎ 5141-1330; www.hotelprim.com; Versalles 46; s/d/tr incl breakfast M$588/672/756; Ⓜ Cuauhtémoc
The hulking Prim does not present an attractive facade, but it's decent value and a quick hike from Reforma, the Zona Rosa or Colonia Roma. The junior suites are the best deal, with cozy living rooms, huge beds and two bathrooms. Several hot nightspots are within walking distance, but if you don't feel like going out, the hotel's piano bar hosts schmaltzy crooners Tuesday to Saturday nights.

HOTEL BRISTOL Map pp74–5 Hotel $$
☎ 5533-6060; www.hotelbristol.com.mx; Plaza Necaxa 17; s/d M$563/656; Ⓔ pesero Reforma-Metro Hidalgo; Ⓟ ✖ ✗ ▣
A good-value option in the pleasant and central Cuauhtémoc neighborhood, the

Bristol caters primarily to business travelers, offering quality carpet, a soothing color scheme and cordial service. Guests should expect to rub shoulders with an array of lower-echelon salarymen from throughout the Republic. They'll be checking their email in the small business center, flipping through the newspaper in the lobby lounge or having lunch with clients at the above-average restaurant.

HOTEL PRINCIPADO Map pp74–5 Hotel $$
☎ 5233-2944; www.hoteldelprincipado.com.mx; Londres 42; s/d/tr incl breakfast M$500/650/750; Ⓜ Insurgentes; Ⓟ 🖵 ♿
Conveniently poised between the Zona Rosa and Colonia Roma, this friendly little place makes a nice cocoon. It has recently adjusted its look, replacing the carpet with faux wood floors, installing light-stained furniture and updating its analog keys with cards. A gratis breakfast buffet includes fruit, *chilaquiles* (fried tortilla chips with scrambled eggs or sauce, often with grated cheese on top) and much more. Look for weekend discounts.

CASA GONZÁLEZ Map pp74–5 B&B $$
☎ 5514-3302; casa.gonzalez@prodigy.net.mx; Río Sena 69; s/d from M$428/588; Ⓜ Insurgentes; 🖵
A family-run operation for nearly a century, the Casa is a perennial hit with mature travelers. Set around several patios and semiprivate terraces festooned with colorful plants and flowers, the general ambience is extraordinarily *tranquilo*. Original portraits and landscapes decorate the rooms, apparently done by a guest in lieu of payment. Guests meet over breakfast, served on old china in the dining room.

HOTEL SEVILLA Map pp74–5 Hotel $$
☎ 5566-1866; www.sevilla.com.mx; Serapio Rendón 124; tradicional s/d M$276/445, nueva M$459/573; 🚌 Metrobus Reforma; Ⓟ 🖵
Opposite the Jardín del Arte this oft-recommended business hotel is divided into traditional and new sections. Rooms in the former have '60s paneling; those in the latter are more slickly appointed with air-conditioning and hair dryers.

HOTEL COMPOSTELA Map pp74–5 Hotel $$
☎ 5566-0733; www.hotelcompostela.com.mx; Sullivan 35; tradicional s/d M$299/320, nueva M$410/475; 🚌 Metrobus Reforma; Ⓟ

There are two sections occupying this large rectangular block across the way from the Jardín del Arte: traditional and new (though 'newer' might be more accurate). Though only slightly pricier, the units in the latter section have much more pizzazz, with bigger bathrooms, cheerier colors and lots of mirrors.

HOSTAL CASSA VIEJA Map pp74–5 Hostel $
☎ 5208-3004; www.hostalcasavieja.com.mx; Cerrada de Londres 7; dm/s/d incl breakfast M$120/250/320; Ⓜ Sevilla; Ⓟ
Just outside Metro Sevilla is this little-known guesthouse, essentially a second-floor apartment outfitted for travelers. Four two-bed rooms and one four-bunk dorm share a large blue bathroom; another room occupies the former maid's quarters on the roof. Guests from all over congregate in the simply decorated sitting room or put together snacks in the kitchen.

VERSALLES 104 Map pp74–5 Hostel $
☎ 5705-3247; www.versalles104.com; Versalles 104; dm/d from M$115/240; Ⓜ Cuauhtémoc; 🖵
Friendly American-Mexican couple Tory and Livier have reconceived a Porfirio Díaz–era home as a boutique hostel-cultural center, contributing their own quirky design elements, and it's a hit with young, mostly European, travelers. Two rooms around a small patio are outfitted as mixed-gender dorms sharing a single tiny bathroom. Otherwise, you might opt for one of a pair of wood-floored private rooms upstairs. Much of the social interaction takes place in the front-end café-theater, where espresso and Japanese elixir tonics are dispensed.

BOSQUE DE CHAPULTEPEC

Checking in alongside the Bosque de Chapultepec makes it easy to appreciate the vast swath of greenery and its multifaceted attractions. See also the Polanco section for lodgings on the park's north side.

CAMINO REAL MÉXICO
Map p78 Luxury Hotel $$$
☎ 5263-8888; www.caminoreal.com; Mariano Escobedo 700; r/ste US$135/340; Ⓜ Chapultepec; Ⓟ 🗙 🕸 🖵 🛒 ♿ ♨

With over 700 rooms and covering 33,000 sq meters of grounds, the Camino Real is a truly monumental endeavor. It's also a national architectural landmark, boldly designed by Mexican Ricardo Legorreta, whose trademark geometric solids and great swathes of color lend it a refreshing simplicity. Murals by Rufino Tamayo and sculpture by Mathías Goeritz further boost the hotel's cachet. Among a set of internationally themed restaurants is a branch of New York's Le Cirque, possibly Mexico City's most exclusive place to dine.

HOTEL PARK VILLA Map p78   Motel $$
☎ 5515-5245; www.hotelparkvilla.com.mx; Gómez Pedraza 68, Colonia San Miguel Chapultepec; r M$660, ste from M$770; Ⓜ Juanacatlán; Ⓟ ⊠

The only lodging on the south (Condesa) side of Bosque de Chapultepec, the auto-oriented Park Villa is in a self contained compound. Terracotta tiles top a double deck of 40 rooms with 'rustic' furniture amid pink pastels and some leafy motifs hand-painted above the headboards. The larger suites are equipped with Jacuzzis and air-conditioning. Adjacent to the rooms through a bougainvillea-draped threshold is the Restaurante Jardín del Corregidor with seating on a pleasant patio, and a tiny zoo containing a couple of sleepy lions and tropical birds in heavily reinforced cages.

POLANCO

The Polanco neighborhood, just north of Bosque de Chapultepec and within walking distance of the Museo Nacional de Antropología, has some of the city's best hotels, mostly geared to international business travelers. Most prominent are the four sentinels of glass and stone standing opposite the Auditorio Nacional, known collectively as the Zona Hotelera. Staying in Polanco may not put you in touch with Mexico's indigenous identity but it will give you a taste of how modern Chilangos see themselves, somewhere between Euro-chic and New York funky.

W MEXICO CITY HOTEL
Map p84   Luxury Hotel $$$
☎ 9138-1800; www.WHotels.com; Campos Elíseos 252; r/ste from US$455/665; Ⓜ Auditorio; Ⓟ ⊠ ⊠ 🖵 🔁 ♿ 🚴

One of the four sentinels opposite the Auditorio Nacional, Latin America's first W

is a 25-floor business hotel that's determined to break away from the stodginess of its neighbors. Rooms skillfully blend style, comfort and killer views, and feature goose-down quilts, high-tech entertainment and waterfall or massage showers (at the balcony end, which may appeal to exhibitionists). A spa takes up the entire 3rd floor, and includes a 'relaxation pool' and *temascal* (pre-Hispanic sauna). There's fine dining at Solea restaurant, which specializes in seafood à la mexicana, and serious imbibing at the Whiskey Bar.

HOTEL NIKKO MÉXICO
Map p84   Luxury Hotel $$$
☎ 5283-8787; www.hotelnikkomexico.com; Campos Elíseos 204; r incl buffet breakfast from US$350; Ⓜ Auditorio; Ⓟ ⊠ ⊠ 🖵 🔁 ♿ 🚴

The Nikko blends modern luxury with Japanese traditions of service in an architecturally striking 38-story tower. The 744-room hotel features four restaurants (two of which specialize in Japanese fare) plus two bars, three tennis courts, a domed and heated swimming pool, a gym, a modern business center and a branch of the prestigious Alberto Misrachi art gallery. You'll pay about half the standard rate by booking online.

CASA VIEJA Map p84   Boutique Hotel $$$
☎ 5512-0832; www.casavieja.com; Eugenio Sue 45; ste incl breakfast from US$350, Ⓜ Auditorio; Ⓟ ⊠ 🖵

Every whim is catered to at this aggressively colonial boutique hotel near Parque Lincoln. Aficionados of Mexican *artesanías* (handicrafts) will be thrilled by the 10 fancifully decorated suites, each inspired by a different artist. Worth the splurge? If you've ever wanted to step into a scene from the film *Frida,* it may very well be.

HÁBITA HOTEL Map p84   Boutique Hotel $$$
☎ 5282-3100; www.hotelhabita.com; Presidente Masaryk 201; s/d US$228/310; Ⓜ Polanco; Ⓟ ⊠ ⊠ 🖵 🔁

Mexican architect Enrique Norten turned a functional apartment building into one of the city's top boutique hotels. Decor in the 36 rooms is boldly minimal, with bone white walls, goose-down quilts on futons, and Japanese-style benches in the bathroom. The sleek rooftop bar, Área, is one of Polanco's hottest nightspots (see p168).

Downstairs, a restaurant called Aura serves sophisticated global cuisine, fusing Mexican ingredients with Asian and Italian favorites.

HOTEL POLANCO Map p84 · Hotel $$$

☎ 5280-8082; www.hotelpolanco.com; Edgar Allan Poe 8; s/d M$1395/1455; Ⓜ Auditorio; ✕ 🄯 🖳
Unlike the nearby high-rises, this resembles a small European guesthouse of the sort Basil Fawlty might run, complete with Italian bistro and snippy desk manager. It's in a quiet, leafy section of the neighborhood, near the French embassy, with easy access to the National Auditorium through a little patch of forest. The hotel's 71 rooms eschew hipness for a sober ambience.

CONDESA

Thanks to the recent appearance of several attractive new lodgings, this trendy neighborhood south of Bosque de Chapultepec can be an excellent base, with plenty of after-hours restaurants and cafés amid tranquil tree-lined streets.

HIPPODROME HOTEL

Map p88 · Boutique Hotel $$$

☎ 5512-2110; www.thehippodromehotel.com; Mexico 188; r from US$230; Ⓜ Chilpancingo; 🄿 🖳
Condesa's hottest new option is just north of the wonderful Parque México. American owner Tom Shortt converted the Edificio Tehuacán, one of the neighborhood's many art deco gems, into a sleek boutique hotel with the help of Contemporary Mexican designer Nahim Dagdug, who restored the interior to a contemporary Mexican aesthetic, using hardwoods and earthy hues. Original modern art complements the stylish furniture, all designed in-house. Getting out of bed, you step onto a luxuriously cushy shag rug that's laid into the marble floor. With just 16 rooms, it's a small, businesslike affair and features a similarly subdued restaurant, the Hip Kitchen (p148), with menus designed by guest chefs.

CONDESA DF Map p88 · Boutique Hotel $$$

☎ 5241-2600; www.condesadf.com; Veracruz 102; r from US$182; Ⓜ Chapultepec; 🄯 ♿
Setting the standard for Condesa hipness since its opening in 2005, this is where Paris Hilton and U2 checked in during recent DF visits. The 1920s structure has been quirkily made over and furnished with an array of specially crafted objects. The rooms encircle an atrium-bar that's become one of Condesa's trendiest nightspots (partitions along the corridors are meant to reduce noise from below but don't count on it), with a fabulous rooftop component overlooking lush Parque España. Room decor is boldly minimal, with marshmallow beds backed by maplewood screens and original arched windows.

RED TREE HOUSE Map p88 · B&B $$

☎ 5584-3829; www.theredtreehouse.com; Culiacán 6; s with private/shared bathroom US$70/50, plus per additional person US$15, penthouse US$150; Ⓜ Chilpancingo; 🖳
Just off the delightful Plaza Citlaltépetl, the neighborhood's first B&B is in a typically idiosyncratic Condesa residence. It has all the comforts of home (if your home happens to be brimming with art and is decorated with exquisite taste). Each of the three bedrooms on the middle level is uniquely furnished; up a spiral staircase is the top-floor apartment with its own terrace. Downstairs, guests have the run of a cozy living room with fireplace, the kitchen and the lovely rear garden, the domain of friendly pooch Abril. Such has been RTH's success that additional accommodations have been built at the rear of the garden.

HOTEL ROOSEVELT Map p88 · Hotel $$

☎ 5208-6813; www.hotelroosevelt.com.mx; Insurgentes Sur 287; s/d M$450/630; 🚌 Metrobus Álvaro Obregón; 🄿 🖳
On the eastern edge of Condesa and within easy reach of the Cuban club district across Av Insurgentes, this friendly if functional hotel should appeal to nocturnally inclined travelers. The large gray building has 74 well-illuminated units, most overlooking either busy Av Yucatán or busier Av Insurgentes Sur – fortunately, they're equipped with well-sealed windows.

ROMA

Close to the center but just enough outside it to possess a distinctly neighborhood character, Colonia Roma makes a convenient and interesting place to stay, with plenty of cafés, bookstores and galleries to browse. Most of the accommodations are along the main thoroughfare, Álvaro Obregón (though a few of these are shady *de paso* places for short-term trysting guests).

LA CASONA Map pp92–3 · Boutique Hotel $$$

☎ 5286-3001; www.hotellacasona.com.mx; Durango 280; r incl breakfast US$217; Ⓜ Sevilla; ⊠

This stately mansion was restored to its early-20th-century splendor to become one of the capital's most distinctive boutique hotels. Each of the 29 rooms has been lovingly restored and uniquely appointed to bring out its original charm. Though they vary in size, color scheme and layout, common elements Include hardwood floors, fine antique furniture and fixtures, and warm colors highlighted by original moldings. The overall effect is wonderfully cozy though not too cutesy. The appropriately French restaurant on the premises spills into a lovely patio.

QUALITY INN Map pp92–3 · Hotel $$$

☎ 1085-9500; www.choicehotelsmexico.com; Álvaro Obregón 38; r M$1222; Ⓜ Cuauhtémoc; Ⓟ ⊠ ▢

Facing Álvaro Obregón's leafy median, Colonia Roma's newest hotel resembles its pricier downtown counterparts. Equipped with iPod hookups and softly illuminated desk nooks, its 91 ultracomfortable units surround a skylight-capped central atrium. Book online for substantial discounts.

STANZA HOTEL Map pp92–3 · Hotel $$

☎ 5208-0052; www.stanzahotel.com; Álvaro Obregón 13; r with/without air-con from M$702/564; Ⓜ Cuauhtémoc; Ⓟ ⊠ ▢

A business travelers' block on the east end of Álvaro Obregón by Jardín Pushkin, the Stanza makes a cushy, relatively inexpensive landing pad or re-entry chamber. The recently renovated hotel offers two categories of accommodation: executive (dark-stained furniture, large table-sized desks, air-con) and standard (cheaper furniture and slightly smaller bathrooms). Skip the bland coffee shop and make for any of Roma's numerous java joints instead.

HOTEL MILÁN Map pp92–3 · Hotel $$

☎ 5584-0222; www.hotelmilan.com.mx; Álvaro Obregón 94; s/d M$390/500; Ⓜ Insurgentes; Ⓟ ▢

Though lacking in character, the Milán is comfortable and stands in the heart of bohemian Colonia Roma. Design and decor are utterly typical of Mexican business accommodations (small box of a shower, artificial flowers, reproductions of Parisian street scenes), but the hotel makes great efforts to keep things spiffy and its level of service and quality of facilities match others at twice the price. The lobby level boasts a well-stocked bar and a restaurant which some claim offers decent fare, though it's not hard to find better options nearby.

CASA DE LA CONDESA Map pp92–3 · Serviced Apartment $$

☎ 5574-3186; www.extendedstaymexico.com; Plaza Luis Cabrera 16; ste from M$643; Ⓜ Insurgentes

Right on the delightful Plaza Luis Cabrera, the Casa de la Condesa makes a tranquil base for visitors on an extended stay, offering 'suites' that are essentially studio apartments with kitchens. With awesome tableaux of the plaza's grand fountains, the front suites far outclass the interior 'junior suites' or the diminutive standard rooms. All are decorated *rústico* style, with the usual swabbed-on bright oranges and deep blues and the odd knickknack from Metepec or Puebla. Mexican-style breakfasts are served in the little ground-floor *comedor* (dining room).

HOTEL EMBASSY Map pp92–3 · Hotel $

☎ 5208-0859; fax 5511-0344; Puebla 115; s/d/tr M$290/340/300; Ⓜ Insurgentes; Ⓟ

Despite a charmless location, this well-maintained modern lodging is conveniently placed a couple of blocks from the metro, and right next door to the excellent Cantina Covadonga (p164). The abundance of mirrored surfaces suggests this hotel appeals to trysting guests, but it's well looked after and the price is right.

HOSTEL HOME Map pp92–3 · Hostel $

☎ 5511-1683; www.hostelhome.com.mx; Tabasco 303; dm M$120; Ⓜ Metrobus Álvaro Obregón; ▢

Housed in a fine Porfiriato-era building, the small (20-bed) Hostel Home is situated on narrow tree-lined Calle Tabasco, which makes a tranquil gateway to the Roma neighborhood. Managed by youthful and easygoing staff, this hostel is a good place to meet other travelers and find out what's going on.

AIRPORT ACCOMMODATION

Aside from the two upscale hotels accessible from the terminal, these more-economical lodgings are just across the street. Exit the domestic terminal and turn left; past the metro entrance, take a left onto Blvd Puerto Aéreo and cross via the pedestrian bridge.

Fiesta Inn (Map pp42–3; ☎ 5133-6600; www.fiestainn.com; Blvd Puerto Aéreo 502; r M$1538; Ⓜ Terminal Aérea; Ⓟ ⊠ ⊠ 🖥 🖥 ♿) Securely enclosed in a compound dotted with tropical greenery, this branch of the business-class chain offers rooms with balconies around the pool. Transport to/from your flight is included, and rates are about 20% cheaper on weekends.

Ramada Aeropuerto México (Map pp42–3; ☎ 5133-3232; www.ramadamexico.com; Blvd Puerto Aéreo 390; r incl breakfast M$1638; Ⓟ ⊠ 🖥) More stylish than its neighbors, the Ramada offers modern comfort for execs between flights, and it offers shuttles to and from the terminal. For entertainment you can hang in the piano bar.

Hotel Aeropuerto (Map pp42–3; ☎ 5785-5851; fax 5784-1329; Blvd Puerto Aéreo 380; s/d M$500/600; Ⓜ Terminal Aérea; Ⓟ) Not as bleakly functional as the aluminum facade portends (or the name suggests), the only nonchain hotel in the zone has helpful reception staff inside a glass booth and neutral modern rooms, some overlooking the airport runway through soundproof windows.

OTHER NEIGHBORHOODS

COYOACÁN

Despite Coyoacán's appeal, the southern community has only one central place to stay, listed below. At the time of research, plans were afoot to open a new HI hostel in the neighborhood; check with the Centro Histórico branch (p200) to see if it's open yet. Otherwise, you might inquire about short-term home stays at the tourist office in the Casa de Cortés (see p260).

HOSTAL FRIDA Map p95   Hostel $$
☎ 5659-7005; www.hostalfridabyb.com.mx; Mina 54; d M$500; Ⓜ Viveros
Run by an English-speaking couple whose kids have moved on, this 'empty nest' is being refilled with international travelers. Each of the five scrupulously maintained wood-floored doubles occupies its own level in two adjacent towers, and all but

one include kitchens. The excellent location is four blocks west of Frida Kahlo's place and just around the corner from a branch of the Café El Jarocho.

CIUDAD UNIVERSITARIA

Staying nearby the sprawling campus of UNAM would afford an excellent opportunity to get to know student life while giving easy access to the southern districts of San Ángel and Tlalpan.

EL CENOTE AZUL Map p105   Hostel $
☎ 5554-8730; www.elcenoteazul.com; Alfonso Pruneda 24; dm M$100; Ⓜ Copilco
This small, laid-back hostel near the campus of the national university has space for 20 occupants in neatly kept four- or two-bed rooms sharing two Talavera-tiled bathrooms. Guests and UNAM students mingle downstairs around the patio, lounging on beds that hang from an overhead loft, sitting in front of a big TV, or snacking at the café, which prepares hearty natural fare.

DAY TRIPS & EXCURSIONS

Vast as Mexico City may appear, getting beyond the sprawl is not as daunting a prospect as you might expect. Indeed, hordes of Chilangos escape the smog every weekend for such nearby destinations as Cuernavaca, Tlaxcala and Malinalco. The capital is linked to the 'interior' (as urbancentric inhabitants refer to any part of Mexico outside the DF) by a network of high-speed toll roads, and frequent bus connections make the whole region easily accessible.

The capital's environs offer much to explore. Almost every visitor makes it out to the awesome pyramids of Teotihuacán but many other nearby places offer copious rewards often overlooked by travelers eager to get to the coast. Venturing outside the capital gives you the chance to get into a Mexico far removed from the DF's asphalt ambience. So-called 'pueblos mágicos' like Puebla and

Taxco boast plenty of colonial splendor, with well-preserved historic centers and a wealth of sacred art, not to mention unique culinary traditions. Pyramids and other majestic remnants of pre-Conquest civilizations dot the region, while indigenous traditions live on in festivals and rituals. And if it's wilderness that pulls you, other-worldly landscapes await around and upon the peaks of nearby mountain ranges. Often overrun with refugees from the capital on weekends, most of these places go practically unvisited Monday to Friday.

While day trips are feasible to such nearby destinations as Teotihuacán and Tepotzotlán, those going farther afield to, say, Taxco or Puebla, should consider staying at least one night to get a real feel for those towns. There are plenty of accommodations and outside of special occasions there's rarely a need to book ahead.

DETOUR: SIERRA DE AJUSCO

The highest point in Mexico City, the extinct Volcán Ajusco (3937m), is part of the Sierra de Ajusco-Chichinauhtzin, a volcanic range that traverses the city's southern edge. The volcano stands southwest of the capital within the 9.2 sq km Parque Nacional Cumbres de Ajusco, a theoretically protected zone that contains most of the Federal District's forestlands. Glorious views of the Valle de México and further east to the peaks of Popo and Izta can be glimpsed from its piney slopes. White-tailed deer, gray fox and the endemic *teporingo* rabbit roam the premises.

A fine access to the mountain is the Parque Ejidal San Nicolás Totolapan (☎ 5644-1280; Km 11.5 Carretera Picacho Ajusco; admission on foot/with bike; M$10/20 ⏱ 8am-4:30pm Mon-Fri, 7am-5pm Sat & Sun), a forested area of 23 sq km between altitudes of 2700m and 3740m. Crisscrossed by more than 50km of trails carpeted with pine needles, the park is popular with local mountain-bikers and hikers. The *ejidatarios* (communal landowners) set up the *parque ejidal* in the late 1990s chiefly to derive some benefit from their land's popularity. Though not an untouched wilderness, it is well-maintained and staff point out that it's safe, meaning that guards keep an eye on activities within. Outside the park's boundaries, they warn, it is not uncommon for hikers to be attacked by bandits.

Mountain bikes are rented by the entrance (M$50 per hour). Around 200m inside, there's a kitchen shack preparing excellent wild mushroom soup, quesadillas and café de olla. At the *granja de truchas* (trout hatchery), you can rent a fishing pole (M$20), and they'll prepare your catch to eat at a terrace by a mountain stream.

The trails are not clearly signed, but with the aid of the rough map provided by the ticket office, you should be able to keep your bearings. If you head southwest and generally upward for 4km, you should come out at a line of *comedores* on the Circuito de Ajusco road, to the south of which rises the volcano.

The park rents four 'chalets' of varying size (M$120 per person), 600m uphill from the entrance, with bunks and mattresses (bring your own sleeping bag), kitchen with hot water and a fireplace. There's also a camping area with tents for rent (M$150 for four persons).

To reach the *parque ejidal*, take metro Línea 2 to its southern terminal at Tasqueña, then continue south on the Tren Ligero to the Estadio Azteca station. Leave the station via the 'Paradero Autobus' exit. Look for a Ruta 39 bus marked 'Six Flags-Santo Tomás-Ajusco,' at the fourth platform. The bus arrives at the park in a little under an hour (M$4). The driver may not know it by name; ask for Las Llantas ('lahs yahn-tahs,' the Tires), a name that refers to lines of tires set in the ground at the *parque ejidal's* entrance to mark out a biking or riding track. The entrance is also marked by a parking lot and a '¡Bienvenido! Parque Ejidal San Nicolás Totolapan' sign.

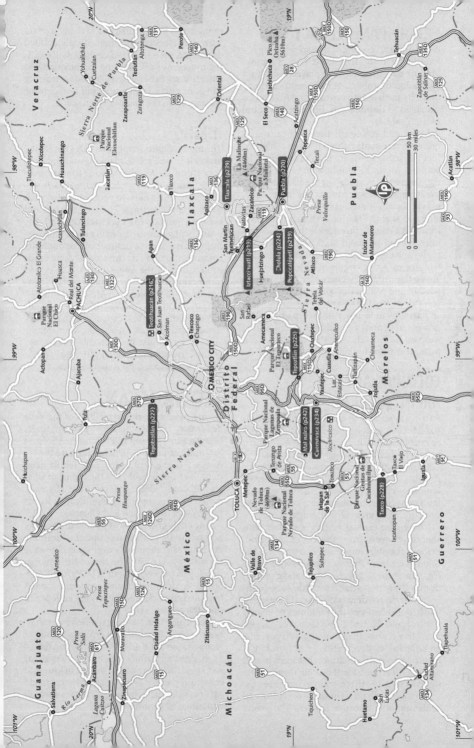

PRE-HISPANIC LEGACY

A cultural and economic crossroads long before the Spanish arrived, the region around present-day Mexico City played host to a succession of important indigenous civilizations. By the late 15th century, the Aztecs had managed to dominate all but one of central Mexico's states.

Many archaeological sites and museums preserve remnants of pre-Hispanic history. Most amazing of all are the Pyramids of the Sun and Moon at Teotihuacán, a major city that flourished northeast of the Valle de México 20 centuries ago. Murals and stone carvings at the site's various palaces and temples attest to the civilization's stunning artistic legacy. An equally formidable though largely unrecovered pyramid stands at Cholula, a lively university town near Puebla. Smaller temples of Aztec origin hold lofty perches above the mystically charged villages of Tepoztlán and Malinalco, south and southwest of Mexico City. The latter features an excellent archaeology museum. Another major collection of indigenous art held by Puebla's Museo Amparo (p220) covers the entire mesoamerican panorama prior to the Spanish conquest.

COLONIAL ART & ARCHITECTURE

Post-conquest, the Spanish transformed central Mexico, establishing ceramic industries at Puebla, mines at Taxco, and wheat, sugar, *pulque* and cattle-producing haciendas. The Catholic church used the region as a base for its missionary activities, leaving a series of imposing churches and fortified monasteries. Today, most towns retain a central plaza surrounded by colonial buildings.

The entire central region is dotted with superb leftovers from the colonial period. Perhaps the most impressive showpiece is the colonial center of Puebla, southeast of Mexico City, where the facades of palaces and churches display the region's trademark tilework. Similarly tiled church domes spring up like painted mushrooms between the buildings of nearby Cholula and Tlaxcala. The legacy of successive silver rushes, the town of Taxco presents an amazing agglomeration of scrupulously preserved colonial structures that seem to spill down a steep hillside. Located three hours south of the capital, it remains a major tourist destination, both for its impressive setting and contemporary silverwork. Fortress-like former monasteries at Tepoztlán and Malinalco retain harmonic cloisters with fantastically painted designs on their walls and ceilings. Outstanding museums in Puebla and Tepotzotlán, the latter just north of Mexico City, house treasure troves of religious painting and polychrome statuary from the Spanish viceroyalty.

HIKING

The mountainous terrain that rings the capital makes for some splendid hiking and climbing opportunities. Whether looking to scale some jagged peaks or just walk in the woods, fresh-air fiends won't have to venture far to reach some pristine settings. The area around and between Popocatépetl and Iztaccíhuatl, the prominent volcano pair rising east of the metropolis, is a favored destination for outdoors enthusiasts. Popo's intermittent activity limits exploration to the lower slopes, but skilled mountaineers can take a stab at Izta's summit. Near the Volcán de Ajusco, southwest of town, is an eco-reserve with miles of trails threading through that extinct volcano's piney slopes. Malinalco and Tepoztlán, atmospheric villages set amidst the spire-like hills south of the city, offer less demanding but serene nature walks to hilltop Aztec temples.

TEOTIHUACÁN

Set in a mountain-ringed offshoot of the Valle de México, Teotihuacán is justly known for its two awesome pyramids, Pirámide del Sol and Pirámide de la Luna, which dominate the remains of the ancient metropolis. Teotihuacán (teh-oh-tee-wah-*kahn*) was the capital of what was probably Mexico's largest pre-Hispanic empire, and compares in significance to the Maya cities of Yucatán and Chiapas.

The city's grid plan was platted in the early part of the 1st century AD, and the Pirámide del Sol was completed – over an earlier cave shrine – by AD 150. The rest of the city was developed between about AD 250 and 600. Social, environmental and economic factors hastened its decline and eventual collapse in the 8th century AD.

The major structures are typified by a *talud-tablero* style, in which the rising portions of stepped, pyramid-like buildings consist of both sloping (*talud*) and upright (*tablero*) sections. They were often covered in lime and colorfully painted. Most of the city was made up of residential compounds, some of which contained elegant frescoes.

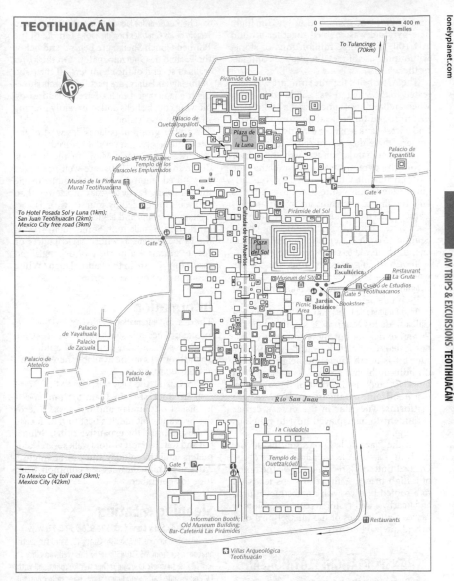

TEOTIHUACÁN

0 ———— 400 m
0 ———— 0.2 miles

To Tulancingo (70km)

Pirámide de la Luna

Palacio de Quetzalpapálotl

Gate 3

Plaza de la Luna

Palacio de los Jaguares; Templo de los Caracoles Emplumados

Museo de la Pintura Mural Teotihuacána

Palacio de Tepantitla

Gate 4

Pirámide del Sol

Calzada de los Muertos

To Hotel Posada Sol y Luna (1km);
San Juan Teotihuacán (2km);
Mexico City free road (3km)

Gate 2

Plaza del Sol

Jardín Escultórica

Restaurant La Gruta

Museum del Sitio

Centro de Estudios Teotihuacanos

Gate 5

Bookstore

Picnic Area

Jardín Botánico

Palacio de Yayahuala

Palacio de Zacuala

Palacio de Atetelco

Palacio de Tetitla

Río San Juan

La Ciudadela

Templo de Quetzalcóatl

Gate 1

To Mexico City toll road (3km);
Mexico City (42km)

Information Booth;
Old Museum Building;
Bar-Cafeteriá Las Pirámides

Restaurants

Villas Arqueológica Teotihuacán

Much of what there is to see lies along the Calzada de los Muertos. Buses arrive at a traffic circle by the southwest entrance (Gate 1), which puts you at the bottom of the Calzada de los Muertos (Avenue of the Dead) by **La Ciudadela**, a square complex believed to have been the residence of the city's supreme ruler. Within its four wide walls is a pyramid called the **Templo de Quetzalcóatl**, with striking carvings of the sharp-fanged feathered serpent deity.

Continuing north along Calzada de los Muertos across the river toward the pyramids, a path to the right leads to the site museum (☎ 958-20-81; admission free with site ticket; ⏰ 7am-6pm), with excellent displays of artifacts, fresco panels, and an impressive large-scale model of the city set under a transparent walkway.

The world's third-largest pyramid, the Pirámide del Sol overshadows the east side of Calzada de los Muertos. The base is 222m long

217

on each side, and it's now just over 70m high. The pyramid was cobbled together around AD 100, from three million tons of stone, without the use of metal tools, pack animals or the wheel.

The Aztec belief that the structure was dedicated to the sun god was validated in 1971, when archaeologists uncovered a 100m-long underground tunnel leading from the pyramid's west flank to a cave directly beneath its center, where they found religious artifacts. It's thought that the sun was worshiped here before the pyramid was built and that the city's ancient inhabitants traced the very origins of life to this grotto. Centuries after its fall, Teotihuacán remains an important pilgrimage site: thousands of New Age devotees flock here each year to celebrate the vernal equinox (March 21) and soak up the mystical energies believed to converge here.

Teotihuacán's most famous fresco, the worn *Paradise of Tláloc*, is in the Palacio de Tepantitla, a priest's residence 500m northeast of Pirámide del Sol.

The Pirámide de la Luna, at the north end of Calzada de los Muertos, is smaller than the Pirámide del Sol but more gracefully proportioned. Completed around AD 300, it's summit is nearly the same height because it's built on higher ground. The Plaza de la Luna, located just in front of the pyramid, is a handsome arrangement of 12 temple platforms. The altar in the plaza's center is thought to have played host to religious dancing.

Off the Plaza de la Luna's southwest corner is the Palacio de Quetzalpapálotl (Palace of the Quetzal Butterfly), reckoned to be the home of a high priest. A flight of steps leads up to a roofed portico with an abstract mural, and nearby a well-restored patio has columns carved with images of the quetzal bird or a hybrid quetzal butterfly.

The Palacio de los Jaguares (Jaguar Palace) and Templo de los Caracoles Emplumados (Temple of the Plumed Conch Shells) are behind and below the Palacio de Quetzalpapálotl. On the lower walls of several of the chambers off the patio of the Jaguar Palace, are parts of murals showing the jaguar god in feathered headdresses, blowing conch shells and apparently praying to the rain god Tláloc.

Another group of palaces lies west of the site's main area, several hundred meters northwest of Gate 1. Many of the murals, discovered in the 1940s, are well-preserved or restored, and perfectly intelligible. Inside the sprawling Palacio de Tetitla, no fewer than 120 walls are graced by murals, with Tláloc, jaguars, serpents and eagles among the easiest figures to make out. Some 400m west is the Palacio de Atetelco, whose vivid jaguar or coyote murals – a mixture of originals and restorations – are in the Patio Blanco (White Patio) in the northwest corner.

Information

There's an information booth (☎ 594-956-02-76; ☽ 9am-4pm) near the southwest entrance (Gate 1). Free site tours by authorized guides (in Spanish only) may be available here if a sizable group forms.

Crowds at the ruins (admission M$45; ☽ 7am-6pm) are thickest from 10am to 2pm, and it is busiest on Sunday and holidays. Due to the heat and altitude, it's best to take it easy while exploring the expansive ruins. Bring a hat and water – most visitors walk several kilometers, and the midday sun can be intense. Afternoon rain showers are common from June to September.

Sleeping & Eating

Hotel Posada Sol y Luna (☎ 594-956-23-68/71; www.posadasolyluna.com, in Spanish; Cantú 13, San Juan Teotihuacán; r/ste from M$330/450; ℗) This well-run place has 16 fine (if unexciting and rather sterile) rooms, all with TV and ensuite bathroom. Junior suites have rather ancient Jacuzzis in them – not worth paying extra for unless you have rheumatism. It's at the east end of town, en route to the pyramids and this is also a good place to get breakfast (from M$60) for guests and nonguests alike.

Villas Arqueológica Teotihuacán (☎ 55-5836-9020; www.teotihuacaninfo.com; r M$875/1000 Sun-Thu/Fri & Sat; ℗ 🖵 🏊) By far the best option in the area is this Club Med-run complex just outside the site grounds. While it's not cheap, the place has plenty of charm and the rooms

TRANSPORTATION: TEOTIHUACÁN

- Distance from Mexico City – 50km
- Travel time – one hour
- Direction – northeast
- Bus – Autobuses México-San Juan Teotihuacán runs buses from Mexico City's Terminal Norte to the ruins every 15 minutes from 7am to 6pm. (Make sure your bus is headed for 'Los Pirámides,' not the nearby town of San Juan Teotihuacán.) Buses arrive and depart from near Gate 1, by the southwest entrance to the site.

are all cozy, clean and well furnished. Amenities include a heated outdoor pool, a lit tennis court, a playground, a billiards table, nice gardens and a refined French-Mexican bar-restaurant. A couple of one-bedroom suites have in-room whirlpools.

Restaurant La Gruta (☎ 594-956-01- 04/27; mains M$200; ⏱ 11am-6pm) This deeply odd restaurant has quite the strangest setting of any in Mexico – a vast, subterranean, dank cave just 75m from gate 5 (don't be put off by the sign on the path that says it's 500m away – it's a misprint). It's aimed squarely at tourist parties and, while the food is very good, it's pricey too – and served in a subterranean, dank cave. On Saturday and Sunday afternoons, there's live music and folkloric ballet (cover M$30). As you'd expect all major credit cards are accepted.

POPOCATÉPETL & IZTACCÍHUATL

Mexico's second- and third-highest peaks – Popocatépetl (po-po-ka-*teh*-pet-l; Náhuatl for 'Smoking Mountain'; 5452m) and Iztaccíhuatl (iss-ta-*see*-wat-l; 5220m) – form the eastern rim of the Valle de México. While the craterless 'Izta' is dormant, 'Popo' is wide awake. Between 1994 and 2001, the volcano's major bursts of activity triggered evacuations of 16 villages and warnings to the 30 million people who live within striking distance of its volatile crater.

Izta's highest peak is El Pecho (5286m). All routes to it require a night on the mountain, and there's a shelter hut that can be used during an ascent between the staging point at La Joya and Las Rodillas. On average, it takes at least five hours to reach the hut from La Joya,

another six hours from the hut to El Pecho, and six hours back to the base.

Near Paso de Cortés, in the saddle approximately halfway between Popo and Izta, there are plenty of lower-altitude trails through pine forests and grassy meadows, some offering breathtaking glimpses of nearby peaks. Trails begin at the La Joya parking lot, 2km beyond the Altzomoni Lodge (see p220).

Information

All visitors must pay the M$10 per day park entrance fee in advance at the national park office in Amecameca, or on Sunday at Paso de Cortés.

Before ascending Izta, all climbers should contact the Parque Nacional Iztaccíhuatl-Popocatépetl (☎ /fax 597-978-38-29/30; http://iztapopo.conanp.gob.mx; Plaza de la Constitución 9B; ⏱ 9am-6pm Mon-Fri, to 3pm Sat), in the nearby village of Amecameca, the usual starting point. To arrange permission, call the office or submit a form that's available online. You'll need the permit to pass the military checkpoint near Paso de Cortés. Alternatively, you can depart from the village of San Rafael, 8km north of Amecameca, a longer and more rigorous climb.

Iztaccíhuatl should *only* be attempted by experienced climbers. Because of hidden crevices on the ice-covered upper slopes, a guide is advisable. Mexico City-based Mario Andrade (☎ 55-1038-4008, 55-1826-2146; mountainup@ hotmail.com), an authorized, English-speaking guide, has led many Izta ascents. His Izta fee is M$3800 for one person, less per person for groups. The cost includes roundtrip transportation from Mexico City, lodging, mountain meals and rope usage.

It can be windy and well below freezing any time of year on Izta's upper slopes, and it's nearly always below freezing near the summit at night. Ice and snow are fixtures here; the average snow line is 4200m. The ideal months for ascents are November to February, when there is hard snowpack for crampons. The rainy season (April to October) brings with it the threat of whiteouts, thunderstorms and avalanches.

Sleeping

The sleepy town of Amecameca, 60km east of Mexico City by road, is the key staging point for an Izta climb. With volcanoes and 16th-century churches as a backdrop, it makes an appealing destination in itself. Most climbers

TRANSPORTATION: PUEBLA

- Distance from Mexico City – 125km
- Travel time – two hours
- Direction – southeast
- Bus – most buses to and from Puebla use Mexico City's TAPO, with additional half-hourly services to Terminal Norte. The deluxe ADO GL (☎ 800-702-80-00; www.ado.com.mx) runs buses every 40 minutes (M$104); Estrella Roja (ER; ☎ 800-712-22-84; www.estrellaroja.com.mx) runs 1st-class buses every 20 minutes (M$104). Puebla's Central de Autobuses de Puebla (CAPU; ☎ 222-249-72-11; Blvd Norte 4222) is 4km north of the zócalo and 1.5km off the autopista. Tickets for most routes can also be purchased downtown via Ticketbus (☎ 222-232-19-52; www.ticketbus.com.mx; Av Palafox y Mendoza 604; ☺ 9:30am-5pm) inside the Multipack office.

sack out at the unassuming Hotel San Carlos (☎ 597-978-07-46; Plaza de la Constitución 10; r M$100), facing the plaza's southwest corner, where the rooms are clean and spartan, but comfortable, and cost M$5 more with TV.

Basic shelter is available at the Altzomoni Lodge (beds per person M$25), by a microwave station roughly halfway between Paso de Cortés and La Joya. Request the keys at Paso de Cortés before hiking up, and bring bedding, warm clothes and drinking water.

PUEBLA

A bastion of conservatism, Catholicism and tradition, Puebla can sometimes feel as if the colonial era in Mexico never quite ended. For the most part this is a positive thing, giving Puebla its fantastic colonial centre, a stunning cathedral and a wealth of beautiful churches, although it also contributes to the (quite unfair) Mexican stereotype of the criollo (people born of Spanish parents in Nueva Espanã) poblanos being snobbish and aloof.

The city itself is well worth a visit, with 70 churches in the historic center alone, more than a thousand colonial buildings adorned with the azulejos (painted ceramic tiles) for which the city is justly famous, and a long culinary history that can be explored in any restaurant or street food stall.

For a city of its size, Puebla is far more relaxed and less gridlocked than you might expect. Its charming architecture and well-preserved colonial imprint in no way make the city feel like a museum piece, and part of its attraction is that it's so clearly a thriving city, yet it still takes great pride in its past.

Founded by Spanish settlers in 1531 as Ciudad de los Ángeles, the city grew into an important Catholic center. Fine pottery had long been crafted from the local clay, and after the colonists introduced new materials

and techniques, Puebla pottery evolved as both an art and an industry. By the late 18th century, the city emerged an important glass and textile producer.

Puebla's superbly impressive cathedral (cnr Avs 3 Ote & 16 de Septiembre; ☺ 10.30-12:30pm, 4-6pm Mon-Sat), whose image appears on Mexico's 500-peso bill, occupies the entire block south of the zócalo. It blends early baroque and severe Herreresque-renaissance styles. Construction began in 1550 but most of it took place under Bishop Juan de Palafox in the 1640s. At 69m the towers are Mexico's highest. Inside, the dazzling interior, the frescoes and elaborately decorated side chapels are all awesome and most have bilingual signs explaining their history and significance.

Puebla's central zócalo, which was being renovated at the time of writing, was originally a marketplace where bullfights, theater and hangings transpired, before it assumed its current arboretum-like appearance in 1854. The surrounding arcades date from the 16th century. The plaza fills with an entertaining mix of clowns, balloon hawkers and ambulatory snack vendors on Sunday evenings. If you're in town on Thursday around 6pm, don't miss the patriotic changing of the flag ceremony, animated by the city's marching band.

By far Puebla's best sight, the superb private Museo Amparo (☎ 222-229-38-50; www.museoamparo .com; Calle 2 Sur 708; adult/student M$35/25, camera/video fee M$50, free Mon; ☺ 10am-6pm Wed-Mon), housed in two 16th- and 17th-century colonial buildings, is a must-see. The first has eight rooms loaded with pre-Hispanic artifacts, which are well displayed, with explanatory information sheets (in English and Spanish) of their production techniques, regional and historical context, and anthropological significance.

Inaugurated in 1999, the Museo Poblano de Arte Virreinal (☎ 222-246-58-58; Calle 4 Nte 203; admission adult/student M$15/10, free Tue; ☺ 10am-5pm Tue-Sun) is

PUEBLA

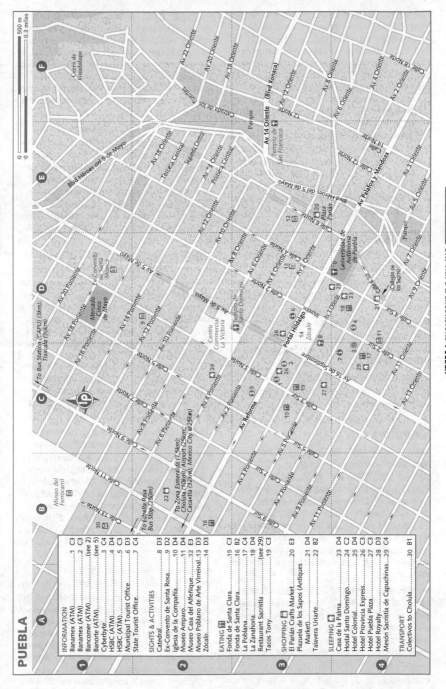

0   500 m
0   0.3 miles

housed in the 16th-century Hospital de San Pedro. One gallery displays temporary exhibits on the art of the viceregal period (16th to 19th centuries); another has temporary exhibits of contemporary Mexican art; and the last houses a fascinating permanent exhibit on the hospital's history, including a fine model of the building. The excellent library and bookstore have many art and architecture books in English.

The Museo Casa del Alfeñique (☎ 222-32-42-96; Av 4 Ote 416; admission adult/student M$15/10, free Tue; ♥ 10am-5pm Tue-Sun) is an outstanding example of the over-the-top 18th-century decorative style, *alfeñique*, characterized by elaborate stucco ornamentation and named after a candy made from sugar and egg whites.

Information

Cyberbyte (Calle 2 Sur 505B) Internet access and cheap international VoIP phone calls.

Money ATMs are plentiful throughout the city. Banks on the *zócalo* and Av Reforma have exchange and travelers check facilities.

Municipal Tourist Office (☎ 222-404-50-08/47; www .puebla.gob.mx, in Spanish; Portal Hidalgo 14; ♥ 9am-8pm Mon-Fri, to 5pm Sat, to 3pm Sun) English- and French-speaking office.

State Tourist Office (Sectur; ☎ 222-246-20-44; Av 5 Ote 3; ♥ 8am-8pm Mon-Sat, to 2pm Sun) Faces the cathedral yard. English-speaking staff.

Sleeping

Hostal Santo Domingo (☎ 222-232-16-71, hostalsto domingo@yahoo.com.mx; Av 4 Pte 312; dm M$100, s/d/t/q M$250/290/350/445; P ✖ ⬜) This is Puebla's only real hostel, offering clean and safe mixed-sex dorms as well as a large range of private rooms. Those at the front of the building enjoy balconies and lots of daylight, while all have high-ceilings. Noise from both the bar downstairs and the street can be a problem, but this is definitely a great place to meet other travelers and have fun. There's web access for M$8 per hour in the courtyard.

Hotel Provincia Express (☎ 222-46-35-57; Av Reforma 141; s/d M$260/350; P ⬜) Tile fetishists on a budget, look no further! This wonderful place has one of the most stunning traditional interiors in Puebla, and all at knock-down prices. Refitted in 2007, the rooms themselves are simple but modern and spotlessly clean, while the corridors and facade are just wonderful.

Hotel Royalty (☎ 222-242-02-02, 800-638-99-99; www .hotelr.com; Portal Hidalgo 8; s/d/t M$465/566/645, ste M$670-840; P ⬜) On the *zócalo*'s north side, with an entrance off the arcade, the 45-room Royalty is a friendly, well-kept colonial-style place. The price hike here is for the superb location. Rooms are nothing special: although they're generally spotlessly clean and comfortable enough, they have the familiar natural daylight problems that haunt the city. The junior suites with cathedral views merit the extra pesos. Downstairs, the sidewalk restaurant-café is perfect for people watching.

Hotel Puebla Plaza (☎ 222-246-31-75, 800-926-2703; www.hotelpueblaplaza.com.mx, in Spanish; Av 5 Poniente 111; s/d M$382/499; P ⬜) This charming place enjoys a great location and has very comfortable rooms and good service. As with many colonial-style hotels though, the rooms at the back are incredibly depressing with little or no natural light, and it's worth paying extra for rooms on the street with little balconies. All rooms have TV, phone, private bathroom and free wi-fi.

our pick Hotel Colonial (☎ 222-246-46-12, 800-013-00-00; www.colonial.com.mx; Calle 4 Sur 105; s/d/tr/q M$590/690/790/890; ⬜) This utter charmer is hard not to love, even though its size and good value has made it a magnet for tour groups. Once part of a 17th-century Jesuit monastery and existing as a hotel in various forms since the mid-19th century, the place oozes heritage from its many gorgeously furnished rooms (half of the 67 rooms have retained colonial décor and half are modern). There's a good restaurant, lobby wi-fi and a fantastic gilt-clad elevator complete with liveried porters. Noise from live music and the street can be a problem, but otherwise this is an excellent choice with an unbeatable vibe and location. Book ahead.

Casa de la Palma (☎ 222-246-14-37; www.casa delapalmapuebla.com; Av 3 Oriente 217; r/ste from M$825/1062; P ⬜) This sumptuous conversion of a colonial town house into a boutique hotel is a winner. If you want to pretend you're a 19th-century *poblano* aristocrat, look no further than the Porfiriana suite, which is stunning for its sheer size and over-the-top rococo flourishes. Opening in 2007, it was still in its early days when we visited. Small qualms such as patchy wi-fi coverage and lack of breakfast options will no doubt soon be resolved.

Mesón Sacristía de Capuchinas (☎ 222-32-80-88, 800-712-40-28, in US ☎ 800-728-9098; www.mesones-sacristia.com; Av 9 Oriente 16; r incl full breakfast M$1600; P ⬜) This wonderful boutique-antique hotel has just six beautifully presented rooms all featuring luxurious four-poster beds and various carefully selected *objets d'art* scattered around. The romantic El Santuario Restaurant is open on guests' request and crafts inspired contemporary takes on traditional Mexican cuisine. Breakfast in bed is simply divine. Perfect for romance, this is one of Puebla's very best options.

PUEBLA'S UNFORGETTABLE SEASONAL TREATS

Puebla is rightly famous for its gastronomy (and most famously of course, *mole poblano,* the classic spicy sauce you must seek out at a top restaurant while you're in the city to really have experienced Puebla). However, the city also has a range of unusual delicacies not likely to make it to your local Mexican restaurant any time soon. These are all seasonal, but any serious foodie should be brave and try whatever's cooking!

- *Escamoles* (March-June) Ant larvae, a delicacy that looks like rice, usually sautéed in butter. Delicious!
- *Gusanos de maguey* (April-May) Worms that inhabit maguey agave plants, fried in a drunken chili-and-*pulque* sauce.
- *Huitlacoche* (June-October) Also spelt *cuitlacoche* (kweet-lah-*koh*-chay). Corn mushrooms are an inky black fungus delicacy with an enchanting, earthy flavor.
- *Chiles en nogada* (July-September) Large green chilies stuffed with dried fruit and meat, covered with a creamy walnut sauce and sprinkled with red pomegranate seeds.
- *Chapulines* (October-November) Grasshoppers purged of digestive matter, then dried, smoked or fried in lime and chili powder.

Eating & Drinking

Puebla's culinary heritage, of which *poblanos* are rightly proud, can be explored in a range of eateries throughout the city, from humble street food stalls to elegant colonial-style restaurants.

Tacos Tony (☎ 222-240-94-31; Av 3 Pte 149; tacos M$10-20) Follow your nose – or ring for delivery – for a *torta* or *pan árabe* taco (made with pita bread instead of tortillas), stuffed with seasoned pork sliced from a trio of enormous grilling cones.

La Poblana (☎ 222-246-09-93; Av 7 Ote 17; mains M$15-30; ☼ 10am-6pm) Around the corner from the Museo Amparo, this small, friendly place whips up (and delivers) a dozen styles of authentic Puebla *cemitas* (a type of sandwich with meat and cheese).

La Zanahoria (☎ 222-232-48-13; Av 5 Ote 206, mains M$20-40, set meals M$49; ⊠ Ⓥ) This entirely meat-free godsend for vegetarians is a great place for lunch, moments from the *zócalo* and the Museo Amparo. The restaurant is split into two – the express service area (including a juice bar and a health food shop) in the front and the more relaxed service of the spacious interior colonial courtyard, where everything from veggie *hamburguesas* to *nopales rellenos* (stuffed cactus paddles) are served up.

Fonda de Santa Clara (☎ 222-46-19-19; www.fondade santaclara.com; Av 3 Pte 920; mains M$75-130) This classic *poblano* restaurant founded in the 1960s by Alicia Torres de Araujo specializes in local seasonal specialties of the region – from maguey worms to grasshoppers. If however, you're not of the bug-eating persuasion, there's plenty of more standard *comida poblana* on offer, including enchiladas and chicken *mole*. This main branch, in a well-restored colonial mansion, is very festive since it attracts locals celebrating special occasions. It also has a gift shop full of Talavera items and typical sweets. There is also a second smaller branch (☎ 242-26-59, Av 3 Pte 307).

Restaurant Sacristía (☎ 222-42-45-13; Calle 6 Sur 304; mains M$85-110; ☼ 8am-11:30pm Mon-Sat, 8am-6pm Sun) This award-winning restaurant, in the delightful colonial patio of the Mesón Sacristía de la Compañía, is an elegant place for a meal of authentic *mole* and creative twists on rich *poblano* cuisine, or a cocktail or coffee and dessert in the intimate Confesionario bar. Live piano and violin soloists lend a romantic ambience most nights from around 9pm. If you like what you taste, inquire about their small-group cooking classes.

Shopping

Several shops along Av 18 Pte, west of the Ex-Convento de Santa Mónica, sell colorful, hand-painted ceramics, known as Talavera. Designs reveal Asian, Spanish-Arabic and Mexican indigenous influences. Bigger pieces are expensive, delicate and difficult to transport. Smaller tiles fetch up to M$50, quality plates upwards of M$100. The finest Puebla pottery of all is the white ceramic dishware called *majolica.*

A wonderful array of quirky antique shops dominates Callejón de los Sapos, around the corner of Av 5 Ote and Calle 6 Sur. Most shops open from 10am to 7pm. On Sunday the Plazuela de los Sapos is the site of a lively outdoor antiques market. It's great for browsing, with a wonderful variety of old books, furniture and bric-a-brac.

Few of Puebla's Talavera shops make pottery on site anymore, but Talavera Uriarte (☎ 222-232-15-98; Av 4 Pte 911; www.uriartetalavera.com .mx; ☼ 9am-7pm Mon-Fri, 10:30am-5:30pm Sat, 11:30am-4:30pm Sun) still does, and it has a factory and showroom. Factory tours (M$60) are offered Monday to Friday until 1pm in English and French, and later in Spanish as groups arrive.

Browse local Talavera, onyx and trees of life at El Parián crafts market, between Calles 6 and 8 Nte and Avs 2 and 4 Ote). Some of the work is shoddy, but there is also some quality handiwork and prices are reasonable.

CHOLULA

Almost a suburb of Puebla these days, but far different in history and feel, the town of Cholula is home to the widest pyramid ever built, the Pirámide Tepanapa. Despite this great claim to fame, it's a surprisingly ignored place, largely because unlike its contemporaries Teotihuacán or Tula, the pyramid has been so neglected over the centuries as to be virtually unrecognizable as a manmade structure. Indeed, the pyramid was so overgrown even when the Spanish arrived that they built a church on the top, not realizing that their 'hill' was actually a native religious site – something that would no doubt have horrified them.

The Zona Arqueológica (☎ 222-235-94-24, 235-97-20; admission M$37, Spanish/English guide M$90/120; ☯ 9am-6pm Tue-Sun) comprises the excavated areas around the pyramid and the tunnels underneath. You enter via the tunnel on the north side, which takes you on a spooky route through the centre of the pyramid. Several pyramids were built on top of each other during various reconstructions and so over 8km of tunnels have been dug beneath the pyramid by archaeologists to penetrate each stage. From the access tunnel, a few hundred meters long, you can see earlier layers of the building. You don't need a guide to follow the tunnel through to the structures on the pyramid's south and west sides, but since nothing is labeled, they can be helpful in pointing out and explaining various features.

The Pirámide Tepanapa is topped by the brightly decorated Santuario de Nuestra Señora de los Remedios. It's a classic symbol of conquest, but possibly an inadvertent one, as the church may have been built before the Spanish realized the mound contained a pagan temple. You can climb to the church for free via a path starting near the northwest corner of the pyramid.

A small museum (Calz San Andrés; admission free with site ticket), across the road from the ticket office and down some steps, provides the best introduction to the site – a cutaway model of the pyramid mound shows the various superimposed structures.

The Ex-Convento de San Gabriel (also known as Plaza de la Concordia) faces the east side

of Cholula's huge zócalo. It includes a tiny but interesting Franciscan library and three fine churches, all of which will appeal to travelers interested in antique books, and early religious and Franciscan history. On the left, as you face the ex-convent, is the Arabic-style Capilla Real, which has 49 domes and dates from 1540. In the middle is the 19th-century Capilla de la Tercera Orden, and on the right is the Templo de San Gabriel, founded in 1530 on the site of a pyramid.

The excellent Museo de la Ciudad de Cholula (☎ 222-261-90-53; cnr 5 de Mayo & 4 Poniente; adult/child M$20/10; ☯ 9am-3pm Thu-Tue) is housed in a fantastically restored colonial building on the zócalo. The small but strong collection includes ceramics and jewelry from the Pirámide Tepanapa as well as later colonial paintings and sculptures. Most interestingly you can watch museum employees painstakingly restore smashed ceramics and repairing jewelry through a glass wall.

Aside from the pyramid and churches, Cholula boasts a buzzing nightlife thanks to the presence of the Universidad de las Américas, plus plenty of good eating and accommodation options centered on the huge zócalo. Nearby, the charming villages of Acatepec and Tonantzintla have splendid churches not to be missed by lovers of colonial architecture.

Information

Banks Facing zócalo's south side; they change cash and have ATMs.

Gioconda Internet (5 de Mayo; per hr M$15) On west side of zócalo.

Tourist Office (☎ 222-261-23-93; cnr Calles 12 Ote & Av 4 Nte; ☯ 9am-7pm Mon-Fri, to 2pm Sat & Sun)

Sleeping

Hotel Reforma (☎ 222-247-01-49; Calle 4 Sur 101; s/d M$180/200; P) If the crumbling exterior doesn't put you off, the interior fares much better – a charming pink

---

TRANSPORTATION: CHOLULA

- Distance from Mexico City – 115km
- Travel time – two hours
- Direction – southeast
- Bus – Estrella Roja runs hourly buses between Mexico City's TAPO and Puebla that stop in Cholula (M$61) on Calle 12 Pte. There are also hourly buses from here to Mexico City's Benito Juárez airport (M$155).

and white painted courtyard divided up into 11 simple but clean rooms, all with their own bathrooms and plenty of character. Overnight parking costs M$20.

Casa Calli (☎ 222-261-5607; www.hotelcasacalli .com, in Spanish; Portal Guerrero 11; s/d M$450/500; P ⌨ ⛶) If you fancy a boutique feel on a budget, this excellent hotel is a great option. Right on the *zócalo*, the hotel contains 40 stripped down, stylishly minimalist rooms, a good pool, free wi-fi, friendly staff and an Italian restaurant.

Plaza Santa Rosa Hotel (☎ 222-247-03-41, 247-77-19; psrosa_reserv@yahoo.com.mx; Portal Guerrero 5; s&d M$400, t&q M$500; P ⌨) Unusually located inside a shopping arcade just on the side of the zócalo, the Plaza Santa Rosa has 27 rather dark rooms but they're spacious and comfortable with phones and TV. Free parking and wi-fi is included in the price.

Villa Arqueológica Cholula (☎ 222-273-79-00, 800-514-82 44; Calle 2 Pte 601; r Sun-Wed M$850, Thu-Sat $950, ste from $1200; P ⛶) This boutique 44-room Club-Med property is within walking distance of the pyramid, across a large field of flowers. Rooms are well furnished and most come with one double bed and one single bed. Other attractions include lush gardens, tennis courts, cozy fireplace-lit common areas and a good international restaurant.

Eating & Drinking

Café Enamorada (mains M$30-60) Facing the *zócalo*, this café is one of the most popular places in town, at least on weeknights and for its Sunday brunch buffet. There's live music most nights and decent doses of the usual sandwiches, tacos and quesadillas.

Güero's (☎ 222-247-21-88; Av Hidalgo 101; mains M$35-80; ⏱ 9am-11pm) Decorated with antique photos of Cholula, Whitey's is a lively family-friendly hangout. Besides pizza, pasta and burgers, hearty Mexican choices include *pozole, cemitas* and quesadillas, all served with a delicious *salsa roja*.

Los Jarrones (☎ 222-247-10-98; Portal Guerrero 7; mains M$45-90) Underneath the plaza's attractive arcade, this casual indoor-outdoor eatery serves set breakfasts and a wide menu of good-value regional dishes. There's a great terrace overlooking the plaza that is a favorite meeting point for young Cholulans.

La Lunita (cnr Calz San Andres & 6 Sur) is a fantastic family run bar (with good food too), decorated with an incredible collection of old advertising posters and other knick-knacks. It makes for a great drinking spot in the shadow of the Pyramid.

Bar Reforma (cnr Av 4 Nte & Calz San Andrés) Attached to Hotel Reforma, Cholula's oldest drinking spot is a classic, smoky corner abode with swinging doors, specializing in

iceless margaritas and freshly prepared sangrias. After 9pm, it's popular with the pre-clubbing university crowd.

TEPOZTLÁN

One weekend trip from the capital that rarely disappoints is to gorgeous Tepoztlán, a wonderfully situated small town with a well-preserved historic centre surrounded by soaring jagged cliffs. As the birthplace of Quetzalcóatl, the omnipotent serpent god of the Aztecs, over 1200 years ago according to Mesoamerican legend, Tepoztlán is a major Náhuatl center and something of a Mecca for New Agers who believe the place has a creative energy. What is indubitable is that this *pueblo mágico* boasts a very impressively located pyramid, a great crafts market and a host of charming restaurants and hotels. It also retains indigenous traditions, with some elders still speaking Náhuatl, and younger generations learning it in school, making it quite unlike most of the other towns ringing the Mexican capital.

The uncontested main sight in town is the 10m-high Pirámide de Tepozteco (admission M$34, video camera M$35, free on Sun; ⏱ 9am-5:30pm), although it's actually some 400m *above* the town, perched atop a sheer cliff at the end of a very steep path that begins at the end of Av Tepozteco. Built in honor of Tepoztécatl, the Aztec god of the harvest, fertility and *pulque*, the pyramid is more impressive for its location than for its actual size. Be warned that strenuous 2km climb is only recommended for the physically fit. At the top, depending on haze levels, you may be rewarded with a panorama of the valley.

The Ex-Convento Domínico de la Natividad (admission free; ⏱ 10am-5pm Tue-Sun) and the attached church were built by Dominican priests between 1560 and 1588. The plateresque church facade has Dominican seals interspersed with indigenous symbols, floral designs and various figures. The monastery's arched entryway is adorned with an elaborate seed mural of pre-Hispanic history and symbolism. Every year, during the first week of September, local artists sow a new mural from 60 varieties of seeds.

Behind the Dominican church, the Museo Arqueológico Carlos Pellicer (☎ 739-395-10-98; González 2; admission M$10; ⏱ 10am-6pm Tue-Sun) has a small but interesting collection of pieces from around the country, donated by Tabascan poet Carlos Pellicer Cámara. The stone fragments depicting a pair of rabbits – the symbol for

Ometochtli, one of the 400 *pulque* gods – were discovered at the Tepozteco pyramid site.

During the five days preceding Ash Wednesday (46 days before Easter Sunday), Carnaval features the colorful dances of the Huehuenches and Chinelos with feather headdresses and beautifully embroidered costumes. On September 7 an all-night celebration goes off on Tepozteco hill near the pyramid, with copious consumption of *pulque* in honor of Tepoztécatl. The following day is the Fiesta del Templo, a Catholic celebration featuring theater performances in Náhuatl. The holiday was first intended to coincide with – and perhaps supplant – the pagan festival, but the *pulque* drinkers get a jump on it by starting the night before.

Sleeping

Hotel Posada Ali (☎ 739-395-19-71; Netzahualcóyotl 2C; s/d M$400-600; P) The best-value option in town, Ali's is a family-run, friendly set-up with 13 good rooms, all with some element of attractive design, most with double beds and cable TV. There's a communal sitting room, *frontón* (court for jai alai, a game like handball) and a small pool.

Hotel Chinelos (☎ 739-395-36-53, www.hotelchinelos.com; Netzahualcóyotl 4A; r M$500; P) Named after the famous dancers of Morelos, this 15-room hotel is excellently located and looks much better on the inside than it does from the street. The airy, spacious and super-clean rooms are set around a charming garden. During the week there's a M$100 discount on the room cost.

Posada Nican Mo Calli (☎ 739-395-31-52; Netzahualcóyotl 4A; s/d M$850/1050, ste from M$1000; P) This is just the place for a romantic weekend away. Brightly painted public areas, a heated pool, stylish rooms (some with balconies and great mountain views) and plenty of animals to keep you company, this is one of the best options in town.

Posada del Valle (☎ 739-395-05-21; www.posadadelvalle.com.mx; Camino a Mextitla 5; r M$1725, d with spa packages daily M$4800; P) Posada del Valle has

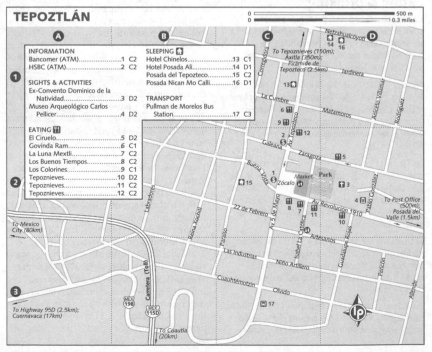

226

quiet, romantic rooms and a good Argentine restaurant. Spa packages include two nights at the hotel, breakfast, massages and a visit to the *temascal* (indigenous Mexican steam bath). Children under 16 are not allowed. It's 2km east of town: take Av Revolución 1910 east and follow the signs for the final 100m to the hotel.

our pick Posada del Tepozteco (☎ 739-395-00-10; www.posadadeltepozteco.com; Paraíso 3; r/ste from M$1890/2640-3900; P ☐ ☑) This gorgeous hotel was built as a hillside hacienda in the 1930s and is the society hotel of choice for Tepoztlán. The 20-rooms are airy and individually decorated in a pared-down way – most with great views over the town. In the age of boutique luxury, some of the rooms may be underwhelming, but the focus of this old-world place is its refined atmosphere, wonderful garden and pool.

Eating & Drinking

Tepoznieves (Av Revolución 1910 s/n; scoops M$10-20) This homegrown ice-cream emporium scoops out some 200 heavenly flavors, including exotics like cactus and pineapple-chili. It's an obligatory stop and has a couple more branches on the road to the pyramid, plus many imitators around town.

Los Buenos Tiempos (☎ 395-05-19; Av Revolución 1910 10; pastries M$10-30) For the best pastries in the state, head here. There's also good coffee and a lively social scene, and it's a great place to buy a pastry breakfast to take up to the pyramid with you.

Govinda Ram (cnr Av Tepozteco & La Cumbre; snacks & set meals M$30-55; Ⓥ) As if you needed it, here's proof that Tepoz is well and truly central Mexico's biggest hippie haunt. A Hindu-inspired vegetarian café, Govinda Ram does a range of snacks and full meals, including an excellent Ayurvedic buffet, good coffee and warming evening meals.

Los Colorines (☎ 395-01-98; Av Tepozteco 13; mains M$60-90; ☺ 9.30am-9pm) Specializing in *la comida sabrosáor* (simply put, 'tasty food'), this is a big two-floor place, vibrantly painted and with a large menu of great Mexican home cooking.

Axitla (☎ 395-05-19; Av Tepozteco; mains M$60-100; ☺ 10am-7pm Wed-Sun) This place is definitely the oddest in town, a Swiss Family Robinson-style sprawling tree-house venue just off the pathway up the archaeological site amid the thick forest. There's a good selection of breakfasts available (M$50) and a comprehensive Mexican and international menu. Avoid the coffee.

our pick La Luna Mextli (☎ 395-11-14; Av Revolución 1910 16; mains M$50-190) Yet another beautifully decorated and adorned space, La Luna Mextli is stuffed with local art, including its own in-house gallery. The food here is also excellent and good value, from Mexican

standards to an entire list of different Argentinean steaks and Argentine-style *parrillada* (mixed grill).

El Ciruelo (☎ 395-12-03; www.elcir uelo.com.mx; Zaragoza 17; mains M$115-196; ☺ 1-6pm Mon-Thu, to 11pm Fri & Sat, to 7pm Sun) Beautifully set out in a courtyard, this long-standing super-smart favorite serves an impressive upscale menu of dishes from *camarones al curry* and *salmón chileno a la mantequilla* to good pizzas, salads and international dishes. Reservations recommended – ask for a table with views of the pyramid.

Shopping

Tepoz has a fantastic, atmospheric daily market that convenes on the *zócalo*, although it's at its fullest on Wednesday and Sunday. As well as the daily fruit, vegetable, clothing and crafts on sale, Saturday and Sunday sees stalls around the plaza sell a huge range of handicrafts, including sarapes (blanket-like shawls), carvings, weavings, baskets and pottery. Shops lining adjacent streets also have interesting wares (some from Bali and India) at more upmarket prices. Popular local craft products are miniature villages carved from the cork-like spines of the pochote tree.

TEPOTZOTLÁN

This little charmer is the easiest single day trip possible from Mexico City, but it's hard to imagine anywhere less like the chaotic streets of the capital, despite the fact that urban sprawl gets closer and closer to Tepotzotlán's colonial streets every year.

There's a very simple reason to visit: the wonderful Museo Nacional del Virreinato (National Museum of the Viceregal Period; ☎ 5876-2771; Plaza Hidalgo 99; admission M$43, Spanish-only audioguides M$40; ☺ 9am-6pm Tue-Sun), comprised of the restored Jesuit Iglesia de San Francisco Javier and an adjacent monastery.

Once occupied by a Jesuit college of Indian languages, the complex dates from 1606, although various additions were made over the following 150 years. Among the folk art and fine art on display are silver chalices, pictures created from inlaid wood, porcelain, furniture and fine religious paintings and statues.

Don't miss the Capilla Doméstica, whose main altarpiece boasts more mirrors than a carnival fun house. The biggest crowds arrive on Sunday, when a crafts market convenes out front. The Iglesia de San Francisco, an extreme example of Churrigueresque architecture, was originally built between

TRANSPORTATION: TEPOTZTLÁN

- Distance from Mexico City – 45km
- Travel time – 1 hour
- Direction – north
- Bus – from Mexico City's Terminal Norte, Auto transportes Valle del Mezquital (AVM) buses stop at the Tepotztláan tollbooth every 15 minutes en route to Tula. From there, catch a local bus (M$4) or taxi (M$30), or walk west for about 20 minutes along Av Insurgentes.
- Pesero – peseros to Tepotztlán leave from Mexico City's Rosario metro station (M$15). In Tepotztlán, returning 'Rosario' buses depart from Av Insurgentes opposite Posada San José.

1670 and 1682; elaborations carried out in the 18th century made it one of Mexico's most lavish places of worship. The facade is a phantasmagoric array of carved saints, angels, plants and people, while the interior walls and the Camarín del Virgen adjacent to the altar are swathed with a circus of gilded ornamentation.

Tepotztlán's highly regarded Christmas *pastorelas* (nativity plays) are performed inside the former monastery in the weeks leading up to December 25. Tickets, which include Christmas dinner and piñata smashing, can be purchased at La Hostería de Tepotztlán (see below), or via Ticketmaster (☎ 5325-9000; www .ticketmaster.com.mx, in Spanish).

Sleeping & Eating

Hotel Posada San José (☎ /fax 5876-03-40; Plaza Virreinal 13; r M$185, with view $250) Within a gorgeous old colonial building on the south side of the *zócalo,* this well-run hotel has a great atmosphere, charming tiled bathrooms and decent rooms, although the furniture is not always as evocative of the colonial-era complex as it could be. Avoid rooms 8 and 9, which are directly below the building's noisy water pump.

Posada Castro (☎ 5876-09-64; Av Insurgentes 11; r M$300-500; P) This friendly, family-run place has 17 smart and comfy rooms a short walk from the zócalo, all with bathroom and TV. The Virgin Mary adorns almost every wall and a selection of religious icons and crucifixes completes the decor of each room.

La Hostería de Tepotztlán (☎ 5876-0243; Plaza Virreinal 1; mains M$60-150; ⏲ 12:30-5.30pm Tue-Sun) The town's most atmospheric place for lunch is the restaurant housed within the monastery in a delightful little court-

yard. It serves hearty soups along with original main courses like *huitlacoche* crepes for brunch and lunch.

Restaurant-Bar Pepe (☎ 5876-0520, Plaza Virreinal; mains M$80-140) Facing the Iglesia de San Francisco Javier across the *zócalo,* Pepe's place has a great terrace and an intimate, gently buzzing interior. Specialties include *camarones empanizados* (breaded shrimp) and there are good breakfasts for around M$65.

Otherwise, join the locals at the *taquerías* (taco stalls) west of the plaza, or in the market behind the Palacio Municipal, where food stalls serve rich *pozole* (a thin stew of hominy, pork or chicken, and avocado), *gorditas* (fried stuffed tacos in fat handmade blue corn tortillas), and fresh-squeezed juices all day long.

TAXCO

The first sight of Taxco across the steep valley as you approach it on the curvy road from Mexico City is enough to take your breath away – scattered down a precipitous hillside, its perfectly preserved colonial architecture and the twin belfries of its baroque masterpiece, Parroquia Santa Prisca, make for one of the most beguiling views anywhere in the central highlands.

Taxco (*tahss*-ko) has ridden the waves of boom and bust associated with the fantastically wealthy silver deposits discovered here in the 16th century and then again repeatedly until the early 20th century. With its silver almost all gone now, the town has turned to tourism as an economic mainstay, and any day of the week you'll find visitors wandering the narrow cobblestone streets peering into the endless rows of silver shops, while at the weekends Taxco is often flooded with weekenders from Mexico City. Nevertheless, Taxco remains a fabulous destination and one of the best weekend trips you can do from Mexico City. Unlike many colonial-era Mexican towns, Taxco has not become engulfed by industrial suburbs, and its status as a national historical monument means that even new buildings must conform to the old in scale, style and materials.

Taxco was called Tlachco (Ball Playing Place) by the Aztecs, who dominated the region from 1440 until the Spanish arrived. Among the town's first Spanish residents were three miners – Juan de Cabra, Juan Salcedo and Diego de Nava – and the carpenter Pedro Muriel. In 1531, they established the first Spanish mine in North America.

The Spaniards came searching for tin, which they found in small quantities, but by

1534 they had discovered tremendous lodes of silver. That year the Hacienda El Chorrillo was built, complete with water wheel, smelter and aqueduct – the remains of which form the old arches (Los Arcos) over Hwy 95 at the north end of town.

The prospectors quickly depleted the hacienda's first silver veins and fled Taxco. Further quantities of ore were not discovered until 1743. Don José de la Borda, who had arrived in 1716 from France at the age of 16 to work with his miner brother, accidentally unearthed one of the region's richest veins. According to legend, Borda was riding near where the Templo de Santa Prisca now stands, when his horse stumbled, dislodged a stone and exposed the precious metal.

Borda introduced new techniques of draining and repairing mines, and he reportedly treated his indigenous workers better than most colonial mines. The Templo de Santa Prisca was the devout Borda's gift to Taxco. His success attracted more prospectors, and new silver veins were found and played out. With most of the silver gone, Taxco became a quiet town with a dwindling population and economy.

In 1929, an American architect and professor named William (Guillermo) Spratling arrived and, at the suggestion of then-US ambassador Dwight Morrow, set up a silver workshop as a way to rejuvenate the town. The workshop evolved into a factory, and Spratling's apprentices began establishing their own shops. Today, Taxco is home to hundreds of silver shops, many producing for export.

The Parroquia de Santa Prisca (9am-6pm) is the symbol of Taxco and was a labor of love for town hero José de la Borda. The local Catholic hierarchy allowed the silver magnate to donate this church to Taxco on the condition that he mortgage his mansion and other assets to guarantee its completion; the project nearly bankrupted him, but the risk was well worth it – the resulting building is one of Mexico's most beautiful and striking pieces of baroque architecture. Perhaps Santa Prisca's most striking feature is the contrast between its belfries with their elaborate Churrigueresque facade overlooking the Plaza Borda and the far more simple, constrained and elegant nave, when viewed from side-on. The rose-colored stone used on the facade is extraordinarily beautiful in the sunlight – look out for the oval bas-relief depiction of Christ's baptism above the doorway. Inside the intricately sculpted, gold-covered altarpieces are equally fine Churrigueresque specimens.

Off an alley behind Santa Prisca, the Museo Guillermo Spratling (762-622-16-70; Delgado 1; admission M$27; 9am-6pm Tue-Sat, to 3pm Sun) holds a small but excellent collection of pre-Hispanic jewelry, art, pottery and sculpture from American silversmith William Spratling's private collection. The phallic cult pieces are a particular eye-opener. On the basement floor there are examples of Spratling's designs using pre-Hispanic motifs.

The rather rag-tag Museo de Arte Virreinal (762-622-55-01; Ruiz de Alarcón 12; adult/student M$20/15; 10am-5.45pm Tue-Sat, to 3.45pm Sun) is in a wonderful old house that is often referred to as Casa Humboldt, even though the famous German explorer and naturalist Friedrich Heinrich Alexander von Humboldt slept here for only one night in 1803! The restored building now houses a small but well-displayed collection of colonial religious art labeled in English and Spanish. There's also an interesting display on the Manila Galleons, which pioneered trade between the Americas and the Far East.

Built by José de la Borda in 1759, the Casa Borda (762-622-66-34; Plaza Borda; admission free; 10am-5pm Tue-Sun) serves as a cultural center hosting experimental theater and exhibiting contemporary sculpture, painting and photography by Guerrero artists. The building, however, is the main attraction. Due to the unevenness of the terrain, the rear window looks out on a precipitous four-story drop, even though the entrance is on the ground floor.

From the north end of Taxco, near Los Arcos, a Swiss-made teleférico (cable car; one-way/round-trip M$20/30; 7:45am-7pm) ascends 173m to the Hotel Monte Taxco resort (p232), affording fantastic views of Taxco and the surrounding mountains. To find the entrance, walk uphill from the south side of Los Arcos and turn right through the Instituto de Artes Plásticas gate.

Information

Net X Internet (Ruíz de Alarcón 11; per hr M$10)

Post office (Palacio Municipal, Benito Juarez 10)

Secretaría de Fomento Turístico (Tourist information office; 622-50-73; Av de los Plateros; 9am-3pm & 4-6pm) At north end of town. English- and French-speaking staff arrange guided tours of Taxco.

TAXCO

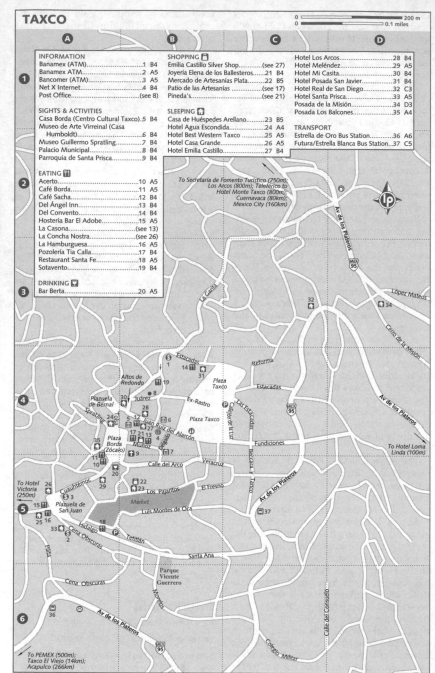

| 0 | 200 m |
| 0 | 0.1 miles |

INFORMATION
Banamex (ATM)...............................1 B4
Banamex ATM.................................2 A5
Bancomer (ATM)............................3 A5
Net X Internet................................4 B4
Post Office.................................(see 8)

SIGHTS & ACTIVITIES
Casa Borda (Centro Cultural Taxco).5 B4
Museo de Arte Virreinal (Casa
    Humboldt)...............................6 B4
Museo Guillermo Spratling...........7 B4
Palacio Municipal..........................8 B4
Parroquia de Santa Prisca.............9 B4

EATING 🍴
Acerto...10 A5
Café Borda...................................11 A5
Café Sacha...................................12 B4
Del Ángel Inn...............................13 B4
Del Convento................................14 B4
Hostería Bar El Adobe..................15 A5
La Casona................................(see 13)
La Concha Nostra....................(see 26)
La Hamburguesa..........................16 B4
Pozolería Tía Calla.......................17 B4
Restaurant Santa Fe.....................18 A5
Sotavento...................................19 B4

DRINKING 🍸
Bar Berta.....................................20 A5

SHOPPING 🛍
Emilia Castillo Silver Shop..........(see 27)
Joyería Elena de los Ballesteros......21 B4
Mercado de Artesanías Plata........22 B5
Patio de las Artesanías ....(see 17)
Pineda's...................................(see 21)

SLEEPING 🛏
Casa de Huéspedes Arellano..........23 B5
Hotel Agua Escondida...................24 A4
Hotel Best Western Taxco 25 A5
Hotel Casa Grande........................26 A5
Hotel Emilia Castillo.....................27 B4

Hotel Los Arcos...........................28 B4
Hotel Meléndez............................29 A5
Hotel Mi Casita............................30 B4
Hotel Posada San Javier...............31 B4
Hotel Real de San Diego................32 C3
Hotel Santa Prisca.......................33 A5
Posada de la Misión......................34 D3
Posada Los Balcones....................35 A4

TRANSPORT
Estrella de Oro Bus Station............36 A6
Futura/Estrella Blanca Bus Station..37 C5

Sleeping

Taxco has a wealth of hotels, from large four- and five-star hotels to charming family-run posadas. It's always best to reserve ahead, and often essential at the weekend, when the hoards arrive from el DF.

Casa de Huéspedes Arellano (☎ 762-622-0365; Los Pajaritos 23; dm $12, s with/without bathroom M$160/140, d M$220/180) There's a large variety of basic but clean rooms in this, Taxco's most backpackery option. The ground floor rooms are the very cheapest as they have no balcony. Other rooms can sleep up to six people and most others have balconies. It's well tended, with lots of flowers, caged birds, a variety of rooms and ample terraces for relaxing.

Hotel Casa Grande (☎ 762-622-09-69; Plazuela de San Juan 7; s with/without bathroom M$230/155, d M$355/230; 🖳) The basic rooms here are very clean, and it's almost worth staying just for the superb terrace overlooking the square. However, it's an extremely noisy place due to both the traffic and the music for La Concha Nostra downstairs. The apartments around the back are quieter, but also a bit rundown – the one with three bedrooms (M$530) is recommended.

Posada Los Balcones (☎ 762-622-02-50; posada_balcones@hotmail.com; Plazuela de los Gallos 5; s/d/t M$300/450/550) This good value, centrally located place has some surprisingly charming rooms, and – as the names suggests – many of these have balconies overlooking the boisterous street below, just moments from Santa Prisca. All 15 rooms have TV and bathroom.

Hotel Santa Prisca (☎ 762-622-00-80; htl_staprisca@yahoo.com; Cena Obscuras 1; s/d/t M$350/500/550; 🅿) The 31-room Santa Prisca has very sweet, traditionally Mexican decor within the walls of a gorgeous old hacienda complete with courtyard garden. It has a great location too, right in the thick of things. Rooms are smallish but most have breezy private balconies with good views. All have two beds and newer, sunnier ones fetch a bit more. The parking lot is reached via a tunnel at the hotel's uphill end.

Hotel Emilia Castillo (☎ /fax 762-622-67-17; www.hotelemiliacastillo.com; Juan Ruiz de Alarcón 7; s/d/t M$400/450/500) The 14 rooms here all have beautiful Mexican tiled bathrooms and are spotlessly clean. Owned by a famous family of silver workers, this intimate place opposite Hotel Los Arcos offers colonial charm at reasonable rates. Sadly it's in a noisy location – ask for a room at the back but don't miss the views from the rooftop terrace.

Hotel Meléndez (☎ 762-622-00-06; Cuauhtémoc 6; s/d M$395/480) Because of its location, street noise penetrates the exterior rooms at this reliable family-run favorite. Upsides include its attractively tiled public areas, a sunny terrace, great views from larger upper-level rooms and an unbeatable central location.

Hotel Los Arcos (☎ 762-622-18-36; www.hotellosarcos.net; Juan Ruiz de Alarcón 4; s/d/ste M$425/475/550; 🖳) This rustic hotel is full of character. A gorgeous 17th-century former monastery, it is furnished in a traditional style. All 26 rooms are charming, if not much more than basic, and the location is excellent.

Hotel Loma Linda (☎ 762-622-02-06; www.hotellomalinda.com; Av de los Plateros 52; s/d M$410/480, r Fri & Sat M$650; 🅿 🐕) The rooms here are larger than most, but it's also not entirely conveniently located, perched as it is on the edge of a vast chasm 1km north of town. At least the back rooms at this well-run motel have some good valley views. There's a restaurant, a heated pool, easy parking and cable TV in the 71 rooms, some of which have terraces.

Hotel Posada San Javier (☎ 762-622-31-77; posadasanjavier@hotmail.com; Estacadas 32; s/d/ste from $460/490/605-1405; 🖳 🅿 🐕) This bizarrely huge place is a combination of hotel and holiday apartments built around a very pleasant, shady garden and pool. There are 22 rooms and numerous different apartments in different corners of the complex. Rooms are comfortable but nothing special, the real attraction is the excellent location and pool.

Hotel Real de San Diego (☎ 762-627-23-30; realdesandiego@hotmail.com; Av de los Plateros 169; s/d/t M$440/500/560; 🅿 🐕) Go for the rooms on the 2nd floor if you stay here – they're bigger and some have balconies. This place is on the main road into Taxco a short walk from the town center. There's a small pool, newly installed bathrooms in the rooms and cable TV.

our pick Hotel Mi Casita (☎ 762-627-17-77; www.hotelmicasita.com; Altos de Redondo 1; s/d incl breakfast from M$550/650; ✖) This absolute gem has 12 beautifully and individually decorated rooms just moments from the *zócalo* and with great views over the cathedral. A colonial-style home run by a family of jewelry designers, this is one of the best bets in town, but bring your earplugs. The comfortable rooms feature original hand-painted bathroom tiles and some have private terraces. Three rooms have rustic Talavera bathtubs, and all have fans and cable TV.

Hotel Victoria (☎ 762-622-00-04; www.victoriataxco.com, in Spanish; Nibbi 5-7; r/ste from M$550/850; 🅿 🖳) This odd place was totally deserted on our last visit. Its 50 rooms are scattered along the hillside amid a dank, overgrown garden that feels more like a primordial forest. Rooms are large and of good quality though, especially the suites with their huge walk-out balconies. The bathrooms are a bit the worse for wear.

Hotel Agua Escondida (☎ 762-622-07-26, 800-504-03-11; www.aguaescondida.com; Plaza Borda 4; s/d M$614/760; 🅿 🖳 🐕) Facing the *zócalo*, the 'Hidden Water' has a couple of pools and a café-bar on a high terrace with unmatchable views of Santa Prisca. The 60

TRANSPORTATION: TAXCO

- Distance from Mexico City – 160km
- Travel time – 2½ hours
- Direction – southwest
- Bus – Estrella de Oro and Estrella Blanca run hourly 1st-class buses between Mexico City's Terminal Sur and Taxco (M$105). In Taxco, the Estrella de Oro station is at the south end of town, while the Estrella Blanca terminal is downhill from the main market.
- Combis – combis (M$4) are frequent and operate from 7am to 8pm. 'Zócalo' combis depart from Plaza Borda, go down Cuauhtémoc to Plazuela de San Juan, then head down the hill on Hidalgo. They then turn right at Morelos, left at Av de los Plateros, and go north until La Garita, where they turn left and return to the zócalo. 'Arcos/Zócalo' combis follow the same route except that they continue past La Garita to Los Arcos, where they do a U-turn and head back to La Garita. Combis marked 'PM' (for Pedro Martín) go to the south end of town, past the Estrella de Oro bus station.
- Taxi – taxis cost M$15 to M$30 for trips around town.

comfy, if sterile, rooms (some remodeled, some not) have Mexican furnishings, cable TV and phones. Rooms with balconies overlooking the street suffer bad traffic noise – try for a room at the back. Prices rise at the weekend.

Hotel Best Western Taxco (☎ 762-627-61-94, 800-561-2663; www.bestwesterntaxco.com; Nibbi 2; s/d M$999/1100, ste M$315-1515; P ⛽ 🖳) If you're not looking for a particularly colonial vibe this rather stylish and well-run Best Western is a good option. Large rooms have small bathrooms but the odd boutique flounce make for a comfortable stay right in the centre of town. Upstairs rooms are larger but lack balconies. No matter, everyone enjoys access to the rooftop sun deck with 360-degree city views.

Posada de la Misión (☎ 762-622-00-63, 800-008-29-20; www.posadamision.com; Cerro de la Misión 32; s/d incl breakfast M$1500/1650; P 🖳 🏊) A short way from the town centre on the top of a steep hillock, the large, rambling grounds of Posada de la Misión are an ideal weekend escape. The charming rooms (some of which have great balconies with breathtaking views of the town) are large, airy and bright. There's also a large pool and Jacuzzi under a beautiful mosaic of Cuauhtémoc and an excellent restaurant with more stunning views. Sadly, the hotel can be over-run with tour groups, although given the space available it's likely you can escape them.

Hotel Monte Taxco (☎ 762-622-13-00, 800-980-0000; www.montetaxco.com.mx; Lomas de Taxco; s/d from M$1638/1735; P ⛽ 🏊) This improbably located country club, accessible via a cable car from the edge of Taxco, is where to come and find the golfing classes. It's hard to see what all the fuss is about though – the hotel is nothing special, and while good for views and a relaxed weekend away, the rooms are plain and somewhat neglected, while Taxco itself is too much of an effort to get to – it'd be much better just drinking by the poolside. Use of the nine-hole golf course is extra.

Eating & Drinking

Café Sacha (☎ 762-628-51-50; Juan Ruiz de Alarcón 1A; mains M$45-85; V) This wonderfully decorated hangout enjoys low lighting, little balcony tables and free wi-fi as well as a collection of antique Lonely Planet guides to most of Central America. It's a good place to come anytime of day – it can get lively in the evenings – while the good vegetarian selection and Thai and Indian specialties grab diners at other times.

La Hamburguesa (☎ 762-622-09-41; Plazuela de San Juan 5; hamburgers from M$15; ☻ closed Wed) For a light meal or a quick lunch, try this popular place on the west side of Plazuela San Juan. It sells burger-and-fries combos and excellent enchiladas.

Pozolería Tia Calla (☎ 762-622-56-02; Plaza Borda 1; mains M$20-40; ☻ 1:30-11pm Wed-Mon) There are no fine vistas or breezy *terrazas* here...just authentic, no-nonsense white Guerrero-style *pozole,* served up in Auntie Calla's basement. Pick your poison: chicken or pork. Pork comes loaded with *chicharrón* (fried pork skin), avocado and all the fixings. No matter your meat choice, the broth is always pork-based. The beer steins are chilled and there's *fútbol* on the *tele.* What more could you ask for?

Café Borda (☎ 762-627-20-73; Plaza Borda 6; mains M$40) This tiny place has the single best view of Santa Prisca going, and if you're lucky you can get the one balcony table and own it temporarily. Good breakfasts, strong coffee, sandwiches and Mexican *antojitos* (snacks) are served here by the friendly family owners.

La Casona (☎ 762-622-10-71; Muñoz 4; mains M$60; ☻ 8am-8pm) Cheaper than its neighbor Del Ángel, La Casona is also less touristy, more relaxed and more traditional in its menu choices. There are equally superb views from the tables at the back, although our favorite table is the one you share with the cigar-smoking skeleton! The excellent *menu del día* is a winner for M$80.

La Concha Nostra (☎ 762-622-79-44; Plazuela de San Juan 5; pizzas M$60) On the 2nd floor of the Casa Grande Hotel, this popular pizza and pasta restaurant serves food and drink until 1am. You can watch the action on Plazuela San Juan from the balcony. Live rock music shakes the house every Saturday night.

Restaurant Santa Fe (☎ 762-622-11-70; Hidalgo 2; mains M$55-90) In business for over 50 years, Santa Fe is a favorite with locals, serving fairly priced traditional Mexican fare, such as *conejo en chile ajo* (rabbit in garlic chili) and fresh shrimp. It offers four different set breakfasts, a hearty four-course *comida corrida* (set menu; $6) and three styles of *pozole* daily after 6pm. The walls are bedecked with photos of local patrons and some excellent black-and-white photos of ye olde Taxco.

Del Convento (☎ 762-622-32-72; Estacadas 32; mains M$40-105) For one of the best views in town, the restaurant of the Posada San Javier is hard to beat, with its vast roof terrace setting. Come by for the elaborate breakfasts, evening meal or cocktail.

Hostería Bar El Adobe (☎ 762-622-14-16; Plazuela de San Juan 13; mains M$45-110) Views here are less captivating than at neighboring touristy eateries, but interior decor is lovely and there's a bar full of cocktails.

Specialties include Taxco-style *cecina* (salted strip steak) and shrimp-spiked garlic soup.

Sotavento (☎ 762-627-12-17; Juárez 12; mains M$50-145) Next door to the Palacio Municipal, the Sotavento has a great terrace and a peaceful interior garden as well as a good in-house art gallery. From breakfasts to cocktails, from enchiladas *de mole* to prime rib, it's all served up here.

Acerto (☎ 762-622-00-64; Plaza Borda 7; mains M$90-190) This strikingly modern, sleek (and rather orange) conversion of a long-standing local favorite now functions as a restaurant, cocktail bar and internet café. The main attraction is the fantastic view across the Plaza Borda to Santa Prisca, although its delicious menu of salads, soups, *antojitos* and *moles* and its superior cocktail making are also good reasons to drop by.

Del Ángel Inn (☎ 762-622-55-25; Muñoz 4; mains M$130-150) Think tour groups and mariachi bands here, at one of Taxco's most enduringly popular restaurants. Despite this, the superb views over the town from the 2nd floor roof terrace are hard to beat, and food quality is good, with a range of Mexican and international cuisine on offer.

Bar Berta (Cuauhtémoc; ☾ 11am-8pm) By rights Berta should be flooded with lost-looking tourists, but remarkably there's a clientele of tough-looking locals knocking

¡QUE VIVA ZAPATA!

A peasant leader from Morelos state, Emiliano Zapata (1879–1919) was the most radical of Mexico's revolutionaries, fighting for the return of hacienda land to the peasants with the cry *¡Tierra y Libertad!* (Land and Freedom!). The Zapatista movement was at odds both with the conservative supporters of the old regime and their liberal opponents. In November 1911, Zapata disseminated his *Plan de Ayala*, calling for restoration of all land to the peasants. After winning numerous battles against government troops In central Mexico (some in association with Pancho Villa), he was ambushed and killed in 1919. The following route traces some of Zapata's defining moments.

Ruta de Zapata

In Anenecuilco, 6km south of Cuautla, what's left of the adobe cottage where Zapata was born (on August 8, 1879), is now the Museo de la Lucha para la Tierra (Av Zapata; donation requested; ☾ 8am-9pm), which features photographs of the rebel leader. Outside is a mural by Roberto Rodríguez Navarro that depicts Zapata exploding with the force of a volcano into the center of Mexican history, sundering the chains that bound his countrymen.

About 20km south of Anenecuilco is the Ex-Hacienda de San Juan Chinameca (in a town of the same name), where in 1919 Zapata was lured into a fatal trap by Colonel Jesús Guajardo, following the orders of President Venustiano Carranza, who was eager to dispose of the rebel leader and consolidate the postrevolutionary government. Pretending to defect to the revolutionary forces, Guajardo set up a meeting with Zapata, who arrived at Chinameca accompanied by a guerrilla escort. Guajardo's men gunned down the general before he crossed the abandoned hacienda's threshold.

The hacienda, with a small museum (Cárdenas; donation requested; ☾ 9:30am-5pm), is on the left at the end of the town's main street, where there's a statue of Zapata astride a rearing horse. The exhibits (photos and newspaper reproductions) are pretty meager, but you can still see the bullet holes in the walls.

From Chinameca, Hwy 9 heads 20km northwest to Tlaltizapán, site of the Cuartel General de Zapata (Guerrero 67; donation requested; ☾ 9am-5pm Tue-Sun), the main barracks of the revolutionary forces. It contains relics from General Zapata's time, including the bed where he slept, his rifle (the trigger retains his fingerprints) and the outfit he was wearing at the time of his death (riddled with bullet holes and stained with blood).

From Cuautla, yellow 'Chinameca' combis traveling to Anenecuilco and Chinameca (M$6) leave from the corner of Garduño and Matamoros every 10 minutes.

back stiff drinks and watching *fútbol* instead. There's a tiny upstairs terrace for people watching over the *zócalo* should you not fancy the charming green painted downstairs bar. Try a *berta* (tequila, honey, lime and mineral water), the house specialty.

Shopping

There are several silver shops in the Patio de las Artesanías (Plaza Borda) building. Pineda's (☎ 762-622-32-33; Muñoz 1) is justly famous; next door, Joyería Elena de los Ballesteros (☎ 762-622-37-67; Muñoz 4) is another worthwhile shop.

Inside Hotel Emilia Castillo, the tableware in the showroom of Emilia Castillo (☎ 762-622-34-71; Ruiz de Alarcón 7) is a unique blend of silver and porcelain. For quantity rather than quality, trawl the vast, haphazardly displayed masses of rings, chains and pendants at the Mercado de Artesanías Plata (☽ 11am-8pm).

CUERNAVACA

There's always been a formidable glamour surrounding Cuernavaca (kwehr-nah-*vah*-kah), the high-society capital of Morelos State. With its vast gated haciendas, year-round warmth, clean air and attractive architecture, it has in the past attracted everyone from the Shah of Iran to Charles Mingus.

Today this tradition continues, even though urban sprawl has put a decisive end to the clean air and you're less likely to meet international royalty and great artists in the street, and far more likely to see vacationing Americans and college students studying Spanish on month-long courses.

While Cuernavaca has lots going for it, including some fantastic boutique hotels, good nightlife and fascinating nearby pre-Hispanic sites, it's fair to say that it's not the most accessible destination for those just passing through. Many of its most beautiful buildings are inaccessible to most visitors behind thick walls in private estates, so unless you're well connected in Mexico City high society or able to spend several weeks getting to know the city, then you may come away underwhelmed. However, the city has a great atmosphere, and definitely merits a stop on your way through.

Around AD 1200, the first settlers in the valleys of modern Morelos developed a highly productive agricultural society based at Cuauhnáhuac (Place at the Edge of the Forest). Later, they were conquered by the Mexica (Aztecs) who called them 'Tlahuica,' which means 'people who work the land.' Under their Aztec overlords, the Tlahuica traded extensively and prospered. Their city was a learning and religious center, and archaeological remains suggest they had a considerable knowledge of astronomy.

When the Spanish arrived, the Tlahuica were fiercely loyal to the Aztecs. In April 1521 they were finally overcome and Cortés torched the city. After destroying the city pyramid, Cortés used the stones to build a fortress-palace, the Palacio de Cortés, on the pyramid's base. He also erected the fortress-like Catedral de la Asunción from the rubble. Soon the city became known as Cuernavaca, a Spanish-friendly version of its original appellation.

In 1529, Cortés received his belated reward from the Spanish crown when he was named Marqués del Valle de Oaxaca, with an estate that covered 22 towns, including Cuernavaca, and 23,000 indigenous Mexicans. After he introduced sugar cane and new farming methods, Cuernavaca became a Spanish agricultural center, as it had been for the Aztecs. Cortés' descendants dominated the area for nearly 300 years.

With its salubrious climate, rural surroundings and colonial elite, Cuernavaca became a refuge for the rich and powerful, including José de la Borda, the 18th-century Taxco silver magnate. Borda's lavish home was later a retreat for Emperor Maximilian and Empress Carlota. Cuernavaca also attracted many artists, and achieved literary fame as the setting for Malcolm Lowry's 1947 novel, *Under the Volcano*.

Cuernavaca's *zócalo*, Plaza de Armas, is flanked on the east by the Palacio de Cortés, on the west by the Palacio de Gobierno and on the northeast and south by restaurants and roving bands of mariachis. Although you can't enter the Palacio de Gobierno, it is a nice spot to contemplate some attractive architecture and enjoy the music. It's the only main plaza in Mexico without a church, chapel, convent or cathedral overlooking it.

Adjoining the northwest corner is the smaller Jardín Juárez, where the central gazebo (designed by tower specialist Gustave Eiffel) houses juice and sandwich stands, and hosts band concerts on Thursday and Sunday evening from 6pm. Roving vendors sell balloons, ice cream and corn on the cob under the trees, which fill up with legions of cacophonous grackles at dusk. Even more entertaining are the guitar *trios* who warm up their voices and instruments before heading to the cafés across the street to serenade willing

CUERNAVACA

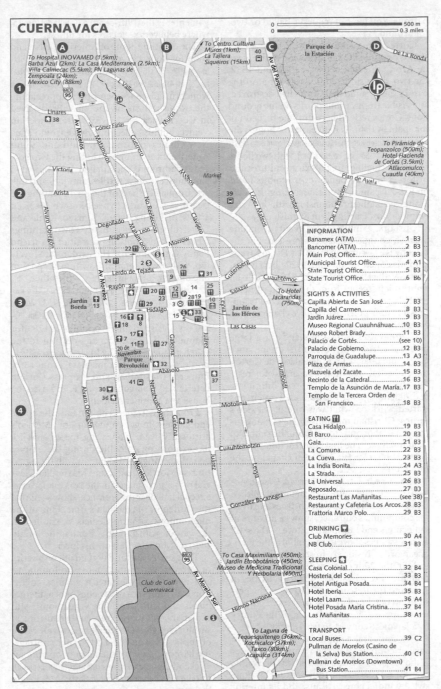

0 ——————— 500 m
0 ——————— 0.3 miles

INFORMATION

Banamex (ATM).................................1	B3
Bancomer (ATM)..............................2	B3
Main Post Office..............................3	B3
Municipal Tourist Office....................4	A1
State Tourist Office..........................5	B3
State Tourist Office..........................6	B6

SIGHTS & ACTIVITIES

Capilla Abierta de San José..............7	B3
Capilla del Carmen..........................8	B3
Jardín Juárez....................................9	B3
Museo Regional Cuauhnáhuac....10	B3
Museo Robert Brady......................11	B3
Palacio de Cortés..................(see 10)	
Palacio de Gobierno......................12	B3
Parroquia de Guadalupe................13	A3
Plaza de Armas...............................14	B3
Plazuela del Zacate........................15	B3
Recinto de la Catedral...................16	B3
Templo de la Asunción de María..17	B3
Templo de la Tercera Orden de	
San Francisco............................18	B3

EATING

Casa Hidalgo.................................19	B3
El Barco...20	B3
Gaia..21	B3
La Comuna....................................22	B3
La Cueva.......................................23	B3
La India Bonita..............................24	A3
La Strada.......................................25	B3
La Universal...................................26	B3
Reposado......................................27	D3
Restaurant Las Mañanitas..........(see 38)	
Restaurant y Cafetería Los Arcos.28	B3
Trattoria Marco Polo.....................29	B3

DRINKING

Club Memories..............................30	A4
NB Club...31	B3

SLEEPING

Casa Colonial................................32	B4
Hostería del Sol.............................33	B3
Hotel Antigua Posada....................34	B4
Hotel Iberia...................................35	B3
Hotel Laam...................................36	A4
Hotel Posada María Cristina........37	B4
Las Mañanitas...............................38	A1

TRANSPORT

Local Buses...................................39	C2
Pullman de Morelos (Casino de	
la Selva) Bus Station.................40	C1
Pullman de Morelos (Downtown)	
Bus Station...............................41	B4

patrons. You too can request a ballad or two, for around M$75.

Cortés' imposing medieval-style palacio stands opposite the southeast end of the Plaza de Armas. Erected between 1522 and 1532, the two-story stone edifice was set atop the base of the pyramid that Cortés had destroyed, still visible from various points on the ground floor. Cortés resided here until he turned tail for Spain in 1540. Today the palace houses the excellent Museo Regional Cuauhnáhuac (admission M$37; ☽ 9am-6pm Tue-Sun, last ticket 5.30pm), with two floors of exhibits highlighting Mexican cultures and history. On the ground floor, exhibits focus on pre-Hispanic cultures, including the local Tlahuica and their relationship with the Aztec empire. Most labeling is in Spanish only.

Upstairs, exhibits cover events from the Spanish conquest up to the present. On the balcony is a fascinating mural by Diego Rivera, commissioned in the mid-1920s by Dwight Morrow, the US ambassador to Mexico. From right to left, scenes from the conquest up to the 1910 revolution emphasize the cruelty, oppression and violence that have characterized Mexican history.

Cuernavaca's cathedral stands in a large high-walled recinto (compound) – the entrance gate is on Hidalgo. Like the Palacio de Cortés, the cathedral was built in a grand fortress-like style, in an effort to impress, intimidate and defend against the natives. Franciscans started work on what was one of Mexico's earliest Christian missions in 1526, using indigenous labor and stones from the rubble of Cuauhnáhuac. The first construction was the Capilla Abierta de San José, an open chapel on the cathedral's west side.

The cathedral itself, the Templo de la Asunción de María, is plain and solid, with an unembellished facade. The side door, which faces north to the compound's entrance, shows a mixture of indigenous and European features – the skull and crossbones above it is a symbol of the Franciscan order. Inside are frescoes rediscovered early in the 20th century. Cuernavaca was a center for Franciscan missionary activities in Asia, and the frescoes – said to show the persecution of Christian missionaries in Japan – were supposedly painted in the 17th century by a Japanese convert to Christianity.

The cathedral compound also holds two smaller churches. On the right as you enter is the Templo de la Tercera Orden de San Francisco; its exterior was carved in 18th-century baroque style by indigenous artisans, and its interior has ornate, gilded decorations. On the left as

you enter is the 19th-century Capilla del Carmen, where believers seek cures for illness.

The one-time home of American artist and collector Robert Brady (1928–86), Museo Robert Brady (☎ 777-316-85-54; www.bradymuseum.org; Netzahualcóyotl 4; admission M$30; ☽ 10am-6pm Tue-Sun) is a wonderful place to spend time appreciating the exquisite taste of one man. Brady lived in Cuernavaca for 24 years after a spell in Venice, but his collections range from Papua New Guinea and India to Haiti and South America. Every room, including the two gorgeous bathrooms and kitchen, is bedecked in paintings, carvings, textiles, antiques and folk arts from all corners of the earth. Among the treasures are works by well-known Mexican artists, including Rivera, Tamayo, Kahlo and Covarrubias, as well as Brady's own paintings (check out his spot-on portrait of his friend Penny Guggenheim). The gardens are lovely too, with a very tempting swimming pool in one of them and a little café in the other.

Beside the 1784 Parroquia de Guadalupe, the extravagant Jardín Borda (☎ 777-318-82-50; Av Morelos 271; adult/child M$30/15, free Sun; ☽ 10am-5:30pm Tue-Sun) was designed after Versailles in 1783 for Manuel de la Borda, as an addition to the stately residence built by his father, José de la Borda, the Taxco silver magnate. From 1866, Emperor Maximilian and Empress Carlota entertained their courtiers here, and used the house as a summer residence.

From the entrance, you can tour the house and gardens to get an idea of how Mexico's aristocracy lived. In one wing, the Museo del Sitio has exhibits on daily life during the empire period, and original documents with the signatures of Morelos, Juárez and Maximilian. Several romantic paintings in the Sala Manuel M Ponce, a recital hall near the entrance, show scenes of the garden in Maximilian's time. One of the most famous paintings depicts Maximilian in the garden with La India Bonita, the 'pretty Indian', who later became his lover.

The gardens are formally laid out on a series of terraces, with paths, steps and fountains, and they originally featured a botanical collection with hundreds of varieties of ornamental plants and fruit trees. The vegetation is still exuberant, with large trees and semitropical shrubs, though there is no longer a wide range of species. Because of a city water shortage, the baroque-style fountains only operate on weekends. You can hire a row boat (M$30 per hour), or take tea at the restaurant (mains M$50-95) inside the entrance without purchasing a ticket.

The city's best art gallery, the Centro Cultural Muros (☎ 777-310-38-48; www.muros.org.mx, in Spanish; Guerrero 205, Colonia Lomas de la Selva; admission M$30, free Tue & Sun; ⏱ 10am-6pm Tue-Sun) is home to restored murals from Cuernavaca's Hotel Casino de la Selva, and a private collection of more than 320 paintings, sculptures, videos and photographs. Highlights include Frida Kahlo's *Diego en mi Pensamiento*, and works by Rivera, Siqueiros, Orozco, Tamayo and emerging 21st-century artists.

In the five days before Ash Wednesday (late February or early March), Cuernavaca's colorful Carnaval celebration features parades, art exhibits and street performances by Tepoztlán's Chinelo dancers. In late March and early April, the Feria de la Primavera (Spring Fair) includes cultural and artistic events, concerts and a beautiful exhibit of the city's spring flowers.

Information

Hospital INOVAMED (☎ 777-311-24-82/83/84; Cuauhtémoc 305) In Colonia Lomas de la Selva, 1km north of town.

Main post office (Plaza de Armas; ⏱ 8am-6pm Mon-Fri, 9am-1pm Sat) On the south side of the plaza.

Municipal tourist office (☎ 777-318-75-61; http://mac .cuernavaca.gob.mx/turismo, in Spanish; Av Morelos 278; ⏱ 9am-5pm) Also has a tourist police office.

State tourist office (☎ /fax 777-314-38-72/81, 800-987-82-24; www.morelostravel.com; Av Morelos Sur 187) and (☎ 314-39-20; Hidalgo; ⏱ 8am-5pm Mon-Fri, Sat 10am-1pm), between Galeanea and Juárez.

Sleeping

A steady stream of upmarket boutique hotels have opened up in recent years, and some of the best in the country are here, squarely aimed at weekend refugees from the capital. On Friday and Saturday nights and holidays, the town fills up with visitors from Mexico City, so it's best to arrive with prior reservations.

Hotel Iberia (☎ 777-312-60-40; www.hoteliberia.com .mx; Rayón 7; s/d M$290/370; P) While rooms may be a little small at this good value student favorite, they have a modicum of style with their iron bedsteads and matching fittings. Staff within the Talavera-tiled reception area are pretty indifferent, however.

our pick Hostería del Sol (☎ 777-318-32-41; Callejón de la Bolsa del Diablo; r with/without bathroom M$400/300; ☑) The moment you enter this perfectly located little charmer it's clear what's wrong with most of Cuernavaca's other budget accommodation. Here prices are rock-bottom, but everything is spotless and beautifully decorated throughout in traditional blue and yellow tones. With just six rooms (half of which share facilities), it's best to ring ahead, although staff don't speak a word of English.

La Casa Mediterránea B&B (☎ 777-317-11-53; www .lacasamediterranea.com; Acacias 207, Colonia La Pradera; s/d incl breakfast $350/500; P ☑) Popular with language students on courses, this seven-room family home is 3km out of town, but features large, well-maintained rooms and a friendly welcome. It's excellent value for the money – you'd being paying twice as much were it in the town center.

Villa Calmecac (☎ 777-313-29-18; www.villacalmecac .com; Zacatecas 114, Colonia Buenavista; dm/d incl breakfast $450/650; P ☑) Crafted from adobe and surrounded by organic gardens, this ecofriendly hostel is 7km from Cuernavaca's center. Yoga classes are offered, breakfast is an all-natural buffet and the bunks are in rustic-style rooms. It's 800m west of Hwy 95, a 20-minute ride from the corner of Av Morelos and Calle Degollado on a Ruta 1, 2 or 3 bus. Zacatecas is two blocks past the Zapata monument on the left. Visitors must check in before 9pm.

Hotel Antigua Posada (☎ 777-310-21-79; www .hotelantiguaposada.com; Galeana 69; r M$800, ste M$950-1100; P ☐ ☑) This exclusive little hideaway boasts just 11 rooms behind its unpromising exterior, a short walk from the center of town. However, once inside there's a lovely courtyard and great service, and all the rooms are of very high standard, complete with wooden beams, rustic touches and full facilities, including free wi-fi, breakfast and valet parking.

Hotel Laam (☎ 777-314-44-11; www.laamhotel.com; Morelos 239; r M$850; P ☑) This new addition to the Cuernavaca hotel scene has the feel of a motel, but its rooms are comfortable, if a little sterile, and some have huge terraces. It's set back from the main road so noise isn't a big problem, although the setting isn't exactly charming either. A small pool and delightful staff compensate though.

La Casa Azul (☎ 777-314-21-41, 314-36-34; www .hotelcasaazul.com.mx; Arista 17; r/ste M$850/1880; P ☐ ☑) This 24-room boutique hotel is a short walk from the town center and has lots of charm, although the suites are a big price jump from the rooms, and they frankly aren't that much bigger. Originally part of the Guadalupe Convent, the hotel has soothing fountains, two pools, free wi-fi and a great selection of local arts and crafts throughout. The staff are delightful, the setting is tranquil and the decor is classic Mexican.

Casa Colonial (☎ 777-312-70-33, 800-623-08-43; www .casacolonial.com, in Spanish; Netzahualcóyotl 37; r from M$985, ste from M$1215; P ☐ ☑) One of the best places in town, the 16-room Casa Colonial oozes thought and style. Set in a charming garden around a large pool, this 19th-century mansion has been lovingly restored and cleverly updated, with beautifully furnished rooms, some of which feature saunas and fireplaces. The cheaper bungalows at the back are still of an excellent standard.

Hotel Jacarandas (☎ 777-315-77-77/76, in Mexico City ☎ 55-5544-3098; www.jacarandas.com.mx; Cuauhtémoc 133, Colonia Chapultepec; rfrom M$1400, ste M$2600-4400; P 🔊) This large five-star place is a true getaway from city life. Set in rambling grounds graced with lots of trees, exuberant gardens, a good restaurant, and three pools of varying temperatures, it makes a great (if pricey) weekend option. It's 1.3km east of the center.

Hotel Posada María Cristina (☎ 777-318-57-67, 800-713-74-07; reservaciones@maria-cristina.com; Juárez 300; r/ste from M$1887/2900; P 🔊) This centrally-located 16th-century estate is one of Cuernavaca's long-time favorites. Highlights include 20 tastefully appointed rooms in a nicely restored colonial building, the charming *nueva cocina mexicana* restaurant and bar Calandria with its popular Sunday champagne buffet, and an inviting pool and Jacuzzi amidst lovely hillside gardens.

Hotel Hacienda de Cortés (☎ 777-316-08-67, 800-220-76-97; www.hotelhaciendadecortes.com; Plaza Kennedy 90; r/ste from M$2350/3525; P 🔊) Built in the 16th century by Martín Cortés, who succeeded Hernán Cortés as Marqués del Valle de Oaxaca, this former sugar mill was renovated in 1980. It boasts 23 rooms of various levels of luxury, each with its own private garden and terrace. There's a swimming pool built around old stone columns. Although several guests have complained that the rooms weren't in the best state when they visited, this is still an incredible place for a memorable night or two.

Las Mañanitas (☎ 777-362-00-00, in Mexico City 800-221-52-99, in US ☎ 888-413-91-99; www.lasmananitas.com.mx; Linares 107; ste incl breakfast Sun-Thu M$2260-4642, Fri & Sat M$2623-5061; P 🔊 🖳 🔊) This utterly stunning place is where to head if you plan to impress someone. It's very much a destination hotel – you may not leave it for the whole weekend, after all – and so the fact that's it's not in the very center is irrelevant. The rooms are large and beautifully decorated yet understated. Many feature large terraces overlooking the sumptuous private gardens, stuffed full of peacocks and featuring a heated pool. As you'd expect it's a home away from home to Mexico's upper crust.

Eating

La Comuna (☎ 777-318-27-57; Morrow 6; mains M$20-30; 🕑 8am-9pm Mon-Sat) One of the friendliest places in town, La Comuna is decorated with handicrafts and serves up excellent organic coffee, as well as cheap beer, cocktails, pies, tamales and fruit salads with granola. Drop by for the daily buffet breakfast, a generous set midday meal, or to browse its small gift shop.

La Cueva (no phone; Galeana; mains M$20-75; 🕑 8am-11pm) This no-nonsense sloped bar opens onto the bustling crowds of Galeana and serves up superb *pozole* and a range of other delicious snacks and light meals. It's a great place to come and eat with the locals at local prices. It's also an excellent place for breakfast, with a range on offer for just M$25.

El Barco (☎ 777-313-21-31; Rayón 5F; mains M$30-90; 🕑 11am-midnight) This popular, no-nonsense joint specializes in Guerrero-style *pozole*, the all-curing Mexican version of matzo-ball soup. Small or heaping clay bowls are accompanied by fine oregano, mildly hot red chili, shredded lettuce, limes and chopped onions. Specify *pollo* (chicken), and *maciza* (unless you'd like your soup to include bits of fat), plus *especial* if you enjoy avocado. For refreshment, there's ice-cold beer, pitchers of *agua de jamaica* (hibiscus water) and top-shelf tequila.

La Strada (☎ 777-318-60-85; Salazar 38; mains M$70-150) On the walking street also known as Callejón del Cubo, this inviting slice of Rome presents authentic Italian-Mediterranean cuisine in a covered interior courtyard. The napkins are linen, the wine cellar is well-stocked, the lettuce is organic and service is attentive. Considering its location near the Palacio de Cortés, it's not too touristy. Romance fills the air Friday and Saturday nights, when there's live violin music and opera singing.

La India Bonita (☎ 777-318-69-67; Morrow 115; mains M$75-150; 🕑 8am-11pm Tue-Sat, 9am-5pm Sun & Mon) Cuernavaca's oldest restaurant is also undoubtedly one of its most charming, set in a lovely courtyard, although with the option of indoor dining available too. The staff are friendly and the traditional Mexican menu with a twist is enticing – from *brocheta al mezcal* to *chile en nogada*. There's an elaborate Sunday buffet brunch, full bar and live folkloric ballet Saturdays from 7pm.

La Universal (☎ 777-318-59-70; cnr Gutenberg & Guerrero; mains M$100) The Universal enjoys a strategic position on the corner of the two central plazas, with tables under an awning facing the Plaza de Armas. This popular place is all about location – the people-watching is great, but you can find better eats elsewhere.

TRANSPORTATION: CUERNAVACA

- Distance from Mexico City – 89km
- Travel time – 1¼ hours
- Direction – south
- Bus – Pullman de Morelos (www.pullman.com.mx) runs frequent 'deluxe' (M$63) and 'executive' (M$75) class buses between Mexico City's Terminal Sur and Cuernavaca's downtown and Casino de la Selva terminals. (From the latter, local Ruta 17 buses head downtown.) The same company offers direct service every 10 minutes to/from the Mexico City airport (M$125).

Restaurant y Cafetería Los Arcos (☎ 777-312-44-86; Jardín de los Héroes 4; mains M$40-120) Right in the thick of things off the Plaza de Armas, Los Arcos is a European-style café which makes for a great meeting place. The huge terrace is nearly always packed. Whether you come for early-morning coffee, late-night cocktails or a meal in between, you'll find friendly and efficient service. There's also a *geletaría* here serving up great ice cream. Happy hours run from 2pm to 4pm and again from 8pm to 10pm.

our pick Casa Hidalgo (☎ 777-312-27-49, www.casa hidalgo.com; Hidalgo 6; mains M$160) Directly opposite the Palacio de Cortés with a great terrace and an even better upstairs balcony, this is one of Cuernavaca's most popular eateries and attracts a well-heeled crowd of local socialites and wealthy visitors. The menu is eclectic (try shrimp tacos with beans wrapped in banana skin, or braided red snapper and salmon in an orange and parsley sauce, for example). Super friendly staff, a strong wine list and great views make this one of the best place in town for a meal.

Reposado (☎ 777-169-72-32; www.reposado.com.mx; Netzahualcóyotl 33; mains M$80-165; 🕑 7pm-1am Tue-Sat, 4-11pm Sun) Reposado is synonymous with its celebrity chef Ana García, a local girl who has made a name for herself both in Mexico and the US with her promotion of *alta cocina mexicana*. Don't miss a chance to come to her intimate and charming restaurant and to try her ever-changing menu of traditional Mexican cooking with exciting twists and innovations. Tables are scattered throughout the colonial complex and romantically candlelit. There's a stylish sofa-bed cocktail lounge in a loft overlooking the pool. Those really interested can organize to stay in the small on-site hotel here and take cookery courses with Chef García – see the website for details.

Gaia (☎ 777-312-36-56, www.gaiarest.com.mx; Juárez 102; mains M$190; 🕑 2pm-midnight Mon-Sat, 1-6pm Sun) This gorgeous, stylish place has a very impressive international menu with dishes such as linguini with shrimp in cilantro sauce and 'fish trilogy' with tamarind and chili, all served in a delightful colonial building that was once the mansion of comic actor Mario Moreno, aka Cantínflas. Reserve a table with a view of the Diego Rivera mosaic that adorns the bottom of the swimming pool. Delivery and take-out is also available.

Trattoria Marco Polo (☎ 777-318-40-32; Hidalgo 30; mains M$60-120, pizza M$45-200; 🕑 1-10:30pm Sun-Thu, 1pm-midnight Fri & Sat) This handy little place does decent Italian dishes in an attractive setting just across from the cathedral. The pizza list alone is huge, and there's friendly service and a decent choice of wine as well. Try for a table by the balcony.

Restaurant Las Mañanitas (☎ 777-314-14-66; Linares 107; breakfast M$60-160, mains M$400; 🕑 1-5pm & 7-11pm) The restaurant and bar of the town's most famous hotel is open to all, and it shouldn't be missed if you want a memorable, romantic dinner in ultra-smart surroundings. The menu has a heavy French accent, with entrecôte bourguignonne and Royal Magret (duck breast) to tempt you, not to mention sumptuous desserts. Choose between tables inside the mansion or on the terrace, where you can watch the wildlife wander around the emerald-green garden among fine modern sculptures. Reservations are recommended.

Drinking & Entertainment

The most accessible bars are around Plazuela del Zacate and the adjacent alley Las Casas. Most offer live music or karaoke and typically don't shut their doors until around sunrise.

The better discos charge a cover of at least M$50, but women often get in free. Some enforce dress codes, and trendier places post style police at the door. Things really get going after 11pm. Some recommended venues are Barba Azul (☎ 311-55-11/55; Prado 10, Colonia San Jerónimo; 🕑 10pm-late Fri & Sat), with fab indoor gardens; centrally located and large NB Club (☎ 318-89-29; Plaza de Armas); and upscale Club Memories (☎ 318-43-80; Av Morelos 241; 🕑 10pm-late Wed, Fri & Sat).

TLAXCALA

Tlaxcala is a delightful Mexican anomaly – despite being less than two hours from Mexico City, the capital of Mexico's smallest state remains a calm and traffic-free place, especially at the weekend. Though there's nothing in particular to warrant a detour here, many visitors fall for the town's refreshingly tourist-free ambience.

In the last centuries before the Spanish conquest, numerous *señoríos* (small warrior kingdoms) arose in and around Tlaxcala. Some of them formed a loose federation that remained independent of the Aztec empire as it spread from the Valle de México in the 15th century. The most important kingdom seems to have been Tizatlán, now on the northeast edge of Tlaxcala city.

When the Spanish arrived in 1519, the Tlaxcalans fought fiercely at first, but ultimately became Cortés' staunchest allies against the Aztecs (with the exception of one chief, Xicoténcatl the Younger, who tried to rouse his people against the Spanish and is now a Mexican hero). The Spanish rewarded the Tlaxcalans with privileges and used them to help pacify and settle Chichimec areas to the north. In 1527, Tlaxcala became the seat of the first bishopric in Nueva España, but a

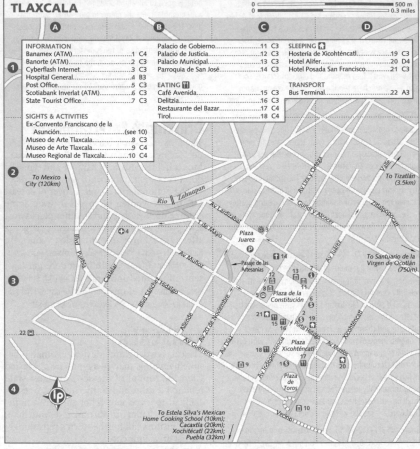

TLAXCALA

0		500 m
0		0.3 miles

INFORMATION
Banamex (ATM)...................................1 C4
Banorte (ATM)....................................2 C3
Cyberflash Internet...........................3 C3
Hospital General.................................4 B3
Post Office...5 C3
Scotiabank Inverlat (ATM)................6 C3
State Tourist Office...........................7 C3

SIGHTS & ACTIVITIES
Ex-Convento Franciscano de la
 Asunción..................................(see 10)
Museo de Arte Tlaxcala.....................8 C3
Museo de Arte Tlaxcala.....................9 C4
Museo Regional de Tlaxcala..........10 C4

Palacio de Gobierno.........................11 C3
Palacio de Justicia............................12 C3
Palacio Municipal.............................13 C3
Parroquia de San José.....................14 C3

EATING
Café Avenida.....................................15 C3
Delitzia...16 C3
Restaurante del Bazar.....................17 C4
Tirol...18 C4

SLEEPING
Hostería de Xicohténcatl................19 C3
Hotel Alifer.......................................20 D4
Hotel Posada San Francisco...........21 C3

TRANSPORT
Bus Terminal.....................................22 A3

To Mexico City (120km)

Río Zahuapan

To Tizatlán (3.5km)

Plaza Juarez

To Santuario de la Virgen de Ocotlán (750m)

Plaza de la Constitución

Plaza Xicohténcatl

Plaza de Toros

To Estela Silva's Mexican Home Cooking School (10km); Cacaxtla (20km); Xochitécatl (22km); Puebla (32km)

---

plague in the 1540s decimated the population and the town has played only a supporting role ever since.

Tlaxcala's shady, spacious *zócalo* is one of Mexico's most fetching. The 16th-century Palacio Municipal, a former grain storehouse, and the Palacio de Gobierno occupy most of its north side. Inside the latter are vivid murals of Tlaxcala's history by Desiderio Hernández Xochitiotzin. The 16th-century building on the plaza's northwest side is the Palacio de Justicia, the former Capilla Real de Indios, built for the use of indigenous nobles. The handsome mortar bas-reliefs around its doorway include the seal of Castilla y León and a two-headed eagle, symbol of the Hapsburg monarchs who ruled Spain in the 16th and 17th centuries.

Off the northwest corner of the *zócalo* is the pretty-in-pink tile, brick and stucco Parroquia de San José. As elsewhere in the Centro Histórico, bilingual signs explain the significance of the church and its many fountains.

Up along a shaded path from the southeast corner of Plaza Xochitécatl, the Ex-Convento Franciscano de la Asunción was one of Mexico's earliest monasteries, and its church – the city's cathedral – has a beautiful Moorish-style wooden ceiling. Next door is the Museo Regional de Tlaxcala (☎ 462-02-62; admission M$37, students free; ☼ 10am-6pm Tue-Sun), with a large collection of religious paintings and a few pre-Columbian artifacts.

The new Museo de Arte de Tlaxcala (☎ 246-466-03-52, www.mat.org.mx; Plaza de la Constitución 21 & Guerro 15; adults/students/under 12 M$20/10/free, Sunday & every day at Guerro 15 free; ☼ 10am-6pm Tue-Sun) is a fantastic addition to the town's cultural scene. The main collection on the *zócalo* contains an excellent cache of early Frida Kahlo paintings. This part of the museum holds excellent temporary exhibits and has a good permanent collection of modern Mexican art. The smaller space (Guerrero 15; admission free) is interactive and aimed at children.

Visible from most of town, the hilltop Santuario de la Virgen de Ocotlán (admission free; ☯ 9am-6pm) stands 1km northeast of the *zócalo*. One of Mexico's most spectacular churches, it's an important pilgrimage site owing to the belief that the Virgin appeared here in 1541 – her image stands on the main altar in memory of the apparition.

The classic Churrigueresque facade features white stucco 'wedding cake' decorations, contrasting with plain red tiles. During the 18th century, indigenous Mexican Francisco Miguel spent 25 years decorating the altarpieces and the chapel beside the main altar. To reach the santuario, walk north on Av Juárez for three blocks, then turn right onto Zitlal-

popocatl. Alternatively, catch an 'Ocotlán' *colectivo* from near the corner of Avs Guerrero and Independencia.

Information

Hospital General (☎ 246-462-00-30/34-00)

Cyberflash Internet (Av 20 Noviembre; per hr M$15) Between Avs Lardizabal and Guridi y Alcocer.

Police (☎ 246-464-52-56/57)

Post Office (cnr Avs Muñoz & Díaz)

State Tourist Office (☎ 246-465-09-60 ext 1519, 800-509-65-57; www.tlaxcala.gob.mx/turismo; cnr Avs Juárez & Lardizabal; ☯ 9am-6pm Mon-Fri, 10am-6pm Sat & Sun) English-speaking staff are keen to sell you tickets to bullfights, as well as to give out a good free map of the town and book you on tram tours of the town (M$20, Friday to Sunday).

Several banks around the *zócalo* exchange dollars and have ATMs.

DETOUR: TEXCOCO

An outing to the little-visited area around Texcoco, 21km northeast of Mexico City's airport, will give you a chance to survey some of Diego Rivera's most spectacular work, as well as a pair of interesting historical sites.

A major city before the arrival of the Spanish, Texcoco proved an important ally of the Aztecs, as part of the Triple Alliance along with Tlacopan. Under the reign of poet-king Nezahualcóyotl in the 15th century, it flourished as a center of music, art and architecture.

Between 1925 and 1927, Diego Rivera painted murals for the Universidad Autónoma de Chapingo, an agriculture school just outside Texcoco that occupies the estate buildings of a former hacienda. Two dozen of Rivera's panels cover the walls and ceiling of the hacienda chapel, now part of the university's administration building (admission M$30; ☯ 10am-3pm Mon-Fri, to 5pm Sat & Sun). These sensual tableaux intertwine images of the Mexican struggle for agrarian reform with the earth's fertility cycles. One depicts buried martyrs of reform symbolically fertilizing the land and thus the future. The curator will give you a brief description (in Spanish) of the murals upon request.

Established in 1585 as the first wheat mill in the region, the Molino de Flores, 3km east of Texcoco, later served as a *pulque* hacienda, before being expropriated by the government in 1937. Many of its buildings are in ruins, but some have been partly restored and opened for exploration within the Parque Nacional Molino de Flores. Works of local artists are exhibited in the *tinacal* (tank) where *pulque* was processed. A walk past the main building will take you to an unusual little church built into the side of a gorge, accessible on one side by a hanging bridge.

The little known archaeological site of Baños de Nezahualcóyotl (Admission free; ☯ 10am-5pm Tue-Sun), 3km east of Molino de Flores, is what's left of a palatial complex built by Nezahualcóyotl, whose engineering skills rivaled his flair for poetry. Ascending to the hilltop site, you'll come across the remains of the spring-fed aqueducts that irrigated the king's terraced gardens in the 15th century. The moderate 2km hike to the summit rewards climbers with views as far as Xochimilco – at least when smog levels are low.

Buses depart every 10 to 15 minutes from Mexico City's TAPO terminal to downtown Texcoco (M$20), from which there is transport to each of the three destinations. The Universidad Autónoma de Chapingo is about 2.5km south, at Km 38.5 on Carretera Federal México-Texcoco (Highway 136). From Calle Fray Pedro de Gante in Texcoco, catch a 'Los Reyes/La Paz' or 'Aeropuerto/Zaragoza' microbus and ask to be let off at Chapingo.

To get to the Parque Nacional Molino de Flores, take a 'Molino de Flores' combi from downtown Texcoco. For the Baños de Nezahualcóyotl, get on a 'Tlaminca' combi and ask to get off at the church. From there, it's a short walk to the park entrance and another 1.5km to the summit. Though there's no public transport between Molino de Flores and the Baños, a taxi between the two points should not cost more than M$50.

TRANSPORTATION: TLAXCALA

- Distance from Mexico City – 118km
- Travel Time – 2 hours
- Direction – east
- Bus – ATAH runs 1st-class 'expresso' buses (M$90) to/from Mexico City's TAPO terminal every 20 minutes until 9pm.

Courses

Estela Silva's Mexican Home Cooking School (☎ /fax 246-468-09-78; www.mexicanhomecooking.com; courses US$1200, nonstudent guests US$600) offers an intimate five-day gastronomic course, with hands-on instruction in the preparation of classic Mexican dishes. Tuition includes all meals, drinks, live music, transfers from Puebla and a trip to local markets, plus six nights of B&B lodging in comfortable private rooms with fireplaces. The bilingual lessons focus on the preservation of traditional French-inflected Puebla cuisine, and take place in the Talavera-tiled kitchen of fun-loving Estela's quaint hacienda-style country home, in a village 10km south of Tlaxcala.

Sleeping

Hostería de Xicohténcatl (☎ 246-466-47-16; Portal Hidalgo 10; s/d M$350/450, ste M$600-1100; P) Of the 16 rooms at this relative newcomer, half are suites. All rooms are clean and quite large, if a little sterile. Staff are friendly enough and location is excellent, just off the zócalo. Check out the collection of crosses in the lobby!

Hotel Alifer (☎ 246-462-56-78; www.hotelalifer.com, in Spanish; Av Morelos 11; s/d M$350/450; P 🖵) One of the best budget options is the reasonable Hotel Alifer, up a small hill just a minute from the zócalo. Some rooms can be a bit dingy and dark (avoid bottom-floor rooms that face echo-chamber hallways and lack exterior windows), but they are clean and spacious with TV, phone and free wi-fi.

Hotel Posada San Francisco (☎ 246-462-56-22; www.posadasanfrancisco.com, in Spanish; Plaza de la Constitución 17; s/d/ste M$980/1155/1700; P 🖵 🐾) The Posada San Francisco is the kind of place where you'd expect to find a famous author drinking himself to death (in a good way) – check out the stained glass lobby roof, the beautiful bullfight-themed bar, the large pool and the airy restaurant. While it's definitely the best place to stay in town, the rooms are something of a letdown.

Eating

Delitzia (☎ 466-38-88; Plaza de la Constitución 14; sandwiches M$40-60; 🕑 noon-midnight Tue-Sun) Just next door to Café Avenida is this great lunch option, serving up good baguettes, crepes, salads and mole in a funky space with outdoor tables overlooking the zócalo. It's also a good bet for a post-sightseeing cocktail.

Tirol (☎ 246-462-37-54; Av Independencia 7A; set menu M$65-90) This sleek place overlooking Plaza Xicohténcatl is all white tablecloths and attentive service and the gourmet Mexican food is excellent. If you don't fancy an elaborate set meal, just get take-out from the gourmet taco stand out front.

Restaurante del Bazar (Plaza Xicohténcatl 7B; mains M$80-90) A new addition to Tlaxcala's eating scene, this upmarket restaurant offers dining in a gorgeous setting with stylish decor and excellent service. The menu is a large and frequently changing roll-call of Mexican favorites with a modern twist.

our pick Café Avenida (☎ 246-466-36-69; Plaza de la Constitución 16; mains M$48-110) On the south side of the zócalo, the Café Avenida makes a refreshing break from the all-day brunches on the square's eastern flank. Its pretty wooden interior is painted green and patronized by a friendly local crowd. The home-cooked three-course lunch for M$56 is a great deal, and on top of that there's a huge choice of Mexican specialties, as well as a full cocktail bar.

MALINALCO

Word has slowly got out about this pueblo mágico, but come soon and you'll still get to enjoy it without the weekend crowds that descend on its more easily accessible cousins. True, there are already a clutch of hippie stores and a couple of boutique hotels, but for the most part life in Malinalco is a far cry from that in Tepoztlán.

In fact the drive to Malinalco is one of the most enjoyable to be had in the area, with dramatic scenery south of Toluca lining the road. The village itself has a charming colonial core set around a well-preserved convent and two central plazas. A short but bracing hike up the mountainside above Malinalco takes you

TRANSPORTATION: MALINALCO

- Distance from Mexico City – 95km
- Travel time – two hours
- Direction – southwest
- Bus – three buses a day run to/from Mexico City's Terminal Poniente (M$52). Otherwise, catch one of the more frequent buses to Tenancingo, and ask the driver to let you off for the colectivo to Malinalco (M$15, 1 hour).
- Car – if driving from Mexico City, turn south at La Marquesa and follow the signs to Malinalco.

DETOUR: TULA

The probable capital of the ancient Toltec civilization is best known for its fearsome 4.5m-high stone warrior figures. Though less spectacular and far smaller than Teotihuacán, Tula is still a fascinating site and well worth the effort of a day trip. The modern town of Tula de Allende is surrounded by a PEMEX refinery and an odoriferous petrochemical plant, but the center is pleasant enough for an overnight stay.

Tula was an important city from about AD 900 to 1150, reaching a peak population of 35,000. It was evidently a place of some splendor – legends speak of palaces of gold, turquoise, jade and quetzal feathers, of enormous corn cobs and colored cotton that grew naturally. It was abandoned by the early 13th century, seemingly after violent destruction by the Chichimecs.

The ruins (☎ 732-0705; admission M$37, use of video M$35; ⌚ 9am-5pm) of the main ceremonial center of Tula are perched on a hilltop with good views over rolling countryside. These make up just a small part of the 16 sq km site, but are where all the sites of interest are located. From the main road, it's a 300m walk to the ticket office and the excellent site museum (entrance included in site ticket price) displaying ceramics, metalwork, jewelry and large sculptures.

Also known as the temple of Quetzalcóatl or Tlahuizcalpantecuhtli (Morning Star), Pirámide B can be scaled via steps on its south side. At the top of the stairway, the remains of three columnar roof supports – that once depicted feathered serpents with their heads on the ground and their tails in the air – remain standing. The four basalt warrior-telamones at the top and the four pillars behind supported the temple's roof. Wearing headdresses, butterfly-shaped breastplates and short skirts held in place by sun disks, the warriors hold spear-throwers in their right hands, and knives and incense bags in their left. The telamon on the left side is a replica of the original, now in Mexico City's Museo Nacional de Antropología (p80).

Now roofless, the Gran Vestíbulo (Great Vestibule) extends along the front of the pyramid, facing the plaza. The stone bench carved with warriors originally ran the length of the hall, possibly to seat priests and nobles observing ceremonies in the plaza.

The plaza in front of Pirámide B would have been the scene of religious and military displays. At its center is the adoratorio (ceremonial platform). On the east side of the plaza, Pirámide C is Tula's biggest structure, and was in the early stages of excavation at the time of research. To the west is Juego de Pelota No 2, central Mexico's largest ball court at more than 100m in length.

First-class Ovnibus buses go to/from Mexico City's Terminal Norte (M$52, 1¾ hours, every 30 to 40 minutes). Autotransportes Valle ded Mezquital (AVM) runs 2nd-class buses (M$40) to the capital every 15 minutes.

---

to one of the country's few reasonably well-preserved Aztec temples (admission M$37; ⌚ 9am-6pm Tue-Sun, tickets sold to 5pm) from where there are stunning views of the valley and beyond.

From the main square follow signs to the zona arqueológica, which takes you up the hillside on a well-maintained footpath with signs in Spanish, English and Náhuatl. The site itself is fascinating, and includes El Paraíso de los Guerreros, a mural that once covered an entire wall, depicting fallen warriors becoming deities and living in paradise.

The Aztecs conquered the region in 1476 and were busy building a ritual center here when they were themselves conquered by the Spanish. El Cuauhcalli, thought to be the Temple of Eagle and Jaguar Warriors – where sons of Aztec nobles were initiated into warrior orders – survived because it's hewn from the mountainside itself. The entrance is carved in the form of a fanged serpent.

Near the site entrance, the Museo Universitario Dr Luis Mario Schneider (☎ 714-147-12-88; admission M$10;

⌚ 10am-6pm Tue Sun) explores the region's history and archaeology in a beautifully set out modern space. The highlight is a mock up of the mural from the temple site and a replica of the Cuauhcalli chamber you aren't able to enter in the temple proper.

A well-restored 16th-century Augustinian convent (admission free), fronted by a tranquil tree-lined yard, faces the central plaza. Impressive frescoes fashioned from herb- and flower-based paint adorn its cloister.

Sleeping

El Asoleadero (☎ 714-147-01-84; cnr Aldama & Comercio; s/d/q from M$300/350/450; Ⓟ Ⓢ) This old-timer offers excellent value for money if you're not looking for a boutique place to stay. The spacious and airy rooms, some with balconies, look over the quiet street, while views from the courtyard overlooking the pool are spectacular.

Hotel Santa Mónica (☎ 714-147-00-31; Hidalgo 109; r M$350) Moments from the zócalo towards the archaeological zone, the Santa Mónica is one of the better budget options, with clean rooms all with private bathroom and TV scattered around a pretty garden courtyard.

Villa Hotel (☎ 714-147-00-01; Guerrero 101; s/d M$300/600) Hardly romantic, the friendly Villa has six rooms: some have cliff views while others (some with better beds) face the plaza. Some rooms were suffering from damp on our last visit. You get a M$50 reduction if you don't have a TV in your room.

Casa Mora (☎ 714-147-05-72; www.casamora.net; Calle de la Cruz 18; ste M$1800-2000; P R) This beautifully appointed oasis is a hotel where you feel more like a house guest than a tourist. It's the pet project of a local artist, who maintains five beautiful rooms, all of which enjoy an intimate and romantic atmosphere.

our pick **Casa Limón** (☎ 714-147-02-56; www .casalimon.com, in Spanish; Río Lerma 103; r/ste incl breakfast from M$2100/2500; P ⌨ R) Malinalco's most famous hotel features beautifully styled, modern, minimalist rooms, enhanced with individually picked pieces of art and the odd antique. A slate swimming pool, classy bar and excellent restaurant complete the scene.

Eating & Drinking

Restaurant El Puente (☎ 714-147-17-43; Hidalgo 104; mains M$40-90; ☿ 9am-10pm Mon-Fri, to midnight Fri & Sat, to 7pm Sun) Just after the tiny bridge as you leave the zócalo for the ruins, this atmospheric colonial house has two smart dining rooms, as well as a great back garden, where you can try a selection of antijitos, pastas, soups and steaks.

Ehécatl (Hidalgo 10; mains M$55-70; ☿ 9am-6pm; V) A beautiful space with a gorgeously verdant courtyard,

Ehécatl is named after the Aztec god of the wind and rain and is one of Malinalco's best choices. As well as good breakfasts (M$40 to M$50) and a large range of fresh fish, it also offers a complete list of traditional Mexican cooking.

Beto's (☎ 714-147-03-11; Morelos 8; mains M$50-95; ☿ noon-8pm Tue-Sun) At Beto's you'll get the best seafood in town by a long way (the fresh trout is superb), as well as ice-cold beer served with salt on the rim. The friendly owner-chef couple will fuss over you until you're stuffed and then bring you a beso de ángel (coffee liqueur and condensed milk on ice, dusted with cinnamon) with the check.

Casa Limón (☎ 714-147-02-56; Rio Lerma 103; mains M$140-180; ☿ noon-10pm Thu-Sun) The restaurant of Malinalco's smartest hotel is also superb: a classy indoor/ outdoor space with white tablecloths, silver service but a friendly atmosphere. Mains are classic international fare – from coq au vin to almond trout – and the wine list is superb.

Koi (☎ 714-147-16-21; Morelos 18; mains M$140-170; ☿ 11am-10pm Fri-Sun) Fusion cookery has arrived in Malinalco in the form of this very trendy (and not particularly cheap) restaurant. The exciting menu runs from camarones al coco to pad thai and fish tempura, all served within a minimalist space you'd frankly not normally expect to find in a Mexican village.

Café La Fé (☎ 714-147-01-77; Guerro; ☿ 11am-8pm Fri-Sun) Between the museum and zócalo, this coffee shop and juice bar is a great place for a drink after having scaled the cliffside to visit the Aztec ruins. Everything sold on site is 100% organic, including locally grown coffee beans.

TRANSPORTATION

For a town of such gargantuan proportions, Mexico City is remarkably easy to get around. Wherever you need to go, there is likely some conveyance heading there momentarily. A swift, extensive and incredibly cheap subway system covers most of the metropolis with frequent service almost round the clock. Above ground, peseros (small buses, also called microbuses or micros), regular buses and electric-powered trolley buses move the city's masses from points A to Z. The metrobus, a recent addition, plies its own lane along the city's principal north–south artery, Av Insurgentes. Taxis are plentiful and reasonably priced, whether you're hailing one off the street or (more securely) phoning one of the radio-taxi services. Of course you can also drive, though pollution, congestion and erratic driver behavior make this the least appealing option. Getting in and out of town is also fairly straightforward, with frequent, inexpensive bus services linking the capital with practically every point in the republic.

AIR

Nearly all sizable cities in Mexico have regular (usually daily) flights to/from Mexico City. Aeroméxico and Mexicana, the country's two largest airlines, cover most of these domestic destinations. The larger domestic airlines serving Mexico City include Aero California, Aeromar and Aviacsa.

Recently started domestic carriers Interjet and Volaris offer very reasonable fares to and from a number of destinations, including Puerto Vallarta (under M$400 each way) and Mérida (M$550). There is a catch, however: they both fly in and out of Toluca, 64km west of the metropolis, a journey of up to two hours by shuttle and taxi to downtown Mexico City.

The peak travel periods of Semana Santa (Easter Week) and Christmas–New Year are hectic and heavily booked throughout Mexico: try to book transportation in advance for these periods.

Airlines

Aero California (Map pp74–5; ☎ 5785-1162; Paseo de la Reforma 332; 🚇 Reforma)

Aeromar (Map pp74–5; ☎ 5133-1111; toll free 800-237-66-27; Torre Mayor, Paseo de la Reforma 505; 🚇 Reforma)

Aeroméxico (☎ 5133-4010) Juárez (Map pp74–5; Paseo de la Reforma 80; 🚇 Reforma); Zona Rosa (Map pp74–5; Paseo de la Reforma 445; 🚇 Reforma)

CLIMATE CHANGE & TRAVEL

Climate change is a serious threat to the ecosystems that humans rely upon, and air travel is the fastest-growing contributor to the problem. Lonely Planet regards travel, overall, as a global benefit, but believes we all have a responsibility to limit our personal impact on global warming.

Flying & climate change

Pretty much all forms of motorized travel generate CO_2 (the main cause of human-induced climate change) but planes are by far the worst offenders, not just because of the sheer distances they allow us to travel, but because they release greenhouse gases high into the atmosphere. The statistics are frightening: two people taking a return flight between Europe and the US will contribute as much to climate change as an average household's gas and electricity consumption in a year.

Carbon offset schemes

Climatecare.org and other websites use 'carbon calculators' that allow travelers to offset the level of greenhouse gases they are responsible for with financial contributions to sustainable travel schemes that reduce global warming – including projects in India, Honduras, Kazakhstan and Uganda.

Lonely Planet, together with Rough Guides and other concerned partners in the travel industry, support the carbon offset scheme run by climatecare.org. Lonely Planet offsets all of its staff and author travel.

For more information check out our website: www.lonelyplanet.com.

Air Canada (Map p84; ☎ 9138-0280, ext 2228, toll free 800-719-28-27; Blvd Ávila Camacho 1, 13th fl; 🚌 Reforma pesero 'Km 13')

Air France (Map p84; ☎ 5571-6150, toll free 800-123-46-60; Jaime Balmes 8, 8th fl; Ⓜ Polanco)

Alitalia (Map pp74–5; ☎ 5533-1240, toll free 800-012-59-00; Río Tíber 103, 6th fl; 🚌 Reforma)

American Airlines (Map pp74–5; ☎ 5209-1400; Paseo de la Reforma 300; 🚌 Reforma)

Aviacsa (☎ 5716-9006, 800-011-43-57; Airport)

Avianca (Map pp74–5; ☎ 5571-4080, toll free 800-705-79-00; Paseo de la Reforma 195; 🚌 Reforma)

British Airways (Map p84; ☎ 5387-0300; Jaime Balmes 8, 14th fl; Ⓜ Polanco)

Continental Airlines (Map p84; ☎ 5283-5500, toll free 800-900-50-00; Andrés Bello 45; Ⓜ Auditorio)

Cubana (Map p84; ☎ 5250-6355; Sol y Son Viajes, Homero 613; Ⓜ Polanco)

Delta Airlines (Map pp74–5; ☎ 5279-0909, toll free 800-123-47-10; Paseo de la Reforma 381; 🚌 Reforma)

Iberia (Map p84; ☎ 1101-1515; Av Ejército Nacional 436, 9th fl; Ⓜ Polanco)

Interjet (Map p84; ☎ 1102-5555, toll free 800-011-23-45; Centro Comercial Antara, Av Ejército Nacional 843B; 🚌 Ejército Nacional)

Japan Air Lines (Map pp74–5; ☎ 5242-0150; Torre Mayor, Paseo de la Reforma 505, 36th fl; 🚌 Reforma)

KLM/Northwest (Map p84; ☎ 5279-5390; Andrés Bello 45, 11th fl; Ⓜ Auditorio)

Lufthansa (Map p84; 5230-0000; Paseo de las Palmas 239; 🚌 Reforma pesero 'Km 13')

Magnicharters (Map pp74–5; ☎ 5679-1212; Guerra 9, cnr Bucareli; Ⓜ Juárez)

Mexicana (☎ 5448-0990, toll free 800-502-20-00) Juárez (Map p64; Av Juárez 82, cnr Balderas; Ⓜ Juárez); Zona Rosa (Map pp74–5; Paseo de la Reforma 312; Ⓜ Insurgentes) Los Morales (Map p84; Pabellón Polanco)

THINGS CHANGE...

The information in this chapter is particularly vulnerable to change. Check directly with the airline or a travel agent to make sure you understand how a fare (and ticket you may buy) works and be aware of the security requirements for international travel. Shop carefully. The details given in this chapter should be regarded as pointers and are not a substitute for your own careful, up-to-date research.

Shopping Mall, Ejército Nacional 980; 🚌 pesero 'Ejército Nacional')

United Airlines (Map pp74–5; ☎ 5627-0222; Hamburgo 213, 10th fl; Ⓜ Sevilla)

Volaris (☎ 1102-8000)

Airport

Aeropuerto Internacional Benito Juárez (Map pp42–3; ☎ 2482-2424; www.aicm.com.mx, in Spanish), 6km east of the Zócalo, is Mexico City's only passenger airport. With a capacity for about 24 million passengers annually, it's the largest airport in Latin America.

A new terminal, inaugurated in 2007, is expected to expand the airport's capacity by 10 million passengers. Delta, Aeroméxico, Continental, Lan Chile, Aeromar and Copa Airlines use the new facility, called Terminal 2, which also features a hotel, a parking garage and shops. Located 3km away from the main terminal, Terminal 2 is connected by monorail, supposedly a five-minute ride. Board the monorail from Puerta 6, labeled 'Crew Parking,' on the upper level of the main terminal. From Terminal 2, you can catch the monorail at Puerta 7. Passengers need to show their plane tickets to get on.

Terminal 1 is divided into eight *salas* (halls):

Sala A Domestic arrivals.

Sala B Check-in for Mexicana and Aero California; Hotel Camino Real access.

Sala C Check-in for Aviacsa.

Sala D Check-in for Magnicharters.

Sala E International arrivals.

Sala F & J Check-in for international flights.

Sala G International departures.

The terminal's shops and facilities include dozens of *casas de cambio*; Tamibe (☎ 5726-0578) in Sala E2 stays open 24 hours. Peso-dispensing ATMs on the Cirrus and Plus networks are easy to find.

Telmex card phones and internet terminals abound; cards are available from shops and machines. Car-rental agencies and luggage lockers (up to 24hr M$80; 🕙 24hr) are in Salas A and E2.

BICYCLE

Mexico City Mayor Marcelo Ebrard has made great efforts to encourage bicycle use (see the boxed text on opposite), and though it still

MARCELO EBRARD, CYCLIST

In a city that is notoriously choked by traffic, Mexico City Mayor Marcelo Ebrard is bullish on bicycling. Addressing the environmental and psychic toll taken by the estimated 4.5 million motor vehicles that clog the streets daily, Ebrard has made an unprecedented attempt to encourage cycling as an alternative form of transportation. He's mandated the closing of Paseo de la Reforma and other major thoroughfares to car traffic on Sundays so that cyclists can enjoy hassle-free recreation once a week. He's installed bicycle-dispensing modules at key points around town, including the Zócalo and Bosque de Chapultepec. And aiming to boost the miniscule ranks of commuters (fewer than 1%) who use two-wheeled transportation to get to their jobs, he's offered breaks to companies that encourage their employees not to drive.

Ebrard doesn't just talk the talk, he rides the ride – once in a while. A resident of the trendy Condesa neighborhood, the mayor rides his bicycle to work in the center of town once a month, accompanied by his (perhaps less enthusiastic) entourage. Bicycle racks have been installed in the patio of the city government offices on the Zócalo for those staff members who show a more serious commitment.

For the moment, the focus appears to be more on recreational cycling than bicycle commuting as an alternative to cars. The lack of a viable bicycle-lane network or parking options, besides a continuing disregard by drivers for their nonmotorized counterparts, means cycling will remain a risky endeavor. Still, the message seems to be getting through on some level, as it's becoming increasingly common to see ordinary Chilangos riding their bikes around town. Or at least around Condesa.

isn't a common mode of transportation in the capital (except by delivery boys), cycling does seem to be catching on slowly. Bicycles can be a viable means to get around town and are often quicker and more pleasant than riding on overcrowded, recklessly driven buses. Although careless drivers and potholes can make DF cycling an 'extreme sport,' if you stay alert and keep off the major thoroughfares, it's manageable.

Bikes are loaned free from a module beside the Catedral Metropolitana (p56). Otherwise, you can rent a bicycle from a module in front of the Museo de la Antropología (p79).

A *ciclovía* (bicycle path) follows Av Chapultepec along a protected median from Bosque de Chapultepec to the Centro Histórico (though a detour through the streets of Colonia Roma is ignored by motorists). Another route runs along Paseo de la Reforma from the Auditorio Nacional to the Museo Rufino Tamayo. Follow the red stripe.

A more extensive trail runs from Av Ejército Nacional in Polanco through the Bosque de Chapultepec, skirting the Periférico freeway from La Feria to Av San Antonio, with several steep bridges passing over the freeways. The trail then continues south to the Parque Ecológico de la Ciudad de México, for a total distance of 90km.

BUS
AROUND TOWN
Mexico City's thousands of buses and peseros (also called microbuses or combis) operate from around 5am until 8pm or 9pm daily;

electric trolleybuses run until 11:30pm. Only a few routes run all night, notably those along Paseo de la Reforma and the metrobus along Av Insurgentes. This means you'll get anywhere by bus and/or metro during the day but will probably have to take a few taxis after hours.

Peseros are generally gray-and-green minibuses operated by private firms. They follow fixed routes, often starting or ending at metro stations, and will stop at virtually any street corner. Route information is randomly displayed on cards attached to the windshield. Fares are M$2.50 for trips of up to 5km, M$3 for 5km to 12km and M$4 for more than 12km. Add 20% to all fares between 11pm and 6am. Municipally operated full-size orange buses (labeled 'RTP') and trolleybuses only pick up at bus stops; fares are M$2 regardless of distance traveled.

Women-only bus routes now run along Paseo de la Reforma and other key routes. The option was recently implemented in response to complaints from female riders that they are often molested on overcrowded buses. Look for the sign, '*Exclusivo Damas.*'

Along Av Insurgentes, a special metrobus plies a dedicated lane from metro Indios Verdes in the northern DF down to the southern end of San Ángel, near the national university (at the time of writing, construction was underway to extend the line 8.5km further south to Tlalpan). These 18m-long wheelchair-accessible Volvo vehicles stop at metro-style stations in the middle of the street, spaced at three- to four-block intervals. Access is by prepaid card, issued by machines at the entrance to the platforms, and rides cost M$3.50 (regardless of distance traveled). Rechargeable cards (M$8) are placed on a sensor device for entry. The metrobus runs round the clock, though frequency is reduced to every 20 minutes between midnight and 5am, when the fare increases to M$5.

Pesero routes ply practically every street that crisscrosses the Centro Histórico grid, while electric-powered trolleybuses follow a number of the key *ejes* (priority roads) throughout the rest of the city.

IN & OUT OF TOWN

Mexico City has four long-distance bus terminals serving the four compass points.

Terminal de Autobuses del Norte (Map pp42–3; ☎ 5587-1552; www.centraldelnorte.com.mx; Av Cien Metros 4907, Colonia Magdalena de las Salinas; Ⓜ Autobuses del Norte) serves points north, including cities on the US border.

Terminal de Autobuses de Pasajeros de Oriente (TAPO; Map pp42–3; ☎ 5762-5894; Calz Ignacio Zaragoza 200, Colonia Diez de Mayo; Ⓜ San Lázaro), usually called TAPO, serves points east and southeast, including Puebla, Veracruz, Yucatán, Oaxaca and Chiapas.

Central de Autobuses del Poniente (Map pp42–3; ☎ 5271-0149; Sur 122, Colonia Real del Monte; Ⓜ Observatorio) is the departure point for buses heading west to Michoacán and shuttle services running to nearby Toluca.

Terminal Central del Sur (Map p95; ☎ 5689-9745; Av Taxqueña 1320; Ⓜ Tasqueña) serves Tepoztlán, Cuernavaca, Taxco, Acapulco and other southern destinations.

All terminals have baggage-check services or lockers (M$5 to M$12 per item), as well as tourist information modules, newsstands, card phones, internet terminals, ATMs and snack bars.

For certain destinations you have a choice of terminals, thus avoiding the need to travel across town for connections. Oaxaca, for example, is served by TAPO, Sur and Norte terminals. Guadalajara can be reached from Terminal Norte or Poniente.

There are also buses to nearby cities from the airport. Direct buses to Cuernavaca, Querétaro, Toluca, Puebla and Córdoba depart from platforms adjacent to Sala E. Ticket counters are on the upper level, off the food court.

GETTING INTO TOWN

The metro is convenient to the airport, though hauling luggage amid rush-hour crowds can be a Herculean task. Authorized taxis provide a painless, relatively inexpensive alternative.

Metro

The airport metro station is Terminal Aérea, on Línea 5 (yellow). It's 200m from the terminal: leave by the exit at the end of Sala A (domestic arrivals) and continue past the taxi stand, to the station.

To the city center, follow signs for '*Dirección Politécnico*'; at La Raza (seven stops away) change for Línea 3 (green) toward '*Dirección Universidad.*' Metro Hidalgo, at the west end of the Alameda, is three stops south; it's also a transfer point for Línea 2 (blue) to the Zócalo.

To get to the Zona Rosa from the airport, take Línea 5 to 'Pantitlán' the end of the line. Change for Línea 1 (pink) and get off at metro Insurgentes.

Arriving at the airport, take the Av Aeropuerto Municipal exit on the *Dirección Politécnico* side, and proceed directly to the terminal.

Taxi

Steer clear of street cabs outside the airport. Safe and reliable 'Transporte Terrestre' taxis, recognizable by their yellow doors and airplane logos, are controlled by a fixed-price ticket system.

Purchase taxi tickets from booths labeled 'Sitio 300,' located in Sala E1 (international arrivals), on your left as you exit customs, and by the Sala A1 (domestic arrivals) exit. Fares are determined by zones (shown on a map next to the booth). A ride to the Zócalo or Alameda Central is M$127, to the Zona Rosa or Plaza de la República M$152. One ticket is valid for up to four passengers and luggage that will fit in the trunk.

Taxi stands for the Sitio 300 taxis are outside Sala A and at the far end of the international terminal. Porters may offer to take your ticket and luggage the few steps to the taxi, but hold on to the ticket and hand it to the driver. Drivers won't expect a tip for the ride, but will of course welcome one.

To reserve a Transporte Terrestre taxi to the airport call ☎ 5571-9344; fares are slightly higher in this direction.

USEFUL BUS ROUTES

'Autobuses del Sur' & 'Autobuses del Norte' trolleybus Eje Central Lázaro Cardenas between north and south bus terminals (stops at Plaza de las Tres Culturas; Plaza Garibaldi; Bellas Artes/Alameda; metro Hidalgo)

'Metro Hidalgo-La Villa' bus or pesero Paseo de la Reforma between Auditorio Nacional or metro Chapultepec and Basílica de Guadalupe (stops at Zona Rosa; Av Insurgentes; Alameda/metro Hidalgo; Plaza Garibaldi; Plaza de las Tres Culturas)

'Metro Sevilla-P Masaryk' pesero Between Colonia Roma and Polanco via Av Álvaro Obregón and Av Presidente Masaryk (stops at metro Niños Héroes; Av Insurgentes; metro Sevilla; Leibnitz)

'Metro Tacubaya-Balderas-Escandón' pesero Between Centro Histórico and Condesa, westbound via Puebla, eastbound via Durango (stops at Plaza San Juan; metro Balderas; metro Insurgentes; Parque España; Av Michoacán)

Metrobus Runs north–south along Av Insurgentes from Metro Indios Verdes to San Ángel (stops at Paseo de la Reforma; metro Insurgentes; Colonia Roma; Parque México; metro Chilpancingo; Monumental Plaza México; Parque La Bombilla)

Check schedules by phoning the bus lines or by visiting their (sometimes functional) websites.

ADO Group (☎ 5133-2424, 800-702-80-00; www .ticketbus.com.mx) Destinations include Campeche, Cancún, Mérida, Oaxaca, Palenque, Puebla, San Cristóbal de las Casas, Veracruz, Villhermosa, Xalapa.

Estrella Blanca Group (☎ 5729-0707; www.estrella blanca.com.mx) Acapulco, Mazatlán, Monterrey, Puerto Escondido, Puerto Vallarta, Tijuana.

Estrella de Oro (☎ 5689-3955; www.estrelladeoro .mx, in Spanish) Acapulco, Taxco, Zihuatanejo.

Estrella Roja (☎ 5130-1800, 800-712-22-84; www .estrellaroja.com.mx, in Spanish) Puebla, Tepoztlán.

ETN (☎ 5089-9200, 800-800-0386; www.etn.com.mx) Guadalajara, Guanajuato, Querétaro, San Luis Potosi, San Miguel de Allende, Toluca, Uruapan.

Omnibus de México (☎ 5141-4300, 800-765-6636; www.odm.com.mx, in Spanish) Chihuahua, Durango, Saltillo, Tampico, Zacatecas.

Primera Plus (☎ 800-375-7587; www.primeraplus .com.mx, in Spanish) Guadalajara, Guanajuato, Morelia, Pátzcuaro, Querétaro, San Miguel de Allende, Uruapan.

Pullman de Morelos (www.pullman.com.mx, in Spanish) Cuernavaca.

You can pick up tickets beforehand at Ticketbus (☎ 5133-2424, 800-702-80-00; www.ticketbus.com.mx), a booking agency for over a dozen bus lines out of all four stations. (A 10% surcharge is added to the cost of the ticket, up to a maximum of M$50.) In addition to the Ticketbus locations below, a couple more are located inside the international-arrivals terminal at the airport. Outlets are generally open 9am or 10am to 7pm or 8pm Monday to Friday with an hour lunch break, and mornings only on Saturday.

Ticketbus also offers purchase by phone with Visa or Mastercard.

Buenavista (Map p71; Buenavista 9; Ⓜ Revolución)

Centro Histórico (Map pp48–9; Isabel la Católica 83E; Ⓜ Isabel la Católica)

Condesa (Map pp74–5; Iztaccíhuatl 6, cnr Insurgentes; Ⓜ Chilpancingo)

Polanco (Map p84; Av Presidente Masaryk, cnr Hegel; Ⓜ Polanco)

Reforma (Map pp74–5; Paseo de la Reforma 412; Ⓜ Sevilla) Across from La Diana Cazadora.

Roma Norte (Map pp92–3; Puebla 46; Ⓜ Cuauhtémoc)

Roma Norte (Map pp92–3; Mérida 156; Ⓜ Hospital General)

Zócalo (Map pp48–9; Turismo Zócalo, La Palma 34; Ⓜ Zócalo)

CAR & MOTORCYCLE

Driving

Touring Mexico City by car is strongly discouraged, unless you have a healthy reserve of stamina and patience. Even more than elsewhere in the country, traffic rules are seen as suggested behavior. Red lights may be run at will, no-turn signs are ignored and signals are seldom used. On occasion you may be hit by a bogus traffic fine, a routine means for traffic cops to increase their miserly salaries. Nevertheless, you may want to rent a car here for travel outside the city. Avoid parking on the street; most midrange and top-end hotels have guest garages.

To help combat pollution, Mexico City operates its 'Hoy No Circula' (Don't Drive Today) program, banning many vehicles from being driven in the city between 5am and

10pm on one day each week. Exempted from the restriction are cars with a *calcomanía de verificación* (emissions verification sticker), obtained under the city's vehicle-pollution assessment system.

For other vehicles (including foreign-registered ones), the last digit of the license plate number determines the day when they cannot circulate. Any car may operate on Saturday and Sunday.

Day	Prohibited last digits
Monday	5, 6
Tuesday	7, 8
Wednesday	3, 4
Thursday	1, 2
Friday	9, 0

RENTAL

Car-rental companies have offices at the airport, at bus stations and in the Zona Rosa. Rates generally start at about M$500 per day, but you will often do better by booking ahead online. For a list of rental agencies, check www.mexicocity.gob.mx, then click 'Transporte' and 'Renta de Autos.'

Avis (Map pp74–5; ☎ 5511-2228; Paseo de la Reforma 308; Ⓜ Insurgentes)

Thrifty (Map pp74–5; ☎ 5207-1100; Paseo de la Reforma 322; Ⓜ Insurgentes)

TAXI

Mexico City has several classes of taxi. Cheapest are the cruising street cabs, though they're not recommended due to the risk of assaults

(see p258). If you must hail a cab off the street, check that it has official taxi license plates. In 2007, the city government began issuing new plates that each have a chip in them for tracking the taxi. The number on the plate begins with a large letter 'A' followed by 5 numbers. All legitimate taxis, whether taken from the street, a taxi stand or a radio dispatcher, should have these plates. Also look for the *carta de identificación* (also called the *tarjetón*), a postcard-sized ID which should be displayed visibly inside the cab, and ensure that the driver matches the photo. If the cab you've hailed does not pass these tests, get another.

In cabs hailed off the street, fares are computed by *taxímetro* (meter), which should start at M$6 to M$7. The total cost of a 2km or 3km ride in moderate traffic – say, from the Zócalo to the Zona Rosa – should be M$40 to M$45. Between 11pm and 6am, add 20%.

A radio taxi costs two or three times as much, but the extra cost adds an immeasurable degree of security. When you phone, the dispatcher will tell you the cab number and the type of car. Hotels and restaurants can call a reliable cab for you.

Some reliable radio-taxi firms, available 24 hours, are listed below. Maps in this chapter show the locations of some key *sitios*.

Taxi-Mex (☎ 9171-8888, 5634-9912)

Taxis Radio Unión (☎ 5514-8124)

RET (☎ 8590-6720, 8590-6721)

Radio Maxi Seguridad (☎ 5768-8557, 5552-1376)

Sitio Parque México (☎ 5286-7129, 5286-7164)

DIRECTORY

BUSINESS HOURS

Government offices are typically open from 8am or 9am to 2pm or 3pm Monday to Friday. Banks operate 9am to 5pm Monday to Friday, and some stay open Saturdays from 9am to 1pm. Most other businesses are open from 9am to 8pm Monday to Saturday, and many stay open on Sundays, too. A few of the more traditional establishments still take a lunch break from 2pm to 3pm or 4pm, closing up for the day on Saturday.

Most museums close on Monday. On Sundays nearly all museums and archaeological sites are free, and the major ones can get very crowded. Some museums may technically limit free admission to Mexican nationals, though the rule is rarely enforced. A few may be free on other days, as noted in the Neighborhood listings.

For opening hours of drinking and eating establishments, see the corresponding chapter introductions.

CHILDREN

As elsewhere in Mexico, kids take center stage in the capital. Sunday is the big day when families go out to parks and museums and fill the restaurants at midday. Many theaters stage children's plays and puppet shows on weekends, and museums often organize hands-on activities for kids. Cartoons are a staple at cinemas around town, with weekend matinees at the Cineteca Nacional (p183), though keep in mind that children's films are often dubbed in Spanish.

Mexico City's numerous parks and plazas are usually buzzing with children's voices. Bosque de Chapultepec is the obvious destination, with the Papalote Museo del Niño (p81), La Feria (p81) and the Chapultepec Zoo (p79), not to mention several lakes with rowboat rentals. But also consider Condesa's Parque México (p86), where Sunday is family activities day. In Xochimilco, kids find the sensation of riding the gondolas through the canals as magical as any theme park.

Children are welcome at all kinds of accommodations and in virtually every café and restaurant – even in some cantinas, which are labeled '*familiar*' (family oriented, meaning children are allowed in).

See 'Top Picks for Children' in the Neighborhoods chapter (p73) for recommended sights and activities.

Children are likely to be excited and stimulated by the colors and bustle of Mexico City, but they may feel the effects of the altitude, the pollution, the noise and the heat more than grownups do. Take care to replace fluids if a child gets diarrhea, and be prepared for minor effects brought on by change of diet or water, or disrupted sleeping patterns. If your kids don't take to typical Mexican food, plenty of restaurants serve up 'international' food, with kiddie menus.

CLIMATE

Visitors who are accustomed to the heat of Mexico's beaches may be surprised by the temperate climate of Mexico City. At this altitude it rarely gets too hot, and even in the summer months you may need a sweater. The warmest months are April and May, before the rains start. From late May or early June through September warm, sunny days often change rapidly to cool, wet evenings. The chilliest time is between November and February, when thermal inversion is also likely to occur. This is also when air pollution tends to be at its worst.

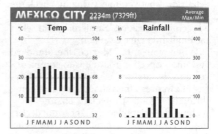

COURSES

Though Spanish-language students more often choose places like Cuernavaca or Oaxaca to work on their verb tenses, the capital offers boundless cultural and historical resources to complement your language studies, plus the chance to mingle with students of Latin America's largest university.

Centro de Enseñanza Para Extranjeros (Foreigners Teaching Center; Map p105; ☎ 5622-2467; www.cepe.unam.mx; Universidad 3002, Ciudad Universitaria) The national university (see p104) offers six-week intensive classes meeting three hours daily (US$340). Students who already speak Spanish may take courses on Mexican art and culture, which are taught in Spanish and run concurrently with the UNAM semester.

Centro Cultural Tepeticpac Tlahtolcalli (Map p64; ☎ 5518-2020; www.tepeticpac.com; Dr Mora 5; Ⓜ Hidalgo) If you'd like to brush up on your Náhuatl – or Mixtec or Otomí – this cultural center offers courses in indigenous languages. On Saturdays you can join workshops on Aztec dance, codex reading or *huehuetl* (indigenous drum) playing.

International House (Map p88; 5211-6500; www.ihmexico.com/eng/espext2.htm; Alfonso Reyes 224, Condesa) The Mexico City branch of the prestigious worldwide chain of language schools is located in Condesa. Classes meet for 20 hours weekly, with a maximum of six students per group (US$200 per week). The institute can arrange homestays.

For cooking courses see p134.

CUSTOMS REGULATIONS

Visitors are allowed to bring certain items into Mexico duty-free, including medicine for personal use, two still or video cameras, one portable computer, 10 DVDs, 30 music CDs, two mobile phones, portable sports equipment, and, if you're 18 or older, 3L of wine, beer or liquor and 400 cigarettes. For more details on what you may bring in, check the Mexican Customs website at www.aduanas.sat.gob.mx. Click on 'Pasajeros', then select the English-language version.

When you enter Mexico the standard customs-inspection routine is to complete a customs declaration form (which lists duty-free allowances), then choose between going through a goods-to-declare channel or a nothing-to-declare channel. Those not declaring items must pass a traffic signal. The signal responds randomly: a green light lets you pass without inspection, a red light means your baggage will be searched.

DISCOUNT CARDS

The ISIC student card, the IYTC card for travelers under 26, and the ITIC card for teachers can help you obtain reduced-price air tickets to or from Mexico at student- and youth-oriented travel agencies. Reduced prices on Mexican buses and at museums, archaeological sites and so on, are usually only for those with Mexican education credentials, but the aforementioned cards will sometimes get you a reduction. The ISIC card is the most widely recognized. A Hostelling International card will save you a few pesos in some hostels in Mexico City.

ELECTRICITY

Electrical current in Mexico is the same as in the USA and Canada: 110V, 60 cycles. Don't use European or Australian 220-240V appliances without a transformer (which will be built into an adjustable appliance). Mexico actually has several different types of electrical socket. If the plug on your appliance doesn't fit your Mexican socket, electrical goods shops have a variety of adapters and extensions. For more information about electricity and adaptors, see www.kropla.com.

EMBASSIES

All foreign embassies in Mexico reside in Mexico City. The following is a selective list. They often keep limited business hours – usually something like 9am or 10am to 1pm or 2pm Monday to Friday – and may close on both Mexican and their own national holidays. Many provide 24-hour emergency telephone contact.

Australia (Map p84; ☎ 1101-2200; www.mexico.embassy.gov.au; Rubén Darío 55; Ⓜ Polanco or Auditorio)

Belize (off Map p78; ☎ 5520-1274; www.mfa.gov.bz; Bernardo de Gálvez 215, Lomas de Chapultepec)

Canada (Map p84; ☎ 5724-7900; www.mexico.gc.ca; Schiller 529; Ⓜ Polanco)

Cuba (Map p84; ☎ 5280-8039; www.embacuba.com.mx; Avenida Presidente Masaryk 554; Ⓜ Polanco)

France (Map p84; ☎ 5282-9700; www.francia.org.mx; Campos Elíseos 339; Ⓜ Auditorio)

Germany (Map p84; ☎ 5283-2200; www.mexiko.diplo.de; Horacio 1506, Los Morales)

Guatemala (off Map p78; ☎ 5540-7520; embaguatemx@minex.gob.gt; Avenida Explanada 1025, Lomas de Chapultepec)

Ireland (Map p84; ☎ 5520-5803; embajada@irlanda.org.mx; Blvd Ávila Camacho 76-3)

Italy (Map pp42–3; ☎ 5596-3655; www.italian-embassy.org.ae/ambasciata_cittadelmessico; Paseo de las Palmas 1994, Lomas de Chapultepec)

Japan (Map pp74–5; ☎ 5211-0028; www.mx.emb-japan.go.jp; Paseo de la Reforma 395; Ⓜ Sevilla)

Netherlands (off Map p42–3; ☎ 5258-9921; www.paises bajos.com.mx; Av Vasco de Quiroga 3000, Edificio Calakmul, 7 piso, Santa Fe)

New Zealand (Map p84; ☎ 5283 9460; kiwimexico @prodigy.net.mx; Jaime Balmes 8, Piso 4, Los Morales)

Spain (Map p84; ☎ 5280-4383; www.mae.es /Consulados/Mexico/es/home; Galileo 114; Ⓜ Polanco)

UK Embassy (Map pp74–5; ☎ 5242-8500; www.embaja dabritanica.com.mx; Río Lerma 71; Ⓜ Insurgentes); Consulate General (☎ 5242-8500; Río Usumacinta 26; Ⓜ Insurgentes)

USA (Map pp74–5; ☎ 5080-2000; www.usembassy-mexico.gov; Paseo de la Reforma 305; Ⓜ Insurgentes)

EMERGENCY

Ambulance, Fire (☎ 060)

Cruz Roja (Red Cross; ☎ 5557-5757)

Hospital ABC (☎ emergency 5230-8161; www.abc hospital.com; Sur 136 No 116, Colonia Las Américas; Ⓜ Observatorio)

Hospital Ángeles Clínica Londres (Map p92–3; ☎ emergency 5229-8445; Durango 64, Colonia Roma; Ⓜ Cuauhtémoc)

HEALTH

It's relatively easy to stay healthy in Mexico City as long as you follow a few common-sense rules to protect yourself from food-borne illness, altitude sickness and air pollution.

Food- and water-borne illness

Mexico City's booming population and sinking infrastructure are a couple of the factors that have combined to create serious sanitation problems that can affect food and water. Most restaurants frequented by travelers are perfectly safe, but be highly selective when eating food from street vendors. If a street stand or restaurant looks clean and well run, the vendor is clean and healthy and follows sanitation rules, and the place is busy with lots of customers, then the food is probably safe. Generally speaking, vegetables and fruit should be washed with purified water or peeled, and dairy products that might contain unpasteurized milk should be avoided. Tap water in Mexico City is generally not safe to drink. Vigorous boiling for three minutes is the most effective means of water purification.

An easier option is to buy bottles of purified water to drink, which are inexpensive and available at supermarkets, street stalls and convenience stores.

Altitude & pollution

Although smog levels have improved over the last decade, Mexico City's air pollution can still be disagreeable, especially during the months from November to February, when thermal inversion traps contaminants and emissions close to the ground. The triple-whammy of the city's high altitude, air pollution and dry climate often causes sore throat, runny nose or eyes, light-headedness, insomnia, slight headaches and shortness of breath. To lessen the chance of altitude sickness, avoid over-exertion, eat light meals and take it easy on the alcohol. If you suffer from severe allergies, asthma, hypertension, and heart, lung or breathing problems, you should consult a doctor before your trip.

HOLIDAYS

Christmas–New Year and Semana Santa (Holy Week, the week leading up to Easter) are the chief Mexican holiday periods. While coastal resorts and other major tourist destinations are quite busy, these can be pleasantly quiet times in Mexico City. There's little point scheduling a business trip to the city between December 15 and January 6, or during the week either side of Easter. Many Mexicans also take holidays in July or August.

Banks, post offices, other offices and many shops are closed on the following days:

Año Nuevo (New Year's Day) January 1

Día de la Constitución (Constitution Day) February 5

Día de la Bandera (Day of the National Flag) February 24

Día del Nacimiento de Benito Juárez (Anniversary of Benito Juárez' birth) March 21

Día del Trabajo (Labor Day) May 1

Cinco de Mayo (anniversary of Mexico's 1862 victory over the French at Puebla) May 5

Día de la Independencia (Independence Day) September 16

Día de la Raza (commemorating Columbus' arrival in the Americas, and the founding of the Mexican mestizo) October 12

Día de la Revolución (Revolution Day) November 20

Día de Navidad (Christmas Day) December 25

INTERNET ACCESS

It's easy to get on the internet in Mexico City these days. For those traveling with a laptop computer, all top-end and many midrange hotels have wireless internet, although some may charge an extra fee (M$40 to M$70 per day) and others may have insecure, open networks. Even the least expensive places are likely to have a computer in the lobby where you can check email for a small price. All of the youth hostels have computers available for guests. Internet cafés abound, especially in the Zona Rosa and Colonias Roma and Condesa. The average rate is M$15 to $M20 per hour. The internet icon in the Sleeping chapter indicates that at least a computer console is available.

The most common local provider is Prodigy Infinitum offered by Telmex (www.telmex.com.mx).

LEGAL MATTERS

Mexican law is based on the Roman and Napoleonic codes, presuming an accused person is guilty until proven innocent.

The minimum jail sentence for possession of more than a token amount of any narcotic, including marijuana and amphetamines, is 10 months. As in most other countries, the purchase of controlled medication requires a doctor's prescription.

It's against Mexican law to take any firearm or ammunition into the country (even unintentionally) without a permit from a Mexican embassy or consulate.

Road travelers should expect occasional police or military checkpoints. They are normally looking for drugs, weapons or illegal migrants. Drivers found with drugs or weapons on board may have their vehicle confiscated and may be detained for months while their cases are investigated.

Useful warnings on Mexican law are found on the US Department of State website (www.travel.state.gov).

Getting Legal Help

Report crimes and get legal assistance at any of three offices of the Agencias del Ministerio Público (www.pgjdf.gob.mx) Centro Histórico (Map p64; ☎ 5346-8720, ext 16520; Victoria 76; Ⓜ Juárez); Plaza de la República (Map pp74–5 ☎ 5592-2677, ext 1114; Paseo de la Reforma 42; Ⓜ Hidalgo); Zona Rosa (Map pp74–5; ☎ 5345-5382; Amberes 54; Ⓜ Insurgentes). All offices are reportedly open between 9am and 5pm daily and have English-speaking personnel. They will help you with forms to report any incident, even if it's just for the purposes of an insurance claim, and give you a receipt number. To follow up your case online, go to the website, click on 'Denuncia los delitos', then 'Seguimiento de denuncias'.

If arrested, you have the right to contact your embassy or consulate. Consular officials can tell you your rights, provide lists of local lawyers, monitor your case, make sure you are treated humanely, and notify your relatives or friends – but they can't get you out of jail. By Mexican law, the longest a person can be detained by police without a specific accusation is 72 hours.

If Mexican police wrongfully accuse you of an infraction (as they have been known to do in the hope of obtaining a bribe), you can ask for the officer's identification, to speak to a superior or to be shown documentation about the law you have supposedly broken. You can also note the officer's name, badge number, vehicle number and department (federal, state or municipal). Pay any traffic fines at a police station and get a receipt, then make your complaint at Sectur or any of the above Agencias del Ministerio Público.

MAPS

Maps handed out free by Mexico City tourist modules include useful plans of the Centro Histórico and some other key neighborhoods, along with a metro map. Those needing more detail should pick up a Guía Roji fold-out map of Mexico City (M$80), or a Guía Roji Ciudad de México street atlas (M$215), updated annually, with a comprehensive index. Find them at Sanborns stores and at larger newsstands.

Mexico's national geographical institute, INEGI (Map pp48–9; ☎ 5512-1873; www.inegi.gob.mx; Balderas 71; 🕒 9am-4pm Mon-Fri; Ⓜ Juárez), publishes topographical maps covering the whole country (subject to availability). Another outlet is at the airport (☎ 5786-0212; Sala C; 🕒 8am-8pm), and INEGI headquarters are in Colonia Mixcoac (Map pp42–3; ☎ 5278-1000, ext 1207; Patriotismo 711; 🕒 8:30am-9pm Mon-Fri; Ⓜ Mixcoac).

MEDICAL SERVICES

For recommendation of a doctor, a dentist or a hospital, call your embassy or Sectur (☎ 078), the tourism ministry. An extended list of Mexico City hospitals and English-speaking physicians (with their credentials), in PDF format, is available on the website of the US embassy (www.usembassy-mexico.gov/medical_lists.html). A private doctor's consultation generally costs between M$500 and M$1000.

Hospital ABC (American British Cowdray Hospital; Map pp42–3; ☎ 5230-8000, ☎ emergency 5230-8161; www .abchospital.com; Sur 136 No 116, Colonia Las Américas; Ⓜ Observatorio) One of the best hospitals in Mexico, with an outpatient section and English-speaking staff.

Hospital Ángeles Clínica Londres (Map pp92–3; ☎ 5229-8400, emergency 5229-8445; www.hospital angelesclinicalondres.com; Durango 64; Ⓜ Cuauhtémoc)

The pharmacies that are found inside Sanborns stores are among the most reliable, as are the following.

Farmacia de Ahorros (Map pp92–3; ☎ 5264-3128; Yucatán 40; 🕒 24hr; 🚇 Metrobus Álvaro Obregón)

Farmacia París (Map pp48–9; ☎ 5709-5349; República de El Salvador 97, Centro; 🕒 8am-10:30pm Mon-Sat, 10am-9pm Sun; Ⓜ Isabel La Católica) Offers allopathic, homeopathic and herbal remedies.

Médicor (Map p64; ☎ 5512-0431; Independencia 66; 🕒 10am-8pm Mon-Fri, to 6:30pm Sat; Ⓜ Juárez) Specializing in homeopathic medicines.

MONEY

Mexico's currency is the peso, which can be denoted by 'M$', 'MX$' or 'MN' (for *moneda nacional*). Any prices quoted in US dollars will normally be written 'US$5' or '5 USD' to avoid misunderstanding. The peso is divided into 100 centavos. Coins come in denominations of 20 and 50 centavos and one, two, five, 10, 20 and 100 pesos. There are notes of 20, 50, 100, 200, 500 and 1000 pesos.

For exchange rates, see inside the front cover. For information on costs, see p13.

The most convenient form of money in Mexico is a major international credit card or debit card – preferably two if you have them. Visa, MasterCard and American Express cards can be used to obtain cash simply from ATMs in Mexico, and are accepted for payment by most airlines, car-rental companies and travel agents, plus many upper midrange and top-end hotels, and some restaurants and stores. Occasionally there's a surcharge for paying by card, or a discount for paying cash. Making a purchase by credit card normally gives you a more favorable exchange rate than exchanging money at a bank, and isn't subject to commission, but you'll normally have to pay your card issuer a 'foreign exchange' transaction fee of around 2.5%.

As a backup to credit or debit cards, it's a good idea to take a little cash and a few traveler's checks. US dollars are easily the most exchangeable foreign currency in Mexico. Euros, British pounds and Canadian dollars, in cash or as traveler's checks, are accepted by most banks and some *casas de cambio* (exchange houses).

Be discreet when changing money or making payments and avoid counting currency in public places or flashing cash when making purchases. For additional tips on keeping your money safe, see p257.

ATMs

ATMs (*caja permanente* or *cajero automático* in Spanish) are plentiful in Mexico City, and are the easiest source of cash. You can use major credit cards and some bank cards, such as those on the Cirrus and Plus systems, to withdraw pesos from ATMs. The exchange rate that banks use for ATM withdrawals is normally better than the 'tourist rate' for currency exchange – though that advantage may be negated by extra handling fees and interest charges.

To avoid the risk of 'card cloning,' use ATMs only in secure indoor locations, not those in stand-alone booths. Card cloners obtain your card number and PIN by means of hidden cameras then make a copy of your card and use it to withdraw cash from your account.

Changing Money

You can exchange cash and traveler's checks in banks or at *casas de cambio*. Banks go through a more time-consuming procedure than *casas de cambio*, and usually have shorter exchange hours. There is often a better rate for *efectivo* (cash) than for *documento* (traveler's checks).

The greatest concentration of ATMs, banks and *casas de cambio* is on Paseo de la Reforma between the Monumento a Cristóbal Colón and the Monumento a la Independencia, but there are others all over town.

AMERICAN EXPRESS

American Express (Map pp74–5; ☎ 5207-7049; Paseo de la Reforma 350; ✆ 9am-6pm Mon-Fri, to 1pm Sat; 🚍 Pesero 'La Villa' or 'Metro Chapultepec')

CASAS DE CAMBIO

Centro de Cambios y Divisas (Map pp74–5; ☎ 5705-5656; Paseo de la Reforma 87F; ✆ 8:30am-7:30pm Mon-Fri, 9am-5pm Sat, 9am-2:30pm Sun; 🚍 Pesero 'La Villa' or 'Metro Chapultepec')

Cambios Centro Histórico (Map pp48–9; ☎ 5512-9536; Madero 13; ✆ 9:30am-6:30pm Mon-Sat, 10am-6pm Sun; Ⓜ Bellas Artes)

Tipping

In general, workers in small, cheap restaurants don't expect much in the way of tips, while those in expensive establishments expect you to be lavish in your largesse. Workers in the tourism and hospitality industries often depend on tips to supplement miserable basic wages. In restaurants and hotels frequented by high rollers, tipping is up to US levels of 15%; elsewhere 10% is usually plenty. If you stay a few days in one place, you should leave up to 10% of your room costs for the people who have kept your room clean (assuming they have). A porter in a midrange hotel will be happy with M$10 a bag. Taxi drivers don't generally expect tips unless they provide some special service. Car-parking attendants expect a tip of M$3 to M$5, and the same is standard for gas-station attendants.

NEWSPAPERS & MAGAZINES

Mexico City's recently resuscitated English-language daily newspaper, *The News*, is sold at many downtown newsstands, as well as by several of the bookstores mentioned in the Shopping chapter. The paper covers the main items of Mexican and foreign news, has long stock exchange listings and a few interesting Mexico features, and will keep you in touch with US, Canadian and European sports. Inside Mexico (www.insidemex.com) is a free monthly in English that covers expat life; pick up a copy at cafés and hotels around town.

ORGANIZED TOURS

Journeys Beyond the Surface (☎ 5922-0123; www .travelmexicocity.com.mx) Offers personalized walking tours on aspects of the DF experience, with a get-off-the-beaten track attitude. Enhanced by expert commentary, tours may cover pre-Hispanic architecture, the muralist movement, or life in low-income neighborhoods, depending on participants' interests.

Mexico Soul & Essence (☎ 5564-8457; www.mexicosoul andessence.com) Culinary-cultural excursions by articulate bicultural guides with a passionate interest in their subject. Tours combine browsing markets for ingredients, kitchen instruction with well-regarded chefs, and dining in some of the city's finest restaurants. Cooking courses are also offered (see p134).

Recorridos Dominicales (☎ 5662-8228, ext 526; www .cultura.df.gob.mx/culturama/visitasguiadas; ✆ 10:45am-1pm Sun) Sunday walking tours organized by the DF cultural ministry. Routes vary weekly, with participants divided between 10 guides; the website lists the week's destination and departure point. Commentary is in Spanish only but even non-Spanish speakers may enjoy seeing some of the little-visited places on the agenda, as well as meeting the middle-class Chilangos who generally attend. There's no cost, but it's customary to tip the guides M$20 or so.

Tranvía (☎ 5491-1615; adult/child M$35/25; ✆ 10am-5pm) Motorized version of a vintage streetcar runs a 45-minute circuit of the Centro Histórico, with guides relating fascinating bits of lore (in Spanish) along the way. On Thursday night there's a special cantina tour (M$100 including wine, reservation required). Tours depart from Av Juárez by Bellas Artes. A similar tour operates in Coyoacán, departing from in front of the Museo Nacional de Culturas Populares.

Turibús Circuito Turístico (☎ 5133-2488; www.turibus .com.mx in Spanish; adult/child 4-12 M$100/50, 2-day pass M$140/70; ✆ 9am-9pm) Provides tourist-eye view of the key areas. The total *recorrido* (route) lasts about three hours, but you can get off and back on the red double-decker bus at any designated stop along the way, which are marked by red banners. Buses pass every 30 minutes or so, stopping at the Auditorio Nacional and the west side of the cathedral, among other places. Tickets are sold on board. The fare includes headphones for recorded explanations in English, French, Italian, German or Japanese.

POST

An airmail letter or postcard weighing up to 20g costs M$10.50 to the US or Canada, M$13 to Europe or South America, and M$14.50 to the rest of the world. Items between 20g and 50g cost M$18, M$21 and M$23. *Certificado* (registered) service costs an extra M$20. Mark airmail items 'Vía Aérea.' Delivery times (outbound and inbound) are variable. An airmail letter from Mexico to the USA or Canada (or vice-versa) should take somewhere between four and 14 days to arrive. Mail to or from Europe takes between one and two weeks.

Oficinas de correos (post offices) are typically open from 8am to 6pm Monday to Friday, and 9am to 1pm Saturday. You can receive letters and packages care of a post office if your mail is addressed to the post office's *lista de correos* (mail list), or poste restante. In the former case, a list of mail recipients is posted; in the latter, you'll need to ask a postal clerk to check. Mail addressed as follows should arrive at the central post office:

Monica CHASE (last name in capitals)
Lista de Correos (or Poste Restante)
Correo Central
México
DF 06010
MEXICO

To claim your mail, present your passport or other identification. There's no charge, but many post offices only hold *lista* mail for 10 days before returning it to the sender.

For assured and speedy delivery, you can use one of the more expensive international courier services, such as UPS (☎ 800-902-92-00; www.ups.com), Federal Express (☎ 800-900-11-00; www.fedex.com) or Mexico's Estafeta (☎ 800-903-35-00; www.estafeta.com). Packages up to 500g cost up to about M$350 to the US or Canada, or M$450 to Europe.

Post Offices

Palacio Postal (Map pp48–9; ☎ 5521-1408; Tacuba 1; Ⓜ Bellas Artes) The stamp windows, marked '*estampillas,*' stay open beyond normal post office hours (until 8pm Monday to Friday, and on Sunday). Even if you don't need stamps, check out the sumptuous interior (see p55).

Other post-office branches, scattered around town, open 9am to 3pm Monday to Friday, 9am to 1pm Saturday, unless noted otherwise.

Cuauhtémoc (Map pp74–5; ☎ 5207-7666; Río Tiber 87; Ⓜ Insurgentes)

Plaza de la República (Map pp71; ☎ 5592-1783; Arriaga 11; Ⓜ Revolución)

Zócalo (Map pp48–9; ☎ 5512-3661; Plaza de la Constitución 7; Ⓜ Zócalo) To the west of the square, inside an arcade of jewelry shops.

Zona Rosa (Map pp74–5; ☎ 5514-3029; Londres 208; ⏱ 9am-5pm Mon-Fri, to 1pm Sat; Ⓜ Sevilla)

RADIO

Of the dozens of radio stations broadcast in Mexico City, the following government-run or independent stations feature especially interesting programming. All can be heard online as well.

Radio Educación (1040AM; www.radioeducacion.edu.mx) Best place to hear Mexican folk and regional music, as well as interviews and programs on political issues. Run by the national education ministry (SEP).

Radio Horizonte (107.9 FM; www.horizonte.imer.com. mx) Mostly jazz, including Cuban and Brazilian varieties, plus some blues and salsa. BBC jazz program (in Spanish) on Sundays.

Radio Ibero (90.9 FM; ibero909.fm) *Rock en español*, presented by students from the Universidad Iberoamericana.

Reactor (105.7 FM; www.reactor.imer.com.mx) Mexican indie scene, featuring some of the upstart bands who perform at Multiforo Alicia (p173) and the Chopo street market (p123).

To hear news and sports updates in English, tune in to Radio Imagen (90.5 FM) at 5:30am Monday to Saturday and 11pm Sunday to Friday.

SAFETY

Mexico City is generally portrayed as an extremely crime-ridden city, so first-time visitors are often surprised at how safe and human it feels. While the incidence of street crime remains too significant to deny the risks – four kidnappings, 70 car thefts and 55 muggings a day in 2006 – there is no need to walk in fear whenever you step outside. A few precautions greatly reduce any dangers.

Robberies happen most often in areas frequented by foreigners, including the Bosque de Chapultepec, around the Museo Nacional de Antropología and the Zona Rosa. Be on your guard at the airport and bus stations, and remember to keep your bag between your feet when checking in. Avoid pedestrian underpasses that are empty or nearly so. Crowded metro cars and buses are favorite haunts of pickpockets. Stay alert and keep your hand on your wallet and you'll be fine.

Unless absolutely necessary, avoid carrying ATM cards, credit cards or large amounts of cash. Most importantly, if you become a robbery victim, don't resist. Give the perpetrator your valuables rather than risking injury or death.

A far more immediate danger is traffic, which statistically takes more lives in the capital than street crime, though things have improved slightly in recent years with the installation of timed crossing signals at major intersections. Obvious as it sounds, always look both ways when crossing streets. Some one-way streets have bus lanes running counter to the traffic flow, and traffic on some divided streets runs in just one direction. Never assume that a green light means it's safe to cross, as cars may turn left into your path. It is useful to take the 'safety in numbers' approach, crossing with other pedestrians.

Despite efforts to remove them, *ambulantes* (mobile street vendors) still clog many downtown streets, impeding movement along the sidewalk and forcing you to walk in the street. Attempting to move through the throngs makes you more susceptible to pickpockets. Metro riders have to contend with the blaring speakers of vendors of pirated CDs.

Expect to be approached by beggars almost anywhere in town, but especially in the Zona Rosa, Condesa, or wherever disposable income is conspicuously spent.

Taxi Crime

Although not as prevalent a danger as in the 1990s, taxi assaults do still occur and visitors are strongly advised to take precautions. Many victims have hailed a cab on the street and been robbed by armed accomplices of the driver. In particular, taxis parked in front of nightclubs or restaurants should be avoided, unless specifically authorized by the management. Rather than taking the risk of hailing cruising cabs, phone a radio *sitio* (taxi service). See p250 for a list of recommended companies.

TAXES & REFUNDS

Mexico's *impuesto de valor agregado* (IVA; value-added tax) is levied at 15%. By law the tax must be included in virtually any price quoted to you, and should not be added afterward. Signs in stores and notices on restaurant menus often state 'IVA incluido.' Occasionally they state instead 'IVA no incluido' or 'más el IVA' (IVA must be added to the quoted prices).

TELEPHONE

Local calls are cheap; international calls can be expensive, but needn't be, especially with widely available discount cards. There are at least six ways you can make phone calls in Mexico:

Calling from your hotel Can be expensive as hotels charge what they like for this service

Cell phones Generally expensive

Internet telephony Services like Skype are the cheapest option if you have an account

Locutorios and casetas de teléfono Call offices where an on-the-spot operator connects the call for you; these can be cheaper than the Telmex card phones

Prepaid long-distance discount cards Cheaper than Telmex card phones or locutorios for long-distance and international calls, and can be used from most phones

Telmax public card phones Operated by the country's main, almost monopolistic, phone operator; these are common and fairly easy to use.

Cell Phones

Like other Mexican phone numbers, every Mexican *teléfono celular* (cell phone) has an area code (usually the code of the city it was bought in). The area code and the phone's number total 10 digits. When calling a cell phone from a landline, you dial ☎ 044 before the 10 digits if the cell phone's area code is the same as the area code you are dialing from; and ☎ 045 if the cell phone has a different area code. From cell phone to cell phone, just dial the 10-digit number. To call a Mexican cell phone from another country, dial your international access code, followed by the Mexican country code (☎ 52), then 1, then the 10-digit number.

If you want to use a cell phone in Mexico, the three main operators – Telcel (www.telcel.com), IUSACell (www.iusacell.com.mx) and Movistar (www.movistar.com.mx) – all sell phones for around M$400 to M$800 including a charger and some call credit. For further credit you can buy top-up cards for M$100 or more. Telcel is the most widespread network, with many sales outlets (including one at Mexico City airport) and coverage almost everywhere that has a significant population. Telcel top-up cards are widely available from newsstands and minimarts. Mexican cell phones generally cannot be used in other countries.

Roaming with your own cell phone from home in Mexico is possible if you have a GSM phone, but is generally very expensive. Much cheaper is to buy a local SIM card or 'chip' from a Telcel or Movistar outlet. You can usually top these up online.

Collect Calls

A *llamada por cobrar* (collect call) can cost the receiving party much more than if they call you, so you may prefer to pay for a quick call to the other party to ask them to call you back. If you do need to make a collect call, you can do so from card phones without a card. Call an operator on ☎ 020 for domestic calls, or ☎ 090 for international calls, or use a 'home country direct' service, through which you make an international collect call via an operator in the country you're calling. The Mexican term for 'home country direct' is *país directo*. Mexican international operators may know the access numbers for some countries, but it's best to get this information from your home country before you leave.

Prefixes & Codes

If you're calling a landline number in Mexico City, simply dial the local eight-digit number.

To call a landline number in another town or city in Mexico, you need to dial the long-distance prefix ☎ 01, followed by the area code (two digits for Mexico City, Guadalajara and Monterrey; three digits for everywhere else) and then the local number. For example, to call from Mexico City to Oaxaca, dial ☎ 01, then the Oaxaca area code ☎ 951, then the seven-digit local number.

The area codes for most Mexican cities and towns are listed in the front section of the Mexico City phone directory. Alternatively, go to www.telmex.com/mx/hogar/ld_clavesld .jsp and input the name of the state and town you're calling.

To make an international call, dial the international prefix ☎ 00, followed by the country code, the area code and the local number. For example, to call New York City from Mexico, dial ☎ 00, then the US country code ☎ 1, then the New York City area code ☎ 212, then the local number.

To call a landline number in Mexico from another country, dial your international access code, then the Mexico country code ☎ 52, then the area code and the number.

Public Card Phones

These can be found on virtually every street corner in town. By far the most common, and most reliable on costs, are those marked with the name of the country's biggest phone company, Telmex. To use a Telmex card phone you need a phone card known as a *tarjeta Ladatel*. These are sold at kiosks and shops everywhere – look for the blue-and-yellow '*Ladatel*' signs. The cards come in denominations of M$30, M$50 and M$100.

Calls from Telmex card phones cost M$1 per minute for local calls; M$4 per minute long-distance within Mexico; M$5 per minute to the USA (except Alaska and Hawaii) or Canada; M$10 per minute to Central America; and M$20 to M$25 per minute to the rest of the world. Calls to cell phones are M$3.12 per minute (local) or M$6.12 per minute (long distance).

Toll-Free & Operator Numbers

Mexican toll-free numbers (☎ 800 followed by seven digits) always require the ☎ 01 prefix. You can call most of these and emergency numbers from Telmex pay phones without inserting a telephone card.

US and Canadian toll-free numbers are ☎ 800 or ☎ 888 followed by seven digits. Some of these can be reached from Mexico (dial ☎ 00 1 before the 800), but you may have to pay a charge for the call.

For a domestic operator in Mexico, dial ☎ 020; for an international operator, dial ☎ 090. For Mexican directory information, dial ☎ 040.

TIME

Mexico City – like all of Mexico except a few western states – is on Hora del Centro (Central Time), which is the same as US Central Time. This is GMT minus six hours, and GMT minus five hours during *horario de verano* (daylight saving time), which runs from the first Sunday in April to the last Sunday in October.

TOILETS

Use of the bathroom is free at Sanborns stores. Public toilets are also found inside most market buildings; look for the 'WC' signs.

Standards of hygiene may vary at these latter facilities, and a fee of M$3 to M$5 is usually charged. Toilet paper is dispensed by an attendant on request, or may be taken from a common roll outside the stalls.

TOURIST INFORMATION

The Mexico City Ministry of Tourism has modules in key areas, as well as at the airport and four bus stations. Attendants can answer your queries on Mexico City and distribute a decent map and practical guide, free of charge. At least one staff member should speak English.

The following offices are all open from 9am to 6pm daily, unless otherwise noted.

Antropología (Map p64; ☎ 5286-3850; Paseo de la Reforma; Ⓜ Auditorio) At the entry to the Museo Nacional de Antropología.

Basílica de Guadalupe (Map pp42–3; ☎ 5748-2085; Plaza de las Américas 1; Ⓜ La Villa-Basilica)

Bellas Artes (Map p64; ☎ 5518-2799; cnr Juárez & Peralta; Ⓜ Bellas Artes)

Catedral (Map pp48–9; ☎ 5518-1003; Monte de Piedad; Ⓜ Zócalo) West of the Catedral Metropolitana.

Del Ángel (Map pp74–5; ☎ 5208-1030; Paseo de la Reforma & Florencia; Ⓜ Insurgentes) On the Zona Rosa side of Monumento a la Independencia.

San Ángel (Map p101; Plaza San Jacinto; ⏲ 10am-6pm Sat & Sun; Ⓜ Miguel Angel de Quevedo)

Templo Mayor (Map pp48–9; ☎ 5512-8977; Seminario; Ⓜ Zócalo) On the east side of Catedral Metropolitana.

Xochimilco (Map pp112–13; ☎ 5653-5209; Mercado) At the Nativitas boat landing. There are additional tourism modules at other landings, open Saturday and Sunday only.

Additionally, these city *delegaciones* (urban governmental subdivisions) operate information offices:

Coyoacán (Map p95; ☎ 5658-0221; Jardín Hidalgo 1; ⏲ 9am-8pm Mon-Fri, 8am-8pm Sat & Sun; Ⓜ Viveros) Inside the Casa de Cortés.

Xochimilco (Map pp112–13; ☎ 5676-0810; Pino 36; ⏲ 9am-9pm Mon-Fri, 8am-8pm Sat & Sun) Off Jardín Juárez.

The office of El Corazón de México (Map pp48–9; ☎ 5518-1869; www.elcorazondemexico.com.mx, in Spanish; Gante 15; ⏲ 10am-6pm; Ⓜ San Juan de Letrán) provides information on these central Mexican states: Hidalgo, Morelos, Michoacán, Guerrero and Estado de México.

The national tourism ministry, Sectur (Map p84; ☎ 3002-6300, toll-free 078; Presidente Masaryk 172; ⏲ 8am-6pm Mon-Fri, 10am-3pm Sat; Ⓜ Polanco), hands out stacks of brochures on the entire country, though you're better off at the above modules for up-to-date information about the capital.

TRAVELERS WITH DISABILITIES

Mexico City is not yet very disability-friendly, though some hotels and restaurants (mostly towards the top end of the market), and some museums and archaeological sites now provide wheelchair access. Museums and hotels with disabled access are indicated on the DF Tourism Ministry's website (www.mexicocity.gob.mx). The absence of formal facilities is partly compensated by Mexicans' helpful attitudes toward others; special arrangements are gladly improvised.

Mobility International USA (☎ 541-343-1284; www.miusa.org) advises travelers with disabilities on mobility issues and runs exchange programs. Its website includes international databases of exchange programs and disability organizations, with several Mexican organizations listed.

In the UK, Radar (☎ 020-7250-3222; www.radar.org.uk) is run by and for people with disabilities. Its website has links to good travel and holiday sites.

Other good sources for travelers with disabilities include MossRehab ResourceNet (www.mossresourcenet.org), Access-able Travel Source (www.access-able.com) and Disability Travel and Recreation Resources (www.makoa.org/travel.htm).

VISAS

Every tourist must have a Mexican government tourist card, which is easy to obtain (see opposite). Some nationalities also need to obtain visas. Because the regulations sometimes change, it's wise to confirm them with a Mexican embassy or consulate before you go. The websites of some Mexican consulates, including the London consulate (portal.sre.gob.mx /conreinounido) and the Los Angeles consulate (www.sre.gob.mx/losangeles) give useful information on visas and similar matters. The rules are also summarized on the website of Mexico's Instituto Nacional de Migración (INM, National Migration Institute; www.inami.gob.mx). The Lonely Planet website (www.lonelyplanet.com) has links to updated visa information.

Citizens of the 27 EU countries, Argentina, Australia, Canada, Chile, Iceland, Israel, Japan, New Zealand, Norway, Switzerland and the USA are among those who do not need visas to enter Mexico as tourists. The list changes sometimes; check well ahead of travel with your local Mexican embassy or consulate. Visa procedures, for those who need them, can take several weeks and you may be required to apply in your country of residence or citizenship.

Immigration officers won't usually keep you waiting any longer than it takes to flick through your passport and enter your length of stay on your tourist card. Remain patient and polite, even if procedures are slow. Anyone traveling to Mexico via the USA should be sure to check US visa and passport requirements.

Passports

US and Canadian tourists can enter Mexico without a passport if they have official photo identification, such as a driver's license, plus some proof of their citizenship such as an original birth certificate. But to return to or transit the USA by air, a passport or other secure travel document such as a NEXUS card is required.

To return to or transit the USA by land or sea, Americans and Canadians must present either a passport, or other documents proving identity and citizenship (for example driver's license and birth certificate), or the recently introduced US passport card, or a NEXUS or other 'trusted traveler' card. Canadians flying back from Mexico to Canada are advised to carry a passport. Further information is available on the websites of the US State Department (travel.state.gov), US Customs & Border Protection (www.cbp.gov), the US Department of Homeland Security (www.dhs.gov) and Canada's Foreign Affairs Ministry (voyage.gc.ca).

In any case it's much better to travel to Mexico with a passport because officials of all countries are used to passports and may delay people who have other documents. In Mexico you will often need your passport to change money and check into hotels.

All citizens of countries other than the US and Canada should have a passport that's valid for at least six months after they arrive in Mexico.

Non-US citizens passing (even in transit) through the USA on the way to or from Mexico, or visiting Mexico from the USA, should also check the passport and visa requirements for the USA.

Tourist Card & Tourist Fee

The Mexican tourist card – officially the *forma migratoria para turista* (FMT) – is a brief card document that you must fill out and get stamped by Mexican immigration when you enter Mexico, and keep till you leave. It's available at official border crossings, international airports and ports, and often from airlines, travel agencies and Mexican consulates.

One section of the card deals with the length of your stay in Mexico, and this section is filled out by the immigration officer. The maximum possible stay is 180 days, but immigration officers sometimes put a lower number (as little as 15 or 30 days in some cases) unless you tell them specifically what you need. It's advisable to ask for more days than you think you'll need, in case you are delayed or change your plans.

Though the tourist card itself is free of charge, it brings with it the obligation to pay the tourist fee of US$22, called the *derecho para no inmigrante* (DNI, nonimmigrant fee). The exact amount of the fee in pesos fluctuates with exchange rates. If you enter Mexico by air, the fee is included in your airfare. If you enter by land, you must pay the fee at a bank in Mexico at any time before you reenter the frontier zone on your way out of Mexico (or before you check in at an airport to fly out of Mexico). Most Mexican border posts have on-the-spot bank offices where you can pay the DNI fee immediately. When you pay at a bank, your tourist card will be stamped to prove that you have paid.

Look after your tourist card because it may be checked when you leave the country. You can be fined for not having it.

A tourist card only permits you to engage in what are considered to be tourist activities (including sports, health, artistic and cultural activities). If the purpose of your visit is to work (even as a volunteer), to report or to study, or to participate in humanitarian aid or human-rights observation, you may well need a visa. If you're unclear, check with a Mexican embassy or consulate.

EXTENSIONS & LOST CARDS

If the number of days given on your tourist card is less than the maximum 180 days, its validity may be extended, one or more times, up to the maximum. To get a card extended you have to apply to the Instituto Nacional de Migración (INM; Map p84; ☎ 2581-0100; Av Ejército Nacional 862; ☺ 9am-1:30pm Mon-Fri). The procedure costs around M$200. You'll need your passport, your tourist card and photocopies of the important pages of these documents.

If you lose your card or need further information, contact the Sectur tourist office (☎ 078, 800-987-82-24), or your embassy or consulate. Any of these should be able to give you an official note to take to the INM office, which will issue a replacement for a cost of about M$450.

WOMEN TRAVELERS

Gender equalization in Mexico has come a long way in a few decades, and the capital is certainly among the more progressive environments. It's no longer unusual for women to take prominent political and corporate roles, and once male-only domains like cantinas and pool halls are generally open to all. Foreign women usually have a great time in Mexico City, whether traveling with companions or solo.

That said, it's wise to remember that many Mexicans still believe in the difference between the sexes (rather than the equality). In general Mexican men are extremely polite, but lone women should expect a few catcalls and attempts to chat them up. Often these men only want to talk to you, but you can discourage unwanted attention by avoiding eye contact (wear sunglasses), dressing modestly, moving confidently and speaking coolly but politely if you are addressed and feel that you must respond. Wearing a wedding ring can prove helpful too. Don't put yourself in peril by doing things that Mexican women would not do, such as challenging a man's masculinity, drinking alone in a cantina, walking alone through empty streets at night, or going alone to isolated places. Keep a clear head. Excessive alcohol will make you vulnerable. For moral support, and company if you want it, head for accommodations where you're likely to meet other travelers (such as backpacker hostels and popular hotels), and join group excursions and activities.

During rush hours, the metro maintains women-only cars at the front of trains to discourage molestation amidst such heavily crowded conditions. A recent initiative by the DF government also mandates buses exclusively for female passengers on certain routes, notably along Paseo de Reforma. Look for the sign, 'Exclusivo damas,' posted on the windshield.

WORK

Mexicans themselves need jobs, and people who enter Mexico as tourists are not legally allowed to take employment. The many expats working in Mexico have usually been posted there by their companies or organizations with all the necessary papers.

English-speakers (and a few German- or French-speakers) may find teaching jobs in language schools, *preparatorias* (high schools) or universities, or can offer personal tutoring. Mexico City is probably the best place to get English-teaching work. The pay is low, but you can live on it. The News and Craig's List (mexico city.en.craigslist.com.mx) are good sources for job opportunities. Pay rates for personal tutoring are rarely more than M$150 an hour. Positions in high schools or universities are more likely to become available at the beginning of each new term; language schools tend to offer short courses, so teaching opportunities with them may come up more often.

A foreigner working in Mexico normally needs a permit or a government license, but a school will often pay a foreign teacher in the form of a *beca* (scholarship), and thus circumvent the law, or the school's administration will procure the appropriate papers.

Volunteering

A great way to engage with Mexican communities and contribute something other than tourist dollars is to do some volunteer work. Many organizations and projects can use your services for periods from a few hours to a year or more.

A good place to find out about what's available is the Casa de los Amigos (p205), a Quaker-run guesthouse in the Plaza de la República area which hosts visiting NGO staff and organizes workshops on nonviolent conflict resolution and economic justice. The Casa's Peace and Service Resource Center maintains a file of current volunteer opportunities and you can discuss the options with knowledgeable staff, look at recent reviews of volunteer stints written by volunteers, and meet people involved in similar projects. The Casa also has informal relationships with other Mexico

City NGOs that do peace and human rights work and can help people get connected with a group. Furthermore, it hires volunteers to carry out its own programs (Spanish language skills are required.)

Cuernavaca-based Por Un Mejor Hoy (www.hoy community.org) is specifically geared to travelers who want to combine volunteer work in varied community projects with cultural immersion and sightseeing. A one-week stay including accommodation and breakfast costs US$300.

VOLUNTEER DIRECTORIES

These sources are good places to start looking for volunteer opportunities throughout Mexico:

Idealist.org (www.idealist.org)

Transitions Abroad (www.transitionsabroad.com)

Volunteer Abroad (www.volunteerabroad.com)

Alliance of European Voluntary Service Organisations (www.alliance-network.org)

Coordinating Committee for International Voluntary Service (www.unesco.org/ccivs)

The predominant language of Mexico is Spanish. Mexican Spanish is unlike Castilian Spanish (the language of much of Spain) in two main respects: in Mexico the Castilian lisp has more or less disappeared and numerous indigenous words have been adopted. About 50 indigenous languages are spoken as a first language by more than seven million people in Mexico, and about 15% of these don't speak Spanish.

Travelers in Mexico City can almost always find someone who speaks at least some English. All the same, it is advantageous and courteous to know at least a few words and phrases in Spanish. Mexicans will generally respond much more positively if you attempt to speak to them in their own language.

It's easy enough to pick up some basic Spanish, and for those who want to learn the language in greater depth, courses are available in Mexico City itself (see p251). You can also study books, CDs and tapes before you leave home. These resources are often available free at public libraries. Evening or college courses are also an excellent way to get started.

For a more comprehensive guide to the Spanish of Mexico, get a copy of Lonely Planet's *Mexican Spanish Phrasebook*.

SOCIAL
Meeting People
Hi!
¡Hola!
Bye!
¡Adiós!/Ciao.
Please.
Por favor.
Thank you (very much).
(Muchas) Gracias.
Yes.
Sí.
No.
No.
Excuse me. (to get past)
Permiso.
Sorry!
¡Perdón!
Pardon? (as in 'what did you say?')
¿Mande?/¿Cómo?/¿Qué?
Do you speak English?
¿Habla inglés?
Does anyone speak English?
¿Hay alguien que hable inglés?
Do you understand? (informal)
¿Me entiendes?
I (don't) understand.
(No) entiendo.

Could you please ...?
¿Puede ... por favor?
  speak more slowly hablar más despacio

  repeat that   repetirlo
  write it down   escribirlo

Going Out
What's there to do in the evenings?
¿Qué se puede hacer en las noches?

What's on ...?
¿Qué pasa ...?
  around here   para acá
  this weekend   este fin de semana
  today   hoy
  tonight   esta noche

Where are the ...?
¿Dónde hay ...?
  places to eat   lugares para comer
  clubs/bars   antros/bars
  gay venues   lugares para gays

PRACTICAL
Question Words
Who is it?   ¿Quién es?
What?   ¿Qué?
Which?   ¿Cuál/Cuáles? (sing/pl)
When?   ¿Cuándo?
Where?   ¿Dónde?
How?   ¿Cómo?
How much is it? ¿Cuánto cuesta?/
                    ¿Qué precio tiene?
Why?   ¿Por qué?

LOCAL LINGO

Spice up your chat with some slang expressions! You'll hear many of these words and phrases around Mexico City.

antro – a bar or a club
antrear – to go clubbing
Vámonos de antro. – Let's go to a club/bar.
¡Bájale! – Don't exaggerate! Come on!
carnal – bro' (brother)
¡Cámara! – Right on!
¡¿Chale?! – No way!
chavo – guy, dude
chava – girl, gal
chela – beer
chido/chida – very cool
¡Qué chido! – How cool!
chingar – literally 'to fuck'; it has a wide range of colloquial usages in Mexican Spanish equivalent to those in English
chingón – crude way to say something is very good, great
¡Fue un reven bien chingón! – It was a fantastic party!
¿Te gustó el concierto? Sí, estuvo bien chingón. – Did you like the concert? Yes, it was great.
la chota – the police
chupar – to drink, but could also refer to oral sex (literally 'to suck on something')
Vamos a chupar. – Let's go for some drinks.
cuate, cuaderno – buddy
un desmadre – a mess
fregada – bad, difficult
llevarse a la fregada – to make angry
¡Me lleva la fregada! – I'm pissed off!
¡Vete a la fregada! – Get the hell out of here!
fregón – really good at something, way cool, awesome; nicer than chingón
Este club está fregón. – This club is way cool.
El cantante es un fregón. – The singer is really awesome.
¡Guácatelas! ¡Guácala! – How gross! That's disgusting!
güey – dude; can also be used for women
huevos – testicles (literally 'eggs')
jefe – father
jefa – mother
kekas, quekas – quesadillas
lana – money, dough (literally 'wool')
Me late. – Sounds really good to me.

ligar – to flirt
¡No manches! ¡No mames! – Get outta here! You must be kidding!
mota – marijuana
Nel. – No.
No hay tos. – No problem. (literally 'there's no cough')
neto/neta – the truth
¿Neta? – Really?
¿Qué onda? – What's up? What's happening? The word onda means literally 'a wave of water'.
ser muy buena onda – to be really cool/nice
Mi novio es muy buena onda. – My boyfriend is really cool.
Eres muy buena onda. – You're really cool/nice.
tirar la onda – try to pick someone up, flirt
¡Órale! (positive) – Sounds great! (responding to an invitation)
¡Órale! (negative) – What the *#&$!? (taunting exclamation)
¡Paso sin ver! – I can't stand it! No thank you!
(un) pedo – (a) fart
No hay pedo. – No problem.
¿Qué pedo? – What's up? What's your problem?
Está re´ pedo. – He's blasted. He's drunk.
¿Qué pex? – What's up?
pistear – to drink booze
Vamos a pistear. – Let's go drinking.
reven – huge, loud party either at someone's house or at an antro
irse de reventón – to go partying
¡Vámonos de reventón! – Let's party!
ruca – woman
Simón. – Yes.
Sale y vale. – I agree. Sounds good.
¡Te pasas! – That's it! You've gone too far!
¿Te cae? – Are you serious?
la tira – the police
¿Qué tranza? – What's up?
Me vale. – I don't care. Whatever.
varo – money, dough
vieja – wife, girlfriend (could be an endearment or derogatory depending on context)

Numbers

0	cero	5	cinco
1	uno	6	seis
2	dos	7	siete
3	tres	8	ocho
4	cuatro	9	nueve
		10	diez
		11	once

12	doce
13	trece
14	catorce
15	quince
16	dieciséis
17	diecisiete
18	dieciocho
19	diecinueve
20	veinte
21	veintiuno
22	veintidós
30	treinta
31	treinta y uno
32	treinta y dos
40	cuarenta
50	cincuenta
60	sesenta
70	setenta
80	ochenta
90	noventa
100	cien
1000	mil
2000	dos mil

Days

Monday	lunes
Tuesday	martes
Wednesday	miércoles
Thursday	jueves
Friday	viernes
Saturday	sábado
Sunday	domingo

Banking & Post

Where's the nearest ...?
¿Dónde está ... más cercano?

ATM	el cajero automático/ el cajero permanente
exchange house	la casa de cambio
post office	el correo

I'd like to change ...
Quisiera cambiar ...

cash	dinero en efectivo
money	dinero
traveler's checks	cheques de viajero

Do you accept credit/debit cards?
¿Aceptan tarjetas de crédito/débito acá?

I want to send a ...
Quiero enviar ...

fax	un fax
parcel	un paquete
postcard	una postal

I want to buy a/an ...
Quiero comprar un ...

aerogramme	aerograma
envelope	sobre
stamp	estampilla

Communications

I want to buy a SIM card/phonecard.
Quiero comprar una tarjeta SIM/telefónica.
I'd like to rent a cell phone.
Quiero un celular para alquilar.

I want to make a ...
Quiero hacer una ...

call (to ...)	llamada (a ...)
collect call	llamada por cobrar

Where can I find a/an ...?
¿Dónde puedo encontrar ...?
I'd like a/an ...
Quiero ...

adaptor plug	un adaptador
charger for my cell phone	un cargador para mi celular
prepaid cell	un celular pre-pagado/ pagado por adelantado
SIM card for your network	una tarjeta SIM para su red

Where's a local internet café?
¿Dónde hay un cibercafé/café internet por acá?

I'd like (to) ...
Quiero ...

get online	usar internet
check my email	revisar mi correo electrónico
wireless internet	internet inalámbrico (also simply wi-fi)

Transportation

What time does the ... leave?
¿A qué hora sale el ...?

boat	barco/lancha
bus (long distance)	autobús/camión
bus (local)	pesero/micro
plane	avión

What time's the ... (bus)?
¿A qué hora es el ... (autobús)?

first	primer
last	último
next	próximo

Is this taxi available?
¿Está disponible este taxi?
Please put the meter on.
Por favor, ponga el taxímetro.
How much is it to ...?
¿Cuánto cuesta ir a ...?
Please take me (to this address).
Por favor, lléveme (a esta dirección)

FOOD

breakfast   desayuno
lunch   comida
dinner   cena
snack   merienda/
                botana (in a bar)
to eat   comer
to drink   tomar

Can you recommend a ...?
¿Puede recomendar ...?
  bar   un antro/bar
  café   un café
  coffee bar   una cafetería
  restaurant   un restaurante

Are you open?
¿Está abierto?
When are you open?
¿Cuando está abierto?
Are you now serving breakfast/lunch/
  dinner?
¿Ahora, está sirviendo desayuno/la comida/
  la cena?
Is the service charge included in the bill?
¿El precio en el menu incluye el servicio?
I'd like to see a menu.
Quisiera ver la carta/el menu.
Do you have a menu in English?
¿Tienen un menú en inglés?
Can you recommend something?
¿Puede recomendar algo?
I'm a vegetarian.
Soy vegetariano/a. (m/f)
I can't eat anything with meat or poultry
  products, including broth.
No puedo comer algo de carne o aves,
  incluyendo caldo.
Is it (chili) hot?
¿Es picoso?
I'd like mineral water/natural bottled water.
Quiero agua mineral/agua purificada.
That was delicious!
Estaba delicioso!
The check, please.
La cuenta, por favor.

Food Glossary

See also the 'Little Whims' boxed text in the
Eating chapter (p151)

a la parilla – grilled
a la plancha – pan-broiled
adobada – marinated with *adobo* (chili sauce)
agua mineral – mineral water or club soda
agua purificado – bottled, natural water
aguacate – avocado
al albañil – 'bricklayer style' – served with a hot chili sauce
al carbón – char-broiled
al mojo de ajo – with garlic sauce
al pastor – 'shepherd style' – cooked on a spit
albóndigas – meatballs
antojitos – 'little whims'– Mexican tortilla-based snacks
like tacos and *gorditas*
arrachera – tender Argentinean-cut skirt steak
arroz a la mexicana – pilaf-style rice with a tomato base
ate – jam, preserves served in slices as a dessert
atole   gruel made with ground corn
atun – tuna fish
avena – oatmeal
aves – poultry
azúcar – sugar

barbacoa – pit-smoked barbecue
bistec – steak
bolillo – French-style roll
brocheta – shish kabab
buñuelos – tortilla-size fritters with a brown-sugar syrup

cabra – goat
cabrito – kid goat
café americano – black coffee
café con leche – coffee with hot milk
cajeta – goat's milk and sugar boiled to a paste
calabacita – zucchini ('courgette' in the UK)
calamar – squid
caldo – broth or soup
camarones – shrimp
cangrejo – crab
carne de puerco – pork
carne de res – beef
carne – meat
carnero – mutton
carnitas – pork simmered in lard
cebolla – onion
cecina – thin cut of meat, salted and hung; served grilled
cerdo – pork
chicharrones – fried pork skins
chiles en nogada – mild green chilies stuffed with ground
meat and fruit, battered and deep-fried; served with a
walnut cream sauce and pomegranates
chorizo – Mexican-style bulk sausage made with chili and
vinegar

chuleta de puerco – pork chop
churros – long doughnut-like fritters
cochinita pibil – pork, marinated in chilies, wrapped in banana leaves, and pit-cooked or baked
coco – coconut
coctel de frutas – fruit cocktail
consome – chicken broth, usually with some vegetables and garbanzo beans
cordero – lamb
costillas de res – beef ribs
crema – cream
crepas – crepes or thin pancakes

elote – fresh corn on the cob
empanizado – breaded
ensalada – salad
esquites – boiled corn kernels served in a cup

filete a la tampiqueña – steak, *tampico*-style, a thin tenderloin, grilled and served with chili strips and onion, *rajas* and an enchilada
filete – filet
flor de calabaza – squash blossom
frijoles charros – beans cooked with sausage, tomatoes, chilies and onions (also called *frijoles rancheros)*
frijoles negros – black beans
frijoles refritos – refried beans
frito – fried

galleta – cookie
gelatina – gelatin; also Jello, jelly)

helado – ice cream
hielo – ice
hígado – liver
horchata – a soft drink made with melon seeds or rice
huachinango veracruzana – Veracruz-style red snapper with a sauce of tomatoes, olives, vinegar and capers
huevos a la mexicana – eggs scrambled with onion, tomato and chili
huevos estrellados – fried eggs, sunny-side up
huevos fritos – fried eggs
huevos rancheros – fried eggs served on a corn tortilla, topped with a sauce of tomato, chilies and onions, and served with refried beans
huevos revueltos – scrambled eggs
huitlacoche – corn mushrooms; a much-esteemed fungus that grows on corn

jaiba – crab
jamaica – a type of hibiscus flower used to make a flavored-water drink
jamón – ham
jitomate – red tomato
jugo de manzana – apple juice
jugo de naranja – orange juice
jugo de piña – pineapple juice

jugo de toronja – grapefruit juice

langosta – lobster
leche – milk
lengua – tongue
lentejas – lentils
licuado – smoothie
limón – lime (lemons are rarely found in Mexico)
lomo de cerdo – pork loin

machacado – pulverized jerky, often scrambled with eggs
mantequilla – butter
mariscos – seafood, shellfish
menudo – stew of tripe
milanesa – thin slices of chicken, beef or pork, breaded and fried
mixiote – chili-seasoned lamb steamed in agave membranes or parchment
mole negro – chicken or pork in a very dark sauce of chilies, fruits, nuts, spices and chocolate
mole poblano – chicken or turkey in a sauce of chilies, fruits, nuts, spices and chocolate
mole – a traditional stew
mollejas – sweetbreads (thymus or pancreas)

nieve – sorbet, sherbet
nopales – sliced cactus paddles, sautéed or grilled; also served as a salad
ostras/ostiones – oysters

pan – bread
papas fritas – potato chips
papas a la francesa – french fries
papas – potatoes
pastel – cake
pato – duck
pay – pie
pechuga – breast
picadillo – a ground-beef filling that often includes raisins and nuts or peas and carrots
piña – pineapple
pipian verde – a stew of chicken, with ground squash seeds, chilies and tomatillos
platano macho – plantain
platano – banana
pollo – chicken
postre – dessert
pozole – a soup or thin stew of hominy, meat, vegetables and chilies
pulpo – octopus

rajas – strips of mild green chili fried with onions, often mixed with cream
sábana – beef filet pounded paper thin and seared
sopa – soup, either *aguada* (wet) or *seca* (dry); in *sopa seca* all cooking liquid has been absorbed by rice or pasta
sopa de ajo – garlic soup

sopa de cebolla – onion soup
sopa de pollo – chicken soup

té de hiebabuena – mint tea
té de manzanillo – chamomile tea
té negro – black tea
te de limón – lemongrass tea
ternera – veal
tinga poblana – a stew of pork, vegetables and chilies
tocino – bacon
tomates – tomatillos, green husk tomatoes
toronja – grapefruit
tuna – cactus fruit

uvas – grapes

venado – venison
verduras – vegetables

EMERGENCIES

It's an emergency!
¡Es una emergencia!
Could you help me, please?
¿Me puede ayudar, por favor?
Where's the police station?
¿Dónde está la comisaría?

Call ... !
¡Llame a ... !
  the police   la policía

a doctor   un médico
an ambulance!   una ambulancia

HEALTH

Where's the nearest ...?
¿Dónde está ... más cercano?
  dentist   el dentista
  doctor   el médico
  hospital   el hospital

Where's the nearest (night) pharmacy?
¿Dónde está la farmacia (de turno) más
  cercana?
I need a doctor (who speaks English).
Necesito un médico (que hable inglés).

Symptoms

I have (a/an) ...
Tengo ...
  diarrhea   diarrea
  fever   fiebre
  headache   dolor de cabeza
  pain (here)   dolor (acá)

I'm allergic to ...
Soy alérgico/a a ... (m/f)
  antibiotics   los antibióticos
  nuts   las nueces
  peanuts   los cacahuates

GLOSSARY

aduana – customs

agave – plant with thick pointed leaves growing straight out of the ground; see also maguey

aguardiente – literally 'burning water '; strong liquor usually made from sugarcane

Ángeles Verdes – 'Green Angels '; government-funded mechanics who patrol Mexico's major highways in green vehicles and help stranded motorists with fuel, spare parts and service

antro – club with (often loud) recorded music and usually some space to dance

Apdo – abbreviation for *Apartado* (Box) in addresses; hence *Apdo Postal* means Post Office Box

artesanías – handicrafts, folk arts

autopista – expressway, freeway

azulejo – painted ceramic tile

balneario – bathing-place, often a natural hot spring

barrio – neighborhood of a town or city, often a poor neighborhood

cacique – regional warlord or political strongman

cafetería – snack bar or coffeehouse

callejón – alley

calzada – grand boulevard or avenue

camión – truck or bus

camioneta – pickup truck

campesino/a – country person, peasant

capitalino – a person from the capital (Mexico City)

casa de cambio – exchange house; place where currency is exchanged, faster to use than a bank

caseta de larga distancia, caseta de teléfono, caseta telefónica – public telephone call station, often in a shop

central camionera – bus terminal

cerro – hill

Chac – Maya rain god

charreada – Mexican rodeo

charro – Mexican cowboy

Chilango/a – citizen of Mexico City

chinampas – Aztec gardens built from lake mud and vegetation; versions still exist at Xochimilco

Coatlicue – mother of the Aztec gods

colectivo – minibus or car that picks up and drops off passengers along a predetermined route; can also refer to other types of transport, such as boats, where passengers share the total fare

colonia – neighborhood of a city, often a wealthy residential area

comedor – literally 'eating place'; usually a sit-down stall in a market or a small, cheap restaurant

comida corrida – fixed-price menu with several courses; cheaper than eating à la carte

conquistador – early Spanish explorer-conqueror

correos – post office

cuota – toll; a *vía cuota* is a toll road

curandero/a – literally 'curer'; a medicine man or woman who uses herbal and/or magical methods and often emphasizes spiritual aspects of disease

de lujo – deluxe; often used with some license

delegación – large urban governmental subdivision in Mexico City comprising numerous *colonias*

de paso – a bus that began its route somewhere else, but stops to let passenger on or off at various points – often arriving late; a *local* bus is preferable

descompuesto – broken, out of order

DF – Distrito Federal (Federal District); about half of Mexico City lies in the DF

defeño – someone from the DF

embarcadero – jetty, boat landing

esq – abbreviation of *esquina* (corner) in addresses

feria – fair or carnival, typically occurring during a religious holiday

fonda – eating stall in a market; small restaurant

giro – money order

gringo/a – US or Canadian (and sometimes European, Australasian, etc) visitor to Latin America; can be used derogatorily

grito – literally 'shout'; the *Grito de Dolores* was the 1810 call to independence by parish priest Miguel Hidalgo, which sparked the struggle for independence from Spain

güero/a – fair-haired, fair-complexioned person; a more polite alternative to gringo

hacienda – estate; Hacienda (capitalized) is the Treasury Department

Huizilopochtli – Aztec tribal god

iglesia – church

INAH – Instituto Nacional de Antropología e Historia; the body in charge of most ancient sites and some museums

INBA – National Fine Arts Institute

indígena – indigenous, pertaining to the original inhabitants of Latin America; can also refer to the people themselves

ISH – *impuesto sobre hospedaje*; lodging tax on the price of hotel rooms

IVA – *impuesto de valor agregado*, or '*ee*-ba'; a 15% sales tax added to the price of many items

lada – short for *larga distancia*

Ladatel – the long-distance telephone system operated by the former monopoly Telmex

larga distancia – long-distance; usually refers to telephones and telephone calls

licenciado – university graduate; abbreviated as *Lic* and used as an honorific before a person's name

licuado – drink made from fruit juice, water or milk, and sugar

local – can mean premises, such as a numbered shop or

office in a mall or block, or can mean 'local'; a *local* bus is one that follows a route within a defined zone or suburb

machismo – Mexican masculine bravura

madre – literally 'mother'; used colloquially with an astonishing array of meanings

maguey – agave plant from which *pulque*, mezcal and tequila are made

mariachi – small ensemble of street musicians playing traditional ballads on guitars and trumpets

mercado – market; often a building near the center of a town, with shops and open-air stalls in the surrounding streets

Mesoamerica – the region inhabited by the ancient Mexican and Maya cultures

mestizaje – 'mixedness'; Mexico's mixed-blood heritage, officially an object of pride

mestizo – person of mixed (usually indigenous and Spanish) ancestry, ie most Mexicans

mezcal – strong alcoholic drink produced from *maguey* sap

microbus – small bus; usually refers to a van converted to allow passengers in and out easily

molcajete – stone bowl with legs, for grinding spices and making sauces

mole – a spicy sauce usually made with chilies, a variety of spices, and sometimes chocolate, served with meat

mordida – literally 'little bite'; a small bribe to keep the wheels of bureaucracy turning

moreno/a – dark, especially a dark-complexioned or dark-haired person

Náhuatl – language of the Nahua people, descendants of the Aztecs

norteamericanos – North Americans; people from north of the US–Mexican border

Nte – abbreviation for *norte* (north), used in street names

Ote – abbreviation for *oriente* (east); used in street names

panadería – bakery, pastry shop

parada – bus stop, usually for city buses

paseo – boulevard, walkway or pedestrian street; also the act of taking a walk

Pemex – government-owned petroleum extraction, refining and retailing monopoly

periférico – ring road

pesero – local city buses, so named because they originally cost one peso

plaza de toros – bullring

propina – tip in a restaurant or bar

Pte – abbreviation for *poniente* (west); used in street names

pulque – thick, milky, alcoholic drink of fermented *maguey* juice

Quetzalcóatl – plumed serpent god of the Aztecs

rebozo – long woolen or linen shawl covering the head or shoulders

retablo – altarpiece or small painting on wood, tin or cardboard

s/n – *sin número* (without number); used in street addresses

Semana Santa – Holy Week, the week from Palm Sunday to Easter Sunday (a major holiday period)

servicios – toilets

sitio – taxi stand

supermercado – supermarket; anything from a small corner store to a large, US-style supermarket

Sur – south; often seen in street names

taller – shop or workshop; a *taller mecánico* is a mechanic's shop, usually for cars; a *taller de llantas* is a tire-repair shop

taquería – taco stand

teocalli – Aztec sacred precinct

tequila – liquor produced from the *maguey* plant; see also *pulque* and mezcal

tianguis – indigenous people's market; weekly neighborhood market

tipico/a – characteristic of a region; particularly used to describe food

Tláloc – Aztec water god

topes – speed bumps; found on the outskirts of many towns and villages, only sometimes marked by signs

trajinera – gondola-like boat punted along the canals of Xochimilco

tzompantli – rack for the skulls of Aztec sacrificial victims

UNAM – Universidad Nacional Autónoma de México (National Autonomous University of Mexico)

zócalo – main plaza or square

Zona Rosa – literally 'Pink Zone'; an area of expensive shops, hotels and restaurants in Mexico City frequented by the wealthy and tourists

THIS BOOK

This 3rd edition of *Mexico City* was researched and written by Daniel C Schechter and Josephine Quintero. The 1st and 2nd editions were written by John Noble. This guidebook was commissioned in Lonely Planet's Oakland office, and produced by the following:

Commissioning Editor Catherine Craddock-Carrillo

Coordinating Editor Penelope Goodes

Coordinating Cartographers Anita Banh & Diana Duggan

Coordinating Layout Designer Margaret Jung

Managing Editor Imogen Bannister

Managing Cartographer Alison Lyall

Managing Layout Designer Adam McCrow

Assisting Editors David Carroll, Susannah Farfor, Sally O'Brien, Joanne Newell

Assisting Cartographers Owen Eszeki, Tadhgh Knaggs, Peter Shields, Amanda Sierp, Andrew Smith

Assisting Layout Designer Indra Kilfoyle, Aomi Hongo

Cover Designer Pepi Bluck

Project Manager Fabrice Rocher

Language Content Coordinator Quentin Frayne

Thanks to Heather Dickson, Evan Jones, Rebecca Lalor Wayne Murphy, Naomi Parker, Michael Ruff, Gerard Walker, Celia Wood

Cover photographs Stone Aztec calendar, Harald Sund/Getty Images (top), Ligaya Restaurant, Mexico City, Mexico, Superstock/Photolibrary (bottom).

Internal photographs p7 (#4) Lightworks Media/Alamy, p5 (#3) Lynsey Addario/Corbis, p5 (#2) Keith Dannemiller/Alamy, p6 (#2) Jan Butchofsky-Houser/Corbis, p6 (#1) Peter M. Wilson/Alamy. All other photographs by Lonely Planet Images: p2, p7 (#3), p7 (#5) Richard I'Anson, p3 Dan Herrick, p4 (#1), p4 (#2), p4 (#3) Greg Elms, p8 (#2) Richard Nebesky, p8 (#3) John Neubauer, p8 (#1) David Ryan, p5 (#1) Daniel C Schechter

All images are copyright of the photographer unless otherwise indicated. Many of the images in this guide are available for licensing from Lonely Planet Images: www .lonelyplanetimages.com.

THANKS
DANIEL C SCHECHTER

Working on my first edition of the *Mexico City* guide, I was able to count on the remarkably enthusiastic assistance of old and new friends. As usual, journalist pals José Fernández Ramos and Jeffrey A Wright offered their invaluable insights on DF issues, Michael K Schuessler and John Rozzo kept me abreast of gay life, and Miriam Martínez translated Chilango slang. *Defeños* and *medio-defeños* Jorge Silva, Monica Campbell, Deborah Bonello, Cynthia Sperry and Michelle Chi Chase all gamely pitched in with suggestions and on-the-scene assessments. Ruth Alegría, María José Serrano, Rocío González Delgado, Mojdeh Hojjati and Pedro Gellert generously shared their voluminous knowledge of cuisine, Concheros and Cubans. Myra, un besote for setting up the office and lots of other stuff.

THE LONELY PLANET STORY

Fresh from an epic journey across Europe, Asia and Australia in 1972, Tony and Maureen Wheeler sat at their kitchen table stapling together notes. The first Lonely Planet guidebook, *Across Asia on the Cheap*, was born.

Travelers snapped up the guides. Inspired by their success, the Wheelers began publishing books to Southeast Asia, India and beyond. Demand was prodigious, and the Wheelers expanded the business rapidly to keep up. Over the years, Lonely Planet extended its coverage to every country and into the virtual world via lonelyplanet.com and the Thorn Tree message board.

As Lonely Planet became a globally loved brand, Tony and Maureen received several offers for the company. But it wasn't until 2007 that they found a partner whom they trusted to remain true to the company's principles of traveling widely, treading lightly and giving sustainably. In October of that year, BBC Worldwide acquired a 75% share in the company, pledging to uphold Lonely Planet's commitment to independent travel, trustworthy advice and editorial independence.

Today, Lonely Planet has offices in Melbourne, London and Oakland, with over 500 staff members and 300 authors. Tony and Maureen are still actively involved with Lonely Planet. They're traveling more often than ever, and they're devoting their spare time to charitable projects. And the company is still driven by the philosophy of *Across Asia on the Cheap*: 'All you've got to do is decide to go and the hardest part is over. So go!'

JOSEPHINE QUINTERO

Josephine Quintero would like to thank coordinating author Daniel Schechter for his patience, suggestions and the canal trip in Xochimilco. *Gracias* also to commissioning editor Catherine Craddock-Carillo for her guidance and email support. I would also like to thank Ruth Alegria who introduced me to *her* Mexico City and invited me to some terrific events. Finally, a wet kiss for my longtime partner and Lonely Planet photographer Robin Chapman for taking care of Marilyn, my cat, during my time in DF.

OUR READERS

Many thanks to the travelers who used the last edition and wrote to us with helpful hints, useful advice and interesting anecdotes:

Horacio Barbosa, Zoe Barker, Rory Bernstein, Brendan Bietry, J David Blagg, Lee Blaylock, Janina Blume, Jannika Bock, James Du Bois, Erik Boshuizen, Travis Boyer, Marko Brescak, Ana Breuer, Amanda Bronesky, Adam Brostow, Anne Cariou, Claire Catanach, Elwin Chouinard, Laura Coloma, Thomas Cook, Bob Cromwell, Jasmyn Davids, Joyce Degens, Cynthia Denton, Yann Deredec, Samuel Eitan Diamond, Kai Artur Diers, Anna Doddridge, Eirik Drogh, Thomas Duke, Diane Elliott, Kilian Engel, Austen Fairbairn, Cecilia Fessler, Stephanie Fleming, Melissa Flore, Daniela Fosado, Dana A Freiburger, David Frier, Cynda Fuentes, Pat Gaudry, Peter & Christine Gaylarde, Kris Genovese, Jonathan Goldberg, Jeff Granger, Yolanda Grau, Kato Guggenheim, Tom Hallinan, Sandi Hammonds, Rickard Hedlund, Margaret Huber, Marian Hudson, Andrew Hulme, Rosa Jakubowicz, Andrew Jessep, Marijke De Jong, Steffen Kahle, Levente Kiss, Leslie Klein, Jo-Ann Kolmes, Josef Kreitmayer, Phyllis Kynas, Stepas Levickis, Irving Levinson, Jonas Lindholm, Beatriz Lopez, Thomas Lunifeld, Mary Markotic, Nicola Martin, Sanna-Maaria Mattila, Clara Mazzi, Daniel Mcgillis, Marianne Mcschnel, Mateja Mikuz, Mari Mizutani, Jeremy Monteiro, Valeria Moy, Roberta Murray, Alex Nekrason, Penny Norman, Petre O'Brien, Peter O'Meara, John Orr, Roy & Velia Ovenden, Steve Patti, Jerry Peek, Jan M Pennington, Melissa Pike, Sandra Ponek, Grethe Rand, Gary Noel Ross, Emma Sadula, Polly Schlodtmann, Rita Seith, Rossana Seitter, Peter & Florence Shaw, Roland & Bettina Shulze, Andreas Spangenberg, John & Tina Sparks, G M Stoffel, Charles Sullivan, Rajat Swani, Martha Tapio, Celeste Tarricone, Ge Teunissens, Christobel Thomas, Barbara Tilford, Essa van Corona, Maurice Der van Holst, Muriel Weadick, Emma Weatherrup, Chris White, Karen Whitlow, Courtenay Wolf, Laura Wong-Pan, Chris Woods, Chris & Judy Woods, Christopher Wortley, Jeffrey Wright, Melek Yaprak, Ray Ydoyaga, Niki Young, Gerhard Zanka

Notes

Notes

Notes

Notes

INDEX

A

accommodations 198, 200-12, see also Sleeping subindex
Alameda Central & Around 203-4
Bosque de Chapultepec 208-9
Centro Histórico 200-3
Ciudad Universitaria 212
Condesa 210
Coyoacán 212
Plaza de la República & San Rafael 204-6
Polanco 209-10
Roma 210-11
Zona Rosa, Cuauhtémoc & Juárez 206-8
activities 188-9, see also Sports & Activities subindex
air travel 245-6
Alameda Central & Around 63-9, **64**
accommodations 203-4
drinking 161
food 139-40
shopping 122-3
transportation 65
walking tours 67-9, **68**
Allende, Ignacio 73
alta cocina mexicana 133, 136, 145

000 map pages
000 photographs

altitude 253
ambulance 253
Amecameca 219
AMLO, see López Obrador, Andrés Manuel
antojitos 151
antros 168-70
architecture 31-3, 216, **6-7**
art deco 33, 86-7
Av México 86-7
colonial 228-9, **7**
pre-Hispanic 31, **6**
subsidence 35
area codes 259
Arias, Sonia 145
art galleries, see Arts subindex
artesanías 26-7, see also Shopping subindex
arts 22-30, 178-86, 216
photography 13, 149
tours 106-8
Atl, Dr 65, 79, 81
Atlante 190
ATMs 255
Audiorama 79
Aztecs, see pre-Hispanic culture

B

Ballet Folclórico de México 180
Barragán, Luis 80, 109
bars 160-6, see also Drinking subindex
antros 168-70
baseball 192-3
Basílica de Nuestra Señora de Guadalupe 116-18
bathrooms 259-60
beaches 22, 190
bicycle travel 188, 246-7
Sierra de Ajusco 214
Blue House, see Museo Frida Kahlo
blues 174
books 30
markets 69
stores 121, 122, 123, 124, 126, 128, 129, 139
Bosque de Chapultepec 77-82, **78**

accommodations 208-9
food 143-4
transportation 79
walking tours 81-2, **82**
boxing 193-4
Brady, Robert 236
bullfighting 191-2
bus travel
to/from Mexico City 248-9
within Mexico City 247-8, 249
business hours 251
drinking 160
restaurants 134
stores 120

C

Cabrera, Miguel 23
Café Tacuba (band) 29
cafés see Drinking & Eating subindexes
cantinas 137, **5**, see also Drinking subindex
car travel 249-50
prevention programs 34-5
rental 250
Carlos I 18
Casa Azul (Blue House), see Museo Frida Kahlo
Castillo de Chapultepec 77-9
Catedral Metropolitana 50-1, **3**
cell phones 258-9
Centro Histórico 46-62, **48-50**
accommodations 200-3
drinking 160-1
food 135-9
shopping 120-3
transportation 56
walking tours 59-61, **60, 61**
Centro Nacional de las Artes 97
charreadas 193
chefs
Arias, Sonia 145
Arzak, Juan Mari 141
Hernandez Oropeza, Titita 147
Muñoz Zurita, Ricardo 156
Ortiz Chapa, Martha 144-5

Oteiza, Bruno 146
Patiño, Mónica 145, 154
Quintana, Patricia 146
chemists 255
children, traveling with 251
eating 142, 143
entertainment 130, 181, 183
shops 122, 125
Cholula 224-6
cinema 30, 183, 197
Ciudad Universitaria 104-8, **105**
accommodations 212
food 155-7
transportation 106
walking tours 106-8, **107**
classical music 178-80, 182
climate 12, 251
clothing sizes 126
clubs 175-6, 197-8
Cocoxtli 15
collect calls 259
comida corrida 133
Condesa 86-9, **88**
accommodations 210
drinking 163, **5**
food 148-50
shopping 126-8
transportation 86
walking tours 87-9, **87**
consulates 252-3
cookbooks 143, 147
Cordero, Juan 23-4
Correa, Juan 23
corridas 191-2
Cortés, Hernán 16-17
costs 13-14, 252
accommodations 200
drinking 160
food 134-5
taxes 258
courses 251-2,
culinary courses 134, 242
dance 171
Coyoacán 94-9, **95**
accommodations 212
drinking 165
food 152-3
shopping 128-9
transportation 96
walking tours 98-9, **98**

lonelyplanet.com

INDEX

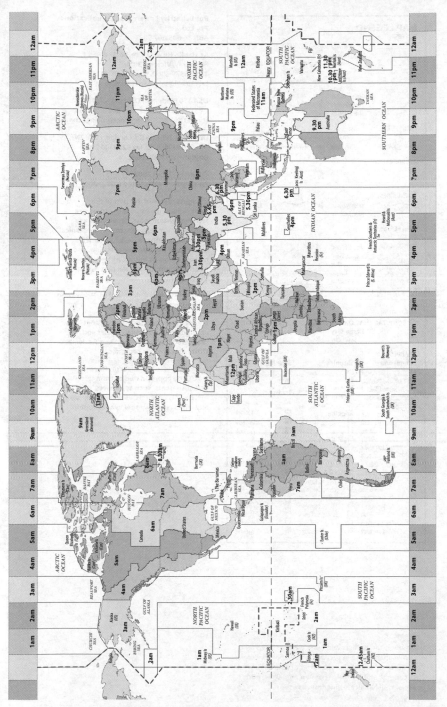

287

MAP LEGEND

ROUTES

Tollway		Mall/Steps
Freeway		Tunnel
Primary		Pedestrian Overpass
Secondary		Walking Tour
Tertiary		Walking Tour Detour
Lane		Walking Trail
Under Construction		Walking Path
Unsealed Road		Track
One-Way Street		

TRANSPORT

Ferry		Rail
Metro		Cable Car, Funicular

HYDROGRAPHY

River, Creek		Canal
Intermittent River		Water

BOUNDARIES

International		Ancient Wall
State, Provincial		Cliff

AREA FEATURES

Airport		Land
Area of Interest		Mall
Beach, Desert		Market
Building		Park
Campus		Reservation
Cemetery, Christian		Rocks
Cemetery, Other		Sports
Forest		Urban

POPULATION

CAPITAL (NATIONAL)		CAPITAL (STATE)
Large City		Medium City
Small City		Town, Village

SYMBOLS

Information
- Bank, ATM
- Embassy/Consulate
- Hospital, Medical
- Information
- Internet Facilities
- Police Station
- Post Office, GPO
- Telephone
- Toilets
- Wheelchair Access

Sights
- Beach
- Castle, Fortress
- Christian
- Monument
- Museum, Gallery
- Point of Interest
- Ruin
- Winery, Vineyard
- Zoo, Bird Sanctuary

Shopping
- Shopping

Eating
- Eating

Entertainment
- Entertainment

Drinking
- Drinking
- Café

Nightlife
- Nightlife

Arts
- Arts

Sports & Activities
- Canoeing, Kayaking
- Diving, Snorkeling
- Pool
- Snorkeling
- Surfing, Surf Beach
- Trail Head
- Windsurfing

Sleeping
- Sleeping
- Camping

Transport
- Airport, Airfield
- Bus Station
- Parking Area
- Taxi Rank

Geographic
- Hazard
- Lighthouse
- Lookout
- Mountain, Volcano
- National Park
- Oasis
- Picnic Area
- Shelter, Hut
- Waterfall

Published by Lonely Planet Publications Pty Ltd
ABN 36 005 607 983

Australia Head Office, Locked Bag 1, Footscray, Victoria 3011, ☎03 8379 8000, fax 03 8379 8111, talk2us@lonelyplanet.com.au

USA 150 Linden St, Oakland, CA 94607, ☎510 250 6400, toll free 800 275 8555, fax 510 893 8572, info@lonelyplanet.com

UK 2nd fl, 186 City Rd, London, EC1V 2NT, ☎ 020 7106 2100, fax 020 7106 2101, go@lonelyplanet.co.uk

© Lonely Planet 2008
Photographs © As listed (p272) 2008